ECONOMIC PHILOSOPHY
OF THE TWENTIETH CENTURY

ECONOMIC PHILOSOPHY OF THE TWENTIETH CENTURY

Theo Surányi-Unger

NORTHERN ILLINOIS UNIVERSITY PRESS
DeKalb, Illinois

Library of Congress Cataloging in Publication Data

Surányi-Unger, Theo, 1898–
  Economic philosophy of the twentieth century.
  Translation of Wirtschaftsphilosophie des 20.
Jahrhunderts.
  Includes bibliographical references.
  1. Economics—History. 2. Economics—History
—20th century. I. Title.
HB75.S8213   330.1'09   72–1387
ISBN 0–87580–016–5

Originally published in 1968 as
Wirtschaftsphilosophie des 20. Jahrhunderts
© *1967 Gustav Fischer Verlag, Stuttgart*

*This first English-language edition has been slightly abridged and edited
for the American reader. Portions of chapter II, dealing with the historical
sources of modern theories of economics, have been deleted. Parts III
and IV of the German edition* (Sozialphilosophische Perspektiven *and*
Sozialethische Aspekte) *have been transposed in this edition, with the
exception of chapter XVIII which remains as the conclusion of the work.*

*Translated from the German by: William Wolf, Foreword, chapters I,
II, VII, XIII, XIV; Allin K. Dittmann, chapter III; Vera Deutsche, chapter
IV, V; Rudolf Schnasse, chapter VI; E. D. Herzberg, chapters VIII, IX,
X; Jeanne Osborn, chapters XI, XII; Jan V. Brodau, chapters XV, XVI,
XVII, XVIII.*

Printed in the United States of America

CONTENTS

CONTENTS

Part Three: Socio-Ethical Aspects

Part Four: Socio-Philosophical Perspectives

CONTENTS

PREFACE

In the Preface to the first volume of my *Philosophie in der Volkswirt-schaftslehre* (Jena, 1923), the manuscript of which was finished in 1922, I wrote: "The field to be investigated lies between and connects philosophy and economics. Such a return to philosophy is demanded by modern economists. The rise of a philosophy of economics is in the making."

Now, a half a century later, this demand has become even more urgent in view of the divisions among national economies. This is stressed in the present volume. Only if this is kept in mind can the investigation of economic foundations deal with the urgent problems of the present. Their solution may lead to a softening of the contrasts of West and East and to the creation of a world-wide economy.

Between the mid-1920s and the 1960s, I was busy with other urgent tasks in the field of the theory and politics of economy. I taught and did research mainly in Hungary, the United States, and the Federal Republic of Germany; I traveled on five continents, particularly in the Soviet Union and the European people's republics.

Nevertheless, I succeeded in gathering much material related to a modern philosophy of economics. From this basis, I had planned for several decades to prepare a third volume of *Philosophie in der Volkswirtschaftslehre*. The present volume is the result of that project. In shaping it, technical considerations of publication played a decisive role. For similar reasons, chapters dealing with business procedures and with econometrics had to be relegated to a separate work.

In arranging the present material, I had the able help of my research assistants at the University of Göttingen. I am especially indebted to Drs. H. Böhme, W. Schneider, D. Fuchs, H. Hellmond, V. Hansen, and Messrs. H. D. Schmitz, E. Világhy, and M. Wolff. I am also grateful to the Deutsche Forschungsgemeinschaft for financial support. My thanks are also due to the Northern Illinois University Press for arranging for the English translation.

Göttingen, July 1972

THEO SURANYI-UNGER

PART ONE

Bases and Previews

I. THE PROBLEM: ITS STRUCTURE AND LIMITS

1. CONCEPT AND METHOD

In Soviet economic policy, the philosophical basis of structural change is often only a neglected stepchild; but in Western thought, more often than not, ethical values are applied to philosophical considerations of economic policy.[1] In the development of this book, too, the ethical point of view plays a leading role—yet today, it cannot stand alone. In the past, up to the time of mercantilism, the ethical point of view was highly valued because the measure of man was seen mainly in terms of political and religious accomplishment. Economic ability was merely a means for making a living, while the ultimate goal of human existence —as determined by the culture of that civilization—lay beyond the realm of economics. Such an approach prevented the rise of economics as a science until well into the eighteenth century.

It was only after the French Revolution that economics acquired its present industrial-capitalistic form. At the same time there developed an increasingly independent theory of economic relationships. Philosophy began to conceive of economics as enriching part of life—almost dominating it.[2] Moreover, a liberal philosophy which was partly responsible for the upsurge in the standard of living created a new image of man. The individual was no longer merely a member of a meta-individual commonweal, but an entity with its own right to existence.

3

From then on the origin and the goal of his way of life were not determined primarily by the culture around him but rather by his own will and private interests. The success of his existence was to be measured by the productivity of his economic achievements, which now aimed at domination of the material world. Therefore, the beginning of modern industrial society was characterized not only by a change in moral philosophy but also by a new and more materialistically oriented basis for evaluating human existence.[3] The always urgent problem of creating a functional economic system is inextricably connected with complex questions of man's metaphysical existence.

Originally, the economic theories of Smith and Marx expressed contrasting philosophies of human freedom. Both were meant to secure the principles of freedom. But that discussion was long held back because philosophy refused to enter into a debate on economic reality. On the other hand, the young science of economics prematurely considered its own subject an almost independent field. Later, it chose to subject itself to a highly mechanistic, exact, and quantitative analysis and to explain itself exclusively in this manner.

But a realistic philosophy of economics becomes possible only when economic structures and ideologies are seen as parts of historical existence. They are mutually dependent. The content of a realistic economic philosophy can be structured so that the practical forms and theoretical concepts of economic activity are seen as being mutually interdependent with the over-all civilization of the time. Thus, certain patterns and systems of economic activity come to the foreground. This does not affect the value of economic-philosophical insights into those realms which they are meant to explain.[4]

In this sense, economic philosophy is not primarily the logic and epistemology of economics but rather an examination of actual systems that incorporate all social sciences. It is a discussion of all human relationships, with special consideration given to economic policies. Economic theories need be taken into consideration only if and when they lie within the scope of such an investigation. Philosophy thus comes to acknowledge the concrete reality of economic activity and recognizes that it is here that man's main drives are to be perceived. On the other hand, economic theory rediscovers a truth which had partly been forgotten: the economic sphere is not fundamentally autonomous.[5]

For we must recognize that economic reality is fundamentally determined by metaphysical, socio-philosophical and ethical interrelationships. It is not quite true that the choice of this starting point is diametrically opposed to the Marxist theory of base and superstructure.

4

New economic and social models always depend on changing forms in active man's view of himself and of reality. There is a problem of priority as far as concerns, on the one hand, objectively forced adaptations created by changing productive forces and methods and, on the other hand, subjective judgments about changes in society and civilization. In the socialistic-communistic economy, for instance, the Russian Revolution answered this problem partly by changing society through political power.[6] * But, from a wider perspective in time and space, the Soviet model can, to a certain degree, be considered a result of the development of productive forces in the West. (As a matter of fact, liberalism is in some ways antagonistic to the development of the ideal humanity of the Enlightenment.) Both forms share not only the formal goal of a rational and free mankind but also an interest in development of an industrial economy.

"Historical laws," which supposedly lead to a certain economic system with a corresponding social structure, cannot really have a metaphysical meaning. "Independent laws" of economics—laws that must be obeyed in order to obtain the best results—are objectively valid only if society institutionalizes the attainment of corresponding aims. The West and the East share a common goal and will continue to do so in the future. Modern industrial society, therefore, creates certain demands which are to be fulfilled in the East through its principle of collective property and planning. With the advent of modern industrialization and an awareness of freedom and equality among all men, economic organization has been determined, on the one hand, by social ideas rising out of the productive process and under the influence of economic development. On the other hand, developments today show that an advancing economic technology calls for revision of unilateral economic systems.

The new state of affairs in the economic "base" is, generally speaking, determined by man's will to dominate nature fully and to satisfy his own needs without restrictions—which is the spirit of modern Europe. But, more specifically, too, that state of affairs is not simply a material necessity but also the result of human inventiveness. Such a spirit is not necessarily guided by needs emerging from the application of innovations. There is always the possibility that innovations might be rejected.[7]

Let us start with the hypothesis that today's economic society is the result of both a new concept of man and a new mode of production. We then have two contrasting models, the East and the West.

* Similar things may be said concerning the liberal concept of the economy, which corresponds to the ideas of classical economics.

5

The Marxist doctrine that economic development follows a natural law is as much an oversimplification as is a voluntaristic idealism which denies that the forces of practical reality have a determining or, at least, contributive power over the development of man. The proper approach is to start out with the premise of reciprocal relations between the concept of man and the means of production—a connection which even Engels had to admit is valid, even though he maintained that "ultimately" the material side is the only determining one.

The metaphysical, socio-philosophical, and ethical concepts are considered first as clearly graspable and expressible and secondly as fundamental factors in the shaping of existence. Marx, Weber, and others have already stated that the problem of the origin of these concepts cannot simply be relegated to chance ideas but must be connected with the origin of general relationships in the historical situation, from its economic base to its religious convictions.[8] If this problem is to be dealt with, all cognate factors must be considered, without priority for material or ideal values. Human actions—of which the economic are only a part—are, from the point of view of phenomenology, an interpenetration of subjective desires and objective needs created by the independent laws of the active world. There is no legitimate priority on either side but rather a mutual conditioning among all factors. It would be an illusion to see any one factor as a "basically ultimate" one. Only in individual cases is it possible to decide which factor is the determining one.

Let us start, synoptically, from the liberal-capitalistic view of citizenry, the humanitarian ideas of the Enlightenment, and the socialist movements. It is obvious that they are connected with one another, and that they have all been influenced by the means of production in the new industrialized society. The East-West conflict may be interpreted as the experimental result of a synthesis of freedom and equality as well as the antitheses of a materialistic and an idealistic foundation of human existence.[9]

There are indications that, in this conflict, the opposing stances of the systems are neither durable nor capable of being permanently institutionalized. Such confrontations are between decentralization and emphasis on consumption, on the one hand, and increasing regulation of society and democratic centralization, on the other.

To point out such connections convincingly would in itself be a difficult undertaking, further complicated by problems of interpretation and selection of facts. Even then not much would be achieved. Next would be the task of explanation, which also allows a critical prognosis of fur-

6

ther development. To this end, it would not do to have acquired merely a certain reservoir of knowledge—of confirmation or rejection of the East, or of historical optimism or pessimism. What we need is a useful theoretical conception. Such a theoretical instrument is, for instance, the doctrine of the interdependence of the species, as anticipated by Hegel and developed by Eucken. Yet, it can only be used in a discussion of the simultaneous interrelationships of political, social, and economic developments. It would not serve us in the investigation of trends of change in such interdependent structures as a whole.[10] * For instance, investigations into a possible convergence between the West and the East must be satisfied with preliminary hypotheses founded on a thorough knowledge of the facts and a neat application of the concepts. What is desired is a general theory based on the history of civilization and anthropology, a theory which could explain the contrasts in the systems and their evolution.

It might go somewhat like this: modern man's acts in society are basically determined through the tension of opposites—the simultaneous striving for individual freedom and for social integration. The two trends are antithetical, yet parallel. The isolated realization of one will, sooner or later, generate the other; or the lack of one tendency will lead to failures in the other field. Thus, Western individual freedom in the Manchester movement produced lack of freedom. This again led to the socialist countermovement. Now it is again menaced by a conformist and anonymous mass society, which stresses lack of freedom. Social critics make themselves heard. In the East, out of planned production for a society of equal men, there arose a hierarchy of Party rulers. In this case, the modern countermovement is the upsurge of individual choice and private property. This again is conditioned by the claims of rising industrialization.

But the relative uniqueness of a historic epoch may make any theoretical explanation *ad hoc* or circular if it is confirmed only by those facts for whose explanation it was invented.[11] It would be better to ask whether it is possible to derive an interpretation from the history of civilization.

Taking the above-mentioned risks into consideration, the philosophical investigation of Soviet economic policy must use a clear-cut theoretical starting point. ("Philosophical" here refers to the attempt to see individuals in their general relationships to one another and to establish general principles for these relationships.) In our case, this relates to the

* Another example is the value theory of the Vienna school.

7

heuristic thesis of abolishing the strict antithesis of materialism versus idealism; individualism versus socialism and communism; and distributive versus corrective justice. The challenge which humanism offered the Enlightenment has not yet been answered. It would consist in the establishment of a social order which is just, combines freedom and equality, rewards achievements and satisfies needs, considers the individual as well as society, and reconciles maximum output with maximum humanity. This challenge is still to be found in the controversy between the East and the West, and the solutions one side proposes are put to the test by the other. There is hardly a more useful starting point for an economic philosophy of the twentieth century.

In the foreground are the structural changes of Eastern economic policy confronted by those of the West. This is philosophically significant, because the contrasts between the two groups of systems are not accidental; rather they are, as described above, fundamental philosophical antitheses. In our own time there is also a trend on both sides toward a weakening of the extremes; that is, toward bringing about a correction of those exaggerations which threaten the optimal functioning of either system. In the West, social policies create a universal and more equal prosperity; in the East, decentralization, greater output of consumer goods, and other policies lead to a loosening of central planning as a whole.

However, vacillations in such self-corrections of the systems cannot entirely be interpreted as convergence, since their premises differ. They are opposing ideological concepts of man—individualistic or communistic.

The reasons for structural changes in Eastern economic policies may be ideological, practical, or political. At the moment, emphasis is placed on the problems of a modern industrial society—its social structure and the type of human being it produces, promotes, or serves. Here the East and the West differ in the direction of their attempts at finding a solution. However, within their individual frameworks there are tendencies which look like the acceptance of heretofore suppressed features of the opposite system, albeit with a change of the ideological sign and thus of the institutional development. In the West, for instance, economic and social policies—and the fundamental submission of mass society to a highly efficient productive process—became an increasingly powerful antidote to individualism; whereas in the East, we find orthodox ideology to be of decreasing importance in social policy.

Philosophical points of view relate mainly to the over-all social framework of the economy; therefore economic philosophy remains primarily within the framework of history and its anthropology is analytical. This point of view alienates it from what economic theory is and does.[12] * We cannot further discuss here the question of the delineation of these two areas.[13]

To a certain extent, the relationship between an evaluative philosophy and "exact" economic theory can be judged in the same vein.[14] While the former is often alienated from reality and its views are not objectively convincing, the same alienation of the latter is based on defining economic acts in terms of a few quantitatively comprehensible factors.[15]

In so far as philosophy criticizes society, it is opposed to functionalism. Such a philosophy demands that the dignity and autonomy of the individual be the only yardstick and goal of the economy. The argument has ended in a draw.[16] The philosophical investigations which successfully grasp reality and those which, rightfully, show concern for the individual lack sufficient reflection.[17] In view of today's economic systems, the investigations of economic philosophy should have the semblence of insight into the antithetic, basic structures of human actions.[18]

Concerning an economic philosophy of the twentieth century, we have, therefore, in the foreground, the idea of a basic confrontation or polarity of human deeds and their interpretations. There is, for instance, an interpretation of an objective course and subjective will, physical needs and spiritual decisions, self-interest and social responsibility, and productivity incentives and economic equality. Ever since the Enlightenment, such antitheses have partly characterized European society. Their source is the awareness that it is up to man to create the best possible economic and human world. Between the extremes there is an infinite number of possibilities. This open horizon characterizes modern European man, who often sees himself not as placed in a divinely or naturally ordained system but rather as standing by himself. Rational self-examination is frequently a guide. Often the norm of his actions is the integration of individuality and community, of world-changing progress and security, and of freedom and organization.

Ideologists approach such problems with solutions which are apparently ultimately valid and which try to realize exclusively one or the other aspect of the whole. But time seems to pass them by, for man's self-shaping practical world contains both elements. We must investigate simultaneously the problems of the interrelated and the opposing tendencies of behavior.

* Compare E. Heimann's challenge of rational economic theory.

9

The object, then, is neither economic regularities nor moral decisions, rather it is the totality of experiences as they interrelate and man's interpretation of these experiences as they apply to certain economic systems. Accordingly, changes in economic policy are based on an interaction of subjective and objective needs, of decision and necessity, and of open possibility and objective regularity.[19] * It is in this interplay of subjectivity and objectivity that the metaphysical, socio-philosophical, and ethical alternatives become centrally important and effective in the resolution of problems in economic policy.[20] †

There is a belief in an increasing predictability of the economic course—including even cybernetic programming—which constitutes faith based on technical and economic success.[21] While it is desirable that the individual be able to develop himself without being enslaved by heavy labor and economic anxieties, it is more probable, the way things are going, that he will become the slave of material wealth.

The framework within which today's controversy over economic systems takes place is determined by alternatives. In the West, individual decisions on the use of private wealth directs the economy; the Eastern economy is guided by the decisions of a central administration. Science must investigate the mechanics of both systems. Economic philosophy in the twentieth century examines the capabilities of the opposing systems to produce freedom and welfare. The systems are at odds as to the proper form of man's self-realization as a free being and how this is possible in an institutionalized society. The philosophy of economics and the science of economics deal with the same subject, but with different problems.[22] The former attempts to find out what economics means to a society of free men; this is the ideal of social science, philosophy, and politics.[23] Such a discussion must also deal with the function of mechanistic, mathematical, cybernetic, and organic models. Economic philosophy is therefore also the scientific and cognitive theory of economics.[24] ‡

The regularities of economic life possess no naturally rigid objectivity

---

* This creates difficulties for all proofs of greater or smaller attainment of welfare by one or another system. Moreover, many a normative demand—be it of retrospective or utopian character—becomes a hopeless illusion.

† These are not necessarily the only valid possibilities nor are the expressions used to characterize them the best possible, but they are at the very heart of the matter.

‡ Consequently, economic philosophy is not merely or primarily logic nor the theory of cognition of an individual branch of science which is concerned with economics. It is rather an anthropologically directed discussion of man's dealings with his world and thus also with the economy. In this connection it may also be the investigation of economic insights.

working upon a merely receptive consciousness. The "market" and the "economy" are natural data, but they arise out of an interpenetration of human will and reality. The changing historical factors lie at the intersection of freedom and necessity, the individual and society, mind and matter, aims and circumstances. Accordingly, the factual bases of the theories change.

Theories are thus the key to, and the expression of, certain forms of social and economic reality. In the East and in the West, today's reality is based on an industrial society formed by science and technology, with its objective and logical requisites.[25] But from a philosophical point of view, even this form of existence is the work of sovereign man.[26]

2. THE COMPLEXITY OF ECONOMIC PHILOSOPHY

A. Metaphysics

In previous investigations of economic philosophy, metaphysics, social philosophy, and ethics have been of central concern. The metaphysical decision is of utmost importance for the shaping of economic thought. The problem is whether or not we see the human scene as a dependent superstructure of material processes; that is, a purely objective mechanism or one with a spiritual source.[27] The exact and deterministic theory of economics represents the materialistic side as opposed to the more idealistic theory of universality and culture.

It is not necessary for the influence of metaphysical thinking on economic theory to be present in the theoretician's consciousness. For example, cybernetic models of the economic process, or equilibrium or game theories, do not call for a metaphysical *Weltanschauung*—a reduction of economic actions to "nothing but physically explainable or mathematically calculable courses of motion." Such theories are mostly estranged from the materialism of old. They are, above all, limited to methods, do not claim any ontological value, and are pragmatic in nature.

The implied relationship to "materialistic" metaphysics is not immediately recognizable. But philosophical investigation sees an essential feature of such research in the trendency to isolate the economy from other cultural structures and to trace it back to calculable basic motives.[28] In this sense, almost independent of the *Weltanschauung,* the above-mentioned theories shall be treated as "materialistic" here.[29] *

---

* Hardly anybody today would think of "isms" in the metaphysical sense; that is, as axioms of reality.

11

B. Social Philosophy

An even greater influence on the shaping of economic thought has been exercised by the socio-philosophical concepts of man either as an individual or as a member of the collective species, although today we have become increasingly aware of a correlation, filled with tensions, of both factors instead of a strict either/or situation. Pure individualism which in politics leads to anarchy and in economics to egocentric self-interest is as undesirable as strict socialism, which is inclined toward political, social, and economic dictatorship.[30] *

One-sided liberals and communists object to any compromise. Nevertheless, current developments favor a new social structure which, in the East and the West, could eliminate both "isms." This happens partly under the influence of industrial and social necessities and partly because of anthropological insights. It is part of the social and historical development that this is done in the West with free individuality in mind, and in the East with an attitude that man is a member of the species.[31]

C. Ethics

Today we assume the fundamental equality of all people as persons—the equality of human dignity—and that every individual is free to guide his own self-development. These two assumptions lead to moral claims.

Therein lies the new historical relationship between socio-philosophical and ethical convictions.[32] † This leads to a third central problem in economic philosophy: the question of the ethical nature of economic policy goals. This is the most important aspect of the philosophical concept of economics—important methodologically as well as objectively. By the latter term, we mean the determination of the aims and definitions of the proper means of economic action—that is, the question of justice and the just. Of predominant interest methodologically is the basis of value judgments and their relationship to scientific statements.

The latter problem can be traced back to the last century. From the writings of its founder to the present day, Marxism refuses to base eco-

---

* This statement does not imply an "interdependence of systems." Whether such exists here is open to question.

† The relationship of propositions regarding "is" and "ought" will be discussed below.

nomics and economic policy on the premises of an ethical *Weltanschauung* but instead refers to "scientific socialism" as derived from Hegel's historical determinism.[33] * The step toward more "social" situations is not a moral claim. It is maintained that such a step is the inescapable consequence of economic and social history, necessitated by scientific calculation, which is applicable in spite of people's varying desires. The deeper meaning of this thought lies in the expectation that the humanism of the Enlightenment and the axiom of a rational shaping of human existence have, in our time, become "objective" powers behind the evolution of society.[34] †

Marxism thus sees the fulfillment of ethical claims to justice as the result of "progress" which would have been achieved in any event through "material" laws, and this has remained its basic attitude in spite of some modifications. In the West there are a number of opposing views, wherein three groups may be differentiated. The earliest tradition was dominated by the idea of man's meta-historical character. Whenever social reality did not conform with the phenomena of natural law, it was considered a deviation of man's conduct from the "natural" norms of behavior as ordained by God. But ever since Herder and Hegel stressed the importance of history, the changeability of moral norms has been taken into account. The Enlightenment saw in reason the ultimately valid basis for ordering man's existence.

In recent times, other concepts have appeared concerning the position and function of normative statements, which have led to a conflict regarding value judgments; the last word has not yet been heard. Those who emphasized the concept of history saw in the established order of any one age the right one. In pragmatism, the individual's absolute benefit became the basis of an "exact" theory. Subsequently, the ethical validity of utilitarianism was interpreted so that it appeared to be a scientifically proven and basic motive of economic activity in general.[35]

Modern positivism calls for a radical distinction between conclusions in the field of economics and norms based on economic policy and ethics [36]—a distinction useful in securing a precise and generally valid science. But the reality of economic activity is already influenced by the human will as motivated by ethical principles.[37] Economic activity is not just the sum of mechanical events utilized to obtain certain goals. Rather, in its day-to-day structure it is also based on previous value

* However, there is an explicit communist ethic and Marxist morality, which will be dealt with later.

† Marx, who was well aware of the historic conditioning of all things human, explicitly rejected a "natural destiny" for man.

judgments. This had already been recognized by Weber, who solved the problem with his concept of the "ideal type." But Weber held that one must not accept as values those aspects of the prevailing economic situation which are part and parcel of it. They must be labeled and accepted as given, factual fundamentals. Likewise, it must be recognized and admitted that the very selection of an object of investigation entails a value judgment.

If a strict point of view is maintained, science must forego evaluation. Instead, it should investigate economic data as regular, or at least as causally explicable, events. Economics as a science has nothing to do with practical moral decisions concerning the economy. This position is in opposition to another which emphasizes the inevitability of value perspectives in every scientific statement, and it recommends, in order to further scientific research, that the dangers and risks in taking such liberties be pointed out.

Science, therefore, in order to preserve the purity and the freedom of its evaluation, tries to avoid any contact with cognition and decision; but this in itself means adopting a value basis—namely, that of a rationally comprehensible shaping of human existence. This value judgment originated in the Enlightenment and thus is an opinion shaped in a particular historical setting. In stating scientific insights are "value-free" and thus may be used to attain irrational aims which menace freedom, there is a risk that one is regressing to the theory of the "tool chest." One must take a stand. Science itself must investigate the social and economic structures and see what functions they perform, positively or negatively, in allowing every individual to fulfill himself consciously and freely. Above all, it is socio-ethical philosophy that works in this direction.[38]

A modernized form of the integration of "is" and "ought" refers to the actualities which must be taken into consideration when setting up goals. Using the concept of "the nature of things," the new approach admits, firstly, the specific requirements and uniqueness of certain areas of life and, secondly, their historical evolution. So far, there has been no resolution of the conflict between this modernized idea of "natural law" and the negative attitude toward value statements.[39]

Another aspect is contained in the problem of whether, in economic policies, there are formal and autonomous goals, such as, for instance, increased productivity, a determination of and obedience to a hierarchy of needs, and preservation of equilibrium.[40] In this connection, the economy must be considered in the entire context of society and cul-

14

ture, and thus also in the valid, more or less unified world of values. Economic ethics are the moral guidelines of economic practice. This requires, firstly, a description of such factors as valid ethical norms and value concepts and, secondly, the application of economic-ethical principles to the entire civilization of the time together with its historical changes. Civilization is to be tested by looking at its practical consequences. Since the Enlightenment, the ethical guideline of social and economic practice has been found in the rational, natural, and multifaceted fulfillment of the free individual.[41] An analysis of both major economic systems—without a value judgment in Weber's sense—can show whether or not they have succeeded in reaching this goal.[42]

3. THE BILATERAL SYNOPTIC SETTING FOR ECONOMIC PHILOSOPHY

A. Individual Sciences

It is difficult to assess the relationship between philosophy and individual sciences. At one time philosophy was "the handmaiden of theology." But since the Enlightenment it has been increasingly harassed by science until today it is at best recognized only as a justifying theory of cognition or perhaps simply as an encyclopedia of scientifically secured insights. Rational metaphysics, which sought to explain the ultimate, little by little acquired a poor reputation. English skepticism maintained that only the impression of our senses can convey truth, but this field of experience has been pre-empted by the individual branches of science, and one of these is the science of economics.

Modern attempts to secure for philosophy an area of its own or access of its own to reality go back to Kant. Milestones on that road are: Kant's proposal of a critical metaphysics based on practical reason; the speculative systems of post-Kantian idealists; the attempts of the neo-Kantians to regain for philosophy its erstwhile position on the basis of the theory of cognition; phenomenology which arose as a counterforce to psychologism; and, finally, existential philosophy.

With existentialism, philosophy was, on the one hand, to become the science of the downfall of capitalism and, on the other, to assist the builders of communism.

In the twentieth century, Western philosophy separated into two opposing trends, one of which (existential philosophy) begins with man's inner being, whereas the other (neo-positivism) leads philosophy into exact science or a generally accepted knowledge of the world. In existential philosophy, science comes off second best; on the opposite side, philosophy ends up either as logic or as mere linguistic therapy.

A beneficial reciprocity of philosophical and scientific investigation has started in the wake of a new trend in research. Here, detailed knowledge of man is presented in the form of philosophical anthropology and an effort is made to combine the problems of human subjectivity and the experience of freedom into a new investigation of structure. This trend is now gaining support even in the East. It arose from biological research, but now it contains elements of sociology, social psychology, and cultural anthropology and looks progressively more like a pragmatic theory in the largest sense.[43] It attempts to establish a concrete definition of man, a task which has been tackled frequently since the time of humanism and romanticism. But we know that the structure of human existence and knowledge of it are historically changeable and conditioned by events.

B. Economic Theory

Today's facts no longer support the traditional dichotomy between a philosophy based on mere concepts and science derived from sensual experiences. In economics and the other social sciences efforts are made to produce a methodically exact deductive theory. But in philosophy, the aim is to experience man by means of induction. No decision has been arrived at in the discussion of whether one or the other system is more realistic.

It is obvious that economic theory cannot content itself with a mere description of the facts but rather must extract out of the wealth of actual events the determining powers and structures. However, even mere description is possible only with the assistance of categories on which to base the description, and these are not abstracted from reality but considered in context. Much of today's economic theory sees economic reality as a field in which mathematically graspable "natural laws" predominate.

Such an inclination is the product of a certain concept of economic activity and how it is shaped. Its historical roots are accessible to historical investigation. With this in mind, economic theory is the expression of a decision to structure and interpret economic activity as a more or less strict natural process. Philosophy sees only relative value in the formation of economic theories. Nevertheless, in many cases economic theory proclaims itself to be universally valid for all economies, inde-

16

pendently of human decisions. This is partly true because, in the age of "capitalistic" order, the greater part of the economy was seen as an independent force in society which obeyed objective rules.

By means of empirical investigation and by looking at the final results, we can judge the relationship to reality of mechanistic, equilibristic, cybernetic, and other model constructions. But their applicability shows that the theories have only a temporary value.[44] They reflect what occurs in a certain historical economic situation or in part of it. Explanation of changes in the entire economic order is at best only limited.

Economic philosophy admits the possibility of the existence of general and formal laws, structures, and interrelationships valid for economic activity in general or, at least, for a modern, rational economy. But it poses the question as to whether any of the existing economic systems may be considered unconditionally best. It sees in the economic systems of the twentieth century attempts to create the best possible human and economic organization.

All economic systems must satisfy vital needs; but otherwise they are more or less dependent on the civilization. The basis of their validity is formed by certain historically definable goals and forms of existence. The aim of modern economics is formally clear: to secure well-being in a community of free men. But such a goal implies also a virtually unlimited need for improvement for every existing order; because the need for well-being is without limits, and the combination of real and complete freedom for the individual with full membership in the community cannot be totally accomplished.

We can conceive of a hypothetical state of affairs in which economics becomes an area dominated solely by technology and obedient to the same goal as described above. In this case, particular historical changes in human desires would call only for the use of well-tried means. Exact theory would then have an unlimited field of activity, undisturbed by outside influences. But consequently we would be faced with a questionable situation in which morally debatable institutions like profit, interest, and large inequalities in income are regarded and treated from a mechanistic point of view.

The greatest difficulty lies in the formulation of goals for the economy, which are in turn dependent on the goals of the culture and hence historically variable. There is a type of theory that generalizes economics by referring to it as a "strategy" of optimally "effective" means, whatever the goal may be. Economics would then be a potentially rational structure of actions in all areas of life and no longer an area of man's activity in which the content has been predetermined. But in reality economics as an area of activity contains a number of contradictory interests, purposes, and values which cannot be fully realized in any one economic system. Actual tasks and interests change. We have, at best, general purposes, such as greatest utility, maximum profit, and a high standard of living for all.

In short, the reality to which the theories must eventually refer is not fixed in nature but is the work of man. Therefore it is very difficult to find in it stable features or to discover universal structural categories that can explain all of the economic relationships that underlie every system.

Finally, even historical changes in the shaping of the economy cannot be fixed by a meta-historical dynamic theory; for the determining forces of the changes originate in economic subjects and their basic interests cannot be traced back to any one permanent motive. Moreover, they are only conditioned, not determined, by the day-by-day situation.

C. Comparative Economic Systems

The same problems arise in theories of comparative economic systems and are further heightened by them. The formation and historical changes of economic systems are not processes to be grasped by an exact theory but must be understood and explained giving due consideration to political and all other social and cultural powers. At least, this is the approach prevailing in the West.

But today there is overlapping of the economic systems of the two major blocs and a contrast in the generic conceptions themselves. Supposedly the East believes that economic laws determine the historical course of economic systems and thus that economic theory is identical with the general theory of civilization. Economic activity, it insists, is the basis of all other human achievements. In the West, theory is, instead, more admittedly used arbitrarily in a political context.

The most pressing problem of twentieth-century economic philosophy is the theory of the structure and changes of economic systems. It takes for granted that economic organization has origins which cannot be traced back to independent laws of economics, no matter how interpreted, but which do arise out of the entire structure of human activity. It does not deny the influence forces of production have had in shaping the economy; but it does refuse to regard that influence as absolute, since economic activity would then become a quasi-natural process. Nor does it decide beforehand whether there exists a certain natural order of economic life which may be studied and comprehended in isolation. It

18

sees the elements of cultural, social, and historical life as the metaphysical, socio-philosophical, and ethical roots of economic systems.

Here, one decisive question is how much attention should be paid, in
any one cultural system, to the economic systems contained within it.[45]
Today, economics is considered the instrument by which nature is increasingly placed at the disposal of man both quantitatively and qualitatively; and, at the same time, economics is expected to help the individual to become freer and more fully developed. The means applied to
satisfy these common interests are what differ in the various systems.

D. Economic Policy

The various methods mentioned above refer to the problems of economic policy. The cultural approach, which places economics within the
entire context of nature and civilization, sees its subject as a product of
human activity, full of contradictions. It becomes a pressing problem
for philosophical investigation as soon as the latter is put in the context
of economic policy. On the other hand, consideration of economic policy is possible only if the economy is considered, not as a self-sufficient
process, subject to natural laws, but instead as a link in the chain of the
social and political aggregate.[46] In this case, economics can only be a
set of tools for economic policies. By applying reason it can predict
consequences of certain actions under certain initial conditions. But a
decision must still be made as to what the goal of economic policy shall
be.[47]

During the Enlightenment, science hoped to be able to show man the
best order of existence by revealing the laws of nature. But in restrict-
ing itself only to the investigation of means, it was bound to fail. This is
one of the strangest features of present-day civilization. Gone is the
possibility of controlling rationally and scientifically the phenomena of
the social sphere which go beyond the mechanical calculation expressible in formulas. Eastern economic thought operates on the basis of
ideas derived from the history of civilization and philosophy. Thus, the
critical clarification of those concepts which give rise to decisions on
economic policy has become an urgent task of economic philosophy.[48]

The difference between Western and Eastern systems arises out of
the dynamics of the modern image of man. Here no existing system is
considered valid for all time but each must be measured against the degree of freedom, community, and material welfare achieved. Although
this would be an infinite task, we can comprehend the differences by
studying the methods employed. Since the individual-centered system of

19

the West does not fulfill all of these claims, the Eastern, collectivistic one rose against it. But since this latter, too, has many faults, there is a tendency to play down the extremes. The perfectionistic goal cannot be attained in any single way. Although the idea of correcting difficulties as they arise may be welcomed, the absolute primacy of humanity would remain. It could be considered a permanent goal which would provide guidelines for the practical measures to be followed at any one time. The belief in the possibility of an ultimately valid system would then be replaced by an awareness of an enduring process of self-correction. Present-day developments make such an assumption probable.

II. THE LEGACY OF MARX

A survey of the economic-philosophical legacy relates to the past role of the economy in social and cultural development. The history of philosophy—or part of it—shows also the mutual relationship between it and other fields of history. This applies as well to economic systems and their changes. Philosophy and economics are thus two intertwined factors of one complicated course.

Only since the French Revolution has this led to the predominance of an economic society of citizens. Human affairs were vastly affected by economic viewpoints. This led to problems which Marx, among others, tried to tackle, and he spoke of the disappearance of philosophy in favor of things practical. Yet philosophy still seeks to understand human activity—particularly the economic side of it—and this claim has become more urgent than ever before, even in the East.

A brief survey of the many historical variations can be found in my *Philosophie in der Volkswirtschaftslehre* (Jena, 1923 and 1926).[1] The discussion below centers on the economic thought of Marx, since in most instances it would be less familiar to the American or British reader than orthodox economic thought.

1. PHILOSOPHICAL SOURCES

Marx's political economy is an outgrowth of his philosophy.[2] Although his concepts can be explained as a development of classical political economy, running parallel with the liberalism of the Manchester school, the accent here is on the labor theory of value.[3] But his concepts derived their specific effect from his philosophy, which was based on German idealism.[4] *

Attacking the liberalism of his time, Marx advocated a radical change of social reality. He confronted the abstract economic theories of the classicists with his view that capitalism is a historical event. His thinking integrated several currents of the spiritual life around him. From utopian socialism he derived the description of more humane conditions. His economic thought derived its emphasis on man's physical existence from the materialism of the Enlightenment. But its determining basis was the philosophy of German idealism, particularly that of Hegel.[5] Previously, Fichte's philosophy advocated "a closed commercial state," that is, economic autarky.

In the history of mankind Hegel had seen "a progress in the consciousness of freedom"—the latter taken as the individual autonomy of Kant and Rousseau. Freedom implies also an intensive community of free men. For Kant, this had merely been a regulative idea, which all men instinctually recognized as valid. With Hegel, it became an objective force, actually shaping history. Nevertheless, Hegel retained the term "idea" in spite of his new interpretation. He defined man as a being which first of all creates itself by its own actions and then becomes that being. Man is originally "purely negative," a productive power which negates or reworks mere natural existence. This harmonized with Marx's concept of work. The form and the content of man's economic, social, political, and cultural existence are not given to him by nature but by his own creative activity.

Nevertheless, according to Hegel, man's self-creation does not come from aimless caprice but is a result of the above-mentioned effective "idea," by which he means the tension between individual freedom and the social order. He assumed that this conflict would tend toward a perfect synthesis of freedom and community.[6] But the idea was assigned a separate, metaphysical existence. Marx, in turn, stressed the superiority of active man. Here we must mention Feuerbach, for he inaugurated

* Lenin wrote: "Marx's teaching . . . is the rightful heir of the best that nineteenth century man has created in the form of German philosophy, English political economy and French socialism." The order of the schools of thought is not coincidental. Engels saw in the German labor movement "the heir of German classical philosophy" and mentions Kant, Fichte, and Hegel. Fetscher stresses that even today's Marxism cannot be thoroughly and critically appreciated without going back to Marx; his opinion is challenged by G. A. Wetter, among others, who denies the possibility of understanding the Soviet system properly by referring to Marx.

and codified the transition from "theology" to "anthropology," and from the primacy of the mind to that of the body and the senses. Marx took from Feuerbach the emphasis on physical and material things instead of on the motivating "idea." From Hegel, he borrowed the idea that man, by his activity, creates his own existence. Marx had only to "turn Hegel right side up" to design his historical materialism.[7]

In the center of Hegel's views concerning economics, in which he had been influenced by Steuart, stands a critical investigation of "civil society" (exemplified by bourgeois, liberal society), which was purportedly based on the personal and commercial relationships of its members rather than family ties or regulation by the state. To Hegel, the antidote to a concentrated accumulation of wealth and to misery and class conflict consisted of the elimination of civil society and its replacement by a society based on the national state, guided by a consciousness and confirmation of universal goals.

Marx condemned Hegel's views in some respects. Hegel did not destroy either the dialectic of master and serf or the configuration of civil society, but only weakened them. His solution lay in the elimination of the civil antagonisms through partnership. Marx maintained that this could only be attained through a radical destruction of the master-serf relationship. Unlike Marx, Hegel looked for the realization of the humanity of the Enlightenment not in the economic-social sphere but in the political one. To Marx, the latter was only a secondary superstructure on an economic base.

From Hegel, Marx took the idea of an "inevitable" historical progress of mankind toward greater freedom. He got his concept of humanity from Hegel, who had borrowed it from Kant, who in turn had taken it from Rousseau. But now Marx rejected the German tradition, stating that, although Hegel's view of man as a self-realizing being was structurally correct, he ought not have limited himself to the intellectual efforts of man. Real man was at stake, and his work begins with the production of food, an activity which is always a social one. This reproach is obviously not quite justified. It originates in Marx's revolutionary and world-reforming proposal of intervention. Secondly, he relied on "materialism," as the dominant spirit in the world then, which had already influenced Feuerbach. Man was to be understood "from the ground up."

Marxian philosophy changed mechanistic materialism into anthropological materialism.[8] For, while materialism, properly speaking, had been purely mechanistic in the thinking of de Lamettrie, von Holbach, Helvetius, and others, Marx the Hegelian assigned a greater role in history to man's more or less conscious acts.

23

Marx's idealistic legacy was too powerful for him to agree to a reduction of what is human to mere natural mechanisms. It was Engels who bore the responsibility for a later weakening of Marxism and for the change of dialectics into "leaps of evolution" based on natural laws. His thinking was ultimately simplified and schematized by Stalin and others.

Another scholar important in the development of Marxism was von Stein. He separated materialism from its ethical basis. Through him, materialistic thinking was transferred to the area of historical determinism. Here, too, we find, before Marx, such important concepts as the proletariat, the class struggle, and revolution. Von Stein combined these elements in his thinking, which was similar to historical materialism.

2. UTOPIAN SOCIALISM

A third related current of the Enlightenment, moral socialism, influenced Marx's image of the world, of history, and of man.[9] Marx became acquainted with this direction of thought during his exile in Paris.

Working man lives in society. Under the conditions of early capitalistic industry, his social actions went hand in hand with an asocial system of property ownership and a striking contrast of misery and affluence. This was the fertile soil which produced the criticism of Saint-Simon, Proudhon, Fourier, and others.[10] * The revolutionary demand for freedom, equality, and harmony of all men was raised against the conditions of the time. But it was not accompanied by the assumption of a scientifically calculable progress toward particular goals; rather it was a moral and pedagogical appeal to man's good will. Utopian socialism demanded that everybody work according to his capacities for the common cause and that he be rewarded according to his achievements. It painted a picture of a future ideal society, which would provide such economic abundance that all of man's needs would be satisfied.

This concept of future society, which was interpreted differently by various thinkers, was taken over by Marx. Although he was reluctant to accept everything his predecessors recommended, he considered the communist system an absolutely just form of life, satisfying all the strivings of mankind.[11] He did not go into details, and even neglected the actual organization in his writings. He was concerned mainly with establishing the next step in history, not with the erection of an ideal organization. Therefore, he was also careful about all utopian demands.

* This was also the starting point for early socialism in England, making the ethical aspects of the problem of distribution—which had been neglected by the classicists—the focal point of its investigations.

This also explains why he became increasingly concerned with the "inevitable" downfall of capitalism and not with the ultimate state of things. Furthermore he took into account Owen and other early English socialists. This was even more true of Engels and his image of the future was therefore more concrete and colorful.[12]

3. MARX AND ENGELS

The starting and focal point of Marx's thinking was Hegel's anthropology of labor—especially the concept of dispossession and alienation.[13] Here, man was presented as a being who "begets" himself through a purposeful utilization and reworking of nature. Thus, he rises to higher and more human conditions.[14] He is a being, growing with history.[15] * Man, who lives, acts, and speaks in human society, experiences his abilities through his own work. In communication with the world, he discovers himself as a creative entity. Through growing capabilities, insights, and thinking he shapes his free personality.[16] At the same time, he experiences himself and his modern concept of self as a product of a necessary process of history.

This Hegelian system of self-creation was made concrete and more restrictive by Marx, according to whom real activity occurs on the economic plane. Economic activity is the conditioning base of all things human. Social conditions, legal norms, constitutions, art, religions, and even philosophical systems are derived from this foundation and in substance depend on its current state.

Marx's theory of history is closely connected with this view of anthropology. Hegel had seen the gradual evolution of free man in history, while Marx saw the growth of economic proficiency and therefore also a chain of transformations in the superstructure.[17] According to him, history evolved from slavery to feudalism and then to capitalism. This is the picture of progress for the economic base; that is, the forces and methods of production. It is a history of class struggles. Marx's historical presentations and proofs do not stand up well under scrutiny. This and other factors prove that this theory of history was only one of several pillars that structured his real sphere of interest—the theory of the inevitable demise of capitalism in favor of communism.[18]

According to Marx, the superstructure lags behind the forces of production. It is an "ideological superstructure," since it preserves the past

---

* Stavenhagen points out that, following Hegel, Marx was the first to recognize the historical side of economics: "His economic system is the first attempt to take seriously the concept of a *dynamic* theory."

for human memory. Again and again, men fettered with outdated methods of production those productive forces which will bring about progress. Thus, to the productive forces developed in feudalism, the system of property and society became, after a certain time, a chain and revolution was the result. For the ruling class did not voluntarily give up its superstructure of antiquated institutions of government and ownership; this could only be brought about by revolution.

The situation is the same for capitalism, according to Marx. He maintained that capitalism, by his time, had fully matured and was about to be "swallowed up" by a new stage in development. The difference between the final stage of capitalism and that of other eras was that the class which would revolt against it—the proletariat—was not interested solely in its own emancipation but the emancipation of all mankind. While the middle class could emancipate itself without freeing the workers, the latter could emancipate themselves only by establishing universally free, that is, communistic conditions.

According to Marx, productive powers are mutually dependent; in other words, production has become completely socialized, in the broad sense. But the ownership of property is anything but socialized. This contradiction, which is manifested in life as exploitation, will kindle the revolution. Because of this contradiction the proletariat is completely alienated. Their labor, which should be the basis for their personality, becomes a commodity. They not only have become alienated from their work but also from the product of their work, from the society in which they work, and finally from their fellow men, whom they can only regard either as masters or as competing "commodities." [19]

Here, two seemingly irreconcilable currents of Marxian thinking meet. On the one side, there is the strictly "scientific" theory of revolution and, on the other, measurement of prevailing circumstances by means of an ideal image of mankind which is not alienated and not a marketable object.[20] But Marx himself adhered to the dialectic in its utmost, which he personally expressed as the dichotomy of "is" and "ought"; of objectivity and subjectivity; of historical immanence and a timeless basis of thinking; of the relative and the absolute; and of theory and practice. Careless followers often treated this aspect of his system of thought as trivial or they destroyed it completely.[21] *

It is also against this philosophical background that Marx's economic theories can be fully understood. From approximately 1849 on, he tried to present his doctrines on capitalism as value-free economic theory.

* Engels had already begun channeling Marx's philosophy into a scientific theory of evolution.

But in reality capitalism has been one of the most important stages in the history of Western civilization. Even Marx tried to emphasize that history is indebted to it for the development of economically productive forces.

The Marxian theory of history presumed a speedy realization of the humanitarian ideal of the Enlightenment, and it presumed to be able to predict that development objectively.[22] But in the West there has occurred only a socio-political evolution, however severe that change may have been. On the other hand, in order to call the Russian Revolution a Marxist one, the theory of imperialism and others must be added. But this leaves both Marx's humanitarian-philosophical position and the dubiousness of his economic concepts unaccounted for.[23] Much of the Eastern criticism of capitalism—derived from Marx's outdated and unrealistic ideas—is debatable.

Marx's economic views are based on his concept of the value of labor, according to which labor is merchandise. Unlike the classicists, his theory considered labor only as that work which is socially useful. He also maintained that the price of labor will never exceed the cost of food and other things necessary for its maintenance. For example, if the time needed to provide subsistence is six hours per day but the actual time spent is nine hours, the capitalist profits from the three surplus hours in those systems where private property rules. With Marx, the basis for such considerations is the fact that the power of labor creates more value than is needed for its reproduction. In the same way Marx tries to explain the recurrent crises in the capitalistic economy. These are generated by overproduction by the capitalist and undercompensation of the workers.

By introducing new procedures in production, capitalists are forced to make additional investments if they are not to lose out in the competitive struggle. Using the ideas of surplus value and the rate of exploitation, sinking rates of profit, and the accumulation of money and concentration of capital, Marx arrived at the thesis of an "industrial reserve army of the unemployed" and the impoverishment of the working class. He held the causes to be the introduction of machinery and technology into the productive process. Furthermore, the accumulation of money and the concentration of capital play a role, since this leads to a continuous unemployment of productive units, which, according to Marx, cannot be absorbed by increasing the amount of capital in existence. The contrast between accumulation, on the one hand, and impoverishment, on the other, manifests itself socially as an increasing class struggle.[24] It will end in a proletarian revolution and the downfall of capitalism.

27

Marxian economics consists in the development of this allegedly necessary evolution. He did not present an operative economic theory of socialism and communism, a lack bitterly to be deplored when the Russian Revolution began.

Engels changed the philosophical accent by stressing instead the supposedly natural bases of Marx's purely sociological and anthropological "historical materialism." He also created the formal framework of dialectic materialism, which was to become important in Russia. In addition, he supported social Darwinism and fatalism.

4. THE MARXISTS

Marx did not consider himself a Marxist. But the explosive power of his ideas is evident from the fact that they produced a number of diverging and competing thoughts and pregnant social movements. Marxian orthodoxy, it is true, did indeed follow Engels. It narrowed Marx's vast intellectual endeavor down to a deterministic theory of economic-historical progress. It finally fell into the domain of social Darwinism.[25] * Austrian Marxism developed only shortly after the turn of the century. It, too, fought for a doctrine of "strictly scientific" observation, stressing an allegedly accomplished change from organized capitalism to socialism. Revisionism derived from Marx the relatively ethical and voluntary idea of an evolutionary and slow socialization, delaying the transition into complete socialism. These ethical derivations prevailed and found their philosophical support in Kantian ethics.[26]

Around 1900, Marxian doctrine appeared as a radical variation of revolutionary syndicalism which sought to bring about the downfall of capitalism and to keep alive the class consciousness of the workers. This was to be done by using all available means, such as boycott, sabotage, and the general strike.

In the Russian leftist socialistic movement (Lenin and Trotsky), the orthodoxy of the Mensheviks was finally stamped out. It was complemented by a voluntaristic strategy of revolution. We also find a certain return to Hegel and to syndicalistic concepts.[27]

After rejecting Lassalle, social democracy in Germany was only partly directed by Marxian ideas. It preferred a reformist line aimed toward social politics and was bent on proving wrong the theoretically

---

* Marx himself was anything but a Darwinist. See his letter to Engels dated 18 June 1862. It was above all Kautsky who represented that doctrine.

"revolutionary" transition stressed in the past by Kautsky and Bebel.[28]
These off-shoots and derivations of Marxism arose around the turn of
the century; therefore, we must not identify Marxism with Russian
Bolshevism.

III. NEW CHALLENGES
OF THE TWENTIETH CENTURY

1. WAR, REVOLUTION, AND ECONOMIC CRISES

The problems of our time, which are novel compared to the questions of all past centuries, came into the foreground as a result of the cataclysmal events of World War II. Among the realities which the war helped bring forth were new social and political issues in the economic realm. These issues have also contributed decisively to the split between East and West.[1]

Progress in the natural sciences during recent history has formed the basis for these social, political, and economic changes. The forces of progress set loose by the natural sciences and which formed the basis for widespread mechanization were a result of the emancipation of the human spirit by the Renaissance and Reformation. Mechanization was intensified through the rapid development of industrialization and erupted in our century as wide-spread technology and rationalization in most areas of life.

Industrialization brought forth the pressing questions of the place and duty of mankind. It is a question which could only be asked in a secularized world. Philosophy was divided by the impact of industrialism into the opposing schools of idealism and materialism. The most extreme of these new philosophies was Marxian socialism. Industrialization as a social problem is still a dominating factor in our time. However, the danger to mankind caused by the polarization of philosophical thought has become even greater.

The rise in economic prosperity—brought about by technology—has led to a permeation of life by economics.[2] Man has paid for his independence from nature with a greater dependence on technology and functional systems of distribution. In addition, rationalism has allowed man to discover how irrational he is, and how much he is influenced by environment, climate, and impulse.

All of this knowledge cannot be mastered within the traditional framework of the academic sciences. Until the nineteenth century, academe at established universities was divided more or less into four faculties—theology, philosophy, law, and medicine. During the nineteenth century, the natural sciences fought for and won academic rank; the humanities were broadened not only by the addition of some new disciplines but also by others within established areas which became independent in their own right; and finally, economics and the other social sciences achieved equal standing with the natural sciences and the humanities. This multiplication of areas of knowledge produced specialization and delineation and with it, expertise and virtuosity in specific areas.

This "isolation" developed *vis-à-vis* the democratization of culture and the idea of man as part of the mass or herd.[3] Cultural, artistic, and literary criticism warned of these negative aspects, but the methods of mass production furthered them, and systems of mass education did little to stop them.[4] Population increased and the growth of cities led—in democratic as well as autocratic systems—to a stage of development also known in antiquity; namely, that extremes become less and community of interests becomes stronger. The "masses" became an object of sociological, psychological, and anthropological studies.[5] Collectively, the mass became the norm for the individual. It gained absolute pre-eminence; the individual was to be valued only as a part of the society in which and for which he lives. Here again, we have the two points of view that are in dispute between East and West.

Advances in the experimental sciences have reached such proportions that general understanding even in the academic world cannot be connected with reality. Everything seems within our grasp—within the realm of possibility—but has at the same time become obscured. From this situation arises the trend toward irrationality, the seduction of the masses, the skepticism of youth, and the instability of our century.

By the turn of the century scientific results had already produced basic changes of which the societal or political sector was not aware.[6]

Although a new era had been signaled by the American and French revolutions, the feudal monarchies of the Russian, Austro-Hungarian, and German empires remained in existence. Since the conservative elements proved themselves incapable of meeting the challenge presented by the new order—especially in the three monarchies mentioned— change by force was inevitable.[7] The downfall of the old order was precipitated by a comparatively trivial event, the assassination at Sarajevo. Shock waves from it continued through World Wars I and II, the Korean war, and the conflict in South Vietnam. The contingencies which produced these shocks show how necessary it was to revise the old order. That this revision broadened into global conflict, however, shows man's limitations.

The importance of national economies became visible in modern states as total mobilization proved the dependence of military achievements on economic production. This was especially noticed by the Central Powers. Soon after the outbreak of World War I, the German Empire broke with traditional economic policy and went over to centralization and a planned economy.

The results of that war were shaped mainly by irrationality. Emotions rather than the somewhat cooler political reasoning of the New World won out. The defeated powers were not only left with ruined economies when peace was made, they faced the breakdown of most European treaties, and as a consequence the predominance of Europe gave way to the rise of the United States. American world pre-eminence—an acknowledgment of an already established fact—appeared in direct contradiction to the results of the Russian Revolution, whose success owes a large debt to the upheaval caused by the war in Europe. The establishment of Marxian socialism as a viable system won importance in the world economy as the "Russian form of a West European idea."[8] The political changes which were brought about in Central Europe by the treaties signed in Versailles effected a complete change in the economic structure of the countries involved. The Central Powers were burdened by loss of geographical areas and reparations payments; the victorious powers, by war debts and changes in their export markets. Russia was almost a non-entity during the early years after the war, and in the same period American and Japanese competition became noticeable in foreign trade. In spite of this situation, which impeded the operation of the international economy,[9] and in spite of inflation and the Communist claim of world domination, liberal economic thought prevailed. There were, it is true, isolated instances of interventionism. In the main, however, the principle of keeping the economy free of governmental inter-

32

ference was maintained. In 1924, the year of the Dawes Plan, an economic revival began after most European countries had been shaken by the economic difficulties from the early part of the decade. This revival led to optimism.[10] But all too soon it became evident that the revival was a mirage. When the New York Stock Exchange shut down, the general world-wide crisis mushroomed; it laid bare the interdependence of national industrial economies. At the same time, the 1929 economic crisis showed the weaknesses of industrialized nations. In face of this effect economics as a science was on the defensive. This was compellingly shown in the difficulties experienced by Germany and Japan.

As two of the nations most affected by the economic crisis, America and Germany chose different solutions for the dilemma. The solutions, although opposite in method, were based on the same principle—government intervention. Germany recovered by supporting a dictatorship which advocated complete economic independence; the United States recovered through Franklin Roosevelt's New Deal.[11] * Roosevelt increased governmental intervention, begun by the Republican president, Herbert Hoover, to such an extent that he met heavy opposition. Important New Deal laws were at first declared unconstitutional by the Supreme Court, but later accepted as constitutional when the membership and mood of the court changed.[12] In spite of his successes, Roosevelt was not able to reduce adequately the number of unemployed by 1939.[13] † In spite of all predictions and attempts of liberal economists, free enterprise was not capable of ending the Great Depression on its own. The opinions that it had not been given enough time or that Roosevelt hindered it overestimate both the possibilities of such an economic system and the insight of industrialists and even of contemporary economists.

The belief in an economic system that could regulate itself was certainly strongly shaken. It had not been possible to find a successful prescription for recovery by pragmatic means. It was not until 1936 when J. M. Keynes's *General Theory of Employment, Interest and Money* [14] was published that a scientific economic basis was given to reform capitalism.[15] A revision in thinking brought about by this work, and new attitudes toward government-regulated capitalism and monetary theory necessitated by the world-wide crisis, made possible internal changes in the earlier economic practices.

* The roots of this tendency lie not only in the ideology of national socialism, the goal of Fichte's "closed commercial state," but also in the general political situation.

† In 1940 unemployment was still over eight million.

Macro-economic thought, which weakened liberal individualism, worked in favor of an organized capitalism. This "third way," somewhere between the collectivism of Bolshevik Russia and the allegedly uncontrolled capitalism as exemplified by the United States in the early twentieth century,[16] forced itself into practical application both in economic ministries and at the managerial level.

While the West was immersed in the global economic crisis, Joseph Stalin pushed through his First Five Year Plan in the Soviet Union. As the armies of the unemployed swelled to frightening proportions in Germany and the United States, the Soviet Union was faced with a shortage of skilled and semi-skilled workers.[17] Soviet Russia proved its capability for survival. The Revolution, begun in 1917 by the bourgeoisie, became a proletarian revolution and was won by Leon Trotsky's Red Army. Just as the discrepancy between the political and economic aspects in Russia before 1917 formed the basis for the domination of politics over economics in the October Revolution, so, too, did the differences between reality and theory reach such proportions in the period of "war communism" that a return to capitalistic economic methods in both agriculture and trade became necessary. This was achieved via private ownership.[18]

This New Economic Policy (NEP) which Vladimir Lenin propounded in 1921 achieved consolidation in Bolshevik Russia. During the First Five Year Plan (1928–1932) Stalin pushed through the collectivism of farming and suppressed all opposition. This was an attempt to make a large country function according to a plan and to shape it according to a theory of history. An ideology dominated in the main by economic concepts became the driving force of the state.

2. THE DETERMINING ANTITHESIS

A. Technological Progress and Neomaterialism Versus Modern Idealism

The discipline of economics emancipated itself from philosophy and developed into an independent science. To the same extent that it gained autonomy in its own right, it closed out philosophical inquiry. This does not mean, however, that an economic system which is composed of pure economics and therefore requires definite specialized thought is immune to philosophical influences. It means that philosophical systems no longer form the only foundation of economic theory. Economic theories, however, often unconsciously contain philosophical as well as ideo-

34

logical elements which in time produce conscious criticism.[19] Very often, therefore, economic theory in itself can clarify philosophical thought.

Clarification of the expressions "materialism" and "idealism" can be achieved by transposing them into the realm of present philosophical discussion. This discussion is shaped by two opposing points of view. One point of view is associated with idealistic traditions, and, speaking in terms of subject-object, is subject-oriented. Man, his thoughts, actions and his relationship to his environment, stands at the center of philosophical reflection in which the cultural structure as well as his individual and social existence are objectivized. One of the philosophical views which pertains to this process is existentialism (the philosophy and ontology of existence), the phenomenology and structure of which are associated with traditions of German idealism. This school of thought recognizes objective structures in the different realms of existence as projections of man's intellectual prowess which reach their fullest development in the social and cultural processes.

Opposed to this idealism stand the teachings of neopositivism. Neopositivism orients itself in the main to the material world and is closely allied with the exact and quantifying sciences. Neopositive analytical philosophy tries to identify itself with the philosophy of science. Neopositivism aims to understand and clarify causal and functional relations, which supposedly may be described by logical statements.[20] *

When this is superimposed on contemporary Western economic views, two interpretations can be made, both of which are defined by their method and the questions they direct themselves to. On the one hand, there is a qualitative view of economics based on intellectual knowledge and cultural theory. It states its questions in terms of man's free will. Its methods are formed primarily by "understanding" and phenomenological observations. On the other hand, there is a quantitative view of economics based on the "hard sciences" such as physics. Its form of questioning is structured by the attitude that the field of economics is guided by its own laws, and its methods are empiricism and mechanical, causal, and functional explication.

The first steps leading to the development of the present polarization began in Freiburg, Germany, at the turn of the century. A battle was fought to decide whether the study of political economy belonged—to use the words of the Freiburg/neo-Kantian school of thought—in the area of the "natural sciences" or the "cultural sciences." Another step

* For the philosophical history of the various materalistic and idealistic points of view on economics, compare this with chapters IV and V.

toward polarization was the debate on value judgments. Max Weber opened the debate—one that still exists today, though in other forms.[21] This debate finally resulted in questioning the logic of the social sciences. Weber, in deciding against using value judgments in the field of social science, led his supporters to treat the social sciences as an area of the "hard sciences." This meant that the logic and methods of natural science were to be applied to the social sciences.

Practically speaking, putting the social sciences to the task of gathering quantified empirical data ("science is measurement") and establishing causal-mechanical connections at first affected only the logic and methods of the social sciences. However, there is a tendency of the science-is-measurement school of thought to turn statements meant to apply only to logic and method into statements of ontology. This happens because qualitative observations are systematically rejected and relegated to the area of philosophy, which is isolated because it cannot claim to deal with objects.

The concrete, visible forms of materialism and idealism in today's economic thought are best grasped by using the following questions as a basis for understanding. What role is assigned to the human being in economics? Should economics be seen as an integral part of a social-intellectual context or should economics be isolated from this context and seen as an independent area guided by its own laws?

The independence of economics is maintained by assigning the meta-economic factors which determine an economic system to the "data area," which represents the stipulated constellation where models based on pure theory are shaped.[22] The quasi-scientific viewpoint tends to absolutize the purely theoretical models in a negative way. By setting up as absolute those methods whose goals are objectivization and quantification, one is led almost unnoticeably to a metaphysical form of economic materialism which might be called "economism." [23] In this context economics deals with the satisfaction of needs and maximization of individual or, interchangeably, social well-being. For this, economic policy goals must be the increase of productivity and the growth rate as well as economic stability.[24] Quantitative economic thought implies that the social optimum is reached simultaneously with economic maximization. Here we can see economics in its traditional context of utilitarian philosophy. This has strongly influenced economics from its inception and—paradoxically enough—has led to the elimination of philosophy from technological economic thought.[25] Such essential certainties imply, in the main, anthropological definitions: to strive for

36

social well-being is essentially a human act, and it is, in the last analysis, on this human characteristic that economics is based.

Functional growth, maturation, and decline of economic systems are treated as objective movements following their own eternal laws.[26] An example is the competitive system of marketing.[27] By making maximum utility its highest goal, the metaphysical element of market economy analysis, whose logic, nevertheless, is materialistic, becomes apparent.[28] Goals other than economic ones interfere and are, consequently, denied recognition in the system by saying that they are "non-economic." The problems of the social order, as well as the freedom [29] * guaranteed or denied by that order, and cultural progress can be reduced to economic dimensions.

The term *homo economicus* denotes yet another form of economic materialism. The theory of a general economic equilibrium is philosophically close to Herbert Spencer's theory of evolution.[30] The prediction of equilibrium is the ultimate forecast for economic development.[31] Predictability means that human economic actions also have to be predictable. According to the original concept, which is a product of the Enlightenment, *homo economicus* acts autonomously in making decisions dealing with economics. It is true that the enlightened man of economics is aware of influences on economics outside his control— something he has to incorporate into his calculations if he wishes to survive in the marketplace.[32] This hint of something outside man's control became more emphatic in successive developments in economic thought. The idea that economics follows quasi-natural mechanical laws tends to lead to the assumption that man cannot act autonomously. For this reason, behavioristic models are used to guide the rational acts of *homo economicus*. These rational acts become "faultless" reactions to known data.[33] The methodical approach of calculating functional interrelationships by omitting the subjective element as such is justifiable.[34] The danger lies in expanding this idea to include all of society.[35]

The approach from the field of cybernetics—an approach which is presently affecting the social sciences and especially economics in many forms—shows a new form of determinism. This school of thought definitely distinguishes between technical functions and the mecha-

---

* The postulation of freedom, which is central to neoliberal theory and which is a thoroughly idealistic concept, as seen from the perspective of economics is formulated as freedom in the economic sense but is made to stand for freedom in general.

nism.[36] Functional thought processes [37] are observed, evaluated, and characterized as being subject to the universal aspect of a social system which functions without friction and has the goal of equilibrium.[38]

This means that the function of the individual is determined by the role he plays in the system, and he functions by expecting to play the roles which fulfill the institutionalized value system.[39] Such a functional social system is consciously analogous with cybernetic, self-directed, and self-correcting systems.[40] Value standards form the basic program, and the ingestion of the value standard forms the programming and the conditions for the self-direction of the special individual system of equilibrium.

The relationship to economics of the above approach is easily derived.[41] True, the functional theory does not view economics as an isolated system, but as a social subsystem. Still, major economic categories can be turned into sociological elements through generalization. All economic terms such as welfare, costs, profits, income, and productivity are functional for the main purpose: continuation of a social system in the most stable equilibrium possible.

Within this "predictable" functional system called society, human action is seen as properly playing out a role. Since it is thought to be a cybernetic system, it can and must be withdrawn from human autonomy and spontaneity. After all, human autonomy and spontaneity could upset the mechanical understanding of economics and thereby these factors can only be seen as a possible disruption of the functional equilibrium. Here we see the development of *homo mechanicus* through *homo economicus* to *homo functionalis*. He becomes the target of social criticism in the Western world today,[42] not because he is just a scientific model, but because he has in part become a reality.[43] Theories dealing with problems of decision-making and natural law also come to similar conclusions. These theories are not based on the model of cybernetic machinery, but rather on the very real and growing influence of technology in the areas of economics and society.[44]

Idealistic by comparison is the point of view which Weippert has described as the cultural theory of economics.[45] For the cultural theorist, economies are a result of man's actions and are all woven into the societal and intellectual contexts of man. Economics has the same cultural reality as, for example, law or language.

In other words, economics is an objective extension of man, who is a creator of culture guided by intellect. This point of view opposes that which sees an economy as a closed system working autonomously to create its own reason for existence. The idealistic picture of economics shows it as a structure which is formed in part by social and cultural life and in part by the varied drives (not just utilitarian or hedonistic drives) of human beings involved with economics. Seen in this light, economics is only a portion of man's social and cultural existence.

It is true that certain objective areas within economics can be understood through pure theory. However, economics as a whole always operates in and relates to the changeable structural whole of cultural reality. This cultural whole, however, is guided by principles outside the world of economics—principles that have been relegated to the area of data by pure theory. Since pure economics has meaning only if it is seen in perspective to the cultural and social whole, it is in a subservient position to that whole. Economics is that part of the cultural whole which produces and offers the means necessary for realizing social, cultural, and individual goals. This means that all economic goals and values are of a derived nature and made up of values that are meta-economical.[46] Therefore, the attainment of *economic maximums* can never be construed as being the same as reaching a *social optimum*. Attainment of economic maximums is not the content and goal of economics. Frictionless functioning can never eliminate the question of the reason for the function. The reason for the existence of economics according to this can never be derived from economics itself; it can only be meta-economic.

This position which does not oppose examination of positive laws does, however, contain the danger of overemphasis. When this happens the objective point of view and the necessity of objectivity to understanding are at times disavowed. Then, an anthropological exposition is turned into a radically subjective one. When this happens, there is an exaggerated idealism in which the idea of economics is, for the most part, one of negation. This type of idealism once again takes up the inimical attitudes of creative idealism.

Existentialism and Martin Heidegger's existential ontology both negatively raise the subjective elements of existence to an absolute power.[47] Anthropological reduction is turned into a radical reduction to subjectivity. According to Heidegger, all objectivity dissolves into the prediction of existence. A thing exists because the human being defines its existence,[48] a thing can have no existence without man (the subjective). Using Heidegger's method of predicting all things as existing, history exists only as the history of mankind; time becomes temporal. Should objects now allow themselves to be "existentialized," or in other words, if they operate of and by themselves according to their own laws, are they to be classified as not-real? All intra-human relationships—in other words, social and economic relationships—are seen as spheres of "man" and of his pronouncements. In all of them the idea becomes replaced again and again by existence.[49] *

Both of the extreme positions—the existential view as well as the purely functional determinist system—are superior to that which uses objective natural law together with subjective purpose as principally equal factors in the formation of economic systems. Both the existential and natural law approaches and their complex lines of intersection demand methodical and unprejudiced research. Such an attitude is present in all of the ideas presented. This attitude toward research is being used increasingly by most researchers in the highly differentiated fields mentioned above. A conscious effort has developed to avoid those methods which cannot be stretched to give a metaphysical explanation for the whole object. This insight provides the possibility of generally reopening the question of the categorical structure of economic spheres. This would be the point of approach for a philosophical anthropology which stands above the various "isms." This approach rests upon man's actions, which form the basic element.[50] Accordingly then, economics is an objectivization of cultural activity. However, economics is at the same time an objective creation governed by its own structural laws (definitely not natural laws) and by man, who is an exponent of this creation and is himself formed and guided by his need for material objects and by historical trends, among other things. This is what anthropology defines as the dual position of man; he is both the creator and the creation of culture.[51] The Kantian concepts of *homo noumenon* and *homo phaenomenon* are equally acceptable to studies of laws and to the standpoint of the freedom of man. This approach strives to grasp (and in doing so goes beyond Kant) and integrate both aspects as tendencies in the history of human self-realization.

B. Private Enterprise Versus the Planned Economy

From the socio-philosophical point of view, the basic problem of the twentieth century is the contradiction between individual and collective interpretations of man.[52] Seen in this light, the questions of greater or lesser economic efficacy and of one or another economic or social

---

* The concept of "dread" or "Being-in-the-World" in Heidegger's ontology thereby offers a fruitful approach to a philosophical explanation of economic activity. Brecht has made some contribution in this direction.

system are methodically diminished. The problem here is the opposing principles.

The Western (noncommunist) world sees the individual human being as the basic element of social and economic activity. In the Eastern (communist) world, man is seen as part of the whole. It would, however, be wrong to say that here only the individual and there only the collective is of interest. Here in the noncommunist world it is expected that sensible actions by the individual will lead to an optimum of communal well-being; in the communist world the collective well-being of all is supposed to bring freedom to the individual.[53]

The sharpness of the conflict is contained only in the historical and systematic point of departure. The two extreme examples in economic thought are those which, on the one hand, oppose control by the middle class and support individual freedom and the market system, and, on the other, those which espouse strong egalitarian control of the actual inequality and misery which are the results of a rigorous system of individualism. (Another less important variant is the popular opinion that sees society as a structured "organism.") Today, the world is divided on, and as a result of, the practical application of the two extremes mentioned above. In spite of their seemingly radical opposition, they are related to each other. The goal of both is that the individual, as a free and whole person, takes full responsibility for himself by realizing his strengths and goals. In order to reach these goals it is necessary to have a social order which furthers them. The design of this order is where the divergency lies.

The Western world stresses individualism which, economically speaking, is unhindered profit-seeking in free markets. Differences in original positions and capabilities have divided society into rich and poor. This was the first negative consequence of unadulterated individualism. The "general welfare" became an abstract which, in truth, only a minority of the propertied class shared in. This mistake has been corrected in part by the socialist movement, labor unions, the challenge of communism, moral insight, and the pragmatic force of utility, incentive, and buying power.[54] Welfare as a whole has increased, and there has been more equality in sharing. It is true that economic equality does not exist, but this is perhaps a utopian goal or rather a task that cannot be realized at this point, as is indicated by continued inequality in the Soviet Union and the people's republics. Traditional interests, the community of interest of both the management and labor hierarchies, the clear need to increase material incentives, and the existing conditions of ownership are some of the things preventing economic equality.

41

Political equality has almost been completely won in democracies. Social goals, however, are seen by some as illusionary. All the same, liberal doctrine maintains a clear conscience. Economic bottlenecks and crises are seen as accompaniments to freedom; lack of freedom of the masses is excused as an accompanying factor in the growth of national prosperity.

As a result of the general increase in prosperity, the question of absolute poverty has been eliminated in the main, and the question of relative poverty has, at least for the majority of people, been weakened. This has happened even though some countries suffer food shortages or have a high rate of unemployment, both of which are disturbing. Major critical conditions are, however, rectified by governmental economic policies. The new social problems in the Western world have developed with the growth of an industrial society which has hardly slackened since the Great Depression. The individual has more and more developed into a functionally important part of a technologically, thoroughly rationalized working world. The goal is no longer so much one of freedom of ownership for all but rather social security for all within an economic system with balanced growth. This situation agrees with the already mentioned basic concept of economic theory, which sees economic activity as a system of functional progression (such as cybernetics). Economics has developed more or less into instrumental, specialized knowledge which offers adequate strategy for any desired result.

The aims of economic policies are themselves in part largely of an economic nature (economic growth, stability, prosperity, effective demand, and full employment) [55] and together with this they also in part tend to encourage the development of a self-consciously free and responsible, generally well-educated human race. Opposition to these goals comes from socialist and liberal viewpoints when economic policies move into the area of meta-economic goals and the whole area of the social and cultural "data circle" which affects economic events.[56] The liberal point of view essentially sees a more productive functioning of the economy and at the same time more individual freedom as the result of competition among privately owned enterprises. The socialist viewpoint believes it can fulfill its duties to the economy and to mankind through state ownership of key industries, joint participation, and abolition of private property.[57]

Experience with the negative conditions produced by the liberal middle-class social order resulted in socialistic and communistic ideas of society in which private property was to be done away with and in which private interests were to be absorbed for the benefit of society. In this

42

way, the equality of class comrades is supposed to lead directly to freedom for everyone. This will happen because every individual is an equal partner in a collective world of work and, beyond that, can use his free time to develop his own image as a human being. In principle, everyone participates equally in cultural goods. This is the way it should be according to the Marxist viewpoint, which sees perfected humanity as a result of centrally directed social and economic relationships. Practically speaking, however, Bolshevism led to totalitarian systems. These totalitarian sysems derived their legitimacy for economic command from a futuristic vision of a productive community of all workers. In order to realize this vision, it was important to have a strong centralist government. Later on, the state would wither away and the general welfare would be taken in hand by associated individuals. This goal justifies dictatorial measures if necessary.

When applied to conditions in Soviet-type countries, the parallel with modes of justification for liberal dogma becomes apparent. Lack of personal freedom is excused by the need for rapid and planned economic structuring. Lower economic productivity is acceptable, because it is necessary to hold on to the principles of communal ownership and the communist work ethic, even if people are not yet mature enough for communism and could be spurred to greater productivity by capitalistic methods. After the true value of the communist economic system has become apparent, work in itself will be the first necessity of life for the free individual.

The first extreme dictatorial phase of the collective experiments began to diminish even during Stalin's lifetime. In the meantime, the Soviet Union, which can be taken as typical, has become a vigorously developing industrial nation. Along with this development came new problems for the Soviet Union. The need for specialists and the increased educational needs of a technological world forced an easing of centralism. The Soviet economy—still for the most part without private ownership and centrally directed—did return to encouragement of individual initiative. Added to this is the fact that private interests have to be acknowledged if the individual is to be content to work toward communist goals. Attainment of communist goals is no longer seen as the automatic result of a developing communal economy. Education in communist morality is being given ever-increasing importance.

Western individualism gave birth to a pluralistic industrial and welfare society. Eastern collectivism is trying to reach a centralized welfare society through an improved economic order. The last word is not yet in as to which of the two systems has the greater or lesser capacity. The

43

differences between them should lessen because pragmatic interest in economic success will keep both sides from becoming bogged down in doctrine.[58]

The problems which arise in both systems come about in different ways but are unmistakably related, and neither has much effect on the original forms of opposition. The real differences are which of the two images of man and which of the two economic systems are most suitable for developing the type of human being that can survive under the conditions of an industrialized world. This person must be, first, an effective specialist. Secondly, he must be a free person who is interested not only in private or group advantages, power, and private consumption, but also must help form and be in part responsible for the general political, social, and economic order. At the same time institutions will be required which allow such democratic participation in all areas of life. In the long run, the most successful form of existence will probably be that which can leave both extreme individualism and extreme collectivism behind it.

If Eucken's neoliberal theorem of the "interdependence of systems" is correct, it is as much against an exaggerated type of liberalism as against a Stalinist system. Economic freedom without any type of intervention may lead to only a formal democracy, in which real control is in the hands of those who have economic power.[59] On the other hand, a forced system of equality directed by a despotic centralized government leads to the loss of freedom for the masses.

In fact, the middle 1960s brought an expansion in the private sector in the East.[60] During the same time the West increased administrative controls on ownership rights, secured subsistence minimums in wages and salaries and in social insurance, and the importance of the private sector was decreasing.

The levels of these two movements, which are heading toward each other, are still extremely different. After all, bits and pieces of private ownership in a collective system of society cannot be equated with economic and social policy restrictions on free enterprise in a societal structure based on the freedom of man and secured by due process of law.[61] * The opposing sides are the ideal of individual freedom with its antisocial consequences and that of the equality of all which works toward the general welfare of workers and its totalitarian consequences.

---

* In Marxist terms, freedom arises from personal participation in the public cause; liberalism regards the private sphere (one's own four walls) as the home of freedom.

Both are a double-edged heritage from the intellectual world of classical liberalism.[62] They have in turn been alloyed with many other socio-philosophical thoughts which are now being fought out between East and West.

C. Eastern Versus Western Justice

Ethics at the middle of the twentieth century, as far as ideas of justice are concerned, can in part be understood in terms of Aristotelianism and the Scholasticism which grew out of it. Aristotle saw the best justice, in general, as that which acknowledged and was compatible with the government which in its ideal form includes the total tradition and general spirit of the *polis*.[63] Seen as an object, justice can, according to Aristotle, be differentiated into two basic forms. These are distributive [64] and corrective [65] justice. The mean, Aristotle believed, must be preserved in all ethical concepts with high standards.[66] This middle point is to be found in equality between too much and too little justice. Equality is defined as "geometric" within distributive justice and as "arithmetic" in corrective justice.

Geometric equality must contain four parts (in a geometrical proportion) and take into account, while disseminating justice, the reputation of the individual in regard to a just allotment: personal value and division of goods are related to each other. Since Aristotle mentioned money, then, too, personal value and the financial capacity of a human being are directly proportionate.[67] Freedom seems to be the correct standard by which to measure properly the ratio of division under a democratic form of government.[68] Arithmetic equality is divided into two parts and disregards the moral status of the individual. This viewpoint, which only regards the circumstances caused by the subject (not inherent in the subject himself), originates in the Attic philosophy of law [69] and is based primarily on reparations ordered by the courts and on the terms of a contract. Finally, arithmetic equality is used in the relationship between demand and supply in order to leave the producer with an incentive to produce.[70]

The metaphysics of the Middle Ages exploded the Aristotelian framework. Legislation became an ethical problem and differentiation based on the material world was subjectivized. Distributive justice appeared as directive justice (*justitia directiva*); for unfulfilled obligations (*obligationes ex delicto*), it was a corrective justice; and medieval law became a commutative justice (*justita commutativa*) for obligations made under contract (*obligationes e contractu*).[71] The structure of the material, which was constant in Aristotelian thought, gradually disappeared.

Political discussion in modern times brought a renewal and a far-reaching change. The demands for justice were, as the demands of the French Revolution had been, brought forth without basis in an explicit idea of justice.[72] The old Aristotelian means of measuring justice (for example, freedom in a democracy, and riches and heredity in oligarchies) were made the slogans in the movement for ideal conditions. Marx proposed the modern theory for this goal. He abstracted from the ideal condition an ethical demand and saw the ideal as the result of an objectively necessary historical development.[73]

The ideal condition against which reality is measured may be called the idea of justice, the abstraction of which in a concrete situation always takes on the form of whatever demand is necessary. The way in which the situation is made concrete would be for the most part determined by the particular historical setting and the particular social, political, economic, and judicial situation. Systematic structural examination of the ability to unify abstract ideas of justice seems difficult and possible only after long historical experience. It is within the area of historical reality that the antithetic ideals of freedom and equality of individual human beings are battling it out.[74] The struggle between liberalism and socialism is the struggle for a possible unification of freedom and equality.

The self-understanding of liberalism was doubtless rooted at the beginning in a religiously understood presentation of the dispensation of justice. The talents and abilities of the individual engaged in economics were seen as gifts of God and their use as a command. The free development of divine gifts was just; inequalities were accepted and discrepancies were evened out in social relationships by altruistic morals. The "unseen hand of Providence" brought human relations into a natural order which within the market mechanism was seen as a pre-established harmony.[75]

However, even in the beginning stages of liberalism theological understanding, with its ideas of predestination, began to weaken. What remained in the consciousness of economic man was an idealistic humanism, which when it was later joined to the rationalism of the natural sciences gradually began to destroy itself. Society began to seek a social order which equaled the order of the natural sciences—an order whose existence was taken for granted. The state, therefore, was only to be allowed a very small function in the economic order. The state should in-

46

tervene, in the main, only if the free economic practices of individuals were threatened.

Modern socialism chose another standpoint according to which a few economically strong individuals eliminated the possibility of development of those economically less strong or those who had not inherited the opportunity to develop themselves. Not predestination but rather barriers erected by men to protect a variety of privileges were the reason many had to endure unbearable economic hardship, and the robust competitive struggle hindered many individuals in developing their personalities in freedom. The guide to free development on the level of human self-understanding should not be one of struggle but rather of corrective justice. From this came the ideal of equality for all men, which is supposed to have gradually evolved since the French Revolution.[76] Societal demands in support of individual freedom were to replace political privilege. The state's *raison d'être,* given it by society, was to establish the equality of all men. The core of corrective justice in socialist and communist countries was related to humanitarian equality in the areas of human and social self-understanding. However, this vision of justice very soon disassociated itself from its structural unity. Its idea of justice was applied freely to any situation, but it was especially used within the field of economics.

The bitter struggle between the exponents of freedom and the representatives of egalitarianism is most easily grasped when seen in light of its saturation with humanitarian, political, and economic ideas. The question of "freedom and/or equality" became removed from concrete problems and was discussed abstractly and passionately.

Liberalism was successful as a protest against the misuse of state power and against the lack of justice for the individual. Its true core sought the greatest possible freedom for all men regardless of their form of government.[77] Equality achieved through governmental compulsion was not compatible with liberalism. Economic liberalism cleared away many of the obstructions to the development of freer forms of life.[78] In spite of a general rise in economic well-being, it was not until economic models of the Manchester type were joined with liberal goals that humanitarian attitudes led to an antiliberal movement. Those who fought for the liberal idea of freedom felt that they would have to give up their barely established freedoms in the areas of politics and economics if a radical invitation were given to egalitarianism.

The dangerous proximity of equality and demagogy in politics was all too well known. The tyrants of antiquity were already well versed in the use of egalitarianism as an instrument to entrench their rule. Aristotle

47

clearly saw how easy it was for the tyrants to play off the masses of the lower classes against the numerically inferior upper classes. He also noted how willingly the masses allowed themselves to be put under the yoke if even the breath of a chance existed that their egalitarian wishes would be fulfilled. The demand for uniformity seemed to be the banner of revolutionary movements with totalitarian goals.

The demand for social equality seemed to the exponents of freedom to be a sortie against the freedom for human development, even though this danger was not seen so clearly then as it is today. The "horizontal pressure" of the masses in the context of a corrective justice stood in danger of producing a homogeneous society and of suppressing the personality of the individual.

Uniformity in the social area was seen to threaten dictatorship. A classless society therefore presented as much danger to freedom as did an egalitarian democracy in which the boundaries between the state and society are blurred. Equality was often seen as leveling and conformist; Burckhardt's "terrifying simplifiers" became a nightmare. John Stuart Mill thought that tyranny had not only political but social characteristics and that freedom could be a danger when adapted to the democratic form of government because it seemed to advance the dangers of leveling through majority rule. Beyond this, many political thinkers began to combine egalitarian thought with the growing threat to freedom caused by the governmental apparatus.[79]

The defenders of freedom saw their ideal gravely endangered by egalitarian tendencies. They fought egalitarianism in every form and sought a governmental form under which freedom would have maximum security. The idea of freedom was made into a bulwark against dictatorship —especially in Western countries which were obligated to the Graeco-Roman heritage.[80] In spite of its many imperfections, democracy seemed to be the proper form in which people could live together in freedom. Many "prophets" saw a future danger coming from Eastern Europe where the idea of freedom was not deeply enough rooted.[81]

PART TWO

Ontological Basis

IV. QUALITATIVE VIEW OF THE ECONOMY

1. METAPHYSICAL ASPECTS

In philosophical analysis of economic goals there is a fundamental difference between material and cultural needs. In human existence, spirit and body, culture and nature, as "ideal factors" and "real factors" are so interdependent that one domain does not exist without the other. However, the relative superiority which is theoretically and practically conferred upon one or the other leads to major changes in the whole structure of human life, including the economic sphere of existence, and will continue to do so until one view or the other is absolutely established.[1]

The history of metaphysics is defined by dualistic rather than monistic (i.e. singularly idealistic or materialistic) concepts. It is difficult to deny that in one's perception of the world, reality has simultaneously an external, objective existence and also a subjective existence shaped by representation and concept—that in actual existence mind and soul, on the one hand, and, on the other, the body frequently work together and within each other. Individual philosophers usually emphasize one or the other when evaluating existence and value.

With the rapid progress of the natural sciences, the material world has clearly been given the dominant position. As early as Descartes, the ambiguity of this position was suggested. Perception of the outside world becomes the main object of methodological reasoning; yet the thinking ego remains the ultimate reference point regarding all certainties of existence. With that also begins its impoverishment, because it shrinks to nothing, a mere insignificant point, which stands *vis-à-vis* with all reality in its varied profusion as the outside world. Because of this, man prepares to become its master and owner.

At present, one is forced to recognize that there still exists a split in philosophy, even disregarding the biased Marxian theory of base and superstructure. The existential school ponders the "I-self," the human subject, but cannot raise it further into a mature configuration. (Rather it is experienced as something fathomless and frightful.) It stands opposed to positivism, which recognizes only objective data, scientifically determined, but which nevertheless tacitly assumes its transition into an ontologically uninformative convention or linguistic rule. Man's position in industrial society reflects this division. Therein man, as an individual, develops into an "empty space" of private existence which is of no public significance except as professional or leader to accomplish and to stimulate.[2] So it happens that today idealism has developed, even in fields outside existential philosophy, into a washed-out appeal to subjective self-existence. Materialism, however, is more simply comprehended as the concept of material stability and scientific objectivity. Chapter VI will show that the communist ideology consists in an amalgamation of the ideal of the fully developed, unalienated, free, and cultured man and of the materialistic basis of existence which keeps man tied to a quantitatively oriented world of work.

The idealistic restriction of economics to a servant role in the formation of the human personality, on the one hand, and the materialistic reduction of man to a personally uninteresting and only functionally important transmitter of the economic structure, on the other, is the important antithesis in this regard. While the East strives to reconcile them dialectically (i.e., historically) and to compensate for them, they confront each other in the West irreconcilably and therefore indeterminately.[3] In the East the Communist party dictates the road to the ideologically expected reconciliation, but in the West each individual is confronted with the conflict between the creation of a "better world" of cultivated humanity and the goals of maximum output and maximum consumption.[4] In the Soviet social theory this tension is overcome by transforming the quantitative increase, once it reaches a certain degree, into qualitative improvement of the society.

The materialistic economic theories of the West [5] * originate in the spirit of the pragmatic and causal-oriented natural sciences. Economic

* Of almost entirely different origin is the economic materialism of Marx. See chapter V.

man, *homo economicus,* is comprehended as a being who is determined by only a few basic instincts and is therefore predictable.[6] The total economy is furthermore considered to be an equilibrating functional system which recently has become subject to cybernetic study.[7] * An idealistic approach, however, cannot conceive of the economy as an isolated or as a seemingly autarkic system. It considers the economy as interwoven with the total environment and as open to the multitude of personal motives from the social and cultural spheres.[8] † It considers the economy as a domain of life which provides and prepares means, which, however, are subordinate to "superior ends," such as the national culture (universalistic) or to the formation of the individual personality (individualistic).

The contrast between the quantitative-materialistic and qualitative-idealistic concept of the economy may be elucidated historically by the parallel developments in philosophy and economics. When Descartes confronted the outside world as a methodically explorable mechanism, the medieval spirit of the guilds simultaneously gave way to modern industry, which was primarily interested in profitable production. Medieval thinking had been qualitatively oriented in two respects: In the domain of workmanship, quality of product stood in the foreground, and macro-economically, the surplus did not serve its expansion and improvement but rather purposes outside the working world. Quantitative thought directed toward mass production lies much closer to the "rational-purpose" spirit of capitalism and industry guided by technology.[9] Only against the background of an extreme materialistic-quantitative point of view can one understand the derivation of the classical cultural idealism of Germany, which considers concern with economic matters intellectually undignified.

It was already indicated that these two patterns of thought are still in conflict in the West and that they have not become "dialectically reconciled." Certainly these two points of view have not been forcibly joined together by an official philosophy as takes place in the East.[10] ‡ On the

* The economy is understood here as a system of feedback in which economic man reacts upon satisfactory or frustrating stimuli with "yes" or "no" answers respectively.

† Note here a difference between Eastern and Western materialism. Marx also stresses, but with reversed causality, the interrelations claimed by Western idealism. Western materialism, however, is rather inclined to disregard these interrelations.

‡ The complicated tension between idealism and materialism is, in communist thinking, based on the starting point of Marx: that is, man realizes himself in free self-creativity; his fundamental activity, as well as everything else, is determined by economic assimilation into nature.

53

other hand, it is difficult to find in the West a philosophical theory of economics which would act strictly materialistically by assigning to the economy a legality entirely independent of the human will. Materialism, however, appears in milder forms. It presents to the penetrating eye an often implicit, even partly subconscious element of everyday economic thinking and also mechanistic, mathematical, and even cybernetic economic theories. Man must, within such theories, be viewed as an object or as a functional member of an objective process.

In idealistic theories, however, man possesses an element which is not integrated into any objective connection with existence. In these subjective depths lies the real basis of man's existence and activities. The erroneous road, which may start here, is idealistic but is antagonistic to work and will reduce man to his spiritual half, substituting this half for the whole. Enlightened idealism does not turn against the material world and economic goods but confirms them without being addicted to them. It will recognize, promote, and use them with regard to man's spiritual sovereignty. The economy is therefore a mechanism or a equilibrating structure of objective character and, beyond that, the domain of freely acting man.[11]

The idealism of individual freedom, as it still exists in the extreme liberalism (von Mises, von Hayek, and Lord Robbins) is even willing, on behalf of individual autonomy, to accept economic and social disadvantages, such as marked social inequalities and partial poverty. In opposition to such liberalism, an idealism of a more social character is gaining influence. Such idealism first emphasizes that the economy represents only a small, subordinate sector of the human realm. Secondly, it is rooted in an anthropological concept which sees the individual as involved in social relations, which provide, in essence, his self-awareness and for which he is responsible.[12] *

It cannot be said of the classic theorists in economics that they were already aware of these two kinds of metaphysics.[13] † The anti-mercantilistic demands for freedom together with the sympathy principle and the legitimization of the profit motive and self-interest went hand in hand. The contrast became acute only later with the advent of "value-free" analytical research.

* Hegel and Marx continued with community-oriented idealism. Kierkegaard's subjectivism, however, stressed the individual. Today, existentialism (Satre) and Marxism (Schaff) are involved in a dispute with each other.

† Also here it can be seen that Marx, in some ways, was the last of the classicists. His materialism is the antithesis of the preferential position given by Hegel to the idea and the state.

2. IDEALISTIC ECONOMIC PHILOSOPHY

The struggle between an idealistic and a more materialistic concept of economics can also be traced back to Aristotle. The man from Stagira considered economic activity as a more or less inferior human activity, mostly relegated to women and slaves in the household. The business of earning a living is mentioned in the materialistic metaphysics of a few Sophists, who considered man as purely a creation of nature. It is only logical that from there on the value-free struggle for existence and the mechanism of concern about commodities stood, even in ethics, in the foreground. For Aristotle, however, man was not merely at the mercy of material impulses not even consciously so, but he was also a spiritual being who is formed and performs in a political and cultural setting. In medieval times an idealistic concept of economics prevailed. The Aristotelian *polis* and its free citizens were, however, replaced by the Church and the faithful, whose concern was the soul after death. Economic activity remained mainly as a device for fulfilling basic needs, even though the feudal caste often developed excessive demands.

During the Renaissance the polarization of idealism and materialism which became so characteristic of the West first appeared clearly.[14] For Machiavelli the human political community was a physical-mechanical power play of passions. In opposition to it stood the ideas of Sir Thomas More, in which spirit, ideals, and science share eminence. More, Campanella, and others, carried on the wings of Platonic political idealism, imagined utopias of an ideal communistic type, in which the economy should be, first, of subordinate importance and, secondly, according to Campanella, completely collectivized.

In the age of mercantilism an economic concept developed that combined individual economic units. It was "discovered" that the economy was a domain that promotes the power and greatness of a nation. Here the ancient predominance of politics was renewed and a conceptual framework was found that put considerably more stress upon the economy. It is not too out of line that today the theories of J. M. Keynes are compared with those of the mercantilist period.[15] The welfare of the political community was supreme, and individual interests could be subordinated and their actions could be regulated in its favor. Only after de Mandeville stated, in opposition, that private vices could work for the public good was a breach struck in the theory of mercantilism through which liberalism penetrated.[16] The philosophical rationalism which prevailed during the period of mercantilism incorporated the world in

55

its spirit and in its eternal truths. Such an idealistic metaphysics cannot, however, be attributed to the centralist tendencies of mercantilism. The national will to power, wealth, and squandering in the courts of absolute monarchs, although sometimes connected with support of the arts and sciences, revealed the dualistic spirit of the Renaissance.

The next important step in idealistic thinking was made by German idealism and its romantic successors in answer to the materialism of the Enlightenment. Kant divided man and his world into a spatial-temporal and empirical part (*homo phaenomenon in mundus sensibilis*) and a scientifically intangible part (*homo noumenon im mundus intelligibilis*). According to Kant all human activity derives from the intellect and finds its meaning by asserting and maintaining its autonomy. The material, economic conception of the individual is, according to this proposition, unthinkable. Material events are phenomena solely of the visible world. The ultimate and most profound aim of all human effort is, however, the realization of a "community of free moral beings." This aim might never be fully realized but remains a task, a regulative guide to action, a perennial duty (Hegel).

Though Kant divided man into a spiritual half and an empirical-material half, he did not plead for a unilateral retreat toward mere thought. Making the monolithic "half man" absolute was reserved for Humboldt, among others. For Kant as for the Platonic school of philosophy,[17] the ideal side had the prerogative of being transcendental—of being introspective—whereas the material side was only appearance. Nevertheless Kant demanded that man actively work toward the realization of the moral ideal. While he did not consider such activity a Sisyphean labor, he nevertheless considered it in principle an impossible goal. For, according to Kant, freedom is not a category of value in the world of appearances. In the end man must content himself with goodwill. It is not objective (because in objectivity everything occurs by necessity) and it cannot be proved empirically. However, its manifestation must always be sought in appearances.[18]

Hegel understood most profoundly this unmitigable duality in Kant's intentions and extended it by explaining man dialectically. For Hegel, man in his practical contact with objective reality is defined neither by subjectivity or objectivity, nor by freedom or scientific necessity; rather he combines these antithetic and irreconcilable tendencies of his activity. Thus human action is a product of contradictory forces, but is neither one nor the other. It unites subjectivity and objectivity, practice and theory. Theory, also in the economic science, therefore can account for only one kind and one aspect of human existence and does not seek to explain the whole with its objective conclusions. To look upon this from the "idealism" of practice and synthesis would be the beginning of a one-sided and therefore fatal and inhuman objectification of mankind.[19] * (This will be discussed in chapters V and VI.) The "objectivity" of the social sciences is, according to Hegel, again balanced by the free subjectivity of essential human existence and vice versa.

For empirical reality Kant invented a more moderate model with diminished demands, which displays a noticeable closeness to liberal ways of thinking. Empirical man, who is the only one considered in real life, is dominated by incorrigible egocentric motives. A wise government will not strive to realize the ideal of a fraternal family of noble-minded and free people but rather to create a republic whose legal system limits the egoism of the individual. Possibly it will provide for a necessary social balance and will finally consider the profit motive and the drive for power as the price to be paid for the preservation of personal freedom. If one's neighbor is to be respected as an end in himself, and this commandment is the foundation of Kant's ethics, he is also corrupted by base instincts and cannot be tempted by ideals. This would violate his freedom.

It appears that idealistic "metaphysics" [20] could be combined with a seemingly materialistic realism. It has already been mentioned that the views of Kant are not free of liberalism. Kant was not only influenced in regard to the theory of perception by Hume, who was a close friend of Adam Smith, but also by the liberal thinking that primarily possesses a thoroughly materialistic appearance and in which the idealism of freedom is essential. Originally the economic motive in the self-related and egotistic psychic urges was a technical abstraction typifying the ideal.[21] Human existence was by no means limited to participation in an economy whose mechanism has been triggered by the urge for profit maximazation. On the opposite side stands Smith's moral theology which preceded his economic theory and which gives central position to the concept of sympathy. This virtue, which is directed toward what is useful and pleasant to others, is founded in the subjective instincts but unrelated to the ego. Viewed from the economic sphere, it is a socially mitigating corrective to strict selfishness; in the metaphysics of puritan liberalism it is an expression of the spirit of Christian brotherhood.

To understand this metaphysics, whose exact elucidation is not only of practical but also of historical interest, the following thoughts are offered. Adam Smith leaves brotherhood and common welfare in the gra-

---

* It is indeed questionable whether, with Kant, one can speak of metaphysics at all.

cious hands of providence, which out of the confusion of individual interests "automatically" sees to the common welfare. This should not be considered cynicism but rather good faith in the harmony of the market economy. Such a harmony should furthermore be guaranteed through emotional social commitments. In economic reality every free individual is primarily responsible for his own welfare and salvation. This promotes the welfare of a nation better than planned mercantile control. It results from competition among individuals who, in turn, consider the wealth acquired in striving for profit as a measure of God's grace. Freedom and equality of opportunities and faith in predestination of the "chosen" could, strangely enough, be channeled into the same line of thought.

The metaphysical foundation of liberalism combined the idealism of individual freedom and an extramundane salvation with a ruthless worldliness in competing for the evidence of eternal salvation. Evidence was economic success which, as a side effect, was supposed to generate the common welfare. This linking of the morality of profits and the metaphysics of freedom determines the neoliberalism of Germany today even if this liberalism grants restraint on competition.

Romantic political economy is based upon Fichte's continued development of Kant's metaphysics of freedom. The early Fichte possessed a broader political picture of mankind, in which the free individual and the liberal state were central. The late Fichte, who was influenced by the wars of liberation, developed, however, the idea of a national state, directed by authoritarian education toward higher culture. The idealism of the ego is now replaced by the idealism of the nation, whose character, according to Fichte, is more that of a commander than of an individual being.[22] But by this time Hegel had called the state the "walk of our Lord on earth," that is, the superior authority in all human affairs. This idealism reached its culmination in the later theories of Müller. The national culture is made up, as Spann wrote after World War I, of different organic fields of activities which together are subordinate to the whole. One of these organic sectors is the economy. Man is not a product of nature but of the nation.

Marx also belongs to the tradition of German idealism, not only in his studies but also in the content of his theories. As he himself confessed, he only wanted to realize Hegel's philosophy. It is generally pointed out that Marx, his materialistic metaphysics notwithstanding, emphasized an idealistic ethics. Since, however, his ethics were derived from assertions of existence based on the theory of history, this does not explain everything. For within the historic materialistic premise itself is

58

hidden a trend of idealistic ontology, that is, the consciously acting man who, disregarding his origin in nature, creates his own objective being through his unhampered productivity. "Matter" is humanly processed nature or, in other words, "industrial" production. Only the liberation of man, who is expressly set as the creative cause of the historical process, is essential in history. To originate in nature was, to Marx, as little conditioned by nature as the basic ego, to Adam Smith, was identical with the ego reference of commerce.

In a dialectic sense man is a product of nature. He reproduces himself freely, is concerned about the humanization of nature and the naturalization of man, and finally obtains these goals from a communistic fraternity in the family of mankind. In this thought appears first a comparatively Romantic interest in the "naturalness" and "wholeness" of man; secondly, one can hardly miss the presence of German idealism. Starting with Kant, through Fichte and Hegel, and up to Marx the human ego was considered the core of all transactions in which the individual and the universal, subject and object, freedom and necessity intermingle. Marx, however, traced this completely socialized way of life, in historical reflection, back to the economic conditions of the late capitalistic era. In this respect he recognized communism only as another step in historic development. Otherwise he characterizes man as a species and, accordingly, communism as the full self-realization of the origin and essence of man.[23]

The other individualistic side of German idealism, or, better, the dual nature of the individual, was made absolute by Kierkegaard. Here the absolute subjectivity of man becomes the basis of his being. Perhaps the way Eastern interpreters assess this Western trend in the philosophy of existence is not completely wrong. They sometimes interpret it as the expression of a naked individualism in which man has detached himself from community life and leaves the objective political, social, and economic events to capitalism's inherent laws and searches for the basis of his existence in subjectivity. In recent times Sartre has tried to combine existentialism and Marxism to a single thought structure. Similar attempts have been made in the East by Schaff.

Western economic metaphysics has today progressed to a more or less detailed, yet clearly recognizable conception which tries to eliminate the division of economic man into a cog in the objective-material mechanism, on the one hand, and a dislocated consciousness, on the other.[24] In modern philosophical anthropology, man, disregarding the more refined differentiations, is seen as a dual being, which as a creature of nature is of material origin but also, considered in his entirety,

59

an intellectually directed person with free will and individual dignity. Here a pattern of metaphysics develops which remains outside idealism and materialism and which views the phenomenon of dualistic, active man as a material body and an intellectual subjectivity which transcends the existing world.

More recent Western economic philosophy is influenced by this anthropological concept in the following manner. Economic development is seen as a branch of man's self-realization which, in general, takes care of the needs of life and of the material culture. But this sphere of producing, processing, and distributing relatively scarce goods is, as a human action, not simply subject to physical causality or determining instincts but is also controlled by freedom in human planning. Both aspects of Western economic thought are now considered as being practically complementary. The orientation toward ever more varied productivity and research in model theory, in order to find deterministic laws, is balanced by socio-political concern for man's independence and self-development.

Finally the idealistic view of the economy has in the meantime proved itself more realistic in one respect, since it has turned out that the subordination of man to supposedly irrevocable economic laws (as for instance, Ricardo's Iron Law of Wages) does not do justice to reality. This was not because of the validity of other laws but because man, determined to change circumstances, was able to adapt them toward more socially desired conditions. It proves, especially today, that man's administrative control of economic development extends to unexpected dimensions. Technical mastery in the scientific control of nature, such as automation, and humanitarian mastery of these acquired abilities are no longer a matter of autonomous economic laws; they are much more a responsibility of intellectual activities.

The "idealism" which is of concern here is no longer identical with the previously mentioned educational idealism of Humboldt, which fled the world of realities in order to find fulfillment in the supposedly pure realm of the spirit.[25] In its place, the idealism of self-realization demands, through productive disposal, the mediation of the mind with objective reality, the ego with society, and the subjective (liberty) with the objective (legitimacy of the real). It is no longer a pleading for a one-sided introspection. It opposes, however, the opposite extreme of "materialism," of the functional man who, estranged from his own creations, exists only to serve technocratic industry instead of being served by it. Educational idealism that disregards "the inferior" as well as materialism that boasts of its "sobriety" regarding natural laws are unreal-

60

istic metaphysics, once "from above" and once "from below," according to a dictum of Hartmann. Serious anthropology begins with the elimination of this contrast in the description and analysis of the whole man.[26]

The Eastern attitude subsumes the entire Western world view under the concept of "idealism"—disregarding all serious distinctions within that concept, which was once in close relationship with subjectivism. Materialism lends, in this view, primacy of existence to objective "material" reality, as it is also the reference point for exact observation by the human intellect of this reality and its laws. This is the picture of material events. From these observations, which will be more closely examined in chapter VI, Western economic philosophy is interpreted, first of all, as the construct of phantoms which provide illusionary reasons for the material events of a true world and, secondly, with respect to perception theory, as a disavowal of the observability of true existence. The idealism of individual freedom is interpreted as the expression of an subjective retreat from the world; and the idealism of the state, as the ideology of political control by the powers of capitalism. Thus the East sees Western philosophy as a "false consciousness," as the ideological justification of a historically outdated reality, and as a falsification of actual present conditions.[27] *

3. RECENT DEVELOPMENTS

The metaphysical implications of economic science and sociology in the West today rest entirely upon the assumption that we must start from socially active and therefore also economic man. Rather than the acceptance or the assumption of ontologies in which man is an object there is now a metaphysical view derived from the actual condition of man in which man is seen, not one-sidedly as body or spirit, but primarily as a comprehending and active being who reduces the universe and himself to mind and matter. Considered abstractly as a phenomenon, man is the unification of both aspects. Present-day economic metaphysics in the West is, therefore, not fixated on one of the two -isms. There are three different types of idealism which shall be described below.

A. Autonomy

The first form of idealism is associated with the principle of individualism. The individual is viewed as the metaphysical origin of all human affairs. His fellowman is another independent subject all to himself.

* However, various modifications and mixed forms may appear here.

Objective reality is where all individual plans of existence are carried out. Supra-individual systems are but annoying forces whose only justification is the preservation of the realm of individual freedom.

Originally this individual idealism tied itself to the Christian religious metaphysics. The individual, who, *vis-à-vis* God, was mostly concerned with the salvation of his own soul, determined all further worldly circumstances. It is known that this principle of individual sovereignty was also the basis of the economic Puritan ethic. It is worthwhile to think about the practical effect of this metaphysical doctrine; in the desire to be among the chosen of the Lord, it led to an asocial establishment which finally resulted in the surrender of inner idealism in favor of a superficial way of life that was determined by the profit motive. This same idealism is also the basis of the opposition to increasing the power of the masses and to economic leveling.

In the East, this world-rejecting subjectivism, which cannot cope with modern historical developments, is also somehow connected with the more modern trends in existentialist philosophy. In the proper sense, however, such subjectivism contains Kant's refusal to found existence upon spatial-temporal manifestations. The human ego is not of the world but the authority for which the world exists and the essence of the dignity of man.

It is understandable that such a philosophy could give birth to concepts of the proper economic and social order which occasionally approach inhumanity, considering its contempt of public, social, and materially determined institutions. Even Kant recognized that there was a wide gap between freedom as an idea and material reality. An important point of this idealism is the emphasis on private property as that over which subjectivity is supreme over all outside forces. Private property is the domain of the individual in which he possesses the power to dispose. His competition with other owners of property occurs in the interest of the material basis of freedom and its maintenance.

B. Community

The idealism of the communal spirit, which today prevails in socialist circles, opposes the predominance of interests based on income and consumption. Here the economy also has an idealistic foundation which, however, is of supra-individual character. The individual economic subject is part of a political, social, and cultural whole.

Occasionally the basis of man's existence in society and history and its "necessary" legality are identified with materialistic metaphysics.

While this is true in the East, it is not generally valid. For instance, the socio-philosophical challenge of the independence of the individual, as Spann presented it in development of Hegel's theories, is of a definite idealistic nature. According to the communal-idealistic concept, the human being is anchored in the collective and from there he demands mitigation of such inequalities as different abilities and energies, inherited wealth, the burden of family, and illness and disability in favor of a leveling, bureaucratic citizenry within a unified social order. Here there appears to be a connection between metaphysics and ethics.

Social idealism sees man as rooted in society. Society, however, is not a simple product of nature but an institution created by man which is responsible for its own norms. The economy is an institution of communal life and serves the interests of the supra-individual social units such as society or the state.[28]

This socio-idealistic premise may have a religious, a nationalistic, or a collectivistic accent. In its present form as a social welfare state, it is threatened by a vulgar materialism on the part of the consumer and by the need for security in a bureaucratic and outer-directed existence. On the opposite side, the idealism of individual freedom is threatened by the materialism of strictly private profit seeking. The possible transformation of the two one-sided idealisms into a coarse materialism causes concern. A synthesis, armed to oppose it, presents a third type of idealism.

C. Modern Idealism

Oscillating between the social whole and the individual, the prevailing idealistic economic thought in the West today occupies an intermediate position between the two views. The metaphysical roots of man and his place in the world, and consequently of economic development, originate today to only a small extent from purely idealistic or purely materialistic sources of existence. Instead, both, the dualism of "the being in the world," form the starting and turning point in ontological thought.

Man is simultaneously a physical object and a subject willing to think. His freedom for self-determination and creative formation of his world is more or less recognized in all variations of contemporary thought. On the other hand, recognition is given—in a more narrow sense—to man's material-physical dependency (such as on climate) as well as to the socio-cultural context of individual action. These views are represented by ontologies which view man as formed of matter, life, soul, and spirit, as Hartmann wrote; existential-analytical philosophy

63

which elucidates being from the premise of human existence (Heidegger); and the various philosophical anthropologies (Scheler, Plessner, Gehlen, Sartre, and American transcendental theories). However, they all are inclined to advocate a metaphysics which accounts for the economy more as a human and historically created institution rather than one that views it as a strictly objective, natural development.

Parallel to this, contemporary economic philosophy views the economic process as invested with many partial autarkies constructed on the same model. It sees the economic process in its totality exemplified in matters of intellectual decision, planning, and evaluation. The origin and goal of the economy is the social person who acts independently and with social responsibility respecting the social structure and at the same time protects his autonomy. Classical language calls him the "citizen." The qualitatively oriented economic philosophy of the West is no longer based on a cosmological monism or dualism.[29]

All new directions of thought have one thing in common which distinguishes them from Marxist anthropology. The relation between the material and the spiritual is seen to be closer to life than in the Marxian historical materialism, which monistically bases man's being upon his economic-materialistic activity. The dualism which prevails in Western philosophies is reflected, on the one hand, in the stress given the autonomous superiority of the material, objective, "outer" aspects of human existence. On the other hand, the ideal, subjective aspect of human existence is presented, partly retreating into privacy, by such features as the isolation of the elite, the reformers' protest and its relative impotency. To some extent it is also said to attempt to give economic reality a personal note.

Western idealism is characterized by the principle of past influence of free man upon the economy as well as by the lack of structure in his actions. According to Scheler, the latter changes into the absolute setting of a metaphysical and ethical objectivity envisioned by the "person." Another risk lies in the pursuit of a consequent pragmatism which measures truth by its pragmatic utility. Finally, a trend of the philosophy of life tries to found human action upon the voluntary setting of aims and ideals.

The freedom of individual decision, as compared to the Eastern submission of man to dictated, objective legality, matches a lack of inner determination on the part of the individual, from which it far too easily succumbs to the charms and forces of the production mechanism. This may be demonstrated by the example of social welfare policies. Social policies are frequently used to improve only material conditions, while the psychological elements remain unchanged. In such a possible re-trenchment of the idealistic side of social politics lies the dilemma which, however, must not be seen as a diminuation of its performance. Today's practical social policies do not stop at material aid; they also try to raise the cultural and political level.

D. Existence and History

A final point should be mentioned. The idealistic view of contemporary economy is confronted by the problem of the historicity of all human beings. First of all, it is no longer certain that man is a timeless being who, beyond the mere form of his self-productive spontaneity, may be defined according to his content, nor is it that man as a type is dissolving in the processes of history, as stated by Dilthey. Secondly, it is an open question whether there are any ethical values which are not subject to change by historical evaluation. The idea of an originally undetermined productive power within or of man took the place of an eternal fundamental being. It peaked in Kant's philosophy of freedom, derived from and going beyond Hegel's historic metaphysics. Its content is subject to historical changes, also in reference to extra-human reality, matter, and life.

In the course of man's conquest of natural forces, the belief in a stable nature, superior to all temporality of human affairs, became shaky and faith in a stable order of creation became weaker. Finally, man sees himself in a world in which all nature is slowly being converted into human creation while man becomes a mere producer without a clearly defined character. Even the natural sciences revise again and again the natural laws, which they themselves had postulated. Science is thus reduced to "if-then" assertions in which the "if" can be modified at anytime.

There is very little left, particularly in social life, that can be considered permanent. Everything seems accessible to man's active power. Simultaneously the same man experiences himself as a more or less impotent individual who came into a historical reality not of his making to whose automatic course he is, however, chained like Faust's apprentice. The economy and society appear to be an arena of aspiration and action, which is partly free and partly determined by nature and history, where the future cannot be forecast.

Hegel, the most influential of the founders of this historical method of thought, held, in the face of a great flood of nihilism, a measure of truth in his convictions about self-achievement and the institutional re-

65

alization of liberty. This he understood as a synthesis of the common will and the self-will, world development and individual, objective and subjective, theory and practice, nature and humanity. His legacy fell partly to Marx, and it is presently exploited by a world movement which was created by its "realizers." This movement has installed itself as the source of presumptively scientifically based knowledge of the "realm of freedom" and how to attain it.

However, to Western consciousness, the march of history does not appear so safe and so well planned. It sees man thrown into a stream of events, which is not fully accessible to human reason and in which man must secure his own way without absolute support. A note of resignation as in "Impotence of the Spirit" (Scheler) also reduces this sovereignty, while Heidegger's solution of the human problems lets man split into mere particularity (*Eigentlichkeit*) and uncontrolled "facticity" (*Faktizität*).[30]

Economic metaphysics, on this basis, threatens to lose its firm grip if it does not simultaneously secure the autonomy and the social responsibility of the individual.[31]

Today man faces himself as an autonomous productive force, no longer as an entity of known nature or as a certain idea. He experiences himself in his activity as a being with increasing power over all reality (Plessner). He is thus compelled to create a new world structure that does justice to nature and promotes humanity. The definite call for a common cause, heard from all sides, to reach a desirable synthesis of these antitheses can only be answered through the interplay of decisions made by individuals. There, however, lies democracy. Democracy is not lost in the struggle among special interests and power groups. The resolution of this task is, in the meantime, being further sought by the Western philosophies in order to give practical dimensions to Western idealism.

V. WESTERN ECONOMIC MATERIALISM

1. QUANTITATIVE THOUGHT

At first glance it appears strange that Western economic theorists can present a seemingly strict materialistic analysis of important economic processes and, simultaneously, idealistic assertions of the ontological basis of the economy. Thereby the apparent materialization of the world of goods into an autonomous state, independent of man, is integrated with the unrestrained trade of men. Even Adam Smith could, on the one hand, describe the automatism of the early capitalistic economy in which man was only the egoistic drive wheel and, on the other, view this economy as the best possible means to wealth and culture.[1]

This particular intertwining of the mechanistic and the ideal became the prototype of Western and partly also Eastern economic concepts. Materialistic and mechanistic thinking generally present an impetus to idealistic thought in the beginning because of a deistically tinged admiration for a divine "world machine." Scientific analysis of the mechanistic model first proved its worth in the inorganic aspects of nature (Galileo and Newton). It was to be expected that this method would also be extended to the organic and the human world. Therefore, since the Renaissance, Occidental thought has been shaped by sober skepticism toward the imponderable as well as by an unlimited urge for knowledge of the obviously comprehensible and the calculable. The rigid philosophical materialism of some of the philosophers of the En-

67

lightenment was an unswerving expression of this spirit of cold truth-seeking directed toward rational knowledge. Their inclination to replace all idealistically coined speculations based upon subjective presumptions which are extravagant and contradictory with an intersubjective, verifiable, and therefore "objective" knowledge led to a narrow view of the world so that it is seen as containing only material things and processes. Thus the qualitative and traditional view of existence was replaced, in the new concept of science, by a quantitative one.[2]

Yet on the Continent the rationalistic systems of metaphysics (Descartes, Spinoza, and Leibnitz), continuing in the medieval tradition, still possessed a propensity for "spiritual," a priori truth. Only with English empiricism, from which also arises classic English economic theory, did the new decisive direction begin. All knowledge was based upon sensory experience and was directed toward discovering those drives, systems, and regularities which determine what happens in the material world.[3]

Classical political economy was in remarkable agreement with its origins—French rationalism in the form of physiocracy, on one hand, and the English empiricism of Hume, on the other. It was essentially the investigation of sensorially perceived economic processes (empiricism), but at the same time it sought to uncover the eternal laws of nature and existence (rationalism). Because of this kind of thinking the economy eventually came to be viewed as a process which performs in an "external world," independent of man's thinking. Even in his economic activity man is no longer a *subject* with a will of his own but primarily an *object* of his selfish motivation for profit and secondarily of the economic laws of co-operation or of competition between individuals.[4] *

2. METAPHYSICAL AND PRAGMATIC MATERIALISM

If the economic process is considered as a creation of exact laws of nature, then a materialistic metaphysics is always implied, even if only philosophically. In human activities the seemingly radical contrasts between the material and the spiritual blend into each other, although one may be presumed inferior and the other superior. Still, every human action, even the most intellectual one, is simultaneously a physical action; and every physical action, even the most simple, is also an intellectual

* It has been demonstrated in chapter IV that in opposition to it stood the influences of Scottish moral philosophy and of the idealistically founded natural law.

procedure. In a society based on the division of labor, the distinction between intellectual and manual occupations is naturally emphasized greatly, even though with advancing technology the human body is increasingly relieved of effort. Nevertheless, beyond individual acts in the entirety of human existence and historical-social context stands the realm of the intellectual—the world of culture and the world of work, in perpetual interplay.

A dualism, deeply rooted in the Western tradition of thought since Plato, has contributed to concealing the simple truth that man is a whole and body and spirit are one. Instead, these two forces have been separated from each other and the philosophers have favored the autarchy of the one or the other. Mostly, however, they held the intellectual to be more "dignified," since in this way man was distinguished from the animals. As with political activities in the Athenian *polis* and religious activities in the medieval period, so the activities in arts and sciences became the modern ideal of culture as the proper goal of man's life. Metaphysically expressed, the spatial-temporal sphere was labeled a mere fantasy or a temporary imprisonment of the "soul."

At the same time modern natural sciences, technology, and economic organization have brought industrious acquisition, use, and production of material goods to a staggering efflorescence. It is not surprising that this has led to a subordination of spiritual life to the material; physical processes and natural instincts made it appear that modern materialism was in opposition to the idealistic aspects of dualism. The absolute emphasis upon the human intellect gave way to an equally absolute emphasis on a "spiritless" natural process. There remained a soberly recording ego which, in a passive way, perceived the presumably pure natural processes. According to such metaphysics, observing man is considered a predictable *homo economicus*.[5]

Nevertheless, in this connection the use of the word "materialism" should be taken with reservations, insofar as the ontological-materialistic assumptions are implied, not stated. The treatment of economics in such terms as a system of equilibrium, a growth process, a game structure, or cybernetic interactions is not identical with materialism as a *Weltanschauung*. Economic research guided by the concept of quantitative relations in production and distribution is a technical process and not a philosophical decision. It can, however, just as easily as not become one if the theoretical interest is mainly in the calculation of such things as maxima, minima, medians, and static or dynamic models. Then the human being becomes a quantitatively measurable executor of production and consumption activities. Such a tendency is contained in all research on economic activity, be it goal-rational or value-irrational.[6]

The idea of a basically universal predictability of economic and social events contains the idea of a general, objective determinism in human actions. Intellect and the will of man appear, within such a theory, to be based upon a concept from natural law, i.e., dependent quantities. Freedom does not exist, or it is defined as the conscious obedience of objective forces or necessities. In any case it is not an autonomous causal determinant of the economy.[7] * Such a deterministic formulation of economic theory began during the classical period simultaneously with the separation of economics as an independent and autonomous realm in the totality of human interrelations (Ricardo). As a seemingly value-free, sovereign system which derives its motivations entirely within itself, economics created its own quantitative theory which confirmed such an isolation.[8] The materialistic commandment concurs very well with the attitude that only quantifiable things are real, while meaningful *qualities* are more or less uninteresting side effects of physical processes.

It is questionable to what extent such a concept may be used as the metaphysical basis of economic development or of a quantitative materialism in the goals of economic policy; consequently, the restrictions put on the social significance of economics on the part of its theorists. There is no necessary connection. An extensive emphasis of research interest in a completely rational computability of the determining factors is, however, able to satisfy the demand for relevancy in that particular school. Methodological, ontological, and ethical schools of materialism are to be strictly distinguished from one another, though they might have a certain tendency to fuse together.

Marx's work provides a good example of the problem under discussion. His "materialistic" economic philosophy establishes rationally intelligible laws of progressive economic development which lead to a society of equality of wealth and the complete emancipation of man.[9] †
The substance of this materialism is not physical-mechanical but consists of the predominant mode of production of the working man, who creates his current historical existence and essential nature in the economic process. Originally and eternally he is solely a productive force in society whose potential lies in the acquisition of objective reality. He objectifies himself and is educated through his work. On this premise,

---

* It is also occasionally understood as independence from outer forces and as the exclusive adherence to instincts, in the colloquial sense.

† It would be false to put everyday materialism or the purely materialistic pursuit of wealth in the same category with Marxian materialism.

Marx is recognized as an "idealist." Nevertheless, the idea of the complete, free personality in a free community (naturalism–humanism–communism) should be considered in combination with the materialistic principle that economic development is based on natural law. However, this synthesis failed in reality. Production at any cost to the means of production gained the upper hand in the East. It degraded man to an obedient tool which plays its part in "scientifically" determined historical development. In the end, practice is determined by the forces of a growing economy and the plans of the party in power and the state. It remains an open question whether the idea of a well-rounded and satisfied individual will once again change the situation or whether the materialism of a conforming member of the masses will prevail.

3. PRESENT TENDENCIES

A. Theoretical Efforts

The interconnections between economic theory and economic policies do not have the base-superstructure relationship as claimed by Marxists.[10] They present, however, the answers of theoretical thinking to the provocations of practice. Western economic systems are, in our time, formally based on the principle of increased affluence with preservation of optimal organic equilibrium and consideration for the priority of needs.[11] Such formal autonomous aims of all modern economic policies invite reinterpretation in a variety of contexts and in combination with heteronomous goals.

Within the framework of a materialistic picture of the world, material needs will generally predominate. Equilibrium is considered as one of the quasi-mechanical forces. Productivity is considered equal to the growth in output of goods and services. In summary, we obtain a picture of an economy for the sake of an economy, which is viewed as a system of subject-independent power plays.

This basic materialistic attitude makes itself felt in everyday thought through belief in the dependence of man on the autonomous world of work, through passivity of consumer consciousness, and through the priority given to material interests.[12] * It appears in such economic policies as an orientation toward increased productivity and a personification of institutions serving the common interest. The expanding bureau-

* This point needs cautious discussion. How far a materialistic attitude toward life and materialistic metaphysics belong together should not be predetermined by falsely equating them.

cratic apparatus of governmental and quasi-governmental institutions suggests the picture of a large machine.

In theoretical discussions these realities are explained in equilibrium theory, growth theory, cybernetic self-regulation theory, and game theory. It must, however, be kept in mind that exact research which disregards sensory categories has little in common with traditional metaphysical materialism. Cybernetic research, for instance, examines the actually existing self-regulatory processes in the economy. The statement that economic activity is basically a mere physical process is not necessarily a statement in cybernetic theory. Such premises and procedures naturally have the tendency to perceive the economy in its quantifiable aspects. There is also frequently a purposeful, rational, profit-seeking concept established which amounts to making consumption and income maximization the sole motive of economic subjects.[13] It is open to dispute whether the principle of self-regulatory processes can also explain intellectual processes, without reservation, and still be called "materialism." In a rigid definition of "spirit," meaning the entire spatial-temporality of the subject, which itself vanishes into oblivion, cybernetics denies all spiritual existence. There is no room in its objectivity for a subjectivity that is incalculable. The mind is recognized as an instrument of data-processing and as a source of "decisions" that are system-serving or derivable from maxims. Otherwise cybernetics does not represent a mechanistic materialism at all, for it deals with processes of learning and information, self-regulation and objective aims of empirical systems, always, of course, in quantitative and analytical ways.[14]

The game theory of economic decision-making is likewise in principle physically oriented. It too challenges the existential meaning of freedom of decision-making. It considers the area of the "arts" identical with that of the "natural sciences" and rejects in principle the noncalculability of economic actions. Discrepancies in individual decisions equalize each other according to the law of large numbers and therefore allow probability forecasts. Connected with this theory is the rejection of qualitative aberrations in resolution, planning, and decision. An objective system of rational modes of behavior with numerous but basically fixed and measurable motives constitutes here the material domain of the economy.[15] "Games of strategy" are behavioral processes in a social structure with generally accepted behavioral standards, in whose framework the individual participants adjust their behavior according to the expected behavior of others.[16] This is the model of an exchange

72

economy. The picture of man derived from such research into human activity reduces the reality which is contained in the entire man to such formal qualities as "satisfaction," "conformity," and "deviation."

This scientific attitude, which considers the social world as pure nature, strives to determine objectively the "mechanisms" of social, political, and economic activity. It considers the values that determine human actions to be objective, system-serving power drives—the "programming" of the cybernetic functional structure called society. Such drives belong to a structure of determinants of the ego in whose network the active subject *as subject* no longer exists. On the other hand, society and the economy become analogous to nature, explorable for every purpose, the objects of a value-free science whose achievements may serve in every social-political technique. From it originates a social structure wherein the theory and the practice of an objectively determined functional structure mutually confirm and create each other. The apprehending and active ego-subject faces the outside world with discretionary and manipulative activity to the same extent as he passively accedes to its calculable developments. This concept overlooks the fact that society consists in and of human beings, none of whom is merely an object for the theoretical or practical manipulation of others but is also a subject in and of himself. Inversely, the objective, searching scientist himself belongs to society. He confirms in his "value-free" description the currently predominant values which aim at the frictionless functioning of society, or at least they are present in its implications. Moreover, the programming practitioner, exploiting this knowledge of society, performs only a mechanistic evaluation.[17]

In Talcott Parsons's theory of action, for instance, the freedom of the subject is only the choice between alternative possibilities permitted by the empirical system, which is solely directed toward maintenance of its "equilibrium" and demands absolute system-conforming action. Deviations from normal behavior are considered irrational disturbances which require "psychological treatment."

B. Trends in Economic Policies

Behind these theories, and formed, described, and justified under their influence, stands an economic structure wherein idealistic impulses and the independence of the individual are neglected in favor of the expansion of a well-organized system of providing for human existence. Thus the intellectual activity is directed not so much toward the classical pur-

73

suit of wealth motivated by personal ambition but rather toward an industrious status-seeking for the sake of social prestige and a consumer-oriented striving toward security.[18]

Here, however, we do not have to consider the subjective side of the matter but its more objective formulation in the economy and in society.[19] * In so doing the economic as well as the social domain will have to be examined.

As a guide line we may presuppose that the growth of cybernetic theories and their application in present-day economic research already point toward actual models which demand such an analysis.[20] †

At the time of Marx critical attention was concentrated on the proletarian who, in doing his work, became estranged from it as well as from his fellow men. Later criticism concentrated upon the monotony of work on the assembly line and the division of labor in factories.[21] ‡ In present society, the well-compensated and well-adjusted organization man is characteristic. The tension between the intellectual and the material as well as between the subjective and the objective has transformed itself into a contrast between autonomy and conformity. The controlling society is a machine in which initiative on the part of individual members is considered a disturbance to "equilibrium." For Parsons, the supreme control devices are the value orientations which individually are intensified (as behavior dispositions) and become effective in the social system (as job expectations).

To Parsons, the origin of the dominating values, however, was no longer a problem. This implies that their determination is left to powers outside the realm of science, which presupposes values as existing and indisputable. Its empirical object is the structural and functional system of society together with the "subsystem" economy.[22]

Mannheim drew a conclusion which Parsons gave little regard. He recognized that the total process could be systematically dominated from the control centers of economic and social life. Control of the rational, fully clarified, functional system of society is ultimately performed by the recognized values of the times. The individual operators act in line with them and, therefore, in conformity with the system.

* This distinction will not be a revival of Marx's image and reflection theory.

† Dahrendorf presents the thesis that the "role sociology" of Parsons is the exact image of a form of society which today shows at least tendencies to dominate.

‡ The counterpart in economic theory of this phase in practical development was the causal-analytical concept of the rational and, therefore, predictable economic man.

74

There is the danger that anybody who is able to enforce these values can arbitrarily manipulate human actions.

In this world of values the purposeful, rational orientation of the subjects of the economy toward personal income maximization will finally also be integrated into the system as maximum consumption. This "materialism" can only be fully apprehended within the framework of the above-described total attitude. The predominance of private interests and the frictionless operation of the system certainly imply a renunciation of individual participation in accordance with the "mathematic" and objective analysis of the structure of social and economic activities. The dominating values are those of an individual who acts rationally within a balanced and stable economy. Pluralistic democracy based on special interest groups and political parties is the playground of its self-development. This picture of reality shows conversely that the individual who wants to act sovereignly is threatened with becoming the passive object of compulsions and corruption in the matters of consumption and production.

At its culmination, however, the industrial society offers a social order which is no longer determined by power and submission and by authoritarian leadership and alluring idols,[23] * rather it will be organized by individuals who act autonomously but in co-operation and who are willing to conform. Reality, which can in considerable measure be analyzed by the "role sociology" of Parsons, therefore does not mean the realization of the "man-machine" of de Lamettrie.[24] The former materialism, together with its causally determined basis, is obsolete. It is eliminated, together with the idealism of freedom, in the new reality, i.e., these concepts are simultaneously repealed and reformulated on a higher level.[25] In the economic life of the individual as well as in economic policy, economic reality today is considered a system of total interdependency, wherein individual initiative and material laws are looked upon as tendencies that encompass the economy, which is recognized as a structure whose resistance to fluctuation and whose equilibrium can be programmed.

Also within the philosophy of classical liberalism, the ethical value of labor was upheld by the idea of individual freedom. According to it the individual was not a mere push button of an objectively functioning control system, nor a private person only when not on the job. There was, however, already the belief in the self-regulating equilibrium of the circulation of goods in the liberal market economy. It is just this belief,

* That was the reality toward which theories from G. Sorel to C. Schmitt were striving.

75

which later proved to be threadbare and caused the socialist-idealistic opposition, that has today become reality through the co-operation of scientific theory and practical attitudes. The behavior of man in the economic organization is directed by the signals of his environment and as a free consumer he is willing to enjoy subjectively the goods of the world of commerce. However, the contents of his search for happiness will be determined by the world of commerce in a feed-back process. Finally, as a producer, he is no longer willing to commit himself fully to his work; he is no longer willing to sacrifice himself on behalf of his personal honor, his power, or his wealth. He considers production as a proper function of the life process which provides the means for living the life he chooses when he is not at work. A participant in this economic organization might represent the modern form of economic materialism, which has little in common with the old materialism as a *Weltanschauung* but which fits modern cybernetic theory well.[26]

It has already been emphasized that a synthesis is developing here with idealism, since the system of programmed control and feed-back processes leaves room for individual initiative. Therefore it does not matter if they are mitigated by the dynamic system or may have effects that disrupt the system. This new world of work is materialistic only by the superiority of the scientific, objectively determined, autodynamic system. This system is characterized by the predominance of the social and economic sphere over the subjective will and actions of its individuals, as well as their subordination under its respective control mechanisms. Even the values that guide individuals are only considered technological in the sense that they guide the economic system at optimal efficiency and with little friction.

By contrast, one should characterize today's idealism by understanding the mechanisms of the apparatus not as subject-independent but as —at least in principle—determined by and subject to revocation by man. Materialism, however, could be called that part of experience wherein the creative activities of man represent, in the autodynamic and self-regulating operation of the objective system, a dependent and somewhat disturbing rather than promoting factor. In any event, creativity has the possibility of free development outside the system.[27]

In agreement with this modern idealistic materialism is an economic practice which—in management as well as in politics—is directed toward stable development, overall balance, security, full employment, and general prosperity; certainly more toward all of these than toward the classical aim of mere income maximization. This practice might, as described above, be called "materialistic." A psychological outlook which is based upon assured maximization of wealth and which seeks to direct optimally all reality through bureaucratically organized, institutional regulation becomes the social and economic scene for an objective nature. The individual is part of this "natural" process.

Idealism sees all this, not as the expression of legitimate and realistic metaphysics, but as the arbitrariness of the empirical aspects of our world. However, idealism itself, in its demands for the self-developed, whole man and, further, in its condemnation of an exaggerated division of labor—that is, a society of roles—goes to the opposite extreme. It forgets that our world of scientific, technical industry is very much determined by the mechanisms stressed by materialism. If economic politics is mainly directed toward the economic power of the state in international relations, maximizing output, and the effective use of human labor, it is materialistically oriented. If educational policies are intended for the training of specialists, materialism also dominates.

At present, economic thought has gone considerably beyond the bias of such metaphysical attitudes. The synthesis of Marx and Hegel, that voids both isms, has already been mentioned. To be sure the latter stressed far too much the idea of a superhumanity, while the former stressed the objective requirements of nature, which is independent of man. But both extremes are sterile. Continuous fertile thinking starts where active man is, as central mediator, a free human personality who, conscious of his historical dependence, actively realizes freedom in his given time. The necessities of the industrial world arise from the free, self-generating productivity of men. In order to offer a relevant picture of the economic scene one is neither permitted to falsify the material basis—man's economic activity—into an alien natural force nor to overstate the intellect as a quasi-divine control.

With the growth of philosophical anthropology and philosophy of language (as previously mentioned),[28] * the trend toward abandonment of fixed isms has been continued in our time. Man, consisting of body and mind, has both kinds of needs and every human action is conditioned by mind, body, and existence. Man is the authority in understanding the true structure of reality. Natural laws and freedom, objectivity and subjectivity are therein so deeply intertwined that they are inseparable. Consequently neither mind nor the objective laws of nature nor free will is any longer valid as the one basic cosmic principle gov-

---

* This is true of the West. More recently, however, the East has also shown new philosophical beginnings which, while still following the Marxian party line, are already inclining, in fact, toward a theory that goes beyond idealism and materialism (A. Schaff).

erning all things. The problematic compatibility and the interaction from both sides, which, since Kant, we have been conscious of is now accepted and considered fundamental. The rigid fronts begin to move. Solutions of the problem are, however, more remote than ever. There is no successful attack that can provide an unequivocal solution. Two facts stand side by side. Knowledge of the law proves that extramundane facts and systems are irrevocable and that man must submit to them. This objective accumulation of knowledge is otherwise contained in the immanence of our spiritual and linguistic consciousness of reality. The latter assures us of our theoretically unlimited, though actually constantly restricted freedom to transform the structure of objective exactitudes. Kant approached this problem by letting both sides stand alone but idealistically emphasizing the whole. Today there is frequently a naturalistic-realistic emphasis.

If we do not consider the question of the relation between man and nature generally but rather that between man and his economic, social, and cultural world of work, then we learn that absolutely free productivity and constraint are interlocked through the prevailing institutions and systems. One and the same action contains both aspects. Subjectivistic idealism that does not recognize established objective systems is in error. Conversely, materialistic exaggeration, which denies freedom of choice as well as its self-realization and considers man as a push button in an entirely objective social system, is false metaphysics. It is just this two-edged nature—to be subject and object simultaneously—that characterizes man in economy and society; and by failing to recognize this, the one-sided metaphysical isms made it too easy for themselves. Practice shows man simultaneously as the determined member of an objective system of intersubjective controls and as sovereign subject who through a constructive criticism of current existence is able to change the total objective pattern of the system.

The contradiction of the isms is today reduced to a difference in emphasis. Materialism gives priority to the programming and organization of the objective structure of functions, leaving to man only his private life as a field for personal initiative. Idealism, as a matter of principle, considers man as an autonomous being in the world of work and therefore places the responsibility for reality on the active citizen. Scheler's claim that our age represents an "age of compromise" appears, according to the above presentation, justified.

VI. EASTERN DIALECTICAL MATERIALISM

1. CHANGE OF ACCENT IN MARXIST PHILOSOPHY

The Marxist-Leninist philosophy is the foundation of Soviet communism.[1] Even the empirical sciences are subjugated to this philosophy which, however, together with its principles, is controlled by the Party.[2] Thus the philosophy is employed less as a science endeavoring to find the truth than as a sphere of thought whose aim is the defense of an ideology raised to the level of dogma.[3] The philosophy on its part is monitored and ordered by the Party when opposing directions of research have developed in the interpretation of the dogma.[4]

The basis of communist ideology is dialectical and historical materialism.[5] It contains notions which vary in their exact definition and use or both, depending upon the position of the philosopher. Materialism varies in its meaning from an unpretentious materialism to realism. The distinction between dialectical and historical is often so hazy that by implication they may coincide.[6] Within the common equation in communist thought of dialectical materialism and Marxism-Leninism, political economy is also incorporated into the philosophic discussion of Eastern ideology.

In the more recent, post-Stalinist philosophy of the U.S.S.R., historical materialism is to be distinguished from dialectical materialism as social science in its broadest sense.[7] In the latter are discussed problems

79

of the philosophy of nature and the theory of cognition, again in the broadest sense.[8]

Historical materialism is concerned with such matters as the condition of material life in society, the development of the means of production, the relationship of base and superstructure, class problems, problems of transition between the individual phases of socialism and communism, the forms of social conscience, the state, and the law. Dialectical materialism, on the other hand, concerns itself mainly with the laws of the materialistic dialectic, the cognition of truth, the role of action, the relationship of thought and language, and the reflection of reality in the consciousness of man.

The materialism of Marxism in substance is social, not metaphysical.[9] The materialistic interpretation of history develops on the basis of an anthropological concept. In it, man, in contrast to other animals, is able and compelled to work for his well-being and his environment. Marx envisioned as the goal of history, in accordance with this anthropological conception, a pervasively humane working environment. The appearance of alienation under capitalism and the necessity of its abolition required a materialistic interpretation of this historical era and a revolutionary overthrow of existing social conditions. Accordingly, history is the history of society and thus the history of man as a socially active being. A dialectical description of historical development embraces the gradual unfolding and realization of an originally imperfect humanity in the social conditions of work. The historical dynamics lie with the means of production. In the sphere of economics, this can conflict with the social conditions of production.

Above all, materialism meant for Marxism that all ideas are derived from reality. The significant presumptions for all men are determined by their social condition in their particular historical era. The laws of economic development significantly mold the content of the political, social, and cultural systems. Consequently, the economic means of production dominate the total reality of human life.

The positive thesis in the theory of cognition of historical materialism is characterized by the general reciprocal relationship between the forms of consciousness, the mind and society. Therefore, the contemplatively perceiving man and the metamorphosing active man depend upon each other in the pursuit of truth. The validity of a theory can only be related to the respective historical practice, and only through this relationship can it prove its "relative" truth. Indeed, this take-off point in the perception theory of Marx's dialectical materialism led to a radical intellectual decline even with Friedrich Engels. It culminates in the idea that the perception of most truths can merely be "relative," in the sense that total knowledge can be gained only through an unending process or not at all.[10] Engels's real work was the transfer of the dialectic into the sphere of nature. It was an attempt which Marx completely endorsed in his time.

The Party's interpretation in the Soviet Union has followed Engels's premise. It has made the dialectical materialism molded by Engels the starting point of all philosophical thought.[11] * In this way dialectical materialism became, by referring to historical origins, the basis of historical materialism; the purely material elements dominated more and more. They were refined and expanded. Also, Marx's materialistic historical philosophy itself was finally interpreted in the vein of dialectical materialism, as formulated by Engels, Plechanov, Lenin, and Stalin.[12]

Deriving all substance of the mind from matter or, as the case may be, nature led to a division of the history of philosophy into idealistic and materialistic directions, even with Lenin. According to the teachings of dialectical materialism, philosophy cannot be anything other than an "ideological weapon of the ruling class." Therefore philosophical idealism became equated with Lenin's notion of imperialism and its "war mongers," whereas philosophical materialism means communism, with its representatives of world peace and "true humanity."

The controversy about the correct comprehension and interpretation of Marx's historical philosophy was already fought before the Russian Revolution. This fight occurred between the ideas of the Narodniks,[13] † who moved predominantly in the tradition of the Slavophiles, and Marxism, which tended toward the traditions of the West. The victory of the latter asserted and established for good dialectical materialism in Russia.[14] However, the combatants who had had a common cause against the Narodniks soon divided over the different interpretations of materialistic historical philosophy and other questions into two camps: the orthodox and the critical Marxists.

2. ECONOMISM

The dissensions among Marxists in the pre-Revolutionary period did not clarify the important economic principles relative to the different types of economy within the socialism to which they aspired. On the

---

* Since the de-Stalinization movement, Stalin's formulation of the dialectic has receded and Engels's original work has again moved into the foreground.

† The Narodniks were adherents of a pre-Marxist socialism which was predominantly built upon an ethical foundation.

contrary, the dissensions were directed toward doubts about the pre-eminence given economic versus other social factors. In a battle for recognition of the social and historical materialism of the Marxists, the obscurity and indistinctness of many fundamental statements of Marx became definitely conspicuous. To be sure, Marx had asserted emphatically that man in the process of living must adopt certain modes of production independent of his will, because of the productive forces in effect at the time.[15] He did not, however, say at the same time that the historical development of the generative economic base develops independently of the will of man. Rather, he emphasized even in *Das Kapital* that the impetus to trade was psychologically determined and that the political conditions of power could decidedly influence the economy.[16] Relative to these thoughts, Engels noted that the view of society as determined primarily by economic conditions would be changed into a "meaningless, abstract, absurd phrase" if "the economic factor" were assumed to be "the single determining" factor.[17] Only the battle against the historical conception of the Narodniks, which emphasized the role of law and justice as well as the role of the individual in historical development, led to a doctrinaire hardening of the position. The intolerant Marxists finally advocated a purely "economic materialism." They denied a free, purposeful role of the individual in the historical process and acknowledged an economic determinism.[18] *

The thought of a consistent, causal dependence of the social superstructure on the economic factors attributed too great a significance to them. This opinion led, in its economic-political consequences, to the assumption that Russia as an undeveloped country had to pass through a capitalistic phase before the introduction of socialism. Even a response to the contrary by Marx, who could still be asked, did not induce the orthodox Russian Marxists to change their minds.[19] By making absolute the theories of collapse and pauperization, together with the deterministic notions of the intolerant Marxists, an economic fatalism developed. This led to the position that the worse economic life became, the better it would be, for then the country could pass most quickly through the transitional process necessary for achieving communism.[20]

Plechanov attempted to escape these consequences. He turned against a factor-analytical dissection of the forces generating history, which he believed could only lead to an excessive emphasis on economic factors.[21] Each economic system is adapted to man as long as it satisfies needs and does not oppose the current mode of production.[22] Plechanov emphasized, in contrast to economic determinism and fatalism, the pos-

* Recently economism has been rejected.

sibility of conscious and free action by man.[23] He declared the freedom of the individual to be a necessary link in the chain of historical events.[24]

His premise principally denies the possibility of breaking through historical necessity by the moral influence of the individual or by realization of ideas. While the course of history is dependent upon man's actions, it transcends the deeds of individuals. At most, they give general events an individual character.[25] Therefore, it does not make any sense for the individual to resist the total social development.[26] Also, the economy has at its disposal rules independent of the will. They cannot be ignored, but they can be consciously manipulated. Freedom, understood as arbitrariness, is as limited by laws in the economic sphere as it is by the laws of nature in the physical world.

The possibility of freedom of the individual within the collective determinism of history has become an official thesis in the Soviet state philosophy. "Inevitability" is understood as social inevitability, analogous with the laws of natural science in the microcosm.[27] This, and the resulting interpretation of the idea of "freedom," make possible a formal and substantive evaluation of the results deriving from this premise.[28]

Plechanov had attempted to eliminate the difficulty of fatalistic determinism during the philosophical debate about the significance of the economy, but the times did not yet demand a concrete substantiation of his thoughts. However, the clarification accomplished with his definition did not at all suffice for the future, when numerous detailed questions growing out of economic practice demanded a substantive definition. Plechanov's premise led in practice, after further alterations, to a restriction of the personal freedom of the individual in favor of material economic achievement, as the later history of the Soviet Union proved. The Party spoke the last word.

Such dangers were recognized early by a group of Marxists who were influenced by Kant. These "critical" Marxists did attribute superior significance to economic factors, but they opposed the thesis that economic progress should be identified with social progress. Consequently, they denied the superstructure's causal dependence upon economic factors. They contemplated the possibility of a real influence upon the total course of history by man himself. Yet, history demonstrated that the struggle of Lenin and Plechanov against the far-reaching critical revisions were justified from the Marxist standpoint. The critical philosophers later turned away from dialectical materialism and acknowledged a transcendental materialism.[29]

83

In early disputes about the significance of the economy in establishing a communist society, it may be noted that the working environment was no longer conceived predominantly as the anthropological sphere of human self-realization. On the contrary, a dualism of the economy and man began to take form. This led to a tension between freedom and necessity in the economic realm. The utilization of ideas such as determinism and free will, however, allowed the thinking to lapse onto a pre-Hegelian level because Hegel and Marx had attempted to surmount the contrast between both, particularly with the help of the dialectic.

3. THE DEVELOPMENT OF LENINISM

Lenin's philosophical activity began with a battle on two fronts. On the one hand, he turned against the Narodniks and, on the other, against revisionist opinions among the Marxists, a heresy which was not yet outlawed at the time. These opinions revealed to him the seeds of far-reaching changes. Initially, he especially fought economism. Later he was drawn into the debate on philosophical principles. This debate had developed through the critically disposed philosophers (Kantianism) and the varied interpretation of new scientific accomplishments (empirical criticism).[30] Lenin's significance for the further development of Marxist philosophy lies in his increasing the profundity of materialism, in the creation of a binding theory of cognition through expansion of the "theory of image," and in his emphasis on Marx's teachings concerning the unity of theory and practice.[31] He also participated in the elaboration of the dialectic argument. The peremptory debate, however, did not occur until the struggle between mechanism and Menshevik idealism.

A. Matter and Image

The materialism of Marx presented itself as a primacy of the economic base *vis-à-vis* the derived intellectual superstructure in historical evolution. By contrast, Engels tried in his *Dialectic of Nature* to prove also for the details in nature what Marx's insight achieved for its whole. He claimed an objective dialectic in nature and attempted to establish the necessity of a conscious materialistic dialectic in the natural sciences. His goal meant at the same time an expansion of the materialist-economic philosophy of history into a complete ideology. He sought to buttress the pre-eminence of material relationships in social life with a naturalistic-philosophical materialism. This led to a crisis of philosophical principles as a consequence of criticism leveled by Marxism and empirical monism.[32] * The reason for the crisis was that the critically disposed Marxists thought it possible to connect a materialistic observation of society and history with an idealistic interpretation of natural sciences and cognition of nature. Lenin wanted to prevent a division of the Marxist ideology through his book *Materialism and Empirical Criticism*.[33] He leaned significantly upon Engels's body of ideas.[34] Furthermore, he defended the Marxist image theory of cognition against the idealism of the empirical critics.[35] To this end, he introduced into philosophical discussion a philosophically, economically, and politically portentious differentiation between a natural-scientific and a philosophical concept of matter.

The natural-scientific concept of matter contains the image of an inner structure and the exterior properties of matter. According to Lenin, the empirical critics arrived at their idealistic conclusions through discovery of the possibility of splitting the atom. They thought of matter, not as being dialectically dynamic, but rather as consisting of "small blocks of reality," which could move in the sense of simple relocation. For such a "metaphysical materialism," which represented a materialization of a scientific theory closely connected with the historically influenced state of knowledge, these new scientific insights had of necessity to cause the collapse of the entire metaphysical structure and to lead its adherents into the camp of the idealists. According to Lenin, the idea of matter in the natural sciences remained dependent upon the state of knowledge in physics and other sciences. It could therefore contain only "relative" truth. Independence of the idea of matter from the prevailing state of scientific knowledge was achieved by Lenin through the division of the idea of matter. While the determination of the structure of matter is reserved for the natural sciences, the philosophical idea of matter is determined from theory of cognition. In this fact lies the cause of almost equal use of the two ideas in ontological materialism and the emphasis on realism in the theory of cognition. However, since 1951, this separation has been retracted step by step by the Soviet state philosophy.[36] The danger of a separation of the natural sciences and dialectical materialism was conjured up and made possible by such a differentiation. Today, only the Leninist philosophical idea of matter is acknowledged. The natural sciences elaborate only single aspects and qualities of objective reality. Therefore, there are only different forms and kinds of philosophically determined matter.[37]

* Bogdanov was the main advocate of empirical monism. This premise presented a considerable danger to the materialistic principle of the philosophy and was therefore attacked sharply.

85

The philosophical idea of matter is defined from the standpoint of a realistic theory of cognition. It proposes an objective reality which exists independently of thinking processes and is "copied" from human consciousness. Thus, the ontological priority of matter is presupposed, although unverified in the philosophical idea of matter, as is the claim of, in principle, the complete cognition of matter. With these premises, Soviet state philosophy rejects any form of agnosticism, skepticism, or idealism. The psychological background of these suppositions becomes tangible in the polemic against Kant's phenomenonological concept. The assertion of an indiscernable view of existence appears, for Soviet philosophers, to interfere with the active transformation of the world, since it allows doubt about the correctness of action. Therefore, Lenin mistakenly moved the disciples of Kant close to the realm of the fatalists and the advocates of economism, who relied on historical development to bring about communism.[38]

According to "image theory," cognition proceeds in two steps. A sensation develops through the change of energy caused by an external stimulus.[39] This sensual cognition must then be converted into an abstract, logical concept. The exterior world's adherence to laws can be recognized only through logical cognition. Although logical cognition leads away from concrete images by abstracting them, it mirrors nature "more deeply, faithfully and completely" through the individual's grasp of the essential from a certain distance.[40]

This, incidentally, also holds true for the social sciences. The perspective of distance from specific industrial activity renders possible the right "generalization" and recognition of the economic processes and the comprehension of political-social reality.[41] * Correctly recognized material reality, however, does not reflect itself simply in a cognizant individual subject but also in the social consciousness. Not just any member of the species can assume the function of cognition, only the active representatives of the leading social class. With this contention, practical application assumes a central significance in the process of cognition.

In his second thesis about Ludwig Feuerbach,[42] Marx discussed the significance of practice for human thought. Not only the thinking of the natural scientists must be oriented toward reality, as has occurred since "discovery" of the experimental method by Francis Bacon, but also so-

---

* The question of whether objective truth can be accorded to human thinking is not a theoretical but a practical question. In practice, man must prove the truth—that is, the reality and power, the applicability to the world—of his thinking.

cial perception must be measured according to the standards of practical application, which is understood foremost as a social and economic working process.[43] The path of perception leads from live observance to abstract thinking and thence to practice.[44] In this process, each individual depends for the development of his capacity for perception and for abstraction first upon his social position and education. Therefore, the process of cognition can only be a social one. Secondly, social practice is at the same time a criterion of truth. The correctness and power of ideas is proven in their practice. Engels's guidelines were predominantly the scientific method and the practice of industry. Lenin and the later Soviet state philosophy shifted the emphasis more and more toward social practice.[45] The perils of this criterion became steadily more apparent in the political sphere. Social practice depends significantly upon the actions of man himself. Furthermore, only one "plan" can be effected for which the "evidence" can be extorted if need be. For these reasons, this type of reasoning amounts to a forcible dictation of political plans by a despot. Control through experience is no longer available in the political realm.[46]

The sphere of production and the "practice of technology" had already been distinguished as the basis of all historically effective change by the philosophy of historical materialism. Engels had fostered this belief in the form of the material dialectic. Lenin made it into a criterion of truth in his theory of the processes of cognition. It had to provide evidence for the correctness of Soviet Russian thinking.[47] * The "practice of technology" became the basis of dialectical materialism—deduced from a historical philosophical context by Marx; ontologically by Engels; and according to the theory of cognition by Lenin. With this, Soviet ideology burdened Soviet industry with a heavy mortgage, even before the beginning of its real work. It had to produce the evidence for the superiority of Soviet society.[48] †

B. Absolute Truth and Proletarian Subjectivism

Lenin perceived the sum of all relative truths to be absolute truth. Absolute truth can at best be comprehended only approximately because the process of perception is infinite.[49] Yet, single truths are absolutely recognizable because, for the objective dialectic, the relative also con-

---

* Adherence to this dogma is still unabated, as indicated by the article "Slava gerojam!" ("Hail to the heroes!") in *Pravda*, 15 October 1964, p. 1.

† Deborin was attacked by Lenin because of the correct conclusion drawn from his nondialectical premise.

tains absolutes.[50] It is true that these relative but absolute truths achieve only a certain degree of depth when reflected within human consciousness by means of the historical situation. However, the existence of such truths, that is, the fact that they deal with a scientifically derived absolute truth, is unquestionable according to Lenin. Therefore, only the degree of correct theoretical penetration, the degree of abstraction, can change in the course of time and not the fact or the object of perception. It is subjugated to the social-historical process.

According to Lenin, the historical-social situation intervenes in the process of cognition in two ways. An objective view of reality is therefore impossible. There is only a class-dependent perception. According to Marx's historical-philosophical premise, however, the proletariat has the task of liberating the entire human race, that is, all classes, from exploitation. Because it does not represent a particular class interest, it has a unique advantage for cognition. Only within the proletariat do the interests of mankind and those of class coincide. So long as there is a class structure, the only prerequisite for any really general human perception is consistent proletarian subjectivism.[51]

The control function of the Party does not conflict with the objectivity of philosophical research according to the Eastern view. The subjective interests of the proletariat coincide with the objective laws of evolution. The Communist party is in harmony with the course of history and reality. With this theory, Lenin claimed objectivity and dialectical absoluteness for all economic findings, even before their substantive elaboration.[52] Accordingly, economic principles reflect the "true" economic production process, which again can be regulated by man. Practice proves the correctness of the derived insights from a proletarian viewpoint.

The opinions derived from cognition theory influenced the political organization of the Party most profoundly. After the Revolution, it gained influence in setting up the economy. In doing this, Lenin referred to Marx's demand that the foundation of all philosophy be the unity of theory and practice.[53] It developed from the dispute with Hegel that it was not enough to surmount the discord between idea and reality in philosophical perception; rather, it must be resolved in concrete practice. Accordingly, theoretical cognition first received the assignment of "critiqueing" (Bauer). Existing conditions were to be measured by the idea or definition.

Marx understood theoretical perception as the conscious awareness of truths already present in reality, as an unveiling of the laws governing history and its economic basis. But the course of history always remains the work of historical development itself. Of necessity it depends upon human activity. Marx believed that becoming aware of historical development would lead to rational activity on the part of man and thus awareness would become reality. On the other hand, he held the opinion that the futile opposition of the human will against the course of history would gradually decline. Lenin, and later Stalin, deviated considerably from this idea. They not only wanted to awaken a latent consciousness but wanted to carry it first into the proletarian society. The unity of theory and practice became an artificial union. The theory arises from the Party, which claims for itself the standpoint which the theory of cognition has proved true. It organizes the enforcement of its ideas and molds practice according to its conceptions.[54]

Since Stalin, the psychologically correct choice of slogans and guidelines, in keeping with the intellectual level of the masses and the exact supervision of their application, became a chief consideration in uniting theory with practice. The connection was seen mainly in the fact that theory needed the performing masses in order to become reality. Leninist theory is thus no longer the discovery of truths and laws which necessarily rest within society and its conditions; it became the guideline for all actions per se. In spite of this, the Party maintained the fiction of being able to conduct "scientifically" founded politics. Initially, this did not mean anything but being in harmony with the laws and tendencies of history.[55]

Lenin's elaborations were generally summarized and subordinated to dialectical materialism.[56] The most important conclusion was that the doctrine of dialectical materialism had become an "exact" science. With this conclusion, Lenin then reversed the direction of the historically developed communist teachings. The materialistic historical philosophy developed by Marx, to begin with, formed the nucleus of historical materialism. This, together with political economy, could be derived from the leading natural sciences—philosophical characteristics of materialism which related to the theory of cognition. They were interpreted as transferences and applications of scientific laws to history and society. Partly for reasons of power politics, Stalin presupposed a closed ideology which was expounded most influencially in the *History of the Communist Party of the Soviet Union*.[57]

4. POST-LENINIST THOUGHT

The philosophical tone in the East was decidedly changed through Lenin's work *Materialism and Empirical Criticism*. Instead of entering a factual debate as, for example, Engels had done against Dühring, Lenin's "line of argument" was closed when he could find a quotation of Marx or Engels which contradicted, or seemed to contradict, the opponent's statement. Thus Eastern philosophy moved out of the field of fruitful discussion and became an apologist of dogmatic, ideological principles, and it also changed to an exegesis of the "classics." Hence, its methods not only became authoritarian but devolved into political, moralistic defamation of the opponent. Conscious neutrality could no longer be tolerated.[58] This conception of the philosophy initiated by Lenin was expanded under the rule of Stalin.

Intense differences of opinion regarding the economic and political development of the U.S.S.R. flared up quite early. As a consequence of the ideological hypothesis which the economy had assumed as its social basis, basic philosophical questions emerged. After the October Revolution, when the forces that had been united against a common enemy and for a common goal separated, there was at first a relatively high degree of philosophical freedom. This freedom was limited, beginning in 1921, by dismissing most of the philosophy professors who were not materialistically oriented. In August 1922, more than one hundred Russian intellectuals were arrested and exiled.[59] The remainder were held together by hardly more than their mutual fight against idealism.

At the end of 1922, the "vulgar materialist," Minin, published a radical proclamation suggesting the elimination of all philosophy from socialist life in favor of the positive sciences.[60] This included Marxist philosophy, which was regarded as a remnant of burgeois society. This radical attack on the existence and justification of philosophy reawakened philosophical discussion. Engels's and Lenin's manuscripts, so very important for dialectical materialism, had not yet been published.[61] The dissertations concerning philosophical and dialectical materialism which had already been published were little known by the "revolutionary" materialists themselves. Therefore, vulgar materialism, stemming from a long Russian tradition, had rather unrestrained rule. Only Marx's socio-critical theories of historical materialism and Lenin's doctrine of the goal-conscious will within the Party were supported and generally acknowledged by the revolutionaries in their active fight.

The increasingly noticeable ambiguity of dialectical materialism within philosophical discussion centered around the position of the dialectic in the system. Between 1922 and 1925, under the leadership of Timirjazev, Skvorcov-Stepanov, and L. I. Aksel'rod, the theory of mechanistic materialism was developed, which was derived from the positivistic thought of Minin and Enčmen. It sought to delimit itself in its

90

ideological consciousness from the vulgar materialism from which it had grown and from the materialism of the eighteenth century.

This orientation, strengthened around 1925, emanated from the Scientific Research Institute of Timirjazev in Moscow. Yet in the same year a new front against this trend developed under the leadership of Deborin. Its objective was to assure a superior role for the dialectic against the promise of Russian materialism, and it was advocated by the editors of the magazine *Under the Banner of Marxism*. Engels' *Dialectic of Nature* was published in the same year. At this point, both sides believed they had found sufficient support for their opinions to dare a debate on fundamentals.[62]

A. Mechanists and Deborinists

The discussions between mechanism and the dialectical philosophy were of a philosophical nature. In spite of this, they had political and economic relevance because they preceded the battles for the introduction of a planned economy. Stalin's program for the socialization of agriculture, liquidation of private real estate, and the annihilation of the kulaks (farmers working large tracts of land) began in 1927. In this he was opposed by the theoretician of mechanism, Bucharin and his followers. Bucharin had been trained in philosophy and economics by Böhm-Bawerk in Vienna.

Economic considerations are tightly interwoven with a theory of cognition in the thought of Bucharin. His vehemently attacked "theory of balance" had its roots in Bogdanov's "empirical monistic" concepts of cognition.

The dialectical structure in the social process tends to assume the form of equilibrium, disruption, and restoration of equilibrium.[63] Bucharin understood disruption as the external shock to a system at rest and could therefore not explain the inner unity of the antithesis. Consequently, his opinion led him into distinct opposition to the theory of revolution and class struggle. The mechanist evolutionary theory of development did not coincide with the hopes of the Bolshevik party for international revolution, especially in the political atmosphere of the 1920s.

Philosophical discussion concentrated more and more around the theme of the dialectic. It was carried on by the mechanists particularly against Deborin and his school.[64] The abandonment of the thesis of inner movement in favor of exterior impulse led to a negation of the dialectical "law" of the change of quantity into quality. The question of

91

the essence of historical determinism was revived in this discussion. On a higher level, mechanistic and voluntaristic dialectical interpretations faced each other, as did the mechanistic and teleological explanations earlier.[65]

The concrete economic and socio-political effects of his theory led Bucharin as well as Rykov and Tomsky to oppose Stalin's economic policy.[66] They found interference with the evolution of socialization unnecessary. Rather, they aspired to an evolutionary view of economics, bound to the conditions of dynamic balance.[67] The conflict between the Bucharin group and official Soviet economic policy culminated in the question of whether the economy should proceed at a slower or faster pace. Stalin treated this conflict in his speech against the deviation of the right-wing of the Party under the catch-phrases of "genetic" or "teleological" thought.[68] With this speech Stalin broke the resistance against the industrialization and collectivization policy which was being imposed by the Party.[69]

Deborin, the leading intellectual of dialectic philosophy, leaned heavily on Engels's *Dialectic of Nature,* as did the mechanists. Lenin's *Philosophical Pamphlets* were also subjected to Deborin's interpretation. He testified to Lenin's thorough consideration of Hegel's interpretation of the dialectic. In contrast to the positivistic trend within mechanism, Deborin attempted to combine inextricably the philosophy of nature and the natural sciences by means of elaboration of the dialectic. Accordingly, the dialectic probes into categories and laws common to reality; it examines the movement of nature.[70]

Engels had described the essence of the materialistic dialectic with three principles: the law of the transition of quantity to quality; the law of mutual penetration of opposites; and the law of negation of the negation. Lenin's description of the dialectic, in contrast to Engels's, consisted of sixteen individual items. He elaborated with greater emphasis the unity of contrasts as the nucleus of the dialectic. The followers of Deborin determined on an abstract level, in constant discussion with the mechanist interpretation of the dialectic, the essence of the dialectic as Hegel had first seen it. They developed the dialectic into a well-honed technique. This abstract and philosophically exact treatment brought upon Deborin's school a reproach for "idealistic treatment" of the dialectic.

Ontologically the most significant law of the dialectic, according to Engels, pertains to the unity of opposites.[71] Inner contradictions are present in all phenomena and objects. The inner turmoil released through the battle of opposites is seen as the motive power behind all

92

change. The assumption of an exterior impetus would unavoidably lead to the metaphysical question of a "prime mover." The ontological development of the social-political phenomena of class struggle and revolution, as shown by Marx, led in the economic realm to a necessary condemnation of Bucharin's theory of balance and the almost equally static interpretation of the dialectic.

The main battle of dialectical philosophy in the Deborin era concentrated on the law of transition of quantity to quality. It was one of the most important pillars in the structure of dialectic-materialist ideology.[72] According to this law, an inner change takes place when sheer quantitative increase of each respective object reaches a limit at which there is a qualitative change through random metamorphosis.[73] Bucharin's concept of a peaceable integration of the elements of a capitalistic economy faltered at this law of the dialectic. Trotsky's radical rejection of an alliance between the proletariat and the peasants, on the other hand, is consistent with dialectical thinking. This, however, did not sufficiently take into consideration historical-political necessity. The later connection of dialectical philosophy (that of Menshevik idealism) with the economic-political views of Trotsky can only be understood on the basis of the Soviet procedure of falsely attributing an incorrect philosophical position to a political enemy.

The law of negation insures the return of the dialectic process to its point of origin, which nevertheless has been raised to a higher level during the dialectical process and can absorb the negation. The law destines the process of evolution to be a steady upward development. Bucharin's economic theory of balance also ran counter to this view of dialectical synthesis because it of necessity understood the final condition as a rapprochement of the opposites. It must be said, though, that the Deborinists removed themselves quite far from Engels's definition through their view of the synthesis as a "rapprochement" of the opposites in Hegel's sense, thus laying themselves open to the accusation of an idealistic interpretation. Their philosophy became taboo, according to the principle of base and superstructure, as an off-shoot of Trotskyism.[74]

B. Philosophical and Economic Discussions

After Lenin's death, the Communist party concerned itself chiefly with practical political and economic questions. Thus relatively free and fruitful philosophical activity could develop in the Soviet Union. Viewed in total, it involved mainly abstract-theoretical problems which

93

attempted to clarify philosophical bases that were still not distinctly defined. Deborin continued to adhere to the elaboration of the materialistic dialectic as the most important task of philosophy, although victory had been won over the mechanists. According to him, even the tangible manifestations of Soviet society would have to be continually measured by Marxist theory. Philosophy should be distilled by philosophers to its greatest purity, in accordance to Marxist principles, and become the supreme and ultimate criterion of truth.[75] With this, Deborin claimed for philosophy "leadership" within the state. Nobody thought of the possibility that the Party might become the supreme arbiter in philosophical questions also.[76]

A newly emerging front within philosophy directed itself particularly against this self-assertion and the comprehensive set of values taken over from a philosophy rooted in the Western tradition. It was especially centered around the Party ideologists Mitin, Judin, and Ral'cevič from the Moscow Institute of the Red Professorate.[77] Their criticism was directed less against the former factual results of dialectical philosophy than against the leadership claim that was becoming more and more evident. This claim to leadership could possibly have led to independent philosophical research, if even on strictly dialectical-materialistic grounds, and thus philosophy might slip from control of the Party. The leadership claim was undermined with the accusation that it lacked "Bolshevik self-criticism"—one of the most important ingredients of the ideology of the Stalin era.[78] The pertinent discussion began by playing off Lenin's doctrine against those of Plechanov, whose work was valued by the Deborinists.[79]

Deborin had already seen, in conjunction with the social-economic upheavals of 1929 and 1930, that philosophy had to enter a new phase. He consequently established a connection between criticism of mechanism and political deviation. In spite of this, the development proceeded only slowly and hesitantly. Stalin spoke, without siding with any philosophical orientation, of a "lagging of theory" *vis-à-vis* Soviet reality. Philosophy had not provided the ideological weapons needed by politicians in the battle for the victory of socialism.[80]

Party ideologists wanted to break philosophy's newly developing claim to power. At the same time, however, they strove to take over the position of power which philosophy had achieved by insisting upon and successfully establishing the primacy of the dialectical method. The claim of supremacy for the dialectic which the philosophers had developed allowed politicians to influence developments in the natural sciences and to wield a certain degree of control. However, it also successfully provided the political direction for society during this controversial transitional phase.[81] Therefore, Party ideologists basically accepted the principles of Deborin's dialectical philosophy. Reluctantly they advanced some criticism of the arguments of the mechanists, who had succumbed in the meantime. The main points to be advocated were the Party, on the one hand, to approach dialectical philosophy and its "social complement" as a total system and to condemn them as "left deviation." On the other hand, the degree of "deviation" measured in this and should be subordinated to the *realpolitik* of the Party. Deborin acknowledged the first part of the critique and had already begun reluctant steps deriving from his own thinking. In spite of this, he opposed the demand for "Party-orientation" and the "politicalization" of philosophy.

Industrialization and collectivization were pushed energetically. The resistance of the right-wing position could have been broken by declaring its philosophical foundation invalid according to the laws of dialectical materialism. However, Party ideologists used a reverse line to break the supremacy of philosophy. They declared dialectical philosophy to be "idealism advancing the Menshevik cause" and labeled it the basic element of already defeated Trotskyism.[82] These tactics permitted the Party, on the one hand, to approach dialectical philosophy and its "social complement" as a total system and to condemn them as "left deviation." On the other hand, the degree of "deviation" measured in this way justified the tough and radical approach of the Party toward Trotsky in the philosophical sphere, just as it had earlier proceeded against him politically.[83] The reproach of dialectial philosophy for separation of theory and practice is also associated with the Party's demand for a stronger political influence upon philosophy.

Dialectical philosophy searched for criteria of truth notably in the dialectically reflected practice arising from the historical process of evolution. In contrast, Party ideologists, along with Lenin, saw proletarian subjectivism as the criterion of truth. The Deborinists understood practice as the totality of all social and economic processes in time and space and surveyed from a distance the dialectical movements active in the socio-economic processes. Party ideologists, on the other hand, viewed practice as the effect of daily political demands within the socio-economic process and as the philosophical justification of the Party's interventions in the socialist society. Elimination of the supposed shortcomings of Deborinism meant the end of relatively free philosophical research.

After the conviction of Deborin in 1930 and 1931, the newly posed problem was characterized by the slogan "the battle on two fronts:" [84] a battle against mechanism and a battle against the idealism of the Mensheviks. The new political "triumphant application of dialectical materialism" [85] was celebrated in this slogan. The decided infusion of politics into current philosophical problems led to the interweaving of philosophy with ideological schemes of thought. Philosophy passed into the executive powers of the Party and was used to justify its economic, social, and political actions. It changed from a relatively free science, based upon dialectical materialism, into an element of Bolshevik ideology during the Stalin era. [86]

C. Economic Theory of the Planned Economy

With the victory of Stalin's general line began the time of complete regulation of Soviet society. Philosophy declined into an instrument for defense of political decisions by the Party. The intertwining of philosophy, economics, and politics became particularly apparent in the tasks and goals of economic theory. However, along with economic theory, economic planning began to appear more and more as an intrinsic area of economic thought. The opinion that the economic base in the socialistic phase had to be differentiated qualitatively from that of capitalism had successfully asserted itself. Consequently, the planned economy could not be determined by the laws of a transitional period that had already been surmounted. [87]

Since Lenin, the economics of Marx had not merely represented a theory which was intended to describe the situation of capitalism, rather it was deduced from the principles of philosophical and dialectical materialism. [88] The price demanded for unity of ideology burdened the new Soviet economic theory with ideological duties. Even today, economic theory has the task of proving Marx's partly obsolete theories of the contemporary capitalistic economy to be true and valid. [89]

The second task of Soviet economic theory developed during the practical construction of the economy after the October Revolution. It had to prove that the Soviet economy was free of the supposedly typical and unalterable vices inherent in capitalism, such as exploitation, consumerism, and crises. [90] But there were no tangible economic theories for the transition period with the exception of the plan to emancipate the workingman in a perfect community. They were also absent in later communism. Marx's few, more academic remarks did not suffice. [91] As a consequence of this dilemma, economic theory and economic planning, which gradually emerged from the economic process, drifted apart. Economic planning assumed more and more the task of solving problems arising in practice. Marxist economic theory, which had with great effort been modernized, was expanded into an instrument mainly of propaganda. It attempted, on a "scientific" basis, to explain the mistakes becoming evident in the West as the expression of a basic inhumanity and growing inability to function on the part of the bourgeois-liberal economic system.

The third main task of economic theory posed an almost insoluble problem for scientists of the Soviet Union. They were to prove that the planned economy is the economic basis for the construction of the ideal communist society of the future. This demand led to an extensive reinterpretation of Marx's original goals in order to maintain the unity of communist ideology. Against the flood of communist literature which attempts to solve these problems stand numerous critical analyses by Western authors.

Economic planning increasingly began to take up Western solutions to economic problems. Without timidity it seized research results of a society it held to be exploitative. The demands of conducting a planned economy led to a softening of the ideological rigor, as became apparent in Stalin's later work, and to some decline in the importance of ideology in economic policy. In spite of this, these demands contained a higher degree of centralism and compulsion for planning in various sectors of the economy than in the West where these conditions were criticized.[92] The ideological connection between the more theoretical-ideological economic theory and the more structural-practical planned economy has become increasingly weaker up to the present. This is also being admitted with discomfort and criticized with obvious nervousness by leading Soviet scholars.[93]

5. STALIN, THE "NEW COURSE," AND ITS AFTEREFFECTS

Political, philosophic-ideological, and economic elements were tightly connected in Stalin's thinking. The significance of this for the Soviet Union rested particularly on its elaboration of domestic politics and its consideration of the main organizational principles of the state.[94] Philosophical theories served Stalin more and more as an ideological justification of his actions after the fact. His position as a philosopher is controversial,[95] but under his rule occurred the most incisive ideological change so far in the philosophic-ideological structure of dialectical materialism. Economic forces were explicitly put to the service of building

97

the economic basis of socialism. The planned economy with its directives and controlled opportunities was developed to this end. The direct metaphysical derivation of economic theory and practice moved into the background to the same degree as the factors determined by the goals of economic and political construction gained influence in the Soviet Union.

Interference in the intellectual life of the Soviet people served, ideologically, to implement the principle of "Party-ization," and, in practice, to secure and tighten Stalin's dictatorship.[96] The *Brief Study of the History of the Communist Party in the Soviet Union (Bolshevik)* was edited by a subcommittee of the Central Committee of the Communist party in 1938. Its philosophical chapter, which has been ascribed to Stalin, was for a long time thereafter the official dogma.[97] Philosophical discussion ceased almost completely after publication of the book, with the only remaining challenge being comments upon the theses offered.

The freeing of intellectual life, which had been the hope of many and which had taken place during World War II, was denied through a number of incisive interventions in the ideological and scientific spheres by the Central Committee under Zdanov, Stalin's son-in-law.[98] During this time, which became known as the "Zdanovscina," when Stalin was at the summit of his power, the unconditional submission of the intellectuals was demanded.

The conviction of Aleksandrov in 1947 invited the beginning of a lively philosophical discussion.[99] * But already in the fourth issue of the newly founded *Voprosy Filosofii* the Party intervened in the discussion, which had hardly begun. Finally a new philosophical "soul-searching" was organized in 1949,[100] because the philosophical "plan" was not fulfilled either in 1948 or in 1949. The atmosphere of planning, control, and pressure did not permit the establishment of philosophical research.[101]

Only Stalin's intervention by letter commenting on specific questions of language led to a certain "liberalization" of the ideological border areas. After a successive application of Stalin's principles to other disciplines, the full scope of the new premise became apparent. Stalin had shaken two main supports of dialectical and historical materialism. He presented the economic consequences in the paper, "Economic Problems of Socialism in the U.S.S.R." Stalin disputed the view held until then that language belongs to the social superstructure. Because of its "direct" correlation to the production sector, which must always avail

---

* Bochenski considers this time as part of a period of "liberalization."

itself of language, it could be part neither of the superstructure nor of the base. On the other hand, it could not be a component of the economic structure of the society. Language is therefore a product of the people as a whole. It is not related to class, and the dialectical law used in the fitful transition period could not be applied. The possibility of continuous change as emphasized by the mechanists had been reintroduced in the realm of language.[102]

The discussion of language stressed the stabilizing elements of Marxism. It formed the beginning of a deactivation of the revolutionary character of the Bolshevik ideology. This began to prove a source of danger for the ruling socialist class.

The justification for the pre-eminent significance of the superstructure instead of economic dynamics in historical evolution could no longer be put forward in the spirit of Marx.[103] The ideas derived from material conditions of society react upon the social being and significantly further the historical process. This thesis is not far removed from the idealistic doctrine that values evolve historically. Actually Stalin's justification theory returned importance to man, upon whom ideals depend for their realization.[104]

Seemingly Stalin had been able to explain forcible collectivization by the theory of a "revolution from above" within the framework of the base-superstructure theme, for the leadership claimed to be the rightful representatives of the proletarian common will.[105] * Consequently, a "reaction" of the intellectual superstructure to the antagonistically divided class society could apparently still be justified. The ideological rationalization for nationalism, however, exploded this scheme. It established language as a phenomenon which unified society and which was subject to a continuous evolution beyond any class struggle.

It was not only that the effectiveness of ideas ceased to be denied, but now the new driving forces of social and economic development could only be found in the intellectual superstructure. This transfer of the history-moving forces into the "superstructure" had effects upon the basic dialectical law of the unity of opposites. Until this point it was the law of development. After the introduction of the Soviet constitution in 1936, the conflicts between classes were surmounted to a large degree. Stalin differentiated between antagonistic and nonantagonistic opposites. The antagonistic opposites could only be eliminated through an "explosion" during the struggle. In the realm of the nonantagonistic opposites,

---

* Fetscher rightly points to the intellectual unification of Hegelian theories with those of Rousseau.

he emphasized the possibility of a gradual, planned elimination of opposites. However, in the ideological justification there loomed the danger of stagnation. An attempt was made to avert this with the theory of new driving forces within the socialist society.

The driving forces deriving from the conflict between the nonantagonistic opposites were conceived to be chiefly intellectual. They were developed by Stalin into the moral-political unity of Soviet society, the mutual friendship of the nationalities in the Soviet Union, Soviet patriotism, socialist competition, and the socialist attitude toward work. The doctrine of these forces led to a rehabilitation of moral values and the creation of a "communist morale." Essentially it provided the inner strength in the development of socialist society. Therefore it was also burdened with the responsibility for economic development. Its ideological position as bearer of Soviet development explains the continued emphasis upon "communist" morals within the framework of economic theory.

Stalin's last work was mainly devoted to the problems of the transition to communism.[106] In this work he reoriented economic theory to fit in with the emphasis on the historical significance of the superstructure for the needs of practice.[107] He had to argue with a group of economists who, following his thoughts too strictly, named the state as the fountainhead of evolution.[108] He emphasized to them the objective character of the laws of economics; man could avail himself of their service but their elimination was not within his power. Furthermore, he underscored the economic laws pervading all social structures and to which socialism had to submit, as did capitalism. As one such law, he regarded the law of unity of productive forces and the mode of production, which connected all stages of society in spite of antagonistic conflicts.

Stalin warded off the premise of a possible revision which passed the responsibility for economic development to the planners who would then set the demands for society. To explain the rigorous actions of the Party, the plan, which had become *de facto* normative, had to maintain under all circumstances the character of descriptive laws.[109] The doctrine of "revolution from above" was to show that as a consequence of elimination of antagonistic opposites within socialism there could no longer be a real revolution "from below".[110] However, it was not to serve in such a way as to put all responsibility for the further development on the central Party leadership. The "activation of the superstructure" meant a total hold on human beings in the material as well as in the intellectual spheres of their lives. Faulty development could be relegated to the immense realm of the intellectual superstructure. This planned development was seen to be a prerequisite if communism was to become a reality.[111]

After the conquest of the antagonistic opposites, economic development in socialism would occur steadily according to the objective "law of the systematic development of an economy." [112] The preference for production of producer goods over consumer goods remained untouched.

The main goal of a socialist economy was to secure the maximum satisfaction of the continuously growing material and cultural needs of the entire society, through uninterrupted growth and constant perfection of the socialist system of production by means of maximally developed technology.[113] This self-evident goal is also accepted by the West, although the socialist production system is not, of course. This goal was sought through conscious economic planning at the price of great suffering on the part of the entire population. Nonfulfillment or overfulfillment of the established plans always led to extensive corrections of the plan, until the present time. For this reason the "plan reserves" of today are intended to prevent economic chaos during disturbing shifts. They correspond in magnitude to the surpluses which also occur in Western market economies.[114] In addition, according to the Soviet view, the socialist economy is still too much involved with "producing to sell" for which it criticizes capitalism. According to Stalin, only if this trait disappears and the state dies away completely, can society itself, through its central economic directorate, assume ownership of the means of production and will the commodity-money relationship be abolished.[115]

After Stalin's death a "collective leadership" assumed the governing of the Soviet Union. No successor was available who could have taken over the leadership alone.[116] The necessity of joint command led to a turning away from Stalin's method of eliminating differences of opinion within top leadership through violence by the secret police. With Beria's demise and the removal from power of Malenkov and Molotov, the prestige of Party leadership under its secretary, Khrushchev, was raised through the use of political power. The conditions of power shifted. The Party regained its former significance *vis-à-vis* the secret police. While the control agencies remained, they were somewhat denied the use of terror, arbitrariness, and dictatorial processes.[117] The change from police to Party rule occurred both because of the leadership's instinct for self-preservation and because of a wide-spread desire for the realization of formerly subjugated ideals.[118]

The leadership found itself obliged during the time of power consolidation to make short-term concessions to the people, which were necessary to prevent a possible revolt, of which there were increased signs.[119] The "New Course" in the economic sphere corresponded to relaxation of control in the intellectual realm, which was called the "thaw" after the play directed by Ilya Ehrenburg.[120] The government had to woo the people into a better relationship.[121] This, however, was possible only by greater emphasis on consumer interests. Therefore the consumer goods industry was to be furthered right along with heavy industry. Agricultural production in particular was to be raised through easing the burden on farmers. Scarce consumer goods were also imported in larger amounts.[122] Malenkov's resignation as prime minister in February 1955, however, was an outward sign of a faltering in the "New Course."

Even during Stalin's lifetime one critic of his doctrine, Josip Tito, had spoken up. Tito demanded a separate path to communism. His views could not be treated as a "deviation" according to proven Stalinist practice because they were based on Marx and Lenin and at the same time had the backing of the political revolution in Yugoslavia.[123] Tito's basic critique culminated in the statement that the Soviet Union had neglected the original goals of communism and had betrayed socialism.[124]

Actually Stalin had already included some elements of the critique in his thoughts, especially in his suggestion of decentralization for the purpose of higher productivity.[125] Only the Twentieth Party Congress, the most important since Lenin's death, brought about a strong reaction (by Mikoyan) to the Yugoslav critique of the New Course.

Changes in political practice found their expression in Khrushchev's secret speech at the Twentieth Party Congress, in which he condemned the "personality cult." [126] All blame for a quarter-century of misguided development was heaped in a quite un-Marxist way onto Stalin.[127]

Soviet imperialism was limited to such an extent that an independent path to socialism was allowed each socialist country. Likewise, limitations were placed on Russian nationalism. In the economic sphere also, "Western" achievements could be acknowledged and used.[128] "Decentralization," however, was not to be interpreted as a departure from a central planned economy. Rather, grievances were to be eliminated and central leadership made more flexible through activation of the local soviets.[129] Despite the officially proclaimed slogan of peaceful co-existence, Khrushchev sharply rejected an ideological co-existence.[130]

It is remarkable that Soviet foreign policy now encompasses principles that can no longer be justified by Marxist theory.[131] The propaganda orientation of the Soviet economy in respect to American productivity also corresponds with this development.[132] Stalin had rein-terpreted ideology for the purpose of justifying previous actions, partic-ularly in domestic politics. In contrast, developments during the Twen-tieth Party Congress more and more approached greater "proximity to reality." This meant a broader ideological perspective vis-à-vis the facts. However, this was only the beginning. Economic practice was also ad-vanced at this meeting, as may be seen from the further rejection of "factological" historical writing.[133]

A major change in the intellectual climate occurred at the beginning of this new approach. The formal aspects of many questions were treated more generously than before. Substantive changes, however, re-mained minor.[134] While considerations of reality penetrated the surface of the metaphysical doctrines, their essence remained untouched.[135] Collective wisdom and experience replaced the Stalinist personality cult and claim to infallibility [136]—a milder form of Lenin's claim that truth was determined by the Party.

Stalin incorporated the useful doctrines contributed by condemned deviators of the 1920s, both right and left, into the body of teaching on Soviet Bolshevism. At the present time, also, some of Stalin's teachings prevail in spite of the disapprobation of him personally.[137] The attempts of a few economists to reintroduce dialectical thought into the realm of economics, however, did not quite succeed.[138]

The time between the Twentieth and Twenty-First Party Congresses was characterized by reform of the planning system. Advocates of cen-tral economic administration (Saburov and Pervuchin) demanded that inherent economic losses be offset through realistic planning, that is, through short-term realistic plans. The crux of the reforms was more rigid economic leadership and simultaneous expansion in authority of the individual Soviet republics and decentralization of economic plan-ning. Soon thereafter, the initially approved plan was modified by Khrush-chev to accommodate his plan for decentralization. The adherents of a centrally administered economy were out-maneuvered, and the reform of management in industry and agriculture was carried out.[139] As part of the preparations for the new "Seven Year Plan" during the Twenty-First Party Congress, the consumer-oriented aspects of production plan-ning in the New Course were recognized and partially approved. The interweaving of economic and educational questions in the Seven Year Plan became increasingly tighter and even became evident in the same year.[140]

The economic goals of the Twenty-First and Twenty-Second Party Congresses were the result of realpolitik insights, ambitions for political power, and the creation of ideological dogmas. They were clearly oriented along Stalin's economic lines.[141] The technological problems of economics were approached according to Western theory and examples.[142] In the course of this development, the use of cybernetics, electronic computers, and automation were officially recommended.[143] The macro-economic plans and goals remained more ideologically bound. There was to be a continuous increase in "social production" for an indefinite period, with increased emphasis on producer goods and the transformation of the *kolhozy* property into property of the people. The philosophical reasoning offered was Stalin's doctrine of the "gradual leaps" of social revolution, which were to lead to increasing perfection of the social body. The elimination of differences between city and country as well as between physical and intellectual labor proceeded slowly.[144] The achievement of communism, whose prerequisite was the creation of a material and technological base, remained a high ranking economic and political goal.[145] The power and continuous growth of the socialist system was further contrasted with the Western economy and interpreted in dialectical terms. The "contradictions" arising in the West were said to be incapable of correction; consequently they should be intensified to the point of "detonation."

The law of contradiction continued to rule the socialist methods of production. However, on the one hand, the evolving differences between the means of production and the progressive development of Soviet society were recognized and exposed with the help of planning.[146] On the other hand, progress was no longer to be determined by this conflict, but by the tension between the increasing needs of the entire population and the concurrent production levels of material and cultural goods. The mainsprings of development, therefore, continued to be found in the superstructure according to the post-Stalinist conception, as Khrushchev explained during the Twentieth Party Congress.[147] They were described in detail, defined, and taught as the mode of behavior in the "Communist morale." [148] The validity of this thesis of such driving forces cannot be brushed off lightly as long as the awakening desire for an education within the population, including its leaders, can be satisfied with Communist doctrines.[149] The current unrest among young intellectuals and college youth points in a different direction.[150]

Marxism-Leninism has lost, during the course of its development from Marx to Khrushchev, its most essential characteristic, namely, the striving for a society of the free and equal. Communism as a socio-economic system has remained the final goal.[151] All principles of human social life and of human existence itself continue to be subordinated to

104

this socio-economic goal. However, the foreign relations policies and social-political situation of the Soviet Union have changed.[152] Maximum economic production is demanded by the arms race, economic competition with the United States and West European industrial countries, political engagement in former colonies, the beginning emancipation of Soviet society with its demands for more security, popular demand for a higher standard of living, and relaxation of totalitarian forms of administration. These can be achieved through decentralization and individualization. This development might be supported by those forces in the Soviet Union that aspire to a profound reform of the Soviet system.[153] The heightening conflict with China and Albania severely tries the former social and historical claims to leadership and truth of the Communist party, which were based upon the theory of cognition.[154]

PART THREE

Socio-Ethical Aspects

VII. ETHICAL VALUES AND ECONOMIC JUSTICE

1. THE INTERTWINING OF ETHICS AND ECONOMICS

An ethical assessment of economic man and economic goods depends in large part upon one's metaphysical interpretation of the world, together with one's socio-philosophical analysis of the economic community.[1] Man's metaphysical speculations illuminate his personal understanding of his place in the cosmos. They determine his scale of values and the nature of their claims to realization through him. The social existence of man has always been acknowledged as a fact, even if deductive and inductive interpretations vary considerably. Its historical expressions extend from transcendental value assumptions to voluntaristic, instinct-oriented teachings, and from individualistic interpretation to the objectivist attitudes of a functional understanding of the social process.[2]

From the theological point of view, the metaphysical determination of values seems to be guaranteed by revelation. In philosophical explication, the problem of the existence of values, as well as that of their eventual hierarchy in a value cosmos, has traditionally led to well-nigh insuperable difficulties. That is to say, attempts have been made to posit an individual, independent existence for values. Nevertheless, more recent efforts to treat the phenomena of value within a context of rules of conduct promise a more propitious outcome.[3]

However problematic the philosophical interpretations of value phenomena may be, they still remain more or less subordinate to socio-eth-

109

ically ascertained reality. So long as human behavior and activity is stamped by the presence of value representations, it is unimportant whether values are possibly more than figments of the imagination or human illusions. Social reality is the sum total of what has come to be socially significant and effective.[4] A society is, therefore, not free from ethical values even though one can, rightly or wrongly, expose them as delusions; this only occurs when such notions grow ineffective within the society. At present it would appear that values are a part of human behavior. To a certain extent they delimit social and economic reality.[5] * As long as values are treated as objective by the social sciences, they can and must be dealt with as actualities. The question whether the tenets and assertions of economics may themselves be taken for value judgments has led, as Max Weber's demands for ethical neutrality have told us, to a set of problems arising from a method of thought that diverges into two extremes.[6] The value judgment controversy touches directly only the question of the feasibility of setting scientific goals in economic policy.[7] As was demonstrated in greater detail in Part One, the danger of confusing science with normative interests can be curbed by a meticulously precise account of the assumptions which penetrate the scientific formulations.[8]

Economics is a sphere of human social life. Its concrete form at any given time is a human achievement. Consequently economics is interwoven into all domains of social living.[9] In the configuration of an economic system, socio-ethical viewpoints play an intrusive role.[10] General economic morality deals with this borderline. The accepted moral values of the society determine the meaning, purpose, and goal of economics. The relation of economics to man, for whose service it exists, is subject to an ethical adjudication. The aim of economics and the formulation of the economic system are largely appraised by whether they are in accord with the ethico-metaphysical self-perception of critical man and with the social behavior norms of his society.[11] Many facets of economics, such as the quantity and methods of production and working conditions, are liable to a moral assessment. Above all, questions of ownership and distribution are the objects of economic morality. They come to be measured against criteria of justice.

The behavior of economic man is moreover determined through the material goal of economics. Morality within an economic system cannot be borrowed from a general morality because things, like man, demand to be considered within the economic context. The social world is but a

* This fact must be especially heeded *vis-à-vis* the frequently expressed counter views of Eastern writers.

historical form of life in which economic goals and ethical norms influence one another.[12] The exclusive adjustment of each economic individual to general human values would lead to a crippling of the economic process. It proves to be just as utopian as the exclusive adjustment toward the commonweal of the citizen in all individual actions. A careful balancing of the material demands given in each case, on the one hand, with man's refusal to be considered exclusively as a means within the economic process, on the other, is the proper task of economic morality.[13] In economics, efficient operation and its organization are fully as important as consideration for humanity. Resolution of these relative tensions is the task of a special and immanent economic morality.

2. CONCEPTIONS OF VALUE

So long as medieval economic morality was grounded on Christian metaphysics, earthly things were incorporated into the value hierarchy of a system of being in which God was the supreme value.[14]

Economic goods were acknowledged as gifts bestowed by God upon man. As such they had their purpose in the divine cosmogony. Covetous accumulation of these goods, which were never considered ends in themselves, was to medieval man the sin of avarice.[15] In connection with the tension worked out by Descartes between the world and the cognitive "I," the ontological/metaphysical interpretation of the world rigidified into ideological antitheses. There was materialism and idealism, which acted characteristically upon the realm of values and variously determined their reciprocal positions. The economic morality of the nineteenth century was to a great extent controlled by this dichotomy. In the economically ethical application of idealistic value systems, the historical school of political economy defended traditionally dominant group values against the classical school, which stood in danger of explaining economically material conceptions as obligatory upon the whole of human life. The basic materialist point of view took the economic means as a goal and oriented all human activity toward the satisfaction of sensual needs.[16] The general aspect of these developments was set forth in chapters II, IV, and V. In this connection, their moral significance stands in the foreground. Moreover, sociology, feeling itself more and more an independent science, exercised a significant influence on the shaping of economic moral values. By and large it abjured a transcendental postulation of values and sought to derive socially ethical relationships from the advance toward rational group formulation.[17]

Marx exhibits a singular combination of materialist and idealist value

111

interpretations. In his effort to bring the philosophical account of the world into harmony with its actual appearance, and this latter with the demands of social justice, the youthful Marx attempted to analyze the "social technique of living." [18] But the working out of an economic philosophy in the center of which stood ethically speculative, practically active man soon became buried under the investigation of economic legalities. Marxist "materialism," which could tolerate no transcendentally established values because all behavior norms must be derived from a historically social methodology, became endangered by a unilateral deterministic and "value-free" formulation.[19] Decisive for the contemporary conflict between two competitive economic systems was the predominence of a more materialistic economic ethic. In the Western sphere of influence it certainly allied itself in the wake of classical liberalism with the fundamental postulate of individual freedom. In the Eastern sphere of influence material values have validity as the basis upon which the spiritual values of freedom and equality become elevated.[20] The danger subsists here in the emerging autonomy of those efforts on the part of national economic planning for material increase.

The far-reaching socially ethical tendency became once more obvious when the question of human freedom and technical/material activity was once again seriously considered.[21] The idea of human nature includes the right of every person to expand, to develop, and to preserve his humanity.[22] The influence of this ethical axiom of the Enlightenment on social and cultural life can be more immediately felt in the East.[23] There the practice of economics is broadly determined by socially ethical, collectively social points of view,[24] whereas the fundamental liberal idea of the West more or less leaves moral decisions up to the individual.[25]

3. LAW, MORALITY, JUSTICE, AND FRATERNITY

The macro-economic ethical view became more importunate than ever through the East-West competition of economic systems. Socially ethical values integral to the founding and historical development of both systems relate preponderately to the universally recognized values of European cultures. Their relationship to each other and the manner of their development are nevertheless separable and ultimately occasion their profound differences.

Law can be defined as the normative side of human interaction.[26] Law is hence most strictly bound to the morality of the social group. So long as the behavior patterns for each member of the community remain clearly visible at a glance, the socially ethical organization can be amply secured through normative behavior schemata as they are displayed and acknowledged in such things as custom, usage, religious conduct, and habit. Yet with the advancing complexity and materialization of life inside a community, a rigid codification of customs into laws shortly reveals itself to be necessary in order that lucid, reiterative legal principles may be invoked and responsible deportment be required of each group member at all times.

A time-honored guiding concept of community-conscious, socially responsible conduct is that of Aristotelian justice. Its essence was a loyal attitude with respect to the laws considered as a union of custom, usage, and social regulations. [27]

In national political practice, the identity of morality and law could not always be maintained. Apart from the domain of morality were prescriptive, universally obligatory statutes which seemed indispensable for the stability of society. Disobedience of them was made punishable; observance of them was compulsory. Giving all citizens a uniform code of conduct for dealing with the persons and possessions of their fellow citizens was an advantage which could be brought about only with the ominous possibility that law and justice might part company. On the one hand, notions of justice often, in practice, evolve away from accepted law in diverse directions. On the other hand, there is a constant danger of abuse in the legislative sphere according to the political distribution of power. Above and beyond this, just prosecution of the law is endangered as soon as one of the litigants is no longer held to be equal to the others and thus finds himself placed under unilateral coercion in areas which affect the elementary concerns of life. Social evolution is spared none of these possible abuses. [28]

In token of the cultural interrelations which have in the meantime spanned the world, a legal system has frequently been more or less taken over by other countries. It has, however, not always been brought into harmony with accepted folk morality. Besides the possibility of the dissolution of law and justice, historical differences in cultures demand special consideration. The prevailing law scarcely requires any other justification within a society than an appeal to the society's own cultural tradition with its acknowledged ethical values. If in such a community a foreign legal system with its underlying concepts of justice is assumed, and if at the same time the possibility of deserting the now-alien corporate body does not remain for group members, the situation readily leads to force and terror. [29] *

* As the events since 1961 in East Germany indicate an alien legality of this kind can lead to extreme bondage for the members of the society.

Justice is not only the comprehensive value in general, but also a special virtue. In its concrete determination, Aristotle differentiated between the two forms of distributive and compensatory justice, which have already been mentioned (chapter II). In Roman law such an analysis led, under the dominant idea of *suum cuique*, to the working out of separate public and private codes, which in principle was taken over gradually by European countries and also later by other civilizations. [30]

As the notion of individual freedom, which had been developed during the Renaissance, became historically effective with the French Revolution through its claims to liberty, equality, and fraternity, law and the sense of justice evolved deleteriously apart from each other. Laws were perceived by the majority in the political arena as an instrument of power for the ruling class. As such, they distinctly permitted, indeed actually supported, injustices. The early French socialists combined their demand for political justice with that for social justice. There is no doubt that the communist social organization also is intended to serve this kind of truly humanitarian ideal. The rational values of the Enlightenment are for East and West the point of departure for truly divergent evolutionary paths. They have nevertheless both grown out of the same presuppositions within intellectual history. [31]

The basic questions of economic morality which are contained in the notion of social justice, and the historic roots of the contemporary cleavage in international economics, can be developed from an economic-ethical analysis of this concept based upon the premises of the French Revolution. [32]

Even at the time of the Enlightment the concept of "fraternity" was disputed. Great political philosophers such as Kant denied that it was a universally binding, rational value, serviceable in the construction of a just social order. Kant believed that the self-interest of individual persons with regard to one another must be so arranged that egoistically based limits could be set for their egoistic strivings. A doubt, constantly corroborated by reality, concerning the ideal of a prevailingly noble human nature loyal to the society as a whole, led to a realistic humanism. It no longer strives to force upon men in the political framework the brotherhood as it exists within the family. The attempts during the French Revolution to substitute morality for selfishness, good men for the social group, and a moral common life for political might, led to the guillotine and to the forfeiture of the hotly contested, scarcely won political and spiritual freedom of the individual. [33]

The development in the Soviet Union had a similar consummation. The attempt to construct a productive economic system predominately

114

upon the principle of solidarity as derived from the concept of fraternity —as well as upon a general political responsibility and idealism for the "just cause"—has had meager results to date in serving to promote productivity. An essential ingredient of the final goal of communist society is true brotherhood. It has, however, been postponed into the future and is to be the result of the training and general development of man under socialism.[34] Even so, socialist education has as yet achieved no great success. Individual enthusiasm for personal renunciation in the interest of a great cause has appeared in every age. The political experiences of the French Revolution have repeated themselves in Stalinist Russia on the political and social levels. The ethically elevated beginning made in the name of humanity led to practical results in which an essential part of personal freedom was lost.

4. ETHICAL-ECONOMIC TENSIONS BETWEEN EAST AND WEST

Philosophical study of the concept of freedom led to the recognition that underlying every theory of freedom is a latent anthropology. When it was determined by Marx, as derived from Hegel, that man was destined to generate his own being through his work and that his particular future existence was essentially self-created, several ancient preconceptions of European culture were considered in a new light. The theoretical weaknesses of capitalist society were quite as pitilessly exposed as was its actual failure to provide any truly human treatment of man in his economic activity. This criticism rested upon a radicalized notion of liberty and equality. In the society of the future such notions were to be the determinative principles of political and social reality. Communist society was in this sense supposed to emerge as the incarnation of a "true, absolute and unlimited humanity." In order for economic practices in the East and the West to be compared, the values of "liberty" and "equality" must be assayed.[35] A distinctive exposition of these two concepts, together with their distinctively determined relationship to each other, has created two different economic systems. These diverse fundamentals have not yet counterbalanced each other to any appreciable extent, and hence they still determine the economic development of the world.

Kant oriented his efforts concerning a social order most appropriate to and just for man toward the notion of individual freedom and personal dignity. Individual freedom found its limits in esteem for the human dignity of the other person, in regarding him as an "end in himself." A compromise was found by giving liberty a value superior to that of equality. In the political movement of liberalism, which in essence determined the evolution of Western economic systems, the individual value of personal freedom was maintained to predominate over societal pressures of all kinds. The fundamentally metaphysical/Christian significance of man assigned to him the task of co-operating in the establishment of a general world harmony, through uninhibited exercise of his natural reason unconstrained by erroneous human dogmas.[36] Freedom of a few individuals, however, was purchased with the bondage of many. The capitalist economic system, with its few wealthy owners and its many poor, dependent laborers, was a visible expression of setting freedom higher than human dignity and the equality of human classes. The balance between liberty and equality was in political practice abandoned in favor of liberty.[37]

This result produced social ferment. Its critique was posited on the fact that freedom was the prerogative of the privileged few and did not serve all men equally. Indeed, it led to repression of the many by the few, to the mastery of man over man. Social equality came to be recognized as the prerequisite if there were to be freedom for all. Equality of all men was the obvious basis for the establishment of a society of free moral beings. Socialism protected, through equality, the possibility of liberty for all in a "homogeneous" society.[38] Marx not only criticized the relationship of liberty and equality, but especially radicalized the concept of freedom that was valid up to that time. The liberal concept of freedom was in general defined formally and negatively, as the opposite of such humanly degrading conditions as slavery, serfdom, and political impotence. It merely assured the individual a chance for freedom; it did not require realization.[39]

Marx's critique of the capitalistic social system made it clear just how few persons could actually use their opportunity for freedom. On the basis of his new image of mankind he demanded not just the possibility but also the realization of freedom. The socially ethical task thus required was not merely the creation of a capacity for freedom, but the self-realization of each member of the society.[40]

The consummation of this demand within socialist practice led to an interweaving of individual personality development with the evolution of economic society. According to the socialist concept of freedom, the community is responsible for the personal development of each individual. The individual, on the other hand, becomes subject to social accountability. Freedom should accordingly become an obligation for self-realization *vis-à-vis* society. Marxism identifies freedom precisely

116

with the total integration of the individual into the collective activity.[41] Since equality was comprehended as the precondition of true freedom in the argument with liberalism, the weight shifted from liberty to equality. At the same time, of course, it conjured up the danger of abrogating freedom. In any case, complete equality for all men implies, at the very least, considerable loss of freedom under presently conceivable conditions.

5. DISTRIBUTIVE AND CORRECTIVE JUSTICE

The notions of social and economic justice in the waning nineteenth century were largely determined by the two socio-ethical persuasions of liberalism and socialism.[42] Aristotle distinguished between two forms of justice, distributive and corrective, and found that in practice they appear side by side. So differentiated had they become under the two modern movements of twentieth century thought that each trend sought to realize but one form.[43] The concept of distributive justice was compatible with the notions of liberalism. Here the state was called upon to sanction the functional differences of each person in the economy. Each was supposed to enter unhindered upon the enjoyment of profits which he had gained by means of his own performance. The principal emphasis, then, was on distributive justice, which was unconditionally advocated as giving sufficient room for independent development of the individual.

Socialism reproached liberalism in that lawful equality must remain formal, the privilege of isolated individuals, as long as the possibility persists that a *legalis homo,* through economic and social sanctions, can subject another person to pressures which jeopardize his existence. Socio-ethical notions of equality in socialism ally themselves with the concept of corrective justice. To achieve freedom for all, a harmonious social equality must be established among the different social classes.[44]

The struggle between liberalism and socialism, to a large extent, involves the correct definition of socially ethical justice. The attempt in modern political economy to define the right proportions of distributive and corrective justice led to considerable divergences. Because of the predominate interest in economic growth, the debate over true justice is, moreover, partially supressed. The point of divergence is the question of uniting equality of social status with freedom for individuals to develop their capacities. At the same time, the social constitution is required to bring about the greatest possible productive power for the economy.

117

Since the French Revolution put an end to any dispute about the equality of all men in relation to their civil status, it accordingly became irrelevant whether equal social opportunities with regard to education, income, and welfare can be dealt with as minimal claims to social equality or whether, as the safeguard of existence and the prerequisites for free development of the individual, they are still considered part of the equalities of citizenship. Although the socialist struggle was ignited by these demands, they number today among the uncontested presuppositions of both Eastern and Western policy. Under liberalism the opportunity for freedom of a few seems to have become, through recognition of social justice, genuine opportunity for all. The question is no longer whether minimum subsistence must be safeguarded but rather how high it must be set for each citizen, with equal socio-economic status, to be guaranteed the greatest possible opportunity for unhindered self-development. The contemporary discussion between neo-liberalism and socialist thought in the economic area centers around the questions of property and the limitation of high incomes, which might perhaps present a threat to the free and equal self-realization of each person. Equality therewith signifies primarily a retrenchment from more than functional control and special privilege.

Extreme egalitarian limitations on social and economic private initiative nevertheless restrict human development as well as economic achievement. This is because social stratification in society acts quite as much as an individual stimulus to personal development as graduation of incomes incites economic activity in the individual. The need for an efficient economy forced the Soviet Union to make concessions in posing an independent life style for the individual: material stimuli (differentiated salaries and rewards) had again to be introduced.

Complete social equality—namely a synchronization in style and manner of developing a life of one's own—means the destruction of freedom. The compatibility of freedom and equality specifies the meaningful domain of civil rights. Their incompatibility points toward the realm reserved for individual development of personal capacities. The applicability of corrective justice ceases at the point where, through a centrally dictated uniformity, freedom for personal development and consequently equal status for every individual are basically destroyed. Distributive justice finds its limit at the point where inequalities arising from unhindered advancement of some obstruct free self-development of all. Between these two limits lies compromise, the area of social justice.[45]

118

The West sees the enemy of freedom as illegitimate private power, which is acquired from an elevated position sanctioned socially, economically, or by right of property. Efforts are now being made to eradicate this threat to freedom. Power will probably remain the motivating element of social development, however, because what takes place in the economic sphere to actualize freedom for all intrudes into the legal and, in part, even the social sphere. In the West, freedom is endangered by private misuse of power. By contrast, the East searches for a better actualization of freedom through abolition of private property and by extensive social equality for all. The price is centrism enforced by administrative law.

The juristic and economic discussion concentrates on the concept of property. It remains to be seen whether in the West, the hitherto existing social function of property will remain if governmental measures are consistently employed to improve the quality of life. It remains likewise open whether in the East, the intrinsic source of the private exercise of power can be choked off merely through consistent abolition of private property. The socially just compromise between distributive and corrective justice is to be found in the area between civil equality and social freedom, or, from the point of view of the East, in the area between social equality and civil freedom.

Although the effort to correlate liberty and equality has led to a withdrawal from extreme positions by both the East and the West, an essential distinction in the definition of freedom nevertheless remains. The West sees a free society as a continuing social union, the fulfillment of which remains the private task of each individual. The East speaks of liberty in which individuals have perceived the opportunity for freedom only in so far as the individual has made himself a voluntary, trained co-worker for the common welfare.

The intrusion of totalitarian power into the private sphere of the individual has long been viewed, and in the final analysis historically confirmed, as the great danger of the socialist idea. Individuality becomes curtailed and is eventually degenerated. Yet the West is also threatened by an unwanted development. The other-directed group member, who orients himself by the behavior and consumption patterns of others, has relinquished his freedom to a uniform social despotism.[46] The liberal concept of freedom is swallowed by the social patterns which it has itself created. As a result, in an attempt to provide a counterbalance, the state gradually becomes the protector of the individual *vis-à-vis* the economic community.

119

VIII. JUSTICE IN THE WEST

1. WORK ETHOS AND PROPERTY-BASED POWER

The ethical issues of modern times are tied in with the value put on work. In earlier tradition, as we have already amplified (chapter II), work was merely what was done to satisfy material needs. In modern times the idea arose that man elevates himself through work to become the controller of nature and a humane personality. Thus the value placed on work is characteristic of the community organization prevailing at any given time.[1] The modern work ethos is suspended between a recognition of the necessity of labor and the task of giving it a human and, above all, free and socially just structure.

Contemporary industrial economy arose in the framework of a religious society in which work was the consequence of human guilt and sin. It could, however, in view of future redemption, be borne cheerfully. Besides, the secularization which came in the train of humanism was already so far advanced that a labor ethic which saw its origins, and those of its accomplishments, in man alone had established itself. It was extensively conceived out of the material present. The joint responsibility of Christians for the secular order was already strongly accentuated in Calvinism. Thus, among other developments, the Puritan work ethic became important for the capitalistic society then establishing itself. Income from labor was the sign of divine approbation. As religious conviction cooled, the rationalistically molded human type remained.

120

Above all, the return from wealth and the enjoyment of goods gained in significance in the consciousness of man and contributed to the development of the capitalistic economic system. The success ethic required, instead of consumption, a continuous reinvestment of profits for the expansion and improvement of the productive apparatus.[2] Especially in the Christian social ethic, there persisted to a large extent a triad of human labor, nature, and product (together with tools). During the first industrial revolution this unity of the labor process was disrupted. Individual labor became a functional segment in a technological "assembly-line" production routine.[3] The human labor ethos was subordinated to economic rationalism. The degree of achievement became the standard, and work was subjected to technical considerations of expediency. Furthermore, through division of labor, a breakdown of the production processes occurred which no longer allowed the individual to manufacture the product from beginning to end by himself.

Man as a mere element of production was scarcely judged according to his personality, but rather seen and treated in the market as a productive unit. This human capability was viewed like any other economic good and had its price. Only in the capitalistic economic system, therefore, could there be conflicts between participation in rationalized production and human self-development.[4] On the social plane, through the separation of labor from the remaining spheres of life, new structures in family, community, and nation arose. Specialized labor in an organized economic process was detached from private leisure and became the proper location of confirmation of one's humanity.[5] In former times the kernel of human existence lay, for instance, more in social ethics, in contemplative education, in faith, or in craftsmanlike production of goods and services. Now maximization of productivity has become urgent. The economic sector has gradually become the determinate force in the total life of society.

A labor ethos based on income also modified the stance of society toward property. In the Christian view, property was first of all a good entrusted by God to man for stewardship. The demand for unlimited power of disposal over private property came forth only in the wake of the concept of justice based on freedom of the individual. The principle of distributive justice permitted the use of property purely in one's own self-interest, without social considerations. On the one hand, there is the notion of a graduated natural order in the idea of distributive justice; on the other hand, the idea of property based on former productivity is approved. This led to the sanctioning of property differentiation that arose from the possession of land as well as ownership of the means of pro-

121

duction because of past labor. The sanctioning of discriminatory distribution of property led to an even greater economic inequality, because productively efficient property guarantees a derived income. A property hierarchy and graduated income led, according to the guiding idea of distributive justice, to a disproportionate pre-eminence of the economically strong.[6] Whoever had at his disposal neither income nor wealth fell into the class of wage laborer, juristically free but impecunious, and therefore dependent upon the individual entrepreneur, who was working for his own profit, and upon circumstances of the market. The wage level oscillated widely in the labor market according to supply and demand, especially where the threat of unemployment often worked as a labor supply incentive. The interest in belonging to the propertied class led more or less to an acknowledgement of egotism, ruthless profit-seeking, a playing-off of those with the more productive capacities against those in need of social and economic protection, and to concentration upon the material values of existence.[7]

2. THE LIBERAL SOCIAL ETHIC

As the Middle Ages waned, freedom was understood as a privilege in a social world ranked according to "estates." [8] A socio-ethical secularization of freedom of conscience became the presupposition for the liberal concept of freedom. The ideas of liberalism directed themselves especially against those dependency relationships which were perceived to be inhuman and against oppression, regimentation, and force.[9] Liberal thought established itself with the rapidly self-emancipating middle class as a formative ethical principle for practical life. Moreover, it had to connect itself in the course of its historical evolution with many types of ideas, especially with the democratic concept of liberty and with Romantic cultural notions. The concretion of the liberal idea led to a multitude of inner contradictions. The abuses and socio-ethical incompatibilities in the old liberalist economic system were seen ever more clearly after the period of the Manchester school.[10]

In the final decade of the nineteenth century, liberalism stood in danger of losing its last remnants of metaphysical and religious introspection and of being forced into a perilously "materialistic" direction. The way had already been opened through its concurrent acceptance of utilitarianism from Mill, Ricardo, Say, and others. The rational and individualist view of man, which even in its early beginnings was too optimistically interpreted, the principle of free competition, and the notion of harmony relative to a market economy threatened to founder under social Darwinism.

122

Such false paths required a new assessment of liberalism.[11] The variety of approaches to international economic neoliberalism makes it difficult to apply the neoliberal label to such diverse thinkers as Knight, Cannan, Villey, von Mises, von Hayek, Lord Robbins, Einaudi, Bresciani-Turroni, Eucken, Röpke, Rüstow, and Müller-Armack.[12] Representatives of the Freiburg school under Eucken sought to achieve a total view of economic and social life which is characterized by the notion of *Ordoliberalismus*. For them the concept of order, in the sense of institutionalism, has become pre-eminently important.[13] Therein the classical liberal ideas of harmony and equilibrium are extensively preserved. The fundamental individualistic conception of the economic system remains firm. The belief in a market harmony naturally establishing itself is nevertheless suppressed through an emphasis on politically regulated competition. This should be guided by economic-ethical considerations and should be the conscientious goal of the market participant.[14] Market arrangements and socio-ethically pursued economic and community arrangements fall together more or less clearly. General human welfare is brought about without further assistance by means of self-regulation, prices, and the free play of forces through politically protected competition. The economic organization with optimal efficiency actualizes at once distributive justice by means of objective selection through competition.[15] The state is to create an economic framework, primarily in the form of constitutionally legalized statutes, which will protect competition against non-conformist market encroachments as well as against degeneration.

The socio-ethical distribution problem is nevertheless neglected by neoliberalism.[16] There is the danger of identifying the market price with a just price, and this overlooks the fact that initial equality positively does not, or does not yet, exist. The ethical presuppositions of individual liberal theoreticians have grown out of a Bentham-stamped utilitarianism, in which materialism is metaphysically superior to rationalistically or ethical-idealistically interpreted humanism. Those structural and organizational laws immanent in a liberal economic system which are especially important for economic-ethical consideration relate themselves more or less to an anonymous market. This corresponds to the picture of a rational economic man in pursuit of profits. In the practice of political economy the neoliberals nevertheless have not always held to their market model. Under the pressure of practical needs they have consented to more or less trenchant, "non-market-conforming" encroachments upon free competition. Otherwise there would arise the danger that unbridled competition might turn into a competitive struggle, which would especially endanger the existence of middle-class industry and small trade. However, for various reasons, the evolution has been toward concentration of resources and of oligopolistic market structures, particularly in large-scale industry.

In spite of the numerous deficiencies of modern liberal theories, the pivotal, ethical idea of freedom and its attendant notions centering on a market economy organization form a major barrier against exploitation, planned-economy despotism, and political repression in the practice of Western forms of life. In the West, detached from temporary ties of liberalism with other spheres of ideas, and independent of the particular theories of its own adherents, the idea of freedom has become an important ingredient of economic practice. The battle centers on how far this market pattern may be interspersed with planned-economy elements without losing its fundamental significance. Economic crises, and the social insecurity that comes with them, could be avoided through Keynesian economic intervention. The social welfare economy endeavors, particularly in matters of distribution, to dissolve the customary formulative task of a compensatory commonweal and to provide a functionally effective market organization with valid socio-ethical standards.

3. WESTERN SOCIALISM AND SOCIAL REFORM

The socio-ethical pivotal idea of Western socialism is contained in the wish to abolish poverty as a mass phenomenon. Absolute as well as relative poverty becomes apparent as soon as obvious social differences emerge in a social system. The group divides into rich and poor and the needs of one confront the affluence of the other. Western socialist thinkers constantly referred their ideas of justice to the individual businessman within the community. Accordingly, the concept of equality stood in the foreground. Their idea of justice was predominately directed toward the equality of human dignity and the possibility of social brotherhood. Western socialist ethical teachings aimed to transform societal organization and economic practice according to egalitarian points of view.[17]

Contrary to its expectations the French Revolution did not realize its demand for the equality of all men, and its realization appeared increasingly unlikely as the middle class established itself in the world. The French Revolution, in contrast to a socialist revolution, was pervaded more and more by a spirit of preservation and perseverance. The utopians, the early socialists, and Karl Marx projected for the first time new social orders in the name of reason and justice. For the most part they envisioned that mature capitalism, which was adjudged to be able to

124

produce goods and services for all, would be an economically sufficient basis for the future society. The primary problem was that of equal distribution. The radical evil of dehumanization under the capitalist economic system was not seen to arise from the intrusion of machinery and of technical modes of thought, but primarily from the private possession of capital goods. Rather than being concerned merely with increased production on a macro-economic level, these thinkers demanded first of all that capital goods be converted to collective goods. In the second place, the combined national income should be distributed according to "natural" and "rational" requirements.

In early communism the idea of fully corrective justice prevailed. Production as well as consumption should be extensively organized in accordance with egalitarian principles. Nevertheless, misgivings concerning the possibility of absolute equality of consumption soon entered the Western socialist movement. Total or circumscribed application of the idea of equality became a distinguishing feature between communism and socialism.[18] The socio-ethical ideas of communism were sweepingly applied by a political dictatorship only in the first half of the twentieth century. Already in the nineteenth century, however, they were attacked by many farsighted persons precisely because of this political danger.[19] Thus communism, among other things, began more and more to absorb the notion of a planned economy. For the Bolshevists, in their early years, the idea of unrestricted equality was uppermost. At the time of the French Revolution the demand for political equality had been identical with pretensions to sovereignty on the part of the middle class, which had already consolidated extensive economic power in its hands and pressed for realization of its own freedom. In much the same way the communist-socialist movement of the nineteenth and twentieth centuries sought at the start the realization of a radical material equality through emancipation of the proletariat.[20] On the other hand, according to the Western view, only certain basic human needs can be classified and satisfied in an egalitarian way.[21]

Marxism viewed evolution toward an egalitarian society as a historical necessity. For this reason it has long renounced every sort of ethic. On the contrary, justice as a regulative or normative idea became a unifying peg for all other socialist forces, from the Christian social reformers, through the Reformation socialists, up to the socialist neo-Kantians. At one extreme, Lassalle, in Germany, sought to carry out social justice with help from the state. At the other extreme, in France and Italy, the same goal was sought through a radical paralysis of the bourgeois economy and the assumption of economic leadership by national trade union federations from the existing branches of industry. (This type of economic organization, known as syndicalism, is less radical than English guild socialism.) The radical socialists strove to actualize unconditionally the ultimate communist goals. However, even during the transition period, the moderate groups, struggling for a bearable life for all, fell in with those groups which, out of Christian or socialist ideas of reform, strove for a greater actualization of social justice. A rigid boundary line between moderate socialists and non-socialistic reformers of society could be drawn only with difficulty. When, under the threat of World War I, the idea of solidarity among all workers proved to be an illusion, the spiritual unity of the socialist movement dissolved in the wake of the breakdown in its organizational unity. Only its ethical demands— abolishment of mass poverty, destruction of economic privilege, and promotion of fraternity—remained the common goals toward which Western socialist thought oriented itself.

With the end of World War I, the socialists of today's Western nations resolved upon a single unequivocal avowal of democracy and partial recognition of the capitalist social order, whose reformulation they would work for under democratic conditions. The more moderate forces in the socialist movement achieved success first of all in the political arena. At the parliamentary level as well as in the labor unions, they submitted to the democratic rules of social ethics. The more urgent the avowal of a democratic life-style became, with the rise of the Soviet dictatorship, and the more social democrats worked together on conditions in their own country, especially on welfare legislation, the more the earlier harshly egalitarian justification of income faded into the background.

A type of "market socialism" arose between the two world wars. A type of socialism which, in addition to the technical and organizational achievements of capitalism, also incorporated the market mechanism of price adjustment was defended in the beginning, particularly by Germans, such as Heimann. Very soon the significance of this theory became apparent and its adherents in Western Europe and America, such as Lange and Lerner, offered a corresponding subspecies of the socialist movement.

The influence of the world-wide economic crisis which began in 1929 and of the newly established Five-Year Plan of the Soviet Union permitted the planned economy to emerge more strongly into the economic thought of Western socialists. Therewith, commensurate with the idea of economic foresight, quantity planning found less acceptance among socialists than did value planning. Here the task fell to the supporters of

126

economic planning to anticipate the price trend on the basis of market fluctuations and to influence the market through control of demand and supply. Notwithstanding, Keynesian interventionism has taken much steam out of the Western idea of a socialist economic order.[22] The original socio-ethical and theoretical economic ideas for socialization through nationalization of private property have lost much of their power of conviction, especially in view of the small success of large-scale nationalization programs by the English Labour government after World War II and of subsequent developments.

The original ethical demands for full equality for men have more or less yielded to a moderate metamorphosis of the economic order. Western socialism no longer directly advocates equal developmental possibilities in freedom through radical displacement of inequalities. The principle of equality has retreated to the realm whence it originally arose, the equality of human dignity. As long as social inequality is not too great it is viewed as acceptable. In the economic realm, the axiom of independent development is valid. The principles of corrective justice find their application in the destruction of economic privileges as well as in the restriction of power derived from property ownership. Egalitarian thought has been replaced by mild elitism. In principle, professional administrators of the society stand on equal terms as fellow citizens with technical manpower in other areas of life. A constitutional state hinders misuse of power. Democracy consists in the temporary transfer of directional authority to freely elected persons who through accomplishment have proved themselves competent for this vocation.

4. CHRISTIAN TEACHINGS AND CONSERVATIVE ETHICS

Recent restoration movements have expressed a socio-ethical desire by an enlightened middle class to ward off assaults on the social organization. In the nineteenth century there existed another conservatism to which radical innovators of every kind were unsympathetic. Edmund Burke stressed *vis-à-vis* the French Revolution the value of historic and social continuity in the life of the people. Catholic-Christian thought, especially, allied itself with the socio-ethical ideas of Romanticism. The Catholic parties, particularly in southern Europe, provided a further adversary to liberalism and consequently also to Western socialism. This common antagonism produced, around the end of the last century, those mixed forms of academic socialism, Christian socialism, and the Christian labor movement which inclined more or less to one pole or the other.

127

In regard to social ethics, the conservatives proved themselves the more progressive in contrast to the liberals. This fact became obvious in the reform efforts of the Pope through his social encyclicals toward the close of the nineteenth century. Notwithstanding that the Roman church declined the socio-economic principles of liberalism (or in other words sought to combine solution of social and economic problems with preservation of the old European order), its efforts were denied a decisive success. Viewed as a whole, the Catholic and evangelical churches had not yet perceived in full their responsibility to the temporal world. Effective help remained overwhelmingly the work of individuals. The English Conservative party, however, succeeded in combining a satisfactory social reform stance with a middle-class Christian system of organization. Thus the Conservative party provided a socio-ethically important opponent to that country's Liberal party (disregarding the Socialist Labour party). In the rest of Europe, conservative endeavors were overshadowed by wide-spread radical nationalism.[23]

Generally speaking, Christian reform of socio-ethical teachings began only after World War I. In explicit form, it actually began only after World War II. The notion of one social order valid for all times and all places has been dropped by the Catholic church. Likewise, the Protestant churches relinquished their cultural programs aimed at realizing the Kingdom of God on earth. These churches saw that a state-imposed social ethic could lead to a decline in convictions of personal responsibility and to a Christian/secular regimentation. On the other hand, the Roman church saw in obligatory social teaching just that possibility of being able to demonstrate conclusively to the individual Christian his personal duty in the specific historical situation. Thereby a maximum approach to actuality was reached through a continuing interpretation of temporally conditioned circumstances, based on the spirit of natural law, as explicated in the social teaching of the Pope. From this basic position the attempt was repeatedly made to bring historical evolution into harmony with the principles of freedom and justice. In the economic sphere the appropriate type of justice is not equality in the general sense but rather patriarchal provision for the disabled and compensation and supplementation aimed at human and material independence.

The Protestant churches aspire to similar goals. They endeavor, however, to renounce empirical and traditional dogma. They deal with the worldliness of men by advocating that man cling to Christ, so that out of their personal freedom they may criticize the social circumstances existing at any time and constructively work together to master new

128

tasks. Faith and Christian freedom are the criteria in the choice between differing socio-ethical possibilities. Beyond this, they would prevent class- and tradition-bound hardening of social teachings as well as
ideological excesses.[24]

IX. INCOME DISTRIBUTION IN THE WEST

1. DISTRIBUTION IN THE MARKET ECONOMY

In classical economic theory, income distribution is of great significance. It is not autonomous but rather the result of price formation, which, however, is influenced by it in turn. What is relevant in economic policy on the distribution of wealth is not so much direct redistribution of existing wealth but, above all, the chance to acquire newly created wealth.[1] In the market economy, prices guide the economic process.[2] The idea of productivity is immanent in competition. From this point of view, productivity is an essential factor in distribution for the market economy.

A. Productivity as a Gauge

The criterion of productivity is not typical only of the Western market economy. In the East the plan determines the output of individual goods. The goal of the factory is to fulfill the plan, and there are certain incentives like bonuses.[3] In the West productivity is based on the economic principle of competition.[4] This can have a variety of forms.[5] The socialistic market economy—a particular hybrid of economic systems —is actually identified with competition in productivity.[6] That principle is usually defined to mean that man's economic success must be measured by his own achievement. But the use of this yardstick is not clear.

130

Differences arise immediately when we ask whether the reason for lower productivity should be taken into account. Must the individual justify the consequences of unequal opportunities? Does productivity mean the result of human effort in a technical sense? [7] Röpke's theory of competition in productivity describes the latter as a quantity which is expressed in increase of income, whose reason and justification is satisfaction of the consumer's wishes.[8] But the "equal conditions" assumed here do not necessarily imply that those sharing in the market must always compete with one another. We may, for instance, think of oligopoly, in which there may be competition and low prices.[9] * The problem would look different if oligopolistic competition were aimed at controlling the market.[10] † By eliminating competitors productivity might disappear as a condition, and then income distribution would be independent of productivity.[11] ‡

A particular market structure does not necessarily guarantee competition in production. Nor are the prevailing micro-economic solutions the only way out. They are often the point of departure by interest groups who try to survive by a ready-made concept of productivity. In the macro-economic sense, the concept is particularly meaningless when it is supposed that it gives the factors of production an adequate share in national income.

B. Equality of Opportunity

There is a close connection between the concept of productivity and the principle of equal opportunity. It is true that the productivity criterion can be applied when the social and material conditions of the subjects differ. But where the achievement of the individual is to be precisely calculated, he must have the opportunity to use his physical and mental power under relatively equal economic conditions. This can be attained through law, a political constitution, and the social structure.[12] Equal opportunity grants the weaker person an advantage, which he can use not only against other individuals and institutions,[13] but also with which he can do his share in bringing about a democratic majority and in put-

* Because of capital accumulation there exists, in oligopolistic market structures, the probability of a greater reduction of costs, a probability strengthened by an accelerated introduction of technology and utilization of internal savings.

† Eucken emphasized that, among producers, competitive acts are not necessarily conflicting.

‡ However, deviating from the principle of productivity does not necessarily imply a less "just" distribution.

131

ting its decisions into practice.[14] This equality is made possible by training the individual and, later, by an occupation that matches his inclination. This equality is also visible in the social field. With proper training, the individual can rise in society, and every competitor is enabled to gain a position appropriate to his achievement.

Individual opportunities, recognized by most social movements,[15] are often secured by general legislation in economic life, although this still has a more or less formal character, as for instance in the term "personal freedom" (Article 2 of the Constitution of West Germany, 23 May 1949) and "free choice of profession" (Article 12). This is based on the idea of a free expression of personality. In the West, material equality is not considered to be entirely compatible with an economic system which is based on incentives and which guarantees private property.[16] Property is "firm, lasting, acquired, secure, and transmittible";[17] were this principle to be weakened, it would also weaken the monetary value.

Unlike economic systems in the East, the systems of the West preserve the right of inheritance.[18] * If an economic system is to develop on the basis of material incentives and, on the other hand, seeks equal opportunity, an antinomy may arise between the interim goals of the economic policy. The principle of productivity may lead to unequal accumulation of capital, possibly to be handed down through inheritance. This in turn may lead to distortions in competition, so that the poor will have less access to the market. If competition in obstacles is to be replaced by a competition in productivity, so that entrepreneurs can be selected according to their efficiency, interference with the acquisition of wealth might be necessary to encourage new competitors.[19] To a certain degree the income tax works toward equality of opportunity, and in the West it is based on progressive rates. Since income may be the source of future wealth, the income tax may also indirectly influence the distribution of wealth. In addition to property tax, inheritance tax does its share in eliminating gross differences in the distribution of wealth.

The British have had vast experience with the inheritance tax, since after both world wars it was used as an instrument of economic and social policy.[20] In the United States a redistributive inheritance tax was not introduced until 1934. Unlike Great Britain and the United States, Germany's inheritance tax, although suggested as a means for influenc-

* According to liberalism, the right of inheritance is a basic right of private property.

ing the distribution of wealth, was mainly intended to enrich the state.[21] As an instrument of redistribution, the inheritance tax must, above all, break up large accumulations of capital. This is evident in the progressive rate structure in the application of this tax.[22] Although it is difficult to prove by statistics what effect the inheritance tax has had on redistribution, it has indeed had some effect, and wealth is distributed more equally.[23] * Even in the United States this has been the result, although not to the extent of the British inheritance tax.[24] In Germany, this effect has been smaller, since that tax is tied in with other aspects of economic policy.

In the West, private decisions concerning saving and investment greatly affect the economy. It is maintained that the inheritance tax is an obstacle to the formation of capital, which in turn leads to a slowing down of economic growth.[25] † Such an argument assumes the accumulation of maximum wealth for the benefit of one's heirs to be an essential incentive for work or saving. But investigations in the United States have shown that people follow a variety of motives.[26] This result is further supported by the fact that in America only a small percentage of property is transferred in the form of gifts, although this may mean a tax saving for the legatee.

Another objection to the inheritance tax is the "destruction of capital" connected with it. But capital—which in reality is the means of production as a whole—cannot be eliminated by such a tax, although this may be the case for the individual.[27] ‡ Thus the individual may be deprived, but the state may use that income for such purposes as public investment and lending.

Therefore the inheritance tax does not necessarily lead to a decrease in existing capital as a whole. If properly handled,[28] § it may rather assist in supporting the structure and the maintenance of a democratic economic society based on equal opportunity.[29] Besides the redistributive effects of the inheritance tax, we must also take into consideration the political aims made possible by it. In the United States, for instance, life insurance means considerable tax savings for heirs. Another possibility that it encourages is the giving of grants to charitable

---

* Property can also be redistributed by war, taxation, and inheritance.

† Smith and Ricardo had already rejected the inheritance tax for this reason.

‡ In certain cases where there is a liquidity problem, as may happen in the case of the inheritance tax, payment may be delayed or made in installments in Great Britain and the United States.

§ For instance, the scale of taxation, current evaluation, exemptions, consideration of hardship cases, and installment payment of taxes.

or scientific institutions. Such possibilities open the road between individualism and collectivism, so that people are persuaded to care for the future, to a certain degree, according to their own wishes, and to combine their own interests with those of the group through voluntary decisions.

In the case of an exclusively materialistic view of opportunity, according to the extreme liberal ideal, the demands of justice are to be realized through continuous, all-embracing competition in production. But the search for justice cannot be dictated by calculations based on economic theories. There is rather a need for creation of certain attitudes which, for instance, in establishing wages, make fruitful negotiations between the bargaining partners possible.[30] Competition of all participants on the market is the result of the individual struggle for economic survival.[31] The ideal of a continuous, substantial equality necessarily presupposes different treatment of materially and spiritually dissimilar individuals.[32] But this would hinder free competition, which is based on the struggle for gain, and such equal treatment would also weaken individual initiative.[33] The liberal demand for equal opportunity does not lead to a perpetually widening material growth; instead it ties unlimited "competition of production" to the maintenance of existing property differences.[34] *

Distribution according to contribution to output is inherent in the theory of marginal productivity. Wages based on value of the product correspond to the output of the product as valued on the market. Pure competition, which is assumed, presupposes a formal equality according to the individual's achievement. But where such a theory is purely economic, it is objected that the relative power of groups, their aims and attitudes, may generate a struggle for the social product and the creation of monopoly.[35] This is based on the assumption that in a freely competitive economy differential gains cannot be eliminated forever, since power structures and adjustment to technological progress maintain dynamic profits in Schumpeter's sense.[36] We must also add monopoly profits and income other than wages, which do not fit a distribution theory based on production techniques and which have little, if anything, to do with special achievements.[37] These are weighty arguments against the theory of marginal productivity. However, that theory is merely intended to deal with a static equilibrium. In the long run there must be adjustment and balancing, which, in this respect, allow that theory to maintain its realistic view.

---

* This is not contradicted by taxation systems. Income tax rates, for instance, are higher for higher incomes; yet they are not a leveling force in a materially equalitarian sense.

The prevailing situation in ownership and wealth also influences the distribution of income. If there is greater equality, labor demand can become more elastic and labor becomes relatively more important than capital. Wages may rise, and this alters the distribution of income.[38]

The "prevailing situation" mentioned above is considered an essential factor in a quantitative and empirical consideration of the problems of distribution.[39] On the basis of statistically proven data, econometric methods of investigation try to incorporate reality as much as possible. On the one hand, there is a lower limit for the rate of return on capital, which at the same time indicates the most favorable distribution for labor. Determining factors are the uncertainty of income and costs and the entrepreneur's sensitivity to risk. On the other hand, the economic system can be maintained only through minimal wages, with a corresponding maximum limit on interest on capital. Accordingly, distribution has little to do with the relative scarceness of capital or labor. Those factors responsible for distribution are, rather, the strength of collective bargaining, monetary policy, market structure, and the traditional yardsticks of the economy.

In this connection the relative constancy of the functional distribution of income over time, i.e., the stability of labor's share, is important. But this does not necessarily imply a status quo in personal distribution. Moreover, every question regarding distribution is also a question of personal distribution. In this respect, in the United States [40] and Great Britain [41] there is a tendency toward leveling off, which means that the highest incomes have risen more slowly than the average, so that their relative share has decreased.

2. MAIN ISSUES IN THE THEORY OF DISTRIBUTION

A. The Interrelationship of Income Distribution and the Distribution of Wealth

In those economies with private ownership of the means of production and orientation toward a market economy, the distribution of income and wealth are closely tied to each other and necessarily influence each other. In Western economies, new wealth can mainly be acquired through three channels: [42] * (1) savings coming from residual income in productive enterprise (internal financing) or contractual income; (2) increase of private savings through agreements made in collective bar-

* The problem here is not the redistribution of existing property but rather how to distribute new property among individuals.

gaining (that is, between management and labor) by sharing gains or invested wages; [43] * and (3) increasing new wealth by granting savings premiums, such as tax relief by the government. [44] †

In Western economies, public saving is almost as important as private savings. [45] ‡ But in spite of its large share in over-all economic savings, it is greatly different from the system in Russia, where wealth is mainly acquired through the state's fixing of prices and wages and by the payments from profits that factories turn over to the state.

Other differences have to do with use of the increase in wealth enjoyed by individuals. [46] § Whereas, in systems with private property, the individual may use his increase, say, by temporarily increasing his demands for goods, collective property offers no such possibility. It is true that the individual shares indirectly in the increase of public wealth, but he has no way to relate to "his" share, since no such thing exists. Although, in Western economies, new private wealth can be encouraged by the state, in many cases such a possibility presupposes the individual's active participation. The aim is to maintain personal incentives and, hand in hand with it, personal responsibility on the part of the individual.

When the economic order changed from earlier, more capitalistic forms to today's welfare state, in which many individuals are granted opportunities according to current concepts of justice, social concepts entered the economic structure to a greater degree. The realization of growing prosperity seems possible only when, on one hand, the material means are provided through higher productivity [47] and, on the other, we can lessen the dependence of socially weaker strata on the powerful and affluent higher strata of economic life. [48] Thus in the Western systems, production is all-important in regard to income, but social aspects must also be taken into account. Such a wage principle is regarded, more or less universally, as ethically just (see chap. VIII). Consideration of such conditions as family status along with wage factors ("social wages") reflects these new Western concepts of justice.

Private ownership of the means of production is regarded by liberalism as a condition for competition. Since, in such a system, concentra-

---

* An example is the so-called Leber Plan in West Germany.

† For instance, measures for promoting the building of private homes, the law promoting ownership by employees, and tax relief for savings in the form of insurance.

‡ In 1963 in Germany, 57.5 percent of all savings were private and 43.4 percent were public.

§ These differences ultimately go back to existing property regulations.

tion of wealth may or should be avoided through competition,[49] that approach believes economic and social grievances to be improbable, since the employees do not depend on each other and may take advantage of opportunities offered by their efficiency.

Catholic social teaching, too, has dealt intensively with the distribution of wealth. It is based on the assumption that income and property greatly influence the social structure. According to this view, the economic helplessness of vast segments of the population more or less turns these people into objects; whereas if they had a share in capital accumulation, they would be subjects in the economy. A broadly based structure of wealth not only stimulates the productivity of the individual but also helps overcome the discrepancies which arise in economic and social reality.[50]

A further variation is pointed out by the neo-socialists. The creation of a socially fair income structure is emphasized as a central aim of socialism.[51] Redistribution, according to the concepts of justice, is possible by a change in economic and fiscal policies—which should disperse wealth instead of concentrating it in a few hands—and by creating capital with the increments in income.[52]

The distribution concepts of these three schools of thought are more or less based on extra-economic considerations, although their correspondence with economic ones must not be overlooked. All three advocate a broader distribution of ownership in which the government is supposed to assist. Yet the question remains whether more equal distribution of ownership is an effective means toward increasing the freedom of the economic "subject."

B. Prices and Capital Formation

There are two main trends in the effort to create a fair system of income and property. For an economy in which "all goes well," the practical effects of such a policy must be felt by every participant, and imbalances must be eliminated. Besides this, as many people as possible should have access to a fund which helps them overcome, by their own efforts, the consequences of economic failures, at least to a certain degree.

During economic depressions, business is faced with low prices, although wages remain stationary. The employee is threatened with loss of his job, and the government is burdened with increased welfare benefits. In order to reduce these occurrences, systems based on a market economy developed compensatory policies aimed at attaining the high-

137

est levels of employment. Along with the supplementary effects of such measures, such as creating a great amount of capital, we must also remember that in a general economic depression the sale—that is, liquidation—of property presupposes an effective market for it. But in a depression such monies are not available. It is true that when there are smaller gains, the wage share of the social product will rise.[53] The unions will hardly allow wages to fall. In the long run, however, reduced investment will lead to unemployment.

In an economy characterized by inflationary tendencies, profits usually rise faster than wages. In West Germany, for instance, ever since 1950 there has been a tendency toward more than full employment of resources. The scarcity of resources effects first of all the structure of wages and costs and then leads to a rise in prices. In the beginning, wages rose more than the cost of living, but, in most cases, not as rapidly as profits. In the middle sixties, as the favorable trade balance decreased at the same time as private households increased their rate of savings and unions continued their wage policies, a change began. The further rise in wages was partly absorbed by industry instead of being passed on in price increases. Generally speaking, fluctuations are overcome by steadier growth, which changes the traditional form of the wage scale.

Prevailing market structures greatly influence the distribution of income and property. In the modern economy we seldom find full-fledged competition. Rather, markets show features of imperfect competition with partly oligopolistic market forms. Greater or lesser attitudes of initiative and personal thrift among economic units work against greater equality in the distribution of wealth [54] and facilitate concentration.[55] * In order to mitigate such differences, many measures have been taken in the field of monetary and credit policy, and in the social system in the widest sense—for instance, workers' taking part in capital ownership. Savings is also an efficient means; if this is done by reinvesting profits, it means a loss to management income, but over-all savings can remain unchanged. If internal finance were not employed, management would be forced to seek funds from the outside, which would entail greater risk. A fall in the propensity to invest can come about with lower profit expectations on the part of management.[56]

According to Littmann, too great a concentration of wealth leads to a self-dissolution of the market economy. Yet, inequality in the distribu-

* The connection between amount of income and the possibility of acquiring wealth through saving is clearly seen in the relationship that Kuznets found between saving and income.

138

tion of wealth is considered a necessary element in the market economy.[57] This does not indicate the degree to which wealth must be distributed differentially in order to maintain the system. This is the main problem of distribution.

C. Policies Regarding Income and Wealth

The increasing prosperity of the masses in the West is paralleled by an emancipation of the worker. He no longer considers himself a member of the proletarian class, pledged to destroying the fetters of capitalism. Rather he takes a greater share in the success of his work and the achievements of technology and in social life, because of the purchasing power accessible to him. Particularly in times of prosperity he is quite conscious of his economic position and, by means of collective bargaining, he can sell his ability at the highest rate.[58] Such a position enables him to become prosperous. His own productivity contributes to a rise in his social stature and, above all, an amelioration of his material conditions.

After World War II, income mainly had to be used for the maintenance of one's physical powers. But it also had to satisfy needs for luxury and durable goods which had been neglected during the war. In West Germany, at least, the sixties showed an increasing propensity on the part of private households to save.[59] In addition, there were the first beginnings of capital accumulation. However, prosperity, because of the dynamics of the economic process, leads to profits, and they in turn accelerate oligopolistic concentration of wealth, as mentioned above. In spite of the general accumulation of wealth, the employee depends upon his income. In crises his voluntarily acquired savings are soon exhausted. In that case unemployment insurance and other social insurance, which are part of the economic system, must be used to help him. In normal circumstances he is less dependent if he owns sufficient property.[60]

In an economy of "full-fledged competition" the owner would make his decisions according to the laws of supply and demand. In such a system he would enjoy complete freedom concerning what means to utilize, but he would not be able to restrict the freedom of others.[61] In accordance with the principle of productivity, the powers of private property can develop so that the economic-social concepts of justice are fulfilled.

The more we deviate from the market structure of full-fledged competition, the greater the potential for concentration, which derives from higher prices and profits. Through the formation of bilateral monopolies, the employee's power, too, increases, which leads to an effort to improve economic well-being. Active support of capital accumulation through such instruments as tax relief, overhead capital, and loans to new business lessens the dependence of weaker economic units, as mentioned previously.[62] The economic policy problem in regard to the social product would then tend toward "better" rather than toward "more." The composition of the social product is ultimately decisive for the life and the viability of individuals.[63]

In this connection it is often said that the claims individual groups have to the social products must be adjusted according to the increase in over-all economic productivity. Advocates of this argument usually wish to preserve the given distribution of income. But this implies a value judgment that the present distribution is the best one, that is, that it reflects the concepts of justice held by the individuals. But efforts made to redistribute income and property make such an assumption questionable. A welfare state, attainable by equalization in capital accumulation, is objected to because it undermines human responsibility, individual efficiency drops, and technological advances are less utilized, i.e., the ability to compete is lessened.[64] It can be argued, however, in opposition to this claim, that a broad-based distribution of wealth can be an incentive to the individual within the limits set by economic laws. This applies to the stimulating effect of tax cuts and other considerations connected with private construction, profits, the government debt, and securities.

There has been a change in preference between income versus wealth over the course of time. Particularly in European feudal systems, wealth provided an open social, political, and economic position.[65] * But when the economic process became more dynamic, the preference changed in favor of income. Wars and subsequent inflation clearly showed that wealth often does not offer sufficient security. Either it is destroyed or devalued or it is quickly absorbed in times of catastrophe. Greater security was often found in having working capacity at one's disposal which could create income. Capital accumulation was carried out through socio-political measures like old-age benefits on an annuity basis.

Efforts also have been made to encourage individual accumulation of capital, which assists capital accumulation in public and private enterprise. These efforts are supported by voluntarily raising private savings, and this is evident in the growth of per capita income. Yet we must ask

* Even today we have such trends in many underdeveloped countries, where "hoarded property" is a sign of prestige.

to what extent a broader basis of wealth which is accompanied by a "de-functionalizing" of ownership can lead to greater independence for the individual.[66] * From a political point of view, too, the dispersion of wealth calls for critical investigation.

Interpersonal competition, such as a laborer's becoming an entrepreneur, can be promoted by such means only in small industry. In many areas modern techniques of production call for an initial investment which can hardly be raised by one or several persons.[67] Past history shows rather that government economic policy has the last word in overcoming a depression. This may, to a certain degree, be supported by the prior existence of a rather equal distribution of wealth, especially when there is a rising trend in the rate of savings.

* Even where full employment is the goal, there are fluctuations in the market. In West Germany there was a drop of 25.2 percent from January 1962 to January 1963; and in individual industries the drop was even greater (for example, paper industry, 52.6 percent and coal mining, 36.4 percent).

X. PROFIT, INTEREST, RENT, AND WAGES IN THE WEST

1. PROFIT

Pure profit (as opposed to business income) is the net gain of an enterprise after deduction of the going rate of interest to cover the invested capital and after entrepreneurial wages. The existence of entrepreneurial activity and the justification of the resulting profit is the most important difference between private enterprise and collectivism.[1]

A. Entrepreneurial Wages

In collectivist economic systems production is directed largely toward fulfillment of a plan.[2] * In the West, on the other hand, management synchronizes demand and supply and thus guides enterprise. Guidance or direction must be based on an optimal combination of the factors of production, and this calls for entrepreneurial wages. The level of these wages is determined by a comparison with the wages of an employee in a similar position (that is, the income of board members of a corporation). Entrepreneurial wages may be considered a fourth factor of pro-

* However, certain changes became evident after Khrushchev's fall in October 1964. Shortly afterwards, the National Economic Council of the Soviet Union seemed inclined toward the reform suggestions made by Liberman, which favored promotion of profit incentives by the state and adjustment of production to demand. Liberman published his ideas first in *Pravda,* 9 September 1962.

duction, provided they are combined with the introduction of new organizational and technical ideas. This entrepreneurial activity in the Schumpeterian sense is recompensed as part of business income, the size of which will be established later. The concept of profit covers that made by proprietorships as well as corporations. Production is determined by profit expectations.[3] External expectations have to do with the growth of the economy, and internal ones refer to the position of the business relative to competitors and to the pattern of demand.

B. The Premium for Risk

From an economic point of view, expectations are normally the basis of current plans for future market situations. In the possible discrepancy between the plan and its realization lies an element of insecurity in the businessman's decision, which cannot be covered by insurance. But in the framework of his arrangements, a corresponding risk premium is allowable. Uncertainty as it presents itself in shifting tendencies in savings, consumption, investment, and future national income appear to be the justification for granting management a profit above entrepreneurial wages as a reward for undergoing risk. Yet it may be objected that taking risk is part and parcel of any economic undertaking and not a distinctive feature of entrepreneurial activity. Even those whose income is based on a contract may lose their jobs or the economic situation may deteriorate due to changes in the demand for certain kinds of work.[4] The same thing may happen to stock owners. In case of a drop in sales they may be without dividends for quite some time, although they do not always gain a full share in corporation profits. In such a situation the liquidation of stocks can only mean a loss.

In discussing risks, we must also take the change in the businessman's position into account. Where ownership is identical with management and the demand for the firm's products increases, its profits rise, whereas in the opposite case they drop. On the basis of the assumptions made above, this means a monetary gain or loss which would influence the owner directly. Today, industrial production in highly developed economies is characterized overwhelmingly by separation of management and ownership. Management must, above all, decide on what productive factors to apply and find new methods in sales and financing. With management thus becoming more independent, profit takes on a different look, and its traditional meaning only partly applies. From the economic point of view, the risk element in the entrepreneurial factor is not unique.

143

Another possible element in pure profit or loss is market conditions and this can be quite important functionally. In the market economy, high profits indicate which goods are to be offered in greater quantity. This influences management decisions. Productive factors must be guided toward the greatest profit. Profit is therefore a tool in co-ordinating the course of the economy.[5] *

C. Market Power

Market power does not necessarily arise from efficiency. Rather, efficiency is often handed down from the past, and, in the course of time, it may, by concentration of economic establishments, change into market power. In that case, the power position is often a result of monopolistic or oligopolistic market forms. Efficiency is, of course, an essential agency in the gaining of such power.[6] † But, because of the structure behind it, such power is in less danger than that of firms exposed to stronger competition on the market.[7] The profit of smaller firms is smaller and, in times of crisis, they can rely on efficiency only, not on efficiency plus monopoly.[8] Sometimes profit arising from market power is considered to contradict the principle of competition, since such a gain is often "without function." [9]

When people wish to make purchases with their incomes, monopoly goods compete with all others for the consumer's money. When fixing prices, the monopolist must also count on outsiders as well as on the development of substitute products. Besides these factors, government policy, when faced with monopolistic price-fixing, may force a reduction of profits or indirectly shape the firm's pricing policy, as is observable in the United States.[10] Whereas, on the one side, profit gained by market power may lead to faulty investment, there is also the possibility of accelerating the tempo of technological progress through monopolistic profits. If others are able to benefit from low costs, general income, as well as the firm's income, may rise in the long run.

---

* In countries where the economy is planned, profit for some time was rejected as a capitalistic phenomenon. But in order to increase the efficiency of such systems, it was finally allowed, mainly, perhaps, because profit can be a guiding factor. In the West, profit has been sanctioned morally in the past. But recently there has been a tendency to reduce exorbitant profits by taxing income and profits and heavily taxing wartime profits.

† Large enterprises make possible decreased costs and—so far as these are passed on to the market—lower prices also.

2. INTEREST

In comparison with other forms of compensation, interest is the price paid for lending capital, as calculated by time units. In a centrally planned economy (such as the U.S.S.R.) the interest rate is precisely determined by the state.[11] In the West, the interest rate is presumed to adjust automatically. It is supposed to provide a close correspondence between investment and economic equilibrium and the direction of maximum yield.

A. The Supply and Demand for Capital

Wicksell was the first economist to present a modern interest theory from the point of view of money. According to him, interest adjusts the supply of savings to the demand of credit. The market interest rate has a tendency to adjust to the "natural" or equilibrium interest rate.[12] Fisher claims that interest arises from human impatience and favorable possibilities of investment.[13] Following Böhm-Bawerk, he arrives at the concept of useful application. Later Keynes gave an exact and successful formulation of modern monetary theory. According to him, interest is the price paid for giving up cash. The amount of cash a person retains from his income depends on the amount of his income and on the amount he wants to retain for transactions and for precautionary reasons, as well as on the interest rate. This proportion is known as his liquidity preference. The interest rate, in turn, is determined by general liquidity preference and the money supply. The source of interest, that is, the reason capital is demanded, arises from the marginal efficiency of capital, wherein expectations and associated risks in using funds must be taken into account. Thus the amount of investment will be determined by the difference between the interest rate and the marginal efficiency of capital. Interest, then, must maintain a macro-economic equilibrium which best guarantees growth and full use of all productive resources. Those who succeeded Keynes have taken this into consideration. They have built models which make the interest rate the instrument of general economic balance. Harrod, for instance, has formulated an equation for the long-term interest rate adjusted to a natural rate of growth which leads to optimal welfare and which arises out of the relationship between the natural per capita rate of growth and the elasticity of utility derived from income.[14]

145

The various schools of modern interest theory have generally neglected the concept of value. Following the classical theory of the value of labor and the previously developed theory of surplus value (see, e.g., Rodbertus), Marx concluded that only labor can create surplus value. As mentioned elsewhere in this book (chaps. II and XII), interest on capital is not justified. This is opposed by those who support the productivity theory of interest (like von Wieser). According to them, not only can more goods be produced by capital goods but the latter also create more value than they themselves possess. This justifies the payment of interest. By turning to functional thinking, and by explaining the formation of prices by means of the scarcity principle (Cassel), the existence and formation of interest are explained functionally and instrumentally.

The market function of interest, which is to limit the time of maturity for investment, enables consumers to have goods which answer their current needs.[15] Every economic system must be concerned with balancing the economy. Whereas in a market economy that adjustment is automatically accomplished through the interest rate, it can be done in other ways. In an economy guided by a central administration, the planning authority can also achieve this.[16] * By assigning interest its due place in the economy, the plan can achieve an optimal combination of productive factors, although interest does not figure as a share in the distribution of income. In a comparison of economic systems, the problem of interest seems to center on whether the course of the economy can be adjusted better automatically or by central planning. In the first case, interest as income would be justified because of its functional character. In planned economies, introducing interest on investment capital would allow it only a limited sphere. Interest rates vary according to goals of economic policy, and the interest rate can be selective only within individual branches. From this point of view, the reintroduction of interest is ultimately based on its instrumental character.

We must make a distinction between the economic-theoretical and the socio-political interest problem.[17] Whereas theory is concerned with the source of interest and its purpose, the socio-political interest problem asks whether interest ought to exist at all and whether it is just. This implies a confrontation of causal and moral views. Proving that the possession of capital must be paid for and that interest must be taken into account in the economy does not justify interest as a special income share. Here is the boundary line between what is decided outside the social order (in this case private property versus collective

* The difficulties raised here shall not be discussed further.

146

property) and what is decided by it.[18] But even this argument does not sufficiently justify interest. For even if we were to admit that without interest the quantity of goods would decrease, the argument would be meaningless to those who place little value on material well-being.

Interest is said to play an essential role in regulating economic growth by equating the supply and demand of capital. In this connection it is even maintained that interest is justified in the creation of capital and the decrease of consumption. Saving facilitates a better economic structure for the future as far as capital and consumer goods are concerned. It would then be justified to award, through interest, those who do save and who therefore do not consume as much as non-savers. They enable the over-all economy to produce more goods in the future. This could mean that additional savings are a real investment.

In an economy where productive capacity is not fully utilized, additional savings not only fail to lead to investment but reduce employment. Nevertheless, interest is paid for savings, although at a lower rate. We thus see that the argument for its justification does not apply to all phenomena.

Another way to justify interest seems to lie in the productivity theory of capital. Since the utilization of capital leads to greater profits, the investor can well afford to pay interest. But such an argument would cover only loans for production. In the case of consumer loans, the debtor uses the money for the purchase of goods. Although unable to produce a greater profit, he must still pay interest.

The problem of justification of interest can also be viewed from another angle. Making interest part of the economic system does not decide who reaps the benefit. In those economic systems in which private property is used in production, the owner of the capital receives the interest. The over-all amount of income through interest is determined by the interest rate and by the capital available at any one time. But in the case of collective property the existence of interest does not by itself answer the question of its distribution. Thus credit may be given out of state funds, and those who use the credit must pay interest to the state. How this should be distributed must be decided by central agencies.

With the choice between private property or collectivism a value judgment is made, although it does not affect the purpose and origin of interest, concerning the distribution of the yield on capital. Nevertheless, even in the East the existence of interest is considered justified and economically necessary.

It seems at first glance that once we admit the validity of the functional theory of interest, the problem of value is eliminated. According

147

to the theory of time preference, interest rates rise until there is an equality of supply and demand. But these two factors are related to the distribution of income. A change in that distribution will also influence the determination of interest rates. Assuming that the marginal rate of savings rises with growing income, a less equal distribution of income leads to increased supply. If demand were to remain stationary, the interest rate would drop. A more equal distribution of income would have the reverse effect, which means that the interest rate would rise. The functional theory of interest assumes a certain distribution. The elimination of the value problem seems, therefore, only illusionary.

B. Market Structure

If, from a purely economic point of view, interest reflects the expected profit on invested capital [19] (which means that it is "normal" and equilibrates savings and investment [20]), there are certain market structures which may modify it. The capital market is far from a full-fledged competitive market. This is so, aside from the influence of central bank policies, because of the trend toward specialization and concentration in the financial system which supplies capital. On the demand side, the strong market position of the seller is weakened by monopolistic firms and co-operative credit institutions. This effect is strengthened by large enterprises which finance their own capital needs.[21]

C. Governmental Interest Rate Policies

There is a tendency for actual interest rates to lead to inflation or deflation or to other frictions and imbalances in the economy which can be traced back to interest rates. Governments try to pattern interest rates on the market so that they can assist in the realization of economic policy goals. Particularly after the depression of the thirties, the size of national income has been of greater interest than its distribution.[22] Governments then became more concerned with the effect of interest rate changes. Following an anticyclical policy, interest rates, during a depression, are kept low, since their rise would serve as a barrier to inflation.

Ever since the 1930s, government interest rate policies—an instrument to offset fluctuation, thus securing full employment, prosperity, and growth of national income—have become less important than modern fiscal policies. Interest rate policies of governments today apply particularly to three areas.

The weakest intervention is the government's participation in the shaping of supply and demand on the competitive capital market. Purchases and sales undertaken by the government influence the interest rate. But more important and effective in some Western economies is intervention by means of the central banks' discount policy, which is adjusted to actual economic development and which influences the interest rate and also the money supply. The third and most incisive intervention is the setting of the interest rate by the government.[23]

3. RENT

In the market economy as well as in the planned economy today, certain costs must be considered in relation to capital and also real estate, if it has become scarce. Only under private ownership is rent charged for the use of land, giving the owner a share in the national income. The rent on real estate thus arising may be a scarcity rent, differential rent, or situational rent; but ultimately all rent is scarcity rent.

A. The Supply and Demand for Land

Rent as a category of personal income is, from a functional point of view, the result of the market process of price formation. When the demand for real estate is determined by marginal productivity, the willingness to pay expressed in demand is decisive for the supplier. It is difficult to evaluate supply since land really does not "cost" anything, a fact which is not contradicted by adding land to the costs of enterprise. Rent is not paid in order to repay the landlord but because real estate is scarce. The amount is therefore determined by the relation between supply and demand.

B. Land Reform

Historically the state has taken measures to minimize monopoly rent, which could arise through exclusive private ownership of the land. These measures worked so that economic systems based on private enterprise developed toward a system with partially collective features. One possibility has arisen in modern land reform, which is aimed at a redistribution of land. The goal is the dispersion of ownership, more intensive utilization through acquired property, broader distribution of income or wealth, or, looked at from a different angle, abolition of the land monopoly. Another form of intervention by the state is land taxation. The physiocrats proposed reduction of rental income through taxation, a modern form of which is rent control by the state. Rent control is mostly a temporary measure taken in times of crisis in order to prevent exploitation or changes in income for only one sector of the economy.[24] Even earlier, technological progress exercised great influence on rent by increasing productivity, which also grew because of technological advances in other areas, as in the use of capital and in production. This entailed a relative decrease in the significance of land. The character of rent as the price for the use of land took on a broader meaning. Previously rent depended on agricultural production, now, because of increasing industrialization, land has become a long-term investment, its price resembling the payment of interest on long-term capital.[25] Aside from the population explosion, more intensive agricultural use and, above all, industrial use of land can change the scarcity factor so that monopoly control of supply is weakened.

C. A Just Rent

Following the economic doctrine of the physiocrats, the existence of rent was justified as compensation for the work done by previous generations, such as restoration and improvement of the soil. Since it is, however, an income not based on current labor, socialists found it unjustified. Because its significance decreased in the course of economic development, the question became less and less important.[26] * Thus, for instance, the establishment of wholesale prices for agricultural products and their continuous support in the more industrialized economies proves that, under free price formation, income from intensity of land use and differential rent would all but disappear.

Contrary to these types of rent, urban location rent has increased in importance. We may assume that changes in this rent are not in accord with attitudes on justice ("to each according to his accomplishment"). If, for instance, a certain area is needed for structures basic to the economy, real estate prices may rise in these localities, a rise brought about, not by greater productivity, but by changed scarcity relationships, which have arisen without effort on the owner's part. (This is true, also, of a drop in such prices.) In West Germany, for instance, in line with attitudes toward economic justice, efforts were made to put a ceiling on land values or to tax the increment.

* We must also remember the share real estate taxes have in tax revenues. In West Germany that share was 17.1 percent in 1961, while taxes from industrial activity, in one form or another, amounted to 75.7 percent.

But, while putting such concepts of justice into practice, there often occur contradictions between necessary measures and the need to conform to a system. If the price of the land is left to the free play of supply and demand, we must assume that in congested areas, real estate prices reach a height which prevents enterprises from investing there. This may lead to high location rents and thus contradict certain concepts of justice, but such a development may also express the rising costs of agglomeration. But if a price freeze is put on real estate, the scarcity portion of rent is changed artificially with the intent to decrease it. The next consequence of this may be the misallocation of productive factors. In order to eliminate such a side effect, it may be necessary to combine the price freeze with a prohibition of investment. Even if, through public intervention, the concepts of justice concerning location rent may be realized, there is a new question of whether such measures can be harmonized with the concept of the freedom to invest.

4. WAGES

A. Historical Development

Modern economic theory in the West defines wages as the price of hiring labor per time unit. But salaries and other types of payment may also be included here.[27] Since it is a price, wages are a determining and a determined variable and are functionally connected with other parameters of the system. There is no single "wage," but rather various wages in relation to different kinds of work. Contrary to Eastern economic systems, wages in the West are, by definition, a result of the interplay of all elements of the supply and demand of labor.[28] In reality, however, social and other factors have considerable and increasing importance in the area of wage determination. Thus the wage shifts from an objective price toward a "just" share in the social product. From almost perfect competition, labor markets changed into the more or less controlled forms such as monopoly, oligopoly, and polyopoly. Modern doctrine on the market structure applies to them. This also allows long-term effects of bargaining and other institutional factors to be taken into account. The bargaining theory of wages, developed earlier, now becomes fruitful. Economic bargaining theory explains the level of wages as relative to the power of social institutions, a power subject to economic laws. Practically this means that today the wage problem is generally solved, since the price is determined by a bilateral monopoly, with the employers or their associations on the demand side and unions as the interested

151

representatives of employees on the supply side. Socio-political points of view are increasingly taken into account. That economically based power has influence is seen in the effort to provide a common share in property for everyone.[29]

According to the social bargaining theory of wages, power works outside economic laws.[30] But the economic bargaining theory mentioned above, which is opposed to the theory of minimum subsistence, shows the connection between wage determination and economic quantities such as output. According to the theory of minimum subsistence, wages —the price of labor—are determined by the actual minimum costs of maintaining the labor supply. It is said that in the long run real wages would be stationary because of the principle of population growth. This means that it would remain at the "natural" level of the cost of minimum subsistence, for any increase would be absorbed by an increase in population. According to Ricardo and his followers in classical wage theory, a wage level determined by population and the free play of economic forces is the only one possible. It was not ethically objectionable since the poverty of the working class was considered to be its own fault.[31] The wages-fund doctrine is another form of the monistic explanation of wage determination, according to which the wage level is determined by demand.[32] The followers of that school rejected socio-political measures by the state and the trade unions to increase wages as obstacles to the accumulation of capital funds.

It is typical of earlier explanations of wage determination that they disregard the connection between the level of wages and the quantity of output. Only von Thünen points out the connection between output and the wage level in the sense of the later theory of marginal productivity and in a micro-economic form. This theory is opposed to the classical theory of the value of labor. The wage formula developed by von Thünen shows the concept of the fair wage. The theory of marginal productivity, applied to wages, was further developed by J. B. Clark at the end of the last century and, in its macro-economic form, transferred to the entire national economy. A major effort was made to find in marginal productivity more than a mere explanation of wage determination. The question of distribution became an important subject for discussion. The conviction arose that wages determined by the marginal productivity of labor were not only economically correct but also just and that they lead to optimal social welfare.[33] Later considerations have shown that the inclusion of imperfect competition, on the one hand, and the negation of power influences, on the other, deprived the theory of marginal productivity of much it had to say on wage determination both then and now.[34] In Western economic systems wages are indeed determined by supply and demand. The basic principle in establishing wages is their relation to productivity. Other factors to be considered are socio-political institutions like family income, unemployment benefits, income tax legislation, and the worker's share in over-all capital formation.[35] These are an expression of a concept of justice and a means to lessen social tensions.

B. Socio-Ethical Wage Determination

According to the liberals and the neoliberals the market structure of perfect competition is also a guarantee for a just balance among those who share in the market. The "pure" wage based on productivity is therefore tied in with perfect competition. But today all existing economic systems in the West and the East are mixed, being more or less removed from one or the other extreme of economic systems as conceived in theory.

In Germany, for instance, there is the tension between the free market economy and social considerations. According to Müller-Armack, the economy seeks "to join the principle of freedom on the market with that of social balance." [36] The socialist market economy thus consciously looks at the entire order. Competition is the first principle, and one of its most important features is that it is safeguarded by institutions.[37] Free initiative is combined with social progress, which is guaranteed by economic productivity through the market.[38]

Social aspects of wage determination are also reflected in the form of social wages, composed of productivity wages and social bonuses. By taking the size of family into account, they are meant to lessen the differences in the distribution of income. A social bonus includes those additional costs of labor which have no bearing on productivity and which may be obligatory or voluntary. Thus premiums for overtime, night hours, and Sunday work represent labor costs which do not depend on productivity. Nevertheless these are part of actual wages, as are increments for families and children. We must also add the often large, but invisible amounts the employer gives employees in the form of old-age and survivors insurance, the cost of cafeteria meals, and building of workers' housing. In this category also belong compensation for absences due to breakdown and shutdown, vacation, sick leave, and holidays.[39]

We must further add the possibilities of profit sharing, an item which has lately increased in importance. Profit sharing that stems from the

153

value added by the worker is paid for by the additional value created. This sharing of productivity increases is known as the Rucker Plan in the United States.[40]

A typical suggestion concerning the leveling of income has come from the entrepreneurs. This proposes buying into the employer's firm as a part of wages. Here the decisive question is which group of employees is to benefit from this proposal. The West German Leber Plan affects only the building trade. A unilateral preference given to certain employees or the exclusion of, say, those not working in a particular industry would lead to a series of social conflicts among employees.[41] The importance of sharing in ownership is that its advocates think of it not only as a social-political measure but as an equalizing agent in the distribution of income.[42] At any rate, here is a new possibility for influencing the determination of wages. But such thoughts must be viewed in the total context of the economy. Doubtless such investment endangers the owner's profits. Under this situation, or if, at least, this weakens incentives for the entrepreneur, we may take the critical arguments of the employers into account.[43] It may be rightly assumed that wage policies can destroy or, at least, influence negatively the stability of the whole economy.[44]

Another means of setting wages is by the cost-of-living index. This is one of the most popular methods among workers. It stemmed from the attempt to accommodate demand and especially to prevent a fall in real income.[45] Whereas West Germany has made little use of cost-of-living adjustments, it has been used in other countries, such as the United States, Canada, and Australia. In some European countries, too, cost-of-living clauses are included in employee contracts, for example, Italy, Belgium, Luxemburg, and Denmark and, to a smaller degree, the United Kingdom, France, Switzerland, and the Scandinavian countries.[46] * The main arguments against further extension of this system are partly social-political, for instance, not all employees benefit from it in the same way. Most pensioners are certainly worse off in a system where wage increases are based on the cost of living.

While the social wage seeks to balance different jobs and productivities, the productivity-based wage corresponds to the contribution the individual makes to the social product.[47] † If a rise in the wage level ex-

* Particular forms of incentive wages are piecework, bonuses, and hourly wages including bonuses. All of these variations are based on productivity.

† This effect is especially pronounced with goods that are relatively price inelastic in response to demand.

ceeds the increase in productivity in any one period, unless the increment is saved the total volume of goods does not increase in proportion to demand. In that case it is easier for the businessman to raise prices in accordance with higher wages.[48]

Business should not adjust wages according to productivity as a whole but rather according to the share the productive factor (labor) has in the additional product. This again emphasizes the problem of calculation, according to which an increase in productivity must be distributed among all productive factors in proportion to their contribution. The difficulty of exact calculation increases with an increasing degree of automation. Therefore a wage policy based on productivity can be justified only to the extent that it is part of an economic or social policy.[49] Rises in productivity cannot be attributed to any one factor unless other goals of economic or social policy are neglected.[50] If productivity growth (in absolute terms, not as a percentage) were ascribed entirely to labor, profit would remain on the same level. With a rise in investment, profit would regress as capital formation increased.

Lower profits could be disadvantageous for the introduction of technical advances among existing firms as well as for new firms that want to participate in the market. On the other hand, wages must be adjusted proportionately to the rise in productivity in the entire economy. If the wage share remains stationary, other factors would then also share in the growth. The price level would not change, and from the point of view of economic policy this is considered desirable. But a constant wage share often has the disadvantage of a stationary distribution of income, which if it is unjust will remain unjust.

In case of a rise in the wage share relative to other productive factors, profits would fall. Then business savings would decrease faster than employee's savings increase, and the rate of saving or investment would be smaller, which might weaken economic growth. It can be argued that long-term perspectives do not advise an increase in the wage share but rather greater growth coupled with a stable price level.[51]

In the interest of a well-balanced economic policy, the demands of collective bargaining must harmonize with the economic situation as a whole. The bargaining parties may be linked to each other by a national social policy. A sound wage policy calls for objective and responsible efforts made by the employees, the employers, and the government. The government can express its rules in laws or guidelines which are relevant to social policy and guide the work of the bargaining parties. This is the foundation of practical decisions in social policy.

155

5. MACRO-ECONOMIC WAGE POLICY

A. Wages and Prices

Free wage determination and maintenance of the purchasing power of money are elementary aims of Western economic systems—aims which concern distribution and production policy. But are these two goals in harmony? Both employers and employees are interested in obtaining guidelines for wage changes which would prevent employment fluctuations and inflation.[52] But it must be remembered that union demands for higher wages must influence other returns, particularly profits.[53] This also touches on the question of an equitable wage policy and the distribution of national income. It is hard to find a scientific theory which takes all this into account and is also practically applicable. Therefore synchronizing wage increments with the growth of productivity by introducing an "improvement factor," as is done in the United States, can be justified only in terms of economic or social policy.[54]

A wage policy based on productivity only therefore has no absolute claim to be a "just" distribution. The increase in average wages must remain within the framework of the average growth of production.[55] Wages that are raised beyond the growth in labor productivity lead to price increases and, therefore, a possible increase in profits. This leads neither to more equal distribution of income nor to price stability.

Furthermore, full employment is an important factor in the stability of the monetary system. Collective bargaining may, in the long run, harm the free economic and social order.[56] If wages are increased beyond productivity, and full employment already exists, inflation can be prevented only if the increment is saved. But in reality only part of that increase is not consumed. Since taxes increase with rising incomes, the government receives and usually spends more money. Unless the increased taxes are paid for out of the individual's previous level of income rather than from the increment, which could then be allocated entirely to savings, aggregate demand will rise and with it prices. This, of course, inhibits the accumulation of wealth and savings by employees.

Constellations of power arising from wage policy are possibly responsible for inflationary tendencies and developments which influence employment.[57] De-emphasis of the power factor in the negotiations of the collective bargaining participants—there is often bilateral monopoly on the labor market—is one condition for objective wage policies. It is not enough for wage demands to be adjusted to general productivity and price stability. The employer must give his employees a wage which is in accord with their particular productive value. As far as the employer is concerned, the play of supply and demand is fully effective in the field of labor. Particularly in cases of high employment and labor shortages, wages rise out of proportion to productivity. But high wages can only be paid as long as profits do not fall too far. When the demand for the products is inelastic, the demand for labor is relatively constant,[58] which creates the probability that high wages are reflected in higher prices. This means that wages and productivity are related factors in inflation.

In practice, even though a reconciliation is attempted between the diametrically opposed principles of individual freedom and responsibility, on the one hand, and collective obligation, on the other, emphasis is on the latter. Where redistribution of income is to be accompanied by price stability, it is generally considered advisable to institutionalize the saving of that portion of wages derived from profit sharing. But we must take into consideration that individualistic, not collectivistic, thinking is to be preferred. In countries where unionization is extensive, there is more to be said for incorporating a return on investment in collective bargaining contracts than for the state to decide on a statutory return on investment. This solution represents a mean between volunteerism and regulation.[59] The increasing importance of the various forms of co-ownership or profit sharing is visible in a number of attempts to solve the problems of income distribution and monetary stability. This should be done through profit and wage adjustment and by means of compulsory savings at a level agreed upon by both parties.[60] The less interference that price fluctuations exert on income distribution and capital formation in Western economies, the more concern with distribution of income gives way to the problem of how income should be used.

B. Wages and Employment Policies

In times of full employment there is a demand for wage increases in accordance with productivity increases.[61] It is hardly probable that wage increases will lead to less employment, for tactically employees are in a favorable position. Employers, too, are inclined to take the rise of costs in stride, since they can raise prices and make up for wage increases.[62] It is therefore not surprising that in times of full employment the influence that unions have on wage determination decreases.[63] It is assumed here that average wages are normally minimal and that in times of pros-

157

perity they rise. In times of depression or recession wages can some-times even be reduced without influencing an existing union contract, as in West Germany, where actual wages are higher than contractual ones because there is a labor shortage.[64]

While in times of full employment, wages and increases in productiv-ity must be adjusted to secure price stability, in periods of depression or recession aggregate demand may require prime consideration and corre-lation of wages and productivity becomes less significant. Perhaps a general wage increase must take preference over productivity.[65] It is true that when labor becomes more expensive, given the price of other factors, the result will be a rise in costs. But since a greater effective de-mand may be assumed, the per unit cost may go down due to better uti-lization of capital through greater output, and employment may also rise. But since there is a time lag between receiving and using income, it is also possible that in times of high unemployment, wage increases will result in a further decrease of employment. Furthermore, in a gen-eral depression the prices of all productive factors go down, and substi-tution must be added to the effects mentioned. It depends on the expec-tations of employers whether during a depression across-the-board wage increases will lead to more employment, and these expectations are unforeseeable, since there are too many unknown quantities involved.[66] It is therefore also questionable whether, in a depression, decreasing wages will result in increased employment. Such an argument takes into account the effect of costs but not their immediate influence on income and, in turn, on demand.

The question of the practicality of a general wage reduction leads us to a significant phenomenon in wage policies. Wage rates have often de-creased during prosperity and risen during downturns in the economy.[67] This may be explained by wage freezing in the former case and the downward inflexibility of wages in the latter. In the complex world of today there are so many variable factors to consider when wage policy is used as an economic tool that it is not well suited as an active policy for employment and production.[68] There are other economic tools for expanding employment. In times of depression, an increase in govern-ment expenditures deserves first consideration.[69]

C. Wages and Economic Growth

Ever since economic theory first emphasized growth, a steady and well-balanced growth of the economy has become a very important goal.[70] In this connection, wage policies became important. The question arises, should real wages be raised by lowering profits or by eliminating them altogether—a policy which could lead to economic stagnation—or should they be raised through economic growth, with profits remaining constant or rising? Unions have become increasingly aware of the importance of long-term and steady growth of the economy.[71] Across-the-board wage increases cut down business profits. If that cut is too large, a short-term redistribution of income may be accomplished from which labor will benefit. But in the long run, investment may fall and growth will decrease. A reduction of dynamic profits, in Schumpeter's sense, does not occur if higher wages are based entirely on increased demands, for the price of consumer goods will rise and, in turn, profits also. This does not occur when the wage increments are saved;[72] in that case, business receives a smaller profit. We must then investigate whether in case of wage increases, the propensity to invest rises and a larger overall income results.[73] In other words, to what extent can wages be increased without discouraging investment?[74] There is a real difference of opinion here. Some economists believe that wage policies adjusted to productivity are not capable of promoting economic growth, since they believe that this would provide only enough profit to keep the same number of firms in the market.[75] Others emphasize that lower long-run profits would eventually be accepted as normal and increases in profit due to a rise in productivity would invite entry of new firms and therefore economic growth.[76]

Recently unions have provided us with an even stronger formulation of the purchasing power theory of wages relative to economic growth, according to which wage policy itself will increase economic expansion.[77] By deliberately raising wages above the increase in productivity, business will be forced to invest more efficiently. This means an increase in productivity and creation of funds for wage expansion. But there is an element of arbitrariness involved, since we do not know which factors are to be measured. Furthermore, this may temporarily force wage earners to save. Where economic policy is concerned with exports, profit reduction may lead to an export of capital. This would weaken domestic investment and the rate of economic growth.[78]

In summary, a rise in real wages through an across-the-board increase is possible in the short run, but this may work against long-term, steady, and well-balanced growth of the economy, which a rising standard of living requires. Therefore, a permanent increase in real wages can hardly be attained by wage policy if long-term, well-balanced economic growth is also a goal.[79] An increase in real wages may be attained, however, if it is properly integrated into the over-all plan for economic growth.[80]

159

XI. JUSTICE IN THE EAST

1. THE LOGICAL-ETHICAL MODEL

The communist social ethic is based on Marx's philosophic speculations. He anticipated a social structure in accord with the ethical principles of equality and justice, not so much motivated by moral impulses as by economic necessity.[1] In contrast to ethical (utopian) socialism,[2] he assumed "objective laws" that are supposed to effect the downfall of capitalist morality and the advent of a communist ethic.[3] Man's "essence," therefore, is considered not as a timeless ethical imperative but as a changeable product of social and economic reality.[4] On the other hand, the existing economic conditions as well as the corresponding political, social, and legal institutions are treated in Marxism as a pseudo-objectivity that is also not governed by "eternal" natural laws but is the changeable product of human endeavor.[5]

The forces of historical development, the contradiction between new modes of production and outdated systems of ownership,[6] therefore manifest themselves in the phenomena of "alienation," "servitude," and "fetishism of material possessions." [7] The worker is alienated because he does not have a chance to develop as a free, ethical personality, but instead must offer himself as a commodity on the labor market.[8] The legal and moral concepts of private ownership constitute, according to Marxist teaching, a "negation of human personality." [9] The communist ethic, in contrast, is based on the direct unity of individual, society, and

160

nature and is supposed to be superior to the idea of the production of goods.[10] The moral idea of Marxism is one of individual social and ethical self-determination. It thus differs from the liberal principle of a simple rejection of external pressures.[11] * The tension between existing reality and the socio-ethically perfect conduct of man in the future can only be resolved through the total destruction of the opposing view.[12] † Economic development proceeds naturally toward abolition of the previously existing dependencies in the economy.[13] Only the Marxist ethic as developed during the last decade has exhibited decisive changes in this determinist position.[14] ‡

Marx's concepts of communist society are the result of a rejection of existing conditions.[15] The fundamental goal of economics, at whose center man is placed, is to create activity that is beyond any biological and social dependency. Everyone is allowed to choose his work freely in accordance with his inner need and his desire to develop as a human being. No member of communist society should be paid in the sense of monetary income for his economically determined contribution to production. On the contrary, physical needs should be satisfied from the real social product so that no individual is hindered in the free, self-determined development of his personality. The slogan "from each according to his abilities and to each according to his needs" [16] is, therefore, a necessary element of the communist society.

As "members of a species" all people are identical in principle. All existing empirical differences in the particular economic achievement of individuals fade into the background by comparison. In general, the economic domain should, as such, lose its importance in shaping peoples' lives. To this extent the idea of "need-oriented" distribution is manifest. What is more, since the needs of people who build their lives in free association instead within a class structure can not differ greatly and since all are equal anyway, equal participation in the gross national product is simply a logical consequence.

Communism, which according to Marx is the next step in the evolution of society, automatically implies a new morality. But the socio-economic basis of this new morality must, in accord with Marxist principles, already be realized before the content of justice can be determined. The Marxist-communist concept of justice thus has only an abstract function in support of the historical process.[17] Justice is real in

* Marx presents his opinion on this topic primarily in his thesis.
† Marx was of the opinion that Hegel identified the theoretical solution of correctly recognized contradictions with their real solution.
‡ Literature concerning Marxist ethics increased noticeably during 1957–1958.

161

the sense that the right to survive is part of the dialectic movement.[18] Distribution of income according to need should not be interpreted as the prerequisite of a communist society; it will develop with this society.[19]

2. SOCIAL ETHICS FOR THE TRANSITION PHASE

There is a difference between the communistic goal and present policies of the Soviet-type economies.[20] But since Marxism postulates a unity of theory and practice, Eastern theorists identify present reality and the desired goal by means of an applied "theory of time." [21] This becomes apparent in the interpretations of Marx's ideas which are specifically tailored to particular historical situations.[22] Lenin is the real theorist of the transition from capitalism to communism.[23]

A. Doctrines from the Past

The pre-revolutionary economic situation in Russia and the social conditions of its people were to some extent worse than in other European countries.[24] The rural population, which was overwhelmingly landless, was not given personal freedom until 1861, when serfdom was abolished. The radicals among the intelligentsia, who had developed under feudal conditions, were to a large extent oriented toward Christian ideals of social justice and human dignity.[25] In face of authoritarian leadership, most of the more important reforms could only be won when the political regime was threatened by external forces. Consequently, the reforms were often in the nature of concessions.

The "Friends of the People" (the Narodniks) viewed the historical goal of society as the establishment of law representing truth and justice in social life. The growth of Marxism, however, soon defeated this populist movement. The measurement of historical reality against an ideal, as the Narodniks did,[26] was considered senseless. Law and morality as criteria for an investigation of history were rejected on principle.[27] That which the Marxists would have supplant these criteria was the "logical" ethic of history.[28]

In opposition to economic determinism, Lenin fought for and won recognition for the possibility of conscious human action. The requirements of the people were still based on social ethics.[29] But Lenin could not totally count on the support of the industrial proletariat, which increased around the turn of the century, although they lived in relative poverty in the few highly concentrated industrial areas. The proletariat

162

was a minor element in the total population. To accomplish the revolution he therefore had to fall back upon the peasantry.[30] He bargained for their co-operation with the promise that the landholdings of large estates would be distributed among them for their own use and there would be simultaneous abolition of all taxes and debts. The Revolution of 1917 finally took on the character of a civil war. It did not, however, develop out of the "ordained inevitability" which Marx predicted for capitalist countries but, like most previous insurrections, from socio-ethical impulses. The communists rode in on the back of the Revolution and then implemented their more extensive programs.

Lenin's position on socio-ethical questions is subtly included in his *Theory of Imperialism*.[31] According to this theory, revolution can also be successful in a less industrialized country and in turn be the initial spark for a revolution in the more industrialized countries. The state which the Bolshevists took over in 1917 had only an agrarian base, interspersed with capitalistic elements, on which they had to build, not the industrial power that Marx assumed in his plans for a communist takeover.[32] Lenin consequently conceded that during the development stage, communism could also make use of capitalist ethics.[33]

Concrete plans for a totally just society were left open by Marx, who reasoned that the form of future practice cannot be theoretically anticipated. The true reason, however, was probably that Marx envisioned an ideal condition of total harmony, which he could not, of course, visualize. The idea that communist society, because it is the result of history, does not require an ethical foundation has been retained unaltered to this day by Plechanov, Lenin, and Stalin. The concept of absolute, equitable justice is thus realizable only through the existence of a communist society itself. As long as such a society does not exist, only the historically relative concept of justice—whose content is determined by economic conditions—is valid. It, in turn, is legitimized by being a phase on the road to total communism. Thus the Russian practitioners of the Revolution who—in contrast to Marx—had to implement certain measures, received a handy as well as delicate tool: handy insofar as a reference to "historical law" justified all practical measures, and delicate because the concept of a humanitarian goal acts as a permanent criticism of the present situation. The alternative chosen in the meantime leads toward the establishment of communism in the sense of a welfare state, i.e., a contemporary mixture of the principles of productivity and of need as applied in distribution policy.

In *The State and Revolution* Lenin, following Marx, insisted that during the first phase of soviet construction, corrective justice is not possible.[34] During the transition phase, therefore, variations in wealth remain as "unjust differences"—a necessity of the economic-historical situation.[35] The transition to communist forms of distribution can only be afforded at a considerably higher level of economic development.

Eastern criticism of Western wage and social policies can be understood in the light of this expectation of the future. Higher wages paid to the proletariat are interpreted as bribery attempts and diversionary tactics by capitalists to deter the working class, through partial concessions, from their revolutionary task and to deprive them of "absolute justice" in the form of a communistic society. Morality in socialist countries has two faces: what is considered just and moral in one's own country—in reference to the relative justice concept of the transition phase (productivity and central control)—is that which is considered necessary to destroy the old social order of exploiters and to bring about the future equality of all.[36] Equalizing tendencies in the West are considered reactionary because they do not aim at the abolition of private ownership of the means of production. That this is, in fact, being partially abolished is overlooked in the East.

While Lenin developed the political strategy for the October Revolution and the following transition phase, the economic program remained relatively undetailed. Since it was not conceivable that all rational needs could be satisfied immediately, distribution was based on a temporary principle of equality. The intended use of incentive wages, however, presumed social concern and disciplined behavior of the people in their work. But practice showed that labor thought of communism as anarchistic consumption. The administrative autonomy of the workers had to be replaced by force.

Liberation from the owners of the means of production was soon replaced by a compulsion to work.[37] The peasants, too, did not live up to the expectations placed on them. They remained skeptical of the stability of the currency and did not deliver their "surplus production" without compensation. This had to be collected against their severe, sometimes bloody resistance in order to provide for the nation.[38] *

Practice also showed that interest in an immediate increase in the standard of living (for workers) and private enterprise (for peasants) was stronger among the Russian people than was the expected communistic solidarity and understanding of the reasons for the government's autocratic measures. When it also became evident that foreign policy—which aimed at spread of the Revolution to other countries—had

---

* Soviet sources designate this resistance as rebellion which was organized by the kulaks and other counter-revolutionaries.

failed, Lenin was forced to carry out the economic construction of communism with the resources of his own country. In 1924, Stalin announced this necessity ("communism in one country") as Party doctrine.[39]

Here the futuristic nature of corrective justice again became evident. Justice is not an ethical imperative that demands immediate realization.[40] * It is supposed to be the result of a deliberately influenced movement in history. This movement was justified in all aspects as the way to final communism. In this manner Lenin and his successors legitimized their strict centralistic approach in the construction of the Soviet economy's heavy industry.

The ethical dilemma of the transition phase lies in the reconciliation of Marx's utopian concept with Bolshevik practice. In this reinterpretation, the unjust differences, in the sense of absolute justice based on needs, would continue to exist for the time being. Only the "exploitation" of man by man had disappeared to the extent that private property had been essentially abolished. According to communist reasoning, capitalistic motives would also change into socialistic motives through these measures. Aside from this, the construction of a communist economy required, in principle, the same economic methods that were employed to conquer similar problems during the early days of capitalism. The only significant exception is that "private exploitation" by employers and their enterprises was replaced by government economic planning, which dictated accelerated growth and correspondingly deferred the material well-being of the masses.

The ethical debate during the transition to socialism, and even during socialism itself, arises from the conflict between two concepts of morality and statutory justice. It is the conflict between the idea of justice as a recognizable improvement in the standard of living and that of complete justice contained in historical materialism, which is oriented toward the future and interpreted philosophically and politically. The real effect of this conflict became obvious in economic practice as a specific oscillating cycle caused, on one hand, by pressures exerted by the Party and, on the other, by concessions forced by the people.[41]

B. Socialist Consciousness and the Socialist Morality

When, in his 1936 constitutional address, Stalin declared that the building of socialism was over,[42] the welfare principle of corrective justice

* Because ethical demands, according to the communist theory of materialism, cannot be derived from freely established ethical views but can only be deduced from societal conditions.

had long since been invalidated because the state's interest in increasing productivity coincided with the desire of the population for better living conditions through higher wages. The main purpose of the distribution policy was no longer the realization of corrective justice but the increase of production. Stalin thus subordinated the goals of communism to the economic goal of higher productivity in principally the same manner as for which the West was and is reproached: the use of better wages to entice the worker to fulfill the goals of the ruling class. In the East, however, the population supposedly shares these goals. The transition from hourly wages to incentive wages became necessary to solve the "extremely difficult and important problem of socialism"—namely, to attract workers to the job. The thesis that after the successful revolution people would joyfully and to their best ability work for society— that is, according to communist teaching, for themselves—because they no longer had to work for alien capitalists proved to be a utopian dream.

As early as 1931, Stalin, in recognition of actual conditions, condemned the principle of equality as a "leveling system" in one of his speeches.[43] The "material incentive" offered to workers, which replaced the profit motive in private enterprise, finally led to egoism and ambitions for personal comfort.[44] The programmatic formula read: Property and background no longer decide recognition by society, but actual performance does. The priority of communism's "materialistic-technical basis" was retained after Stalin up to the present by the leaders of the Party and of the economy. Industrial expansion and electrification still occupy first place in economic planning, despite stronger emphasis on consumer products.[45]

The theories of socialist ethics in the socialist phase, which have been discussed for the last ten years, are intended to justify morally the means and methods that have been necessary for realization of the Party's as well as the economy's goals. Even the creation of a "new man" is no longer considered the automatic result of changed economic conditions; it is the task of deliberate education in communism. To be sure, morality is part of the socio-economic base. Social property and government economic planning are the materials for creating a new type of man motivated by a sense of collective responsibility in his work and in his needs.

So reads the official doctrine. But actual conditions no longer correspond to this. A more mature economy, relaxed in its centralistic character, has produced—in the ranks of managerial personnel and the working class—a rather bourgeois prosperity ethos which, on the one hand, is conducive to future growth but which, on the other, moves further away from the goal of communist solidarity.

Together with the statement that the building of socialism was complete, a decree against "pedology" was issued,[46] which caused difficulties for Soviet psychologists.[47] In the past, human conduct had been attributed to environmental factors. Consequently, the system created by the Party after the introduction of socialism could be held responsible for the bourgeois attitudes of the people. On the other hand, this same theory stood in the way of effective education. With the justification that the "material basis" was established and completed but was not of itself sufficient, emphasis now had to be shifted to the human being himself.[48] Moral motives were no longer supposed to develop simply in compliance with and in support of objective-historical progress but now had to prove their teleological alignment with certain goals and socialistic values. If, therefore, the socialist production plan did not bring forth the desired consciousness, a socialist ethic that relied on fundamental socialistic principles like collectivism, socialist internationalism, and Soviet patriotism became necessary.[49] The dilemma is obvious. Originally it had been expected that the transfer of the economy into common ownership and the quantitative as well as qualitative increase in production would lead to quasi-automatic participation in the community by a free, equal, and prosperous people. But in fact it became evident that a higher economic base tends to lead in other directions. The initial tendency toward authoritarian hierarchy of command is—for economic, social, and technical reasons—increasingly opposed by a trend toward decentralization, plant autonomy, and personal and individualistic styles of life.

For Engels, freedom of the personality was comprised of the ability to make decisions with "expertise," that is, in obedience of the "material," socio-economic laws of development. Under socialism man is supposed to shape consciously his behavior.[50] According to the revised teaching, he is no longer directly subject to the impulses of the situation; instead he meets them always via his own consciousness. It is now demanded that this consciousness examine and shape reality in accordance with the communist goal.

The new formulation of the concept of freedom, therefore, unites man's free will with his understanding of an objective-materialistic, but also comprehensible, inevitability. For the communist subject who desires liberty and equality, elimination of the obstacles on the way to communist society appears to be a legitimate concern. Concrete, freedom-promoting deeds are just. Inevitability, in the sense of objective forces independent of consciousness, is now claimed for capitalism alone. On the one hand, freely formed interests and demands allow the state completely unhampered manipulation of goal determination. For Engels and Marx, freedom meant the ability to do what is consciously recognizable as inevitable. This concept of freedom makes it possible to subjugate the individual and his needs to the system.[51] On the other hand, the new freedom opens up a more flexible and instrumental relationship with the economic structure. Concepts of leadership and organizational forms are no longer sacrosanct but are open to discussion. It becomes possible to make a more concrete and relatively flexible determination of what communism is. Justice is no longer postponed to a utopian future, nor is it the inevitable product of developmental forces; it is a contemporary problem.

The new concept of human motivation retains the thesis that needs and interests are already determined by a communist society, but analysis of the complex of socialist motives is the task of socialist ethics. Motives no longer simply arise spontaneously but are induced by economic forces in the consciousness of man. Of particular importance to the old communist doctrine was the theory that under communism, if not sooner, the individual can satisfy his needs and develop all his abilities. Since all needs are social, differences of interest between the individual and the society will no longer exist in a classless, communistic society. Differing individual and social needs would be an expression of conflict in society itself. But according to official theory, the abolition of private property, the very source of conflict, has already largely eliminated inequalities among people. Individual needs or concepts of justice that deviate seriously from those of society—whose voice is Party doctrine—consequently cannot exist. Justice is what society does, because it serves progress toward a greater humanity. Adaptation of the social and economic system to demands for freedom by the people, which was originally intended and was later retained as an ideal, has in practice given way to adaptation by the individual to the system.

The system itself had retreated from its position of strict despotism. It has become an industrial state in which the economy is run by power politics. At the same time it is increasingly oriented toward a combination of the force of productivity and needs—as has already occurred in the West—in its social welfare and wage policies. The latter idea is expressed through benefits (e.g., cafeterias, education, vacations, and health care); these are defined as elements of communism. With this development, communism partially loses its status of a future goal and be-

168

comes the epitome of practical social measures and welfare policies, even if on a moderate level. The one-time utopia of free development of all human talents has become the socialist duty of self-development and voluntary involvement in the common cause. It now means the subordination of individual interests to those of the state and holds the individual personally responsible for the conformity of his actions to the system.

The Marxist point of view, which exposes in the liberal economic system a split between the capitalists and the wage earners, considers individualism to be the ideology of the ruling class. In the meantime, experience has taught—whether it is admitted or not—that modern industrialism, even after abolition of private property and the introduction of central planning, did not necessarily result in automatic egalitarian distribution. First of all, the complexity of the modern economy itself brings with it problems of organization and production incentives, which cannot be dealt with through tight hierarchical centralism alone. Furthermore, industrialism does not necessarily lead to a condition of totally collective, frictionless egalitarianism and prosperity for all. Finally, it shows that the citizenry has little interest in sacrifice for the utopian goal of total equality as comrades in a collective. Rather, people strive for personal betterment and independence in their private lives. Consequently, the concept and function of the Soviet ethic changes. It becomes the required norm, which demands of the individual an interest in solidary and diligent, conscientious productivity in order to achieve complete justice in the future. Thus everything is just that increases the strength of the Soviet political power and economic policy, for it derives its legitimacy from that future goal.[52]

According to communist opinion, ethics and justice do not come from the same root, because, while justice is the expression of the will and interests of a ruling class, the people derive ethics from generalized experiences. Since socialist society does not sanction "inhumane" production conditions, it receives the moral approval of the working class. It must make its rigor felt only upon those who place themselves outside the socialism that has been recognized as scientifically correct. Historical justice in socialism becomes a moral dictate. Morality is that form of social consciousness in which "objective social laws"—the historical guidelines for development of the proletariat—are alive. In the classless Soviet society, viewed as the institutionalization of the moral interests of the masses, the socialist ethic can completely supersede and negate socialist law. On the other hand, socialist values direct the ambi-

169

tions and efforts of the people toward the needs of society, because they correspond, by definition, to their own interests, which is fully comprehended by them.[53]

In socialist ethics the liberation of the individual from his material needs, from his spiritual egoism, and from his "slave" existence under capitalism—as Marx originally hoped—has become the "coercion for self-development." According to the teachings of "socialist humanism," "valuable traits of man's personality" would otherwise remain underdeveloped. This "new man" reaches his highest conscious freedom (that is, his most valuable ethical state) when he integrates into egalitarian society as represented by the Bolshevik system.[54]

Thus returns Marx's ideal of the complete congruity of both personal freedom and equality among individuals, although it is partially denied its content of individual autonomy and spontaneity. Only recently has the right of the individual to express his individuality gained increased consideration. To be sure, the promotion of progress remains the supreme criterion for the historical legitimacy of existing conditions. The Party determines into which category an issue belongs. At the same time, the distant goal of individuality and free self-development influences the present more and more. Simultaneous realization of both individuality and continual progress requires that individuals voluntarily consider public matters as their common cause and work toward a free community. For example, they must agree, on their own volition, to work for the collective and egalitarian satisfaction of needs. This is why training in socialist ethics is required. If it fails, there remains only the alternatives of planning by decree as it now exists and a private, egoistical "bourgeois-ization" of the workers.

The socialist work ethic represents the "heart" of all ethical relationships in the socialist society. Consequently, work that is considered degrading in the capitalist society because of exploitation and suppression receives a new value in socialism. Such labor allows man to test his capabilities and to develop creatively, that is, to form his personality. In "socialist competition" and self-commitment, new "values" are created —according to Marxist expectations—which place the relationship of the individual to society on an ethically higher plane. The ethical norms for the individual grow out of the demand for such attributes as work discipline, quality workmanship, and increased productivity. The work ethic thus is characterized as voluntary and conscious and is interwoven with the interests of society. To work in socialist terms means ultimately to plan and organize one's life consciously and purposefully so

170

that each individual is able to make his own maximum contribution to the development of socialism.[55]

According to this point of view, all individuals are, without exception, members of one community. As such they are both "the same and equal," even if functional differences remain. All have, in principle, an equal share in the social product, because only the will and total commitment of effort on behalf of the collective are important. Differences in capabilities are no reason for social privileges. As a community conscious human being, each individual will develop only such needs as are sensible for his leisure interests, his physical needs, and the size of his family. Thus it is possible in a sufficiently developed industrial society to have everyone participate in the social product according to his needs. It finally appears that egalitarian distribution in socialism is not identical with an abstract "equalization" of individuals, regardless of differences in capabilities and needs. During the transition phase it was applied no further than the abolition of personal income from investments and rent from tenant farmers. Otherwise it remained, with certain limitations, distribution according to productivity.[56] But as a final goal, the Soviet ethic demands the integration of the individual into the collective, to which he then contributes his utmost and from which he receives his fair share for consumption.

XII. INCOME DISTRIBUTION IN THE EAST

1. ABOLITION OF PRIVATE PROPERTY

The Marxist theory of value is the starting point for Eastern theories of income distribution. It is the pivotal point between socio-ethical and economic views. The demand that the capitalists be dispossessed grew from the Marxist labor theory of value, which grants only labor a value-creating function in the economic process. The Bolshevik nationalization of "the commanding heights" in the economy [1] was not only significant for the status of property but also for distribution policy. Simultaneously with the abolition of private property (even if certain remnants of private enterprise remained), the most conspicuous differences in income were also abolished. It would, however, be a mistake to think that the consequences for distribution policy were a mere side effect of these measures; with them disappeared all types of income that were not based on a person's own labor.

These measures, which were also, indirectly, distribution policies, can be directly connected with Marx's thought. But the views of communist theoreticians concerning distribution policies for disposition of the income left over after wages and salaries are quite general. Of course, these distribution policies are based on the general formula that under complete communism every member of society will partake of the social product according to his needs,[2] especially since in such an economy money—and with it, monetary compensation—will be abolished.[3] But

172

then again, Marx does not explain how to put such a formula into practice. In addition, it must be remembered that there is no assumption of an immediate transformation of the capitalist system into complete communism;[4] there are to be several distinct phases of transition.[5] In keeping with Marx, Soviet literature always points out that during the transition period compensation will be related to performance.[6]

With this, attention is focused on the transition period in its different stages, in which, of course, a concrete distribution policy is pursued.[7] It would be difficult to make more specific statements concerning this policy. This is especially true of the interrelationships of various wage scales. Even its macro-economic aspects (that is, its share of the national product) have not been clearly established,[8] and it has fluctuated during the transition that has so far taken place. Decisive here is the question of economic growth, that is, the formation of capital, whose level and rate of increase determine to a large extent the portion of the social product that is available for consumption.[9] *

Varying opinions can also be noted in regard to the micro-economic structure of income distribution. It is appropriate to associate these opinions with the course of the so-called transition economy in the Soviet Union. In contrast to the people's republics, the economy of the Soviet Union is an innovative development, whereas the people's republics essentially adopt the basic characteristics of the already existing Soviet distribution model. Basically, two ideas were pursued. Although the principle of equality borrowed from the French Revolution was extended to mean equality in the material satisfaction of needs, the stimulating effects of a differential wage system could not be ignored and were considered indispensable for the transition period.

For a "typically ideal" view of communist economic theory it must be assumed that the underlying, basic premise is an egalitarian income distribution. In conjunction with the dispossession of private property and the abolition of interest and rent from this source—which was accomplished during the initial revolutionary phase—the idea of equality in the remaining income from labor was introduced. The Second Moscow Program of the Communist party in 1919 retained equality of distribution as a primary goal, but the idea of its immediate realization was partially rejected.[10] Along with the tendency toward progressive taxation, which had existed in most Western countries for a long time, the program of 1903 had demanded the introduction of this type of tax-

---

* Quickly and steadily increasing productivity is cited as a prerequisite. Only in this way does it seem possible to secure the economic growth needed for the transition from socialism to communism.

173

ation for czarist Russia.[11] However, a decision on concrete questions of income policy was never made. The final phase in the economic policy of the transition period is supposed to be the elimination of monetary compensation. At the same time, according to Eastern theoreticians, the transition to distribution consistent with needs will then have been accomplished.[12]

2. NEEDS AS THE BASIS OF INCOME DISTRIBUTION

In practical economic life a distinction must also be made between the "model of the future" aspired to by a communistic society and actual developments until it is achieved. The seeds of the "self-realization of man," which Marx emphasized as the outstanding goal of communism's final phase, are especially to be cultivated in the economic sector.[13] Once there is socialization of the societal and economic structures, the former wage-slave will labor for the community and thereby work for himself.[14] Wages will be paid according to need [15] and will therefore correspond to the socio-ethical requirement for "corrective justice." [16] These goals will have been attained when all people can voluntarily integrate into the work process according to their abilities. During the transition phase there is the constant need to make people view work as the first requirement of life, so that the individual is self-motivated to become creatively active in accordance with his abilities.[17] Communist development will be complete only when there are abundant material and cultural products for satisfaction of the people's needs. In communism, everyone, then, should receive consumer goods appropriate to the needs of highly culturally developed human beings.[18] When communism is complete, all previously necessary product-money relationships will be replaced by the more productive economic forms described above.[19]

Until the final maturity and realization of the model communist society, there is a difference between this theory and that of the transitional socialist economy. Marx and Lenin emphasized that income differences in socialism continue to exist, even if they are unjust from the point of view of pure communist theory.[20] The need to distribute the product among members of society therefore ceases in communism only when "we have created a surplus of everything, in order to be able to satisfy the needs of all people." [21]

The realization that this goal cannot be attained without a considerable increase in labor productivity made the socialist form of compensation ("from each according to his abilities, to each according to his abilities") seem fair and consistent with the development theory.[22] Aided

174

by the material interest of the workers in the yield of their labor, productivity will be increased, so as to encourage the quickest possible development of the growing economy into communism.[23]

A. Distribution According to Needs

For a long time it remained unclear just how one was supposed to picture the actual realization of communism. A basic change seems to have
occurred with the publication of the Party Resolution of 1961,
concerning the transition to communistic forms of distribution. The humanitarian prophesy was more or less implemented as a realistic program. For the first time the attempt is being made to define the previously rather general and hazy concepts of distribution under
communism and during the transition phase. The distribution principle
("to each according to his needs") has been retained. However, the idea
that all wishes for "material and intellectual goods" should be satisfied
free of charge has yet to be realized.[24]

The more recent discussions of communism led to the establishment
of requirement norms. They refer to the quantitative as well as the
qualitative area of need satisfaction.[25] For the former this concept becomes particularly clear in the establishment of "scientific (rational)
consumption norms" for food, clothing, and durable consumer goods.[26]
According to Soviet opinion, even people's tastes will be developed and
refined in the communist system, for communist conditions should educate a human being "to whom spoiled tastes and unnatural needs" are
alien.[27] Thus the qualitative composition of need satisfaction is also
subjected to a certain standardization.

B. Social Consumption

According to Soviet opinion, the increased consumption by society is
characteristic of the transition to communism, that is, consumption ultimately becomes a gratis and moneyless distribution of income.[28] Present
plans, however, do not yet provide for abolition of compensation in
money. Nevertheless, a progressive expansion of communistic distribution is planned. Its growth rate to the year 1980 is to be double that of
monetary wages.[29] This advance in communal consumption is supposed
to encompass essentially the areas of education, housing, and health
care, as well as local public transportation, certain other community
services, cafeteria meals, and care in vacation and rest homes.[30] The attainment of such consumption standards must not be interpreted to

mean that each economic unit receives clearly defined amounts of goods. Rather, the possibilities for compensation exist within a limited framework. The significance of the standards lies more in the overall economy. They make it possible to gauge production volume for various types of goods needed in the national economy. However, the possibilities for need satisfaction remain limited when contrasted with consumer freedom in the West, which is restricted largely only by income. Thus the communist distribution principle has lost some of its attraction; at the same time it has become somewhat more realistic and has made the "abundance concept" of the final stage of communism more concrete.[31]

Still the communist "society of abundance" appears utopian with respect to a boundlessness of consumer needs and the scarcity of productive factors available for their satisfaction. In the Soviet Union, on the other hand, human needs are no longer regarded as a largely limitless, individual-psychological condition. Rather it is believed that individual needs under communism develop rationally and that communist consciousness effects a limitation of general need standards. Khrushchev expressed this point of view when he said, "As far as the adult population is concerned, one has to consider that the need of the people for means of existence is not unlimited." [32] The standardization of needs in connection with the abundance concept makes distribution according to needs in communism seem economically more feasible.[33] *

3. FUNCTIONAL AND PERSONAL INCOME DISTRIBUTION

Beginning with the socialist transition economy (that is, abolishing private ownership of the means of production), a sweeping change in the functional distribution of income took place in the Soviet Union and the people's republics. Rents on property and interest on capital that were withdrawn from their recipients did not, however, receive consideration as functional income categories in the economic plan. But, especially since the 1960s and in conjunction with the Liberman plan, a decisive change has set in. The functional income categories, profit, interest, and rent, once again entered economic planning.[34] † Even if these measures

* The increase in "social consumption" expected by the Soviets during the transition to communism is, however, by no means limited to the Eastern economic system. The phenomena appearing in the Western world in conjunction with the formation of the welfare state indicate a similar process.

† As early as 1959, Kantorovic used the expression "efficiency norm" in the U.S.S.R. for the concept "rate of interest"; and in 1960, Cholmogerov spoke of it

were primarily intended to improve productivity, their relationship to distribution must also be taken into consideration. In the ideal situation, "profit" would indicate the difference between a market economy (with unequal ownership distribution) and a centrally administered economy (without private ownership of the means of production). If the owners of the means of production and the recipients of profit are one and the same, a change in the profit share of the national product would also entail a change in personal distribution. This is true because the change in profits does not touch all consumers, only those who own the means of production. In a centrally administered economy, on the other hand, a change in functional shares of income does not *necessarily* change personal income distribution. Since the means of production are collectively owned, society as a whole receives the revenues accruing from them, and a central authority *can* distribute additional profits to economic units as a whole, without changing personal income distribution. Even the reintroduction of interest and rent does not effect a change in distribution. The inclusion of profit, interest, and rent in the people's republics of Eastern Europe does not, therefore, necessarily impede the desired leveling tendencies in personal income distribution.

The independence of functional and personal distribution in the people's republics, however, needs to be examined in conjunction with reform proposals for improvement of the economic system of the Soviet Union. To what extent can the goal of egalitarian distribution be reconciled with a system of material incentives and increased freedom of decision at the factory level? According to Liberman's proposals, premiums for working personnel are to be determined by the rate of profitability, that is, the ratio of profit to income from production. A factory's premium fund is supposed to be the only source of premiums in the economy and the individual firm should have more freedom in the use of "its" share of profit.[35] If such proposals were realized, profits would no longer be distributed through the central authority alone but also through the management of individual enterprises. The income shares paid to individual employees through the premium fund are thus

as a "sort of burden of the age." In his linear programming, Kantorovic used prices to measure the use of capital and land as well as profits. During the most recent discussion in East Germany, the concept of interest as a tax on production funds was also used. The latter corresponds to "interest," while the first concept comes closer to a profit tax. The Bulgarians call interest "taxing of production funds," while in Hungary "duty" or "fee" is preferred. Only in Poland and Yugoslavia does one speak of the "interest rate." An annual duty has existed in Hungary since January 1964, and in Yugoslavia collection of interest has been used since 1961.

dependent upon the profitability of the particular enterprise. A differing level of profitability can then cause a differentiated individual distribution between the employees of different enterprises, due to variation in the functional income share, profit. The consequences for personal distribution can be buffered by increasing the percentage of profit that must be turned over to the state as profitability increases. Provisions for this have also been made in Liberman's proposals.[36]

The question of distribution of the goods and services produced by society is considered "a very important problem of scientific communism." [37] Its forms and principles are supposed to depend, on one hand, upon the method of production and, on the other, upon the quantities produced. Therefore, the material basis for the transition to communistic distribution must be created first of all. This hypothesis is manifested in the demand for "creation of the material-technical basis of communistic society." [38] The necessity of regulating distribution of the product among members of society is supposed to disappear. If one considers the standardization of needs, their effects upon distribution, and the concept of the society of abundance, then only size and composition of the total product to be distributed represent decisive variables in the system.

The micro-economic aspect of compensation raises an additional question for income distribution. It has not been explained how a practical substitute for the price function of wages should be realized in the final stage of communism. The differentials in compensation under capitalism, which partly function as guides and also provide incentives to work, are rigorously rejected for this phase. Their functions are relegated to the unproven area of change in the concept of work, according to which the altered character of work itself will cause a sufficient work output for the society.

4. TRENDS IN REDISTRIBUTION

In Western economies changes in income structure seem to be possible only on a long-term basis. Recent studies have even revealed a relative stability of income distribution and the differences between economic systems become more apparent. For example, in the United States in 1939, the income of the top 5 percent of families accounted for 25.8 percent of the total of all family income. Averaging the years 1950 to 1955, this share was only 20.7 percent. These figures refer to income before income taxes. The relative share was thus reduced by one-fifth. If, however, undistributed corporate profits and the corporate taxes are

178

included, then the relative share of the upper 5 percent of family incomes is reduced only by about one-twentieth.[39] In the Soviet Union the ratio of average income of the upper 10 percent of families and the lower 10 percent changed by 37 percent from 1959 to 1965.[40]

The Seven Year Plan of the Soviet Union from 1959 to 1965 provided for a substantial increase in the minimum wage. Whereas the average wage was supposed to grow by approximately 26 percent, as compared to 1958, a growth rate of 70 to 80 percent was the goal for the lowest wage category.[41] In addition, an increase in minimum social security benefits, the abolition of income taxes, and a lowering of restaurant prices and prices of other specific goods were included in the plan. Together with an expansion of government expenditures for social services, these measures were also calculated to bring about a reduction in the existing income differences. According to the calculation of Yanowitch, considerable equalization should occur in the income structure with the realization of these measures.[42] Bearing in mind the comparatively short time span, Yanowitch remarks that the expression "Soviet income revolution" is hardly an exaggeration.[43]

The reasons for an equalization of the income structure in the Soviet Union can be traced to the following factors:

1. The educational and vocational training level of new economic units entering the production process is higher. Therefore, the large wage differentiation of the earlier industrialization period has become less necessary.

2. Even with increasing industrialization, there are still jobs and job areas that can be filled by unskilled or semi-skilled workers in the Soviet Union. To retain the work force needed for this, the wage differential between skilled and unskilled workers must not become too great. (Similar tendencies can also be observed in Western economic systems; for example, wage premiums must be given for particularly dirty or noisy work.)

3. With increasing industrialization it becomes more and more difficult to determine the productivity of the single worker and to compensate him according to his performance. This is also expressed in the increasing number of jobs with hourly wages in contrast to piecework wages.[44]

These reasons are the result of economic development and are common to Western and Eastern economic systems. They are thus not due to differences in economic organization.

In analyzing the income structure based on Western cost factors (including interest, rent, and undistributed corporate profits), it becomes evident that, for example, in the United States, distribution has shown little change in recent years. More equalized distribution can be shown in an economic system based on private property if corporate earnings are excluded. But, the leveling process is limited because of unequal ownership of the means of production. Such differentiating effects do not necessarily occur with collective ownership and a largely central distribution.

The aspiration for and realization of more equal income distribution in the Soviet Union, even within short time spans, is favored by developments which are indifferent to the system. This is further augmented by the system-related factor of property distribution and its effects upon income distribution. The objection that a stronger emphasis on material incentives in the Soviet Union hinders the equalization of income distribution or will even lead to growing differences in income distribution is only partly correct. In the United States, where wages are basically paid according to productivity, it was possible to reduce differences in wage incomes, as may be seen if the 1929 figures are compared to the average for the years 1950 to 1955.[45] Even a pronounced decentralization of control over distribution by means of a more extensive granting of income from premium funds of enterprises does not necessarily prevent reduction of income inequality, as shown above.[46] *

* According to this analysis of Eastern income distribution, the possibility is opened, as it turns out, for the granting of bonuses to and the preferential treatment of top Party members in the form of handouts. This readily allows considerable gradation of incomes, since it permits the setting of arbitrary figures.

180

XIII. WAGES AND OTHER TYPES OF INCOME IN THE EAST

1. SOVIET WAGES AND SALARIES

The major objective of wage policies in the East is to increase labor productivity.[1] This is a prerequisite for the desired increase in national output. For this purpose aspects of welfare and corrective justice have to be partially shelved for the duration of the transition economy, at least as far as actual wage policy is concerned.

The U.S.S.R. has essentially two types of wage regulations. One is based on geographical area and the other, on types of industry.[2] Variations in geographical wage regulation encourages settlement in underpopulated areas. Compensation in various regions of the country also depends partially on different costs of living. Of greater importance, however, seem to be the variability of working conditions and the degree of worker qualification in the different types of industry. Added to this is the importance given in economic policy to particular branches of industry.[3] *

Wages based on productivity are the type of compensation used in industry.[4] Historically the development of types of wages in Soviet industry since the October Revolution has gone through roughly the follow-

* The branches of industry most important for further industrialization (coal, ferrous and nonferrous metals, petroleum, chemicals, machinery, and power) thus show the highest average wages.

ing stages: [5] an equalizing stage from 1917 to 1921; a differentiating stage from 1921 to 1926; an equalizing stage from 1926 to 1931; and a differentiating stage from 1931 until approximately 1955. Judging by this, the development in those decades fluctuated repeatedly between an emphasis first upon incentive wages and then upon somewhat more fixed forms. It is the peculiar trait of the Soviet economic system to swing between the desired supply principle and the required incentive principle. Only since the Twentieth Party Congress in 1956 has there been a noticeable approximation of the various income extremes, and this has been achieved mainly by an increase in lower incomes. [6] *

Industrial wages exhibit varying forms: [7] (1) a straight piecework wage; (2) a progressive piecework wage; (3) an hourly wage; (4) a premium wage; and (5) a special form of piecework wage which will be explained. In the first case each completed unit is paid for according to a fixed rate, that is, the total compensation has no fixed limits, but is governed solely by the level of output. The progressive form of piecework wages pays the worker, after completion of a certain quantity, at progressively increasing rates for all units that are additionally produced. The hourly wage is dependent upon the amount of time expended and the standard wage for the worker's level of qualification. The bonus wage exists as premium pay as well as an hourly premium wage. It represents a combination of the straight piecework wage and bonuses for certain established qualitative and quantitative indices. Similarly, in an hourly wage bonus scheme the worker receives a bonus for special qualitative or quantitative productivity above the standard wage for actual working time. The fifth type of wage is seldom used. It is found in certain types of work in the coal mining industry. In this case compensation is not in accordance with individual incentive wage scales but is adapted to the whole range of work involved. If types of work occur that cannot be performed by a single worker alone, then the group incentive wage is introduced, which operates in a similar way. In this case the time or work norm for the total collective (brigade) is applied. The individual's wages are in accordance with the work time and wage scale to which he has been assigned.

In order to obtain comparison scales for productivity of different workers and enterprises, objective measuring scales or labor standards had to be introduced early. The urgency and importance of these standards was emphasized by Stalin: "Without technical standards, a planned economy is impossible. Furthermore, technical standards are a great regulating force, which organizes the broad masses of workers as

---

* This includes also wage increases for persons who primarily work in education, health services, trade, and other service areas.

well as the advanced worker for production." [8] Those standards that are based on practical experience have to be differentiated from technical standards. The technical standard depends on the capacity of the single machine and the effort of the worker.

The accomplishments of the Soviet economic system are in many respects dependent upon the quality of these standards. The economic effect of incentive wages as well as adherence to the total amount of wages stipulated by the over-all plan for the economy are determined by the quality of the standards.[9] Labor standards are subject to constant change due to technical progress. They are closely tied to the exact measurement of productivity. Labor productivity is understood as the efficiency of "living labor."

The further improvement of standards seems to have partially changed the type of compensation.[10] Added to this is the technical progress of the last few years. Both have required that wages, which until recently were mostly piecework wages, take on the appearance of hourly wages. This type of compensation is now most frequent in the manufacturing industries.[11] But even in mining some deviation from the piecework wage has accompanied increasing conversion to automated or mechanized mining. The change in the compensation system obviously arises from the highly mechanized production processes, for which productivity standards on a time basis are easier to obtain. This development must not, however, obscure the fact that, for the time being, piecework wages and progressive wages are common. In 1956, 77 percent of the workers received piecework wages and of those 43 percent received progressive piecework wages.[12]

The productivity principle is also applied for compensation of managerial technicians and employees. Their salaries are substantially governed by the degree of their responsibility and their importance in the production process. Added to this is the degree of difficulty in the work assignment to be carried out or supervised. Furthermore, the importance of the branch and the complete industrial sector for economic policy play a considerable role in determining monthly compensation. The wage level of the plant workers is also considered.[13] Bonuses for increasing production and lowering costs are paid through salaries according to the same principle that is applied to wages of workers.

All in all, wages and salaries in the U.S.S.R. have risen considerably since 1950: real wages were 50 percent higher in 1959 than in 1950.[14] * The rising productivity of all workers with partial preserva-

* Real wages of all laborers and white collar employees rose from the base year, 1950, to 1955 to the index figure 141 and from 1950 to 1959 to the index figure 156.

tion of more or less differential wage schemes may have played a role.

Agriculture differs from industry in regard to wages and salaries. The pecularity of agricultural compensation lies in its dependency upon the type of operation, such as individual, single-unit operation; the farm collective or co-operative; and the wholly state owned and operated farm.[15] Co-operative operations, as is generally known, constitute by far the most predominant part of agriculture. The following criteria decide the income level of the members of co-operatives: [16] crop yield, number of days worked, total number of co-operative members, prices of agricultural products stipulated in the state plan, and exceeding or non-fulfilling of plan quotas. The difficulty in the U.S.S.R. of strong centralistic planning for total agricultural production led to a new direction that was taken in 1955 during the Stalin era. Increased success was expected from a progressively decentralized type of planning.[17]

The level of compensation for all collective farmers was not predetermined in the plan. Each collective farmer receives his total compensation only at the end of the year, since the profit of each collective depends substantially upon crop yield. Recently it seems, however, that weekly or monthly advances are being made to the collective farmers.[18] With this, the manner in which he is compensated approaches that of a farm laborer. The compensation actually paid for a day's work varies and depends on the geographical location of the collective.[19]

2. WAGES IN THE PEOPLE'S REPUBLICS [20]

Hungary's wage system has been considerably influenced by the uprising of 1956. One result was the departure from incentive wages which, following the Soviet example, was rigorously practiced until then in Hungary and a more pronounced use of hourly wages.[21] Around 1957 the wage system consisted of norms and incentive wages, a changeover to the so-called system of average wage controls later took place. Previously wages were based solely upon productivity and could be improved only by increased work intensity or by exceeding quotas, which were perhaps fixed at too low a level.

However, the new system makes compensation independent of the results of plant productivity. If possible, wages are to be set so that there are no differences between plants. This new type of compensation on the basis of hourly wages still has, nevertheless, aspects that can lead to improved productivity. Qualitatively better work earns a wage increase just as classification in a higher work category stimulates an improvement of quality and consequently may also lead to wage increases.

184

Real as well as nominal wages have been raised considerably since 1956.[22] * But in Hungary it was significant that until 1956 prices for basic foods rose with wages. After 1956, wages under the new system shifted in favor of non-agricultural employees. The real-wage index has since risen. However, the considerable rate of increase in wages and salaries from 1957 to 1960 could not be maintained in succeeding years.

The decisive break in Rumanian wage policies after 1945 occurred as a result of political events in Hungary in 1956. Only from this time on were wages again differentiated to any significant extent. They were raised considerably, partially in anticipation of increased social production in following years. In addition, new standards were introduced.[23] During the earlier years only minor differences existed between the wage levels of a skilled worker or a technician and the many unskilled laborers. But the political atmosphere of 1956 upset this wage system, which had long been criticized. At the same time, analogous to Hungary, the system of incentive wages changed in favor of an hourly wage.

The development of wages and salaries in the various Rumanian production sectors has been more or less the same as in Hungary.[24] However, the rise of industrial incomes was steeper in Rumania where the degree of industrialization at the beginning of the socialist transition economy was comparatively minor. On the other hand, the more industrialized Hungary had at that time already reached a relatively high income level in industry. Therefore, the development of real wages in Rumania moved upward with more consistency although the standard, to be sure, was lower than in Hungary.[25] †

An almost uniform and rather rapid rise in agricultural income suggests similarities in this production sector for both countries. The differences in the pace of growth in industry and agriculture were not so great in Rumania as in Hungary, where distribution policies were supposed to equalize the existing differences in the level of agricultural and industrial incomes. The Rumanian construction, forestry, and trade industries, which at that time were evidently viewed as relatively unim-

---

* The real wage index for laborers and white collar employees (1949 = 100) indeed fell by 1952 to 82.3. But in the following years a steady increase took place: 1954, 102.3; 1956, 118.3; 1958, 145.4; 1960, 156.0; 1961, 156.3; 1962, 158.6; 1963, 165.7; and 1964, 170.0. The index for the net money income (1949 = 100) rose from 147.4 (1952) to 293.3 (1964).

† The increase in real wages of the workers (1950 = 100) for the years 1955–1963 is as follows:

1955: 128	1958: 161	1961: 193
1956: 138	1959: 172	1962: 201
1957: 153	1960: 189	1963: 213

portant, suffered most when compared with average real wages in all production sectors. Generally speaking, the incomes in all production sectors in Rumania grew at a steadier pace than in Hungary.

In Bulgaria, too, the shift toward the hourly wage system and compensation of workers not working on an incentive basis has created a number of problems.[26] Here, too, to promote the material interest of employees, the reduction of norms and their standardization have been considered essential.

Since the early 1950s, industrial income received preference over agricultural income.[27] The goal of the quickest possible industrialization was more prominent than in Hungary and Rumania, especially since Bulgaria lagged behind those two countries in economic development. Because of this, a pronounced disparity between industrial and agricultural incomes developed, particularly in the early 1950s. It stemmed from a one-sided interest in industrialization which led to promoting income increases in industry. However, the New Course from 1953 to 1955 lead to a change; a trend to raise agricultural incomes began and continued into the following years. The disparity between industry and agriculture still existing in Bulgaria until 1959, as well as the relatively high income level in the construction industry, suggests that—as in the case of Hungary—there was no basic change in the course of industrialization, but rather a reduction of differentials.[28] *

Real wages in Albania rose between 1955 and 1958 by 20 percent, while the corresponding increase in Hungary was 33 percent.[29] Evidently in Albania too, industrial wage development received preference above agricultural, although statistical sources permit only indirect conclusions. The reason for this development was that Albania, the least developed country among the four southeast European people's republics, had the longest road to travel toward a Soviet-type economy. It began with the transition to socialism on a level that was almost com-

* Annual average wages (in Bulgarian lev) for workers and white collar employees according to economic sector (excluding agricultural co-operatives).

Year	National Average	Manufacturing	Construction	Agriculture
1948	485 (= 100)	457 (= 100)	640 (= 100)	383 (= 100)
1952	646 (133)	663 (145)	812 (127)	472 (123)
1955	754 (155)	793 (174)	946 (148)	623 (163)
1959	864 (178)	895 (196)	1029 (161)	844 (220)
1962	1020 (210)	1040 (228)	1206 (188)	907 (237)
1963	1051 (217)	1075 (235)	1263 (197)	930 (243)

pletely agriculturally oriented. Albania, therefore, exerted special efforts to achieve the quickest possible industrialization, which in turn influenced income policy.[30]

A much stricter centralist regulation exists for standards in the Albanian wage system than in that of the Soviet Union, where since 1957 standards are examined by the enterprises themselves.[31] In general, Albania to some degree still employs regulations that were affected in the U.S.S.R. before World War II, but which have long since been revised on the basis of new knowledge.

The overriding wage policy of East Germany is directed toward a steady increase in labor productivity. Paragraph 43 of the Work Edict of 12 April 1961 stipulates, in each case, application of the wage that "directly engages the material interest of the workers in a maximum increase of their productivity, the accomplishment of their tasks as to quality and delivery time, the thriftiest employment of time, money, and material, the fullest utilization of their working time, and the worker's constant qualification."

The type of wage that corresponds most closely to this principle is the bonus piecework wage, which is paid for quality as well as quantity of work. The simpler piecework wage and the bonus piecework wage are therefore most frequently used. The hourly wage, on the other hand, is a type of compensation that corresponds least to the strict productivity principle and which, consequently, is seldom used.[32] The wage system is supplemented by a multitude of bonuses. They all serve exclusively the goal of increased labor productivity. Thus, this step in the various wage groups serves the qualitative increase of labor productivity, while quantitative productivity is encouraged by the piecework wage.[33]

A comparison of changes in the index of real wages between East Germany and other Soviet-type countries discloses a faster growth rate in the other countries.[34] * Although the index bases vary, this is partly because in East Germany production of consumer goods vis-à-vis heavy industry has been disproportionally neglected. In contrast, a trend toward increased production of consumer goods has been obvious for several years now in the southeast European people's republics and in the U.S.S.R. itself.

Developments in Poland are marked by the Six Year Plan from 1949 to 1955, the worker rebellion in Poznan in June 1956, and the subse-

* The real wage index (1958 = 100) for full-time laborers and white collar employees (excluding apprentices) in nationalized factories rose from 81.0 (1955) to 122.3 (1963).

quent changes in the system. Until 1949, wage payments were partly in food stuffs. After abolition of this system, incentive wages, according to the Soviet example, were introduced to increase work productivity, although a noticeable improvement in real wages in Poland was not accomplished until after 1956. The actual real wage increase in 1955 was not even 28 percent as compared to 1949.[35]

Poland, too, following the Soviet example, began, in 1949, to push the development of heavy goods at the expense of consumer goods. This necessarily neglected the generally low standard of living for the Polish people. As a consequence of the Poznan rebellion in 1956 a certain restructuring of wage policies can be noted.[36]

The situation in Czechoslovakia was shaped by the struggle for higher labor productivity. As in East Germany, a material interest in socialism is the most important work incentive. A slight reorganization of the wage system, effecting a greater differentiation, took place after 1957.[37] Comparisons of real wages and investigations of the standard of living are difficult because of the differing nature of developments in Czechoslovakia.[38]

The wage system of the People's Republic of China is characterized by the state of development of the country. Compensation according to needs is not possible at present and is reserved for a future communistic order. In the meantime a type of compensation according to productivity is in effect.[39] Basically it can be noted that nominal wages in China, past or present, are still low. Even the minor increase during the last few years could not achieve a noticeable improvement of real wages.

A special part is played by work projects that employ huge masses of people. None of the other Soviet-type economies can form its economic policy on capital investment without at the same time creating a substantial increase in purchasing power.[40] However, while China's extensive "voluntary" and involuntary irrigation projects by farmers and, in a large part, also by the army create productive resources for the future, these capital investments are not immediately inflationary. This is because they are not accompanied by increased wages, which would be inflationary because of a relative scarcity of goods in stock or in production.[41] In this respect China occupies a special position regarding her wage system *vis-à-vis* the European people's republics as well as the U.S.S.R.

3. WAGE POLICY AND TAXATION

The New Economic Policy announced in Russia in the fall of 1921 brought the first wage differentiations.[42] The new system of rates created a considerable range between particular maximum and minimum wages.[43] Only the wage reform of 1956 effected essential changes in this graduated compensation in the form of bonus and piecework wages. The reorganizations which began with the Twentieth Party Congress in 1956 not only extended to a step-by-step increase in wages but also to a general reduction of prices.[44] *

A correlation of distribution policies with the general goals of the transition economy was also in part the basis for tax policies in the southeast European people's republics, especially income taxation in agriculture.[45] These taxes, detrimental to private business, partially softened the differentiating effects of price policy. Thus they contributed to an equalizing tendency of distribution policy for the different types of agricultural operations, especially in the years 1957 to 1959. In contrast to the collectives, which were taxed principally according to their actual yields, private farmers, for instance, had to carry financial burdens based on possible future output.[46] Because of such measures, collective farmers as a rule had to pay only about 60 percent of the taxes that were levied against private farmers with comparable income.[47] On the other hand, independent farmers were frequently granted tax advantages if they decided to join an agricultural production co-operative.[48]

The tax policies for private enterprises in other economic sectors, which were essentially also geared toward strengthening the income potential in the socialistic sector, partly for ideological reasons, provided for several graduations in taxation. Thus, for example, additional taxes were leveled against private tradesmen and merchants employing wage earners in their enterprises. The amount of tax was based on the number of employees. Marx's surplus value doctrine concerning the siphoning off of business profits through "exploitation of the worker" apparently played a role here. Still, tradesmen and merchants who were, for example, more than two-thirds disabled were exempted from these additional taxes. Also enterprises whose owners were either drafted into the armed forces or had died received tax immunity for one employee only.[49] On the other hand, the principles of taxation also contained exceptions to these leveling tendencies. Thus the income of tradesmen and merchants who operated in communities with a low population and who did repair work received a favored status.

Tax relief measures for workers and white collar employees in the U.S.S.R. took up a substantial part of Khrushchev's speech before the

---

* On the raising of minimum wages according to the decree of 8 September 1956, see *Izvestija,* 9 September 1956, p. 1. On the pension law of 14 July 1956, see *Pravda,* 15 July 1956, p. 2. On price decreases, see *Pravda,* 1 March 1960, p. 2.

Supreme Soviet on 5 May 1960.[50] The state's income from socialist enterprises rose sharply with the growth of the national economy.[51] At the same time, not only a general reduction but a partial abolition of personal taxes was contemplated.[52] * The tax relief measures of 1960 were important. The elimination of taxes on wages was supposed to proceed in steps beginning in 1960 and concluding in 1965. The law of 8 May 1960 provided for raising the tax exemption limit to 500 (old) rubles on 1 October 1960 and to 600 (old) rubles on 1 October 1961. Income taxes for workers and white collar employees earning up to 2000 (old) rubles per month in wages or salaries were also to be eliminated. Khrushchev emphasized that in this way the wages and salaries of over 99.4 percent of the workers and white collar employees would be increased by the total amount of the previous income tax. Yet it was clearly pointed out that at the time of his speech only 0.6 percent of all employees earned in excess of 2000 (old) rubles.[53] All measures were supposed to be realized in a comprehensive step-by-step plan.[54]

In his statements Khrushchev pointed out that the measures to be enacted were to achieve—within the framework of tax abolition—an equalization of compensation for workers. But this should by no means lead to a "depersonalization in the compensation of the working people." [55] The leveling of incomes through tax reduction partly stemmed from wage disparities after World War II. They were held to be too large, and attempts were made to narrow them without depriving workers of the stimulus for individual labor. The socio-ethical motives of an equalizing income policy are quite apparent.

The discrepancy between low and high incomes was clearly expressed in the debate on "equalization" during the Twentieth Party Congress in 1956. The measures initiated at that time extended not only to the leveling tax policy previously mentioned but also to wage policy itself. However, data are lacking as to how total national income is distributed among the individual income classes.[56] Wage differentials were substantially reduced again between 1956 and 1959, that is, between the Twentieth and Twenty-First Party Congresses.[57]

The convergence of workers' wages had several causes.[58] Differences in compensation for skilled and unskilled work have been considerably reduced during the past years. Although payment of bonuses was not affected by this, these measures nevertheless caused a change in the basic compensation of the workers. The minimum wage was raised from

* For example, the reduction of the agricultural tax for collective farmers by 60 percent in 1953.

190

40 to 45 (new) rubles per month in 1962. (In 1957, it had been raised from 27 to 35 rubles per month.) Thus, equalization of the wage level, even though minor, was also accomplished in this way.[59] Beyond this, piecework wages were gradually replaced more and more by hourly wages. But here too, care was taken not to diminish the principle of material interest.

It is probable that equalization of wages will continue to be important for Soviet economic policy. After all, the plan provides for even smaller differences in workers' incomes as was the case before the attack on so-called equalization, that is, in the early 1930s.[60]

The ratio of salaries of technicians to those of white collar workers also deserves attention.[61] The most important aspect of the more recent developments in wage policy in the U.S.S.R. is, without doubt, the convergence of wages and salaries among different employment categories. Besides efforts to close the gap between salaries of the two former categories, after the end of the war there was a pressing desire to reduce income differences between laborers and technical personnel. The incomes of 30 percent of the workers in the coal mining and machine tool industry in 1956 exceeded the average incomes of all technical, managerial personnel in these sectors.[62] At the same time, average wages for workers in certain industries, coal mining for example, exceeded those in other industries considerably.

In respect to real wage increases in the Soviet Union during the last decade, one also arrives at the same conclusions as previously discussed. The frequently used opportunities for various price reductions were gradually used to increase real wages. In the years after World War II the Soviet Union has, because of differing methods, changed the growth rate of real wages three times.[63] Increases in real wages can, after all, be brought about not only via general price reductions of consumer goods but also by raising actual wages. Whereas in the first instance all levels of the population are more or less equally involved, the second method can much better be directed to certain parts of the population. Price reductions and wage increases—at times also in combination—were interrupted at the close of the 1950s. In an effort to raise the purchasing power of laborers and white collar employees, as well as the minimum wage, general price reductions were relinquished.[64] * The Seven Year Plan, too, provided for an immediate

* According to Khrushchev, it was far more important to raise minimum wages, pensions, and general wages than to advocate a further price reduction. Here, too, the idea of more equal compensation comes to the fore.

increase of average wages by 26 percent during the years 1958 to 1965, as compared to 1958. Seventy to 80 percent of the total planned wage increase again went to the lowest income group.[65]

Comparisons of real wages within the U.S.S.R. often suffer from the lack of suitable statistical material in the West. Nevertheless, the 1935 *Statistical Handbook* gives comparatively instructive data: [66] 130 rubles per month was the typical wage of the farm worker; 190 rubles, that of the industrial worker. It can be assumed that such wages increased fivefold until the 1950s. This also agrees with the calculations of American economists.[67]

Material incentives find comparatively little consideration in Soviet agriculture. The allocation of profits to increase production funds and material incentives was extremely small in 1963, for instance. In 1963, only 3 percent of total capital investments by state farms in the U.S.S.R. came from their own funds; the remainder was supplied from the state budget.[68] Equally unimportant, for the time being, is the role of profit in encouraging the productivity of state farm workers. More recent tendencies indicate that, in the future, profit may become the sole source of incentives for increasing agricultural output.[69] During recent years collective farmers have been paid a guaranteed monetary wage.[70] State bank credit plays a special role in financing these wage payments.[71] Moreover, the improvement of the economic condition of previously weak agricultural operations is to acquire greater importance.[72]

Although in the transition economy of socialism, labor was to be the only source of personal income for the worker, other forms of income still exist in Soviet-type economies to varying degrees.[73] In the U.S.S.R., property constitutes only a minor source of income. Basically, all income is a remuneration for service—independent of its amount.[74] Only recently has there been a demand that private initiative be allowed more latitude.[75] This could have a noticeable, though not permanent, effect on the income structure of the population.

In contrast to its neighboring countries, Hungary attained a special position rather early because of its higher level of industrialization.[76] The consequence was that Hungary again permitted limited entrepreneurial initiative. Of course, the events of 1956 and their aftermath had a significant influence upon this development. In the remaining southeast European people's republics—Rumania, Bulgaria, and Albania—such tendencies can be observed only to varying degrees. Hungary, because of its economic development during the past decades, was more inclined to accept private enterprise than the others. Chiefly smaller enterprises in trades, commerce, and industry participate in this process.

A similar situation can be noted in Poland since the October 1956 uprising. To a larger degree than before, private initiative in commerce and industry has not only been tolerated but promoted. The easing of credit for private industrial, commercial, trade, and service enterprises testifies to this.[77] These "private industries" are supposed to have no more than fifty employees in each case, except for export and seasonal enterprises, as well as those in particularly important industries, such as coal mining. Nevertheless, an expansion of private entrepreneurial initiative can be observed, although precise data are lacking.

In East Germany the 1950 "law to promote the trades" is still in effect.[78] During the past ten years, however, most of the measures within the framework of a private market economy were in the end aimed at the repression of private initiative. Actually, private initiative plays less of a role in East Germany than, for instance, in Hungary or Poland.[79] In the analysis of such problems, however, the accurate compilation of statistical data is difficult. For the time being only rough approximations of a trend in this direction can be made.

In the transition phase, to be sure, still another form of personal income is derived from agricultural side operations. Each collective farmer is granted a small parcel of land for his personal use.[80] This form of private enterprise is well defined in Soviet-type economic systems. During the transition phase, the side operations will continue to constitute an important part of agricultural income. Precise information concerning the actual proportion of income received by collective farmers from side operations is not available. However, it is known that it is a substantial part of money income.[81] The sale of fruits, vegetables, and animal products plays a considerable part in this. The receipts from these small, private, farm operations represent in some instances an important additional source of income for those collective farmers who are lowest on the income scale. It remains to be added that the amount of such income depends upon various factors: the number of family members, and the size, volume, and quality of the soil. The Soviets, too, admit that these side operations play an important role at times.[82]

In the southeast European people's republics small farm operations are also important. Certainly this agricultural activity shows better results than collectivized farming. In 1962, for example, only 3.4 percent of the farm acreage in Hungary was not collectivized. On the other hand, the share of small farm operations—that is, the noncollectivized part of agriculture—amounted to approximately 14 percent of total government purchases for farm produce.[83] In this way it can be understood that sometimes the wage of a farm worker constitutes only one-half of his disposable total income.[84]

Several things indicate that, in the future, earnings from private operations by collective farmers will slowly decrease.[85] This will occur as improvements in the compensation of collective farmers are undertaken. It should especially be noted that there is a tendency to reduce family farm acreage by a predetermined, but not accurately defined, amount as soon as monetary compensation is introduced. Approximately 0.175 acres has been stipulated as a suitable size for future small farms.[86]

4. THE LIBERMAN PROPOSALS

With the proposals of Evsei Liberman to decentralize over-all economic planning and to use earnings as the criterion of profitability and the awarding of bonuses, there immediately arises the question of how far enterprises, as decentralized decision-making bodies, should be part of the distribution process. Liberman advocates that enterprises should be granted more rights in the use of operational bonus funds.[87] The question is, then, what consequences a stronger emphasis on material stimuli have, or could have, in the future as far as income distribution is concerned.

At present, technical engineering employees in the Eastern economies receive bonuses for meeting or exceeding quality indices. In this case fulfillment of the earning and profitability plan as well as of the plan for reduction of prime costs is particularly important as an index. An absolute prerequisite for the granting of bonuses is, in general, fulfillment of the commodity production plan. The above-mentioned indices and bonus conditions are usually established by the responsible governmental department. They serve as a basis for bonuses to the leading members of the plant management team. On the other hand, indices and bonus conditions for the personnel of individual production departments are established by plant management. Recently the granting of bonuses to managers and personnel of individual production departments of plants has occurred independently of the fulfillment of tasks by the whole enterprise.[88] For example, until 1964, bonuses to foremen of a brake manufacturing plant in Moscow were not granted according to the indices for their particular sector but according to those for the entire department. Under the existing system, the amount of bonus varies because of differences in output.[89] A differentiation of wage incomes therefore begins in the plant and at the same time helps to overcome the "equalization in bonus determination."[90]

In this connection the granting of interplant bonuses must also be considered. In Poland allocations to plant bonus funds, which depend upon profit, are determined by the government for all branches of the economy. If profit increases between 0.01 and 6 percent over the previous year, then the allocation to the bonus fund is increased by 0.2 percent for each 0.1 percent of profit increase. Above 6 percent, allocations amount to 0.52 percent for each 0.8 percent of profit increase.[91] In plants with large profit increases, allocations to the bonus fund rise progressively and with them also the means available for granting bonuses. The importance of the diverse bonus fund allocations for interplant purposes is clarified by the Soviet government. For the machine tool industry in Moscow, the highest bonus ever given was 23.5 percent of base salary and the lowest was 15.6 percent. Even greater are the differences in the textile industry, where the allocations fluctuate between 30 and 12 percent of base salary.[92]

The phenomena mentioned so far lead, *ceteris paribus,* to greater differentiation in the distribution of wages. This process is weakened, however, by a limitation on bonus size. In Poland, for instance, the size of the bonus fund for technical engineering employees in particular industries is fixed at 10 to 30 percent of the salaries. Added to this are further payments from the supplemental bonus fund, although the individual bonus from this fund is not permitted to exceed 15 percent of annual income.[93] Limitations upon the size of the bonus for technical engineering employees (40 to 60 percent of the salary) also exist in the other Eastern economies.[94] * With the newer bonus systems, income differentiating effects are tolerated in order to achieve further industrialization and a rise in economic productivity. Thus, in Poland the basic bonus fund for the steel industry was established at 19.1 percent of the wage fund; for the nonferreous metal industry, at 17.8 percent; for the machine tool industry, at 10 to 20 percent; and for light industry, at 15 percent.[95] Similar differentiations were also planned in 1962 for allocations to the supplemental bonus fund.[96] †

There have been indications in the U.S.S.R. during the last few years

---

* In Czechoslovakia, maximum bonuses may not exceed 60 to 75 percent of wages in heavy industry and 40 to 50 percent in other branches. The range of bonuses in Bulgaria is also from 40 to 60 percent of annual wages. In the past, the percentage of the bonus increased with increasing wages. Now it is the same for all employees. This has produced a certain leveling effect.

† Grants to the bonus funds are given as a percentage of plant wage funds: heavy industry, 3 percent; chemical industry, 2.5 percent; light industry, 2 percent; mining and power, 1.9 percent.

suggesting greater independence of plants and with it greater participation in the distribution process by the production units. Thus, the production co-operatives Bol'sevicka in Moscow and Majak in Gorki (both garment-making plants) were granted the right to determine, in addition to other plans, their own wage fund based on the manufacturing orders received from their trade organization. Now only the rate of earnings and the volume of goods produced relative to orders received are reported.[97] Wage determination has been delegated to the plants to an increased degree. Consequently, great differentiation in income distribution becomes possible.

Profit has been introduced as the chief factor in determining bonuses since earnings are affected by the bonus indices, such as reduction of prime costs, increase in work productivity, reduction in the proportion of inferior products in over-all production of textiles, and increasing utilization of capacity.[98] * A distinction, however, must be made between scheduled profits and profits in excess of the plan. The first are mainly paid into the state budget; [99] † on the other hand, 60 to 90 percent of the "accumulation in excess of the plan" is retained by the plants. From this, payments are then made for "material recognition" of productivity. According to Soviet information, the absolute amount of profit kept by the plants in 1955 amounted to approximately 5.8 billion rubles; for 1960, the amount was reported to be 9.9 billion rubles; and for 1965, 12 billion rubles. These profits, however, were divided among several funds (for instance, the fund for collective consumption, the fund for social and cultural purposes, the plant fund, and others).[100] ‡ Among the stimulation funds, the plant fund gained increasing importance. Nearly 134 million rubles in 1950 and 644 million rubles in 1962 were dispensed out of this fund; of this, approximately 46 percent was spent for individual bonuses, cultural and social services, medical treatment, and relief payments.[101]

The sums set aside for bonuses represent only a small share of total profit. Further lowering of funds for stimulation of productivity can exercise a braking effect upon the increasing inequality of income distribution in the future. By reducing the funds set aside for this purpose the effect

---

* In connection with economic experiments in the Soviet Union, production in physical terms and profit have been the primary yardsticks for some plants since 1965.

† Profit transfers to the state budget were supposed to reach 74 percent in 1964 and 1965.

‡ In addition so-called general consumption and bonus funds existed, which were only partially used for payment of individual bonuses.

of higher bonus rates for technical engineering employees versus the lower rates of laborers can be diminished. The collective consumption funds, which are created directly within the plants, exercise an influence in the same direction. According to Soviet predictions, their size should increase with time as plant profit attains increasing importance as the source of such funds. According to 1 January 1963 figures, in the U.S.S.R. 2.13 billion rubles were granted from these funds, whereas in 1950 only 367 million rubles were paid out; [102] thus there has been nearly a sixfold increase. Such payments are not distributed to individuals; rather, they are used to provide services for the community (plant collectives, for example) in the form of housing and day-care centers for small children, as well as other social and cultural institutions. The income-leveling tendency of such collective consumption funds comes about because distribution is not according to individual productivity but primarily according to need.

A partial realization of Liberman's proposals could cause a widening inequality of income distribution through internal and interplant differentiation of labor income. A lower proportion of bonuses relative to plant profits available to individuals and, especially, a planned, rapid expansion of the collective consumption funds, however, would in all likelihood largely prevent inequalities of income distribution from growing bigger than can be tolerated from the socio-ethical point of view of the East.

5. SOCIAL COMPENSATION IN THE TRANSITION ECONOMY

Part of social income in the U.S.S.R. is through the constant improvement in health protection and medical care. Both are free of charge for Soviet citizens, although most medicines still have to be purchased by the patients.[103] The question then arises, however, whether the expansion of modern hospitals—which is necessary under present conditions—may be retarded due to the extraordinarily high costs of medical care. However, efforts to increase the number of beds and to equip hospitals with high quality technical instruments are being made.[104]

A large, if not the largest, element of government social policy since approximately 1958 has been the payment of social insurance, aid benefits, and pensions. The funds for the satisfaction of social needs have had a considerable influence upon this. Expenditures for an extensive health system, for educational and cultural projects, and for care of the aged are serviced through the social funds. The volume of payments and allowances from the state budget and from the central funds of enterprises and co-operatives increased correspondingly from the First Five-Year Plan until the end of the 1950s.[105] These services included care by a physician, free tuition for vocational training, full or partial payment for stays in health resorts and spas, social security payments, and subsidies to social security insurance, as well as sustenance stipends for students and allowances for families with many children and for mothers without husbands.

The constant improvement of national education occupies a large area within the framework of social income. Free use of libraries and expansion of the scholarship program for students occupy the focal point. Of special importance is the improvement of housing conditions.[106] The Soviet government is trying, with the help of the collectives and the local soviets, to provide cheaper housing for at least the agricultural population. Modern single- and multiple-family dwellings are considered in this context so that at the beginning of the 1960s there was even an overfulfillment of the planned quota for housing space.[107]

The real wages, previously discussed, in the people's republics of southeast Europe are modified by numerous income components which cannot be directly included in wages.[108] Free health protection, modeled after the Soviet example, has, without doubt, contributed considerably to the decrease in the over-all mortality rate. In Rumania, for instance, it dropped from 21.1 percent in 1932 to 8.7 percent in 1960.[109] The situation is similar in the other southeast European people's republics. Comparatively high expenditures for general welfare, better housing, and old-age protection, for example, has led to progressive collectivization. For Rumania, the state budget since 1951 has contained the following (approximate) expenditures for social and cultural purposes: 4 billion lei in 1951; 6.8 billion lei in 1955; 13.7 billion lei in 1960; and 20.0 billion lei in 1965. The considerable increase in social income in other southeast European people's republics can be roughly gauged from these figures.[110]

In Hungary, in 1955, income not directly related to wages amounted to roughly 73 percent of total actual wages. As a consequence, the consumption fund of the workers employed in collectivized industries was comprised of only 57.6 percent in wages and 42.4 percent in direct allowances.[111] Besides the expenditures paid from the state budget, laborers and white collar workers received additional allowances for plant cafeteria meals, work clothing, and rent from the various enterprise

198

funds. In 1958, these grants actually amounted to an increase of up to 55 percent of actual wages.[112]

Bulgaria and Albania, too, have free medical care, as well as allowances for pre- and post-natal care, health resorts for vacationers, and other social benefits.

Social income in the southeast European people's republics corresponds essentially to that in the U.S.S.R. This also includes regulations for the improvement of working conditions and social insurance. Actual wages are even greater if the quite extensive measures for rapid development of low-cost housing are taken into consideration. Rents for such government-constructed housing average as a rule only 1 to 3 percent of average family income.[113]

Social insurance in East Germany is also quite similar to the U.S.S.R. system. Here too the administration was turned over to labor unions (in 1956). The funds are part of the state budget. Social insurance in East Germany includes—in addition to unemployment insurance—pensions and accident and hospital insurance. Of significance for social insurance is the relatively large number of persons insured. Self-employed persons who hire more than five workers, clergymen, and members of religious orders are exempt from the insurance; also exempt are spouses who work for the other partner without compensation, as well as persons who work only occasionally and whose work does not constitute the main source of their livelihood.[114]

The most essential characteristic of this social insurance—aside from the principle of social care which characterizes it—is that it is largely governed by requirements defined in the national economic plan. Consequently, services still serve the interests of the state and are less intensively oriented toward the needs of the individual; thus they are used as a tool of economic policy.[115]

At present, social insurance in East Germany also differs from that of the Soviet Union in its method of collecting dues. In the former, laborers and white collar employees (including employees of the public agencies who replaced civil servants) [116] pay their contributions in the traditional manner. In the U.S.S.R., however, social insurance is entirely financed from contributions by industry, government agencies, and other employers. However, the social insurance system in East Germany is, in principle, little by little approaching the Soviet method. Part of this arises from the varying degrees of service rendered by social insurance in which the special abilities of the insured are of prime consideration. Such peculiarities tend to materially influence care for the aged.[117]

199

In Poland too, as in the other people's republics, the basis of social insurance is the principle of social care. As in the U.S.S.R., the employer alone (the state) pays the social insurance for incapacity due to age, illness or disability; social insurance involves no direct costs for citizens.[118] Since 1955, the organization of social insurance has been in part the responsibility of labor unions. However, there are plans to replace this arrangement with an administration organized according to occupational branches.

The social insurance system of Czechoslovakia can be traced back to the 1930s.[119] Even then Czechoslovakia already had good medical institutions. The costs of accident, health, and old-age insurance were borne jointly by employee and employer. After the events of February 1948, individual branches of the social insurance system were nationalized. Then, in 1951, the whole system was placed in the hands of unions. With this, the system which the U.S.S.R. had instituted in 1932 was introduced in Czechoslovakia. Services, too, do not lag behind those in the U.S.S.R.; in fact, medicines are free. Loss of pay because of pregnancy is fully reimbursed and in Czechoslovakia is paid for eighteen weeks. All costs of social insurance are, following the Soviet example, borne by the employer, which means with increasing collectivization and nationalization of industry they are paid by the state.

The People's Republic of China has for some years now attempted to realize the goal of corrective justice partly by way of people's communes, for which they have been criticized by the Soviet ideologists. This approach to a communistic society by the Chinese has become one of the most important points in the Sino-Soviet conflict. In essence this is a dispute over power, about economic questions of a quite general nature, and about the speed of revolutionary progress inside the country. In the final analysis the pros and cons of the people's communes can essentially be traced back to ideological differences.[120]

The program of people's communes encompasses, among other things, medical care, old-age pensions, cafeterias, nurseries, and better housing.[121] Many of these measures are still in their infancy. The problem seems to be the basically different approach to economic policy by the Chinese; they believe their program will enable them to attain the communist goal more rapidly than any state with a Soviet-type economy.

Only one type of compensation is supposed to exist in the final communist state: corrective justice, hopefully in conjunction with compensation according to the principle "each according to his needs." However, as long as the material prerequisites for this distribution principle do

200

not exist during the transition phase of socialism, other yardsticks are still used. The concrete distribution policies, therefore, are directed more toward increased economic growth than toward egalitarian distribution of income.[122] * On the one hand, material incentives are created to increase production and over-all economic performance, for example, by means of wage differentiation among various industries or bonuses for plant and labor productivity.[123] † Also, the reduction of income disparity between laborers and white collar employees serves primarily to stimulate productivity. On the other hand, existing and developing income differences are reduced through tax policies and deliberate channeling of plant profits by the state, as well as by expansion of collective consumption funds.

The goal of equal distribution of income has not been abandoned. The latest developments in income distribution policies suggest that income based on productivity will continue to be viewed as necessary for economic growth. At the same time, the magnitude of income differences is—according to the principle of corrective justice—to be kept as low as possible.

* Realization of the goal: rapid economic growth coupled simultaneously with optimal equality of income distribution.

† A uniformity in the granting of bonuses is emphatically rejected.

PART FOUR

Socio-Philosophical Perspectives

XIV. WESTERN INDIVIDUALISM

1. IDEAL LIBERALISM

Although a discussion of Eastern social philosophy can be based on an officially accepted doctrine, this is impossible in the case of the West,[1] * where various types of socialism, products of Western thinking, appear side by side with liberalism. Nevertheless, classic liberal individualism is the basic principle of all the different socio-economic theories in Western countries. This Western "pluralism" is itself the expression of an individualistic blueprint. Just as in the East, the image of economic and social forms is determined in the West by the collaboration of tempering tendencies of the strict ideal type and preservation of the basic position.

The following analysis presumes that economic man stands at the border between subjective decisions and objective forces, between subjective interpretation and objective facts.[2]

Although capitalism did not develop in the way predicted by Marx and his successors, it has definitely produced a social pattern which, in some respects, is rather close to the original pure type and, in others, is opposed to it. This new society is described with terms such as "social ethos," "secondary systems," "leveling," "organization man," and "mere role playing." Such categories have a somewhat critical undertone; the present time is characterized as fraught with risks and dangers.[3]

* The present analysis refers to a variety of trends among apparently opposing theories.

The West does not possess an integrated and allegedly redeeming social philosophy and practice. Nevertheless, out of the wealth of analyses and suggestions a more or less unified hypothesis may be developed. One thing is clear, however: such a hypothesis cannot be developed by following Marxist doctrine, which would mean embracing the utopianism of the nineteenth century. It is more likely that liberalism can explain the motives and forces of Western progress.[4] Probably, however, neither of these ideologies is sufficient for our purposes; rather we must turn to socio-philosophical thought as it relates to the problems of our time. Such a hypothesis must overcome the defects of older concepts and yet preserve the insights derived from them. So far such a hypothesis has not been developed; although some signs point to its possibility in the future,[5] an integrated ideology is not yet feasible.

Adam Smith's liberal social philosophy shaped the budding industrial society of private enterprise. Even many central features of the opposing Marxist philosophy are based on liberalism.[6] Economic and technological developments in big business and capitalist society and increasingly monopolized markets have led to an industrial structure in which the private entrepreneur plays only a secondary role as owner.[7] With the changed situation and new problems, hardly anyone today adopts liberalism in its ideal type. Yet von Mises, Hayek, Lord Robbins, and others—representatives of an extremely strict liberalism—still consider the present-day economy entirely or at least highly determined by private initiative.[8] The Mont Pelerin Society, an association of liberal Western political economists, was of major influence after World War II in its deliberations on important economic problems and decisions in the East and West.

Even during Smith's lifetime, liberal thinking, a descendant of French physiocracy, invaded the European continent, and its first powerful consequences were seen in the American Declaration of Independence, which in turn influenced the program of the French Revolution. In doing so, it was, however, gravely changed, since the "communist fiction" (Myrdal)—the principle of equality inherent in liberalism—came to the fore. This means that Anglo-Saxon liberalism was joined or opposed by another version of democracy.[9] Following Rousseau and wavering between anarchy and the totalitarian idea of equality, the concept thus differed greatly from the English view. In Great Britain and the United States the original type of liberalism always remained predominant.[10] Only in the last decades, influenced by the world depression and its effects, did it yield to a new social structure and to different concepts of man.[11]

As far as economic philosophy is concerned, another factor was important: the rise of national republics, a result of liberalism.[12] On the one hand, the policy of national sovereignty has led to an intensification of capitalist expansion; on the other hand, nationalism promoted the state's influence in the economy and at the same time blocked development of freer international economic competition. The state was influenced by society, and vice versa. In addition to what has been said so far, this implies that politics increasingly became the battlefield of economic and social interests.

For some time, liberalism in its ideal form was the historically justified, objective, and progressive doctrine of a new epoch.[13] But because of the increasing complexity of economic activity and the decline of competition without substitution of over-all planning, liberalism has changed into a merely academic model instead. It is true that, in the West, it still determines the economic-political concepts to a great extent. In the West the actual competing concepts are, on the one hand, the attempt to re-establish small business enterprises and, at the other extreme, an economic philosophy which does not advocate liberalism but rather democratic socialism. The latter aims at having all people share in production and distribution. There are many variations, reaching from all-out competition to socialization of basic industries. In spite of such differences, the standard Western concepts share the most important element in the philosophy of liberalism; namely, the belief in the pre-eminence of the individual in the structure and goals of society.

Organic views, influenced by romanticism, have become less predominant. In the modern welfare state and in Catholic social doctrine the superiority of the individual has become rather restricted.[14] It is true that many schools have stressed the importance of the "thou" and "we" as the root of all humanity, as against the "I" or "I-thou" relationship. But all of this remains within the range of Smith's ethics of sympathy.

The individual is never entirely absorbed by a collective concept like folk, state, fatherland, or class. He never loses his roots entirely by becoming a member of one of these. We may therefore correctly see in Western individualism the antithesis of Eastern Marxist anthropology,[15] which sees man primarily as a member of a species, in consequence of which private property becomes the very root of self-alienation.

In Soviet thinking, freedom means adjustment to the laws of history as established by the Party,[16] whereas Western anthropology insists that it always refers to freedom of the individual. Whether motives are supplied from the outside or are innate in all men, the source of all decisions made by the individual must be found in his own self, although

207

motives which thus emanate from the individual may also relate to the group.[17]

2. PLURALISM

In spite of the significance of these philosophical-anthropological principles and the need to cling to them, the actual structure of Western economics has changed to a degree that an apology of classical liberalism, presented with Smithian optimism, must seem strange as an ideology today.[18] In the course of the past decades small enterprises have been replaced by large corporations. The planning of private production and the molding of demand have injected calculated determination into the formerly free market.[19] The "guardian state" has become an institution that seldom opposes a political interest.[20] Instead we have a wealth of desires and demands made by competing interests of employers and employees.[21] The individual, theoretically the pillar of society, is gradually being pushed out by group interests.[22]

It is true that Marx's prediction of an intensification of class conflict did not come true. But the advent of the opposite situation led to new and as yet unsolved problems, which, incidentally, Soviet society must also face.[23] Private property loses its influence. The business crises pointed out by Marx have been analyzed as to their causes and have been minimized through the application of countercyclical measures. The imperialism described by Lenin was turned into foreign aid.[24] The Great Depression led to Roosevelt's New Deal. J. M. Keynes authored methods of increasing employment for a capitalist society. The free market was replaced by a "social" market economy, more or less strongly influenced by the state.[25] The question of how the individual can fulfill himself in an industrial world becomes more and more pressing.[26]

An essential feature of the new situation is its ambiguity. This is seen, for instance, in the contrast of empirical sociology and social criticism. Some observers see society as a harmoniously balanced structure, ruled by democratic equality. To others it is a wrestling ground of self-alienated men, no longer able to find a dignified place between highly specialized production and the demand of consumers. No unified picture can be obtained by analyzing the Western social consciousness and situation. It is dispersed—from class consciousness to the hectic striving for social prestige, and even contains major elements of rigid social adjustment in a merely functional hierarchy.[27] This in turn is opposed by the increasing power of managers and of experts who have become influential because of their scientific training.

Critical analysis is usually followed by good advice, ranging from the extremes of building man's democratic and social consciousness, on the one hand, to thorough institutional reform of the system, on the other. Since analysts have become specialists, perspectives of economics, sociology, and political science are only rarely viewed together, and thus we find side by side, without any connection, research concerning interest, rent, wages, markets, monopoly, social role structure, and democratic procedure.

The present situation may be generally characterized as Western man's satisfaction with economic and social accomplishments. At the same time, however, he is somehow displeased with a merely formal democracy, on which the future growth of his welfare depends.[28] * The feeling of insecurity is often so strong that we occasionally hear the dangerous demand for an "idea" for the West.[29] This again is countered by the defense that pluralism is the arena of freedom.[30] † Sober, pacifying voices speak of the possibility of shaping one's personality according to the demands of our times, so that the contradictory aspects of the economic and social structure may be balanced.

While the East clings to a theory of history, sociology, and economics which has become doctrinaire and partly ideological, Western discussion covers the entire area of possible aspects of social order. All that the Western concepts share is their more or less anti-Marxist propensity. Besides their individualistic and anti-Marxist character, most forms of Western social philosophy have in common real or alleged solutions.[31] There is, for instance, much discussion about Tocqueville's antinomy of freedom and equality;[32] of purely economic and social aims of the economic system; and of the contrast of what is historically conditioned and what is timelessly valid in ethics and human nature. Further emphasis must be placed upon the central problems of the relationship of the individual to society and of mass society to individual representation. Finally, there is the alleged dilemma of a discrepancy between the benefits of the technological age (and the striving for it) and the lack of personality growth in modern man.

A. Historical Sketch

As far as social philosophy and economic policy are concerned, classical liberalism is the most important common root both of today's West-

* Liberalism rightly sees the favorable development of the welfare-oriented society as a result of liberal economics.
† Pluralism here means a variety of socio-philosophical systems.

ern neoliberalism, which is based solely on the idea of freedom, and of Marxist socialism.[33] Both were founded on English liberalism.[34] * However, the development of liberalism in the West, following the line of an ideally complete freedom of production, soon showed that the other element of classical teaching was missing, namely, the one Smith had optimistically tied in with freedom. This was wage distribution proportionate to the value of labor and therefore "just" and equal opportunity for all workers—an extremely important element of free competition. This latter element, which was revolutionary and progressive, was adopted by and became the theme of French and English socialism.[35] † But it also became a source of Marx's thought. In this view, Western neoclassicism and Eastern Bolshevism are two offsprings of classical liberalism itself.

The essential feature of the Western economic and social order is to be found in the play of trial and error, corresponding to an Anglo-Saxon attitude of compromise; its tools being drawn from the reform capitalism presently associated with Keynes.[36] At the same time its practices—based on a classic liberal market economy, but in its result rather a "social" one—tend to strengthen that economic and social structure which is known as modern industrial society.[37] ‡ Therefore social philosophers who are concerned with problems of humanity are concerned with economic problems too.

Keynes's general theory of employment, particularly his explanation of business cycles and crises, is directed toward anticipating or preventing, through measures taken by the state, the negative consequences of the capitalist mechanism. Here, too, the goal is a state dedicated to the general welfare of its people, but without crises.[38] Keynes saw fluctuations in investment as the basic cause of crises. He pointed out that a new equilibrium comes about with unemployment.[39] Like Marx, Keynes maintained that crises were unavoidable consequences of unlimited laissez faire. But in his case this led to the opposite result: economic and political stabilization of capitalism instead of communistic revolution.[40]

Keynes's socio-philosophical attitude considers man as an individual whose main goal in the economy is to increase his income as much as

---

* We do not deny that many ideas in economics are of different origins, but in view of the dominant East-West conflict of today, they are merely secondary variations of the basic theme.

† For this reason Myrdal believes liberalism itself to have split into conservative and social-revolutionary liberalism.

‡ The East rejects attempts to interpret its problems as phenomena connected with an industrial society.

possible. Such an individual becomes aware of the dangers of classical liberalism. He must see to it that, by systematic planning for maximum employment, the income of the entire economy, as well as his own, becomes as high and as stable as possible, in order to further improve human life.[41] Scholars are undecided as to whether Keynes's teaching merely reflects the particular anxiety of the Great Depression or whether it is a theory valid for all times.[42] The author himself was optimistic as far as the future is concerned and saw in his doctrine a description of forthcoming development.[43] Labor socialists regard him as an advocate of socialistic practices,[44] although he interpreted his "liberal" position as a progressive synthesis between the two out-dated concepts of a laissez-faire capitalism and Marxism.[45]

Whereas Keynes's thinking was guided by the problems of creating income, theoreticians of welfare economics turned to questions concerning distribution of income. No longer is size of the social product the yardstick of national welfare but rather its socio-economic and cultural dividend, which is conceived as the sum total of well-being of all individuals. Such a naive philosophical-anthropological starting point confronts welfare theory with the difficult problem of measuring individual utility.

Pigou applied the principle of marginalism to the entire economy.[46] His definition of welfare maximization was a situation in which all individuals enjoy the maximum benefit. But here a subjective element is introduced. Ultimately, such a concept is identical with equal income for all. Neither Pigou nor Keynes adopts an independent socio-philosophical position. The basis of that doctrine is still the utilitarian principle of the "greatest good for the greatest number," and the sole modernization lies in the fact that "all" replaces "the greatest number."

Although "maximum benefit" is not measurable, the possibility of calculating the national welfare is somehow taken for granted. Behind it all is the tacit assumption that what individuals are interested in is the greatest benefit to be derived from the largest income available for free and private consumption. There is no longer any talk of man possibly preferring other aims. In the thinking of these economists, therefore, the two levels of welfare economics—the quantitative one, unattached to values, and the ethical one—are integrated to a high degree.[47]

When Europe emerged from World War I, in which excessive nationalism had spent its strength, striving for greatness seemed a disappointment. Social philosophy received a complex and partly confused legacy.[48] Up to that time, the rise of the socialist movement had really only reflected the evolutionary rise of internationally minded workers.[49]

Now it was suddenly split up into the opposing lines of a Marxist-radical movement and a social-democratic one.[50]

On the social-theoretical level the aimlessness of Western economic nonchalance manifested itself in many contradictory social doctrines. There was an irrational trend in the philosophy of life toward the dissolution of self in history. The defenders of pluralism were opposed to a romantic, "folkish" idea of the whole. Positivistic empiricism, in rejecting values, was accused of being a reactionary imitation of reality. Finally, we must consider the idealistic analyses and anthropological interests which, by offering new definitions, try to resolve the problem of man's humanity.

The political economy of progressive industrialization generated two non-classical schools, the historical school and Marxian socialism. From a philosophical point of view, the other tendencies are variations of the market principles of classicism, which increasingly developed into often unrealistic, yet exact patterns of thought. American institutionalism was better prepared to deal with the complexity and the modern structure of economic life.[51] The institutionalism in turn ended in a functionalism which features the principle of balanced growth.

Present-day problems—they are social rather than economic—developed with the rise of macro-economic and structural-functional views. Only here does economics radically forsake the classical viewpoint. It sees the individual as a statistical unit, a quantity irrelevant in itself, living in an expanding maze of factors, which are complex and which tend toward equilibrium. Such a structural theory becomes the common soil for liberalism and social democracy, as is evident in Keynesian thinking.[52]

Sociology (which, judging by its origins, ought to be connected with the fourth estate and not with the third) became disillusioned with the belief in progress and developed extreme theories such as, for instance, those connected with social Darwinism. Eventually it branched off into two directions, the structural-functional theory of equilibrium and social criticism, the latter preserving the displeasure with loss of humanity caused by modern developments.[53] Gradually feeling its way carefully and after many false starts, the two paths remerged to form a unified theory of the present.[54] After 1945, in the West, the socio-philosophical debate on economic systems therefore became a presentation of variations of a social structure and of social problems based on the model of the United States.

212

B. Social Doctrines

At present, in broad perspective and neglecting national particularities, neoliberalism, economic socialism, and Catholic social teaching are in the foreground, while organic thinking has lost much of its significance. Social economics and welfare economics are merely special cases of these trends.

In general terms, the situation may be described as a polarity between an analysis which confirms the present-day state of things and a consciousness of crisis. We see a confrontation of a sociology based on the concept of equilibrium, offering the image of a society which functions without conflicts, and a strict criticism of society, which judges the world with the yardstick of freedom and equality.[55] A somewhat similar confrontation may be found in the philosophical foundation of economic theory, where a structural-functional theory of equilibrium faces a socialistic will to reform. Opposing both of these tendencies, Catholic social teaching stresses a social organism which encourages community. Below only those problems of today's social philosophy which have to do with economic questions are discussed.[56] *

Orthodox proponents of neoliberalism and of institutional or "establishment liberalism" seemed to assume that the classic liberal axiom, which is basically true, had only been changed for the worse by all subsequent "reforms." Consequently they usually rejected change.[57] With the assertion that "free competition" is highly effective, the basic liberal position is therefore defended against socialist objections. A criticism based on economics is countered with philosophical allusions to the meaning of freedom.[58] † Therefore, the neoliberals follow loyally the tenets of private property and unlimited competition. But this theory has become questionable because of the separation of ownership and management in socialized industry. The same effect is achieved in the West by the increase in the number of wage earners with little property [59] and the increasing influence of organizations.[60] Such changes call for a rigid control of trusts and other measures aiming at the restoration of free market conditions that fit the model. The existence of innumerable impediments is admitted, and yet it is maintained that the capitalistic "principle" is dominant.[61] For all that, people recognized

* Nevertheless we must not neglect the connection with the corresponding political-philosophical concepts.

† Thus some say that restriction of freedom is too high a price to pay for greater "justice" in distribution.

213

that the belief in the power of market mechanics, founded in Christian ethics, failed in classical liberalism. This in turn led to the demand for a strong, regulatory state to safeguard fair competiton.[62]

The liberal view maintains that the West is not in need of a "new idea" but of the rebirth of basic liberal thought.[63] Following this, the natural order will lead to an equilibrium, making social policy all but superfluous.[64] This, however, must be considered mere theory. The socio-philosophical basis of neoliberalism suffers from a fundamental difficulty. It speaks of classical economic freedom, identifies this with business risk, and identifies the latter in turn with human freedom. The "ideal" way means private economic initiative directed toward personal profit-seeking in competition with others. But if liberalism is not to continue with only the illusion of a restoration, it must look at personal autonomy from the viewpoint of an economic system which is characterized by mutual dependence and responsibility that goes beyond the individual.[65]

Taking our departure from the merely personal-ethical aspect and taking this one-sided ideal as the yardstick, we can easily see it as being no less absolute in its demands than communism. It demands complete individual freedom, while communism demands complete solidarity of men. Both of these are apparently required only in initial stages of development. Abstract consideration of the consequences of unlimited realization of the two would show their utter failure. Communism, forcibly pursued and practiced, leads to totalitarianism. On the other hand, uncompromising liberalism would end, not in a just equilibrium, but in exploitation of profit opportunities and in capital accumulation by a few individuals.[66] The modern development of liberalism has taken two separate paths. One is solely interested in profit and private consumption, and the other—the societal one—is ruled by complete dependence on an anonymous market. The economic sphere is strictly separated from the political one, where formal democracy is actually carried out by interest groups.[67]

Liberal thinkers readily admit that this economic system does not aim at an ideal humanity. They look upon certain deficiencies in the system as unavoidable, such as inequalities in the distribution of income and opportunities as well as property. But this is not too high a price to pay for freedom in production.[68] Thus economic freedom, which according to Smith was allegedly the best means for attaining social goals,[69] became an end in itself and the ultimate ethical goal of human action.[70] But neither the abstract pattern nor its abstract refutation have much to do with the facts of the present time. Rather, the complex and

214

ambivalent structure of society in the second half of the twentieth century seems to tend toward a balancing of conflicting ideologies.[71] After all, the economic freedom recommended by classical liberalism was not supposed to serve particular class interests and private advantages but rather to promote general welfare. Liberalism was a philosophical movement, whose political concern coincided with the advance of the doctrine of free trade advocated in the eighteenth century.

The "establishment liberalism" of the period following World War II was realized in the theory and practice of a "social market economy," which is often influenced by state intervention regulated by socio-political considerations. Its aim is general welfare and policies favoring the middle class. In the theoretical foundation of such an economy, the state does not have to make free competition possible, but, having the general welfare in mind, it must be a guardian and a guide, and this allows for a restriction of competition.[72] From this emerged a reformed capitalism, which leaves so much competition and incentive unimpeded that productivity increases. This type of capitalism also added so many corrective measures that broader distribution of the consumer goods weakened the idea of a socialist revolution.[73]

Today's socio-democratic philosophy, too, is based on the same image of man.[74] Like liberalism, it sees in man a primarily autonomous individual, and not, as Marxism does, a member of a species.[75] However, social democracy pushed into the foreground the idea of the solidarity of men which had originally been part of Smith's ethics of sympathy but which was disregarded later on. Herein lies its difference from liberalism, to whose representatives the future opportunities of the West lie in a social partnership of well-trained and politically interested men. In this case the individual is expected to share in decisions concerning social, economic, and political relations of the group.[76] The corresponding economic programs run all the way from the idea of a more strictly socialized market economy to that of economic socialism. The latter goes very far in the establishment of a welfare state,[77] for it also includes state control and an all-embracing planned economy.[78]

There are few Marxist elements left in such a structure.[79] The interest in collective control of the economy is seen in a striving toward socialization of basic or "key" industries.[80] * The state is not to be abolished [81] and revolution is rejected. Nor are there any communist features in the way democratic socialism thinks of man. It adheres rather to individualism, with some traits of existentialism.[82]

* In Germany, there are differences of opinion between a "right-wing" SPD and the trade unions.

Starting with its first and modern declaration, the *Rerum Novarum* of 1891, the Catholic Church's philosophy of society and economics adopted a moderate position between socialism and capitalism,[83] although it opposed the temporal immanence of the human image inherent in either view. From the beginning it maintained that the immanent philosophy of liberalism absolutizes economics. Without denying economics its separate realm of affairs, it maintained that it was not an end in itself. Most important it could not dictate the ultimate aim and the supreme value of human action in general.[84]

According to that doctrine, the goal of an economy is the material and spiritual civilization of all men.[85] It was pointed out that, above all, liberal capitalism has not yet been able to solve the problem of distribution satisfactorily. The opinion that the free play of economic forces leads to harmony of human interests and the best possible well-being for the greatest number is declared to be unrealistic.[86] In reality, it was said, the free market mechanism led to a monopolization of the economy and thus defeated its own purposes.

Therefore the social teaching of Catholicism affirms the social politics of the state, albeit on a subsidiary basis.[87] This shows clearly what distinguishes it from socialism. Declaring capitalism to be inhuman does not justify a socialistic change in the state of affairs. Here, too, the economy is left to private initiative, since the economy is neither a state institution nor a social relationship.[88] The "natural claim" to private property is adhered to without limitation, although in turn it is subordinated to extreme social need for output.[89] Moreover, where public welfare demands it, "public property" is admitted. There is an interplay between justification of competition as a means for increased productivity and the criticism of the faulty distribution of the social product.[90]

In this sage eclecticism the social teachings of Catholicism come increasingly close, on the one hand, to welfare economics and, on the other, to the most recent approaches taken by democratic socialism. For example, there are suggestions for a wider distribution of property and a greater share for the workers in the ownership and control of industry —in effect, a fair wage and a share in management.[91] From this, the idea of an independent professional organization has been suggested, which would abolish differences between capital and labor, management and the working class, and would lead to social solidarity, replacing the plurality of interest groups. Here "the common cause" in organic arrangement is the thesis and goal of the common effort.[92]

3. THE MARKET ECONOMY

Basic conceptions of the individual have also greatly influenced the economic realm in the West. These dominate not only the intrinsic liberal ideas in economic theory and policy but also more socialistically colored thought.[93] Around the middle of the twentieth century there was an increasing tendency toward group individualism and a pluralistic societal structure with rather collectivist inclinations. Economic freedom is therefore the basis of economic conceptions in the West. Here classical liberal ideas of the early nineteenth century have been preserved to a large degree. This is valid for economic policy and even more so for the construction of scientifically planned, theoretical models. Nevertheless, under the influence of changes in the real world and the abundantly proven unreality of its assumptions, the original purity of the economic model of liberalism has undergone many metamorpheses. They point to the stressed situation in which, in his economic activity, the individual feels himself torn between unlimited personal responsibility and social restraint. Modern economic programs try to overcome these stresses by a compromise based on social philosophy. Indeed, there have been more or less profound changes in the organization of Western economics.

At the same time, modern technical and organizational requisites in the economy have increased in significance. Nevertheless, reviewing the differences in socio-philosophical ideas between the East and West, we clearly recognize peculiarities and boundary lines in their economic systems. In the West we still see a tendency toward the principle of economic freedom.

A. Individual Needs

An important expression of that principle is the preference given the satisfaction of individual needs, which are seldom restricted by the state.[94] Therefore the economic theory of the West is mostly based on the individual, whose physical existence must be guaranteed, since this is the very purpose of the economy. The satisfaction of needs is thus always connected with the individual organism. This concept survives even under the modern conditions of higher living standards when such a task is less immediately visible. Therefore individual needs are fundamentally considered as taking precedence over all types of collective needs, and they are the sole basis for determining the common good. In

217

Western economic theory, public institutions are thought to derive their function from the individuals who support them. Accordingly, from the point of view of logic, the concept of collective need is not on the same level with individual need. If the latter is directly associated with the proper task of the economy, the former falls rather in the sphere of a purposeful organization of the economy. The foundations of fiscal theory for the activities of the state and the terms which even modern fiscal theory applies to such activities show the derived nature of collective needs.[95]

However, Western fiscal theories are based on views other than the one that social institutions are an imposition on the product (even if only at the bidding of the individuals in society after careful weighing of their utility). Particularly the secondary role of collective action is firmly anchored in broader economic models which serve as the foundation of economic policies. From the main goal mentioned above—to enable and to secure human existence—they try to create rational systems for the realization of these aims. Herein the consumer occupies a basic role and all systems take him into consideration.[96]

The overwhelming importance of the individual and his personal needs and wishes becomes even clearer if we try to set up a well-formulated goal for such models of economic policy so that, for instance, society can satisfy its needs through the rational shaping of the economy. For decades this has indeed been attempted with theories of welfare economics. Definitions of what is best for society must always go back to the concept of individual utility and have failed because of the impossibility of making interpersonal comparisons of utility. Chief among the attempts to deal with this field are theories of marginal utility, with their purely subjective tendencies.[97] They find an emphatic and theoretically formulated, as well as allegedly valueless, expression in the thesis that the shaping of the economy must be subordinated to consumer sovereignty.

The basis for such a dominant economic position of the individual and his needs, which must be cared for and satisfied, is his personal achievement in the economy and the income deriving from it. Here, too, we find ideas rooted in individualism. Taking the principle of distribution into consideration—it will be considered later in connection with socio-ethical aspects—such ideas may be rephrased "to each according to his output." [98] Theoretically, freedom of individual choice in consumption is only limited by personal income and the share allocated to social institutions which are necessary for technical or organizational reasons. Except for romantic rather than practical ideas, Western con-

218

cepts mostly did away with any further social obligations of the individual. Only in the last decades have some changes been made, and these originate in a critical investigation of actual results of an economic model based on such a high degree of individualism.[99] *

Finally, there is a connection between freedom in the use of income —seen in unlimited individual choice and a limited obligation concerning societal demands—and the division of one's income between spending and saving. Of course, the resulting determination of the time horizon of the economic activity is restricted. Even in classical liberal economics the individual was subject to the influence of the credit system, which plays an equally essential role in determining savings and investments as a whole. But even more important is the fact that a scientifically structured extension of the time horizon, by way of government economic policies (that is, a social investment plan) is not considered meaningful, and efforts in that direction are felt as a disturbance of the economic equilibrium based on individual decisions. Therefore economic development, recently appearing in the foreground as a problem of the state, was liberalized and left to the unplanned interplay of individuals.

Hand in hand with the progress of industrial economic systems, problems arose which led to restrictions in the free satisfaction of individual needs and which threw doubt on the allegedly sovereign character of individual decisions. However, an abstract theory of economics will not completely clarify such needs. Particularly, where the origin and foundation of economic activity are concerned, parrot-like statements cover up the psychological problem. Here we see that, under the influence of advertising and similar agents, the supposedly efficient freedom of the consumer is only a formal one, since he is constantly influenced in his economic decisions from the outside.[100] There is also a discrepancy between the alleged isolation of the individual—systematized in economic theory—and reality, once we take the increasing uniformity of economic life into consideration.[101] Striving for social prestige and similar motives reveal the social ties of the individual and also influence the decisions concerning use or non-use of his income, since in the latter case his standing in the community may deteriorate.[102]

Although not taken into account by pure individualism, the dual nature of man, even where his economic activity is concerned, is a mixture of many elements which originate in economic situations.[103] Thus there is frequently a close connection between sales policies of produc-

* This applies particularly to common responsibility as a foundation of modern social policy.

ers and the technological conditions under which they produce. Where competition forces the introduction of modern production methods that lead to greater output, equally modern methods must be used to sell the product and to make the job of management profitable. The resulting influence on the attitude of the consumer can thus only be considered a consequence of a technical situation. This is quite different from using advertising to attain a monopoly position.[104]

Other limitations on an individual's free disposition of his economic resources and on his choices come from the effort to offset the functional failures of the liberal economic system which have been generated by industrial conditions. In their firmly based theories Keynes and his followers have found causes for these failures. From them they have drawn conclusions regarding cycles and crises in the case of major economic disorganization. Such phenomena threaten the individual's economic and even his physical existence. They may be countered by policies from above, which lead also, however, to more or less major interference in the private sphere. An example of this interference is taxation, which means a loss of income.[105] On an economic basis, neoliberalism emphasizes a similar influence on the economy where there is a channeling of private interests and a corresponding restriction of individual liberty. Here too there is competition of the private interests of individuals; there is also co-ordination of enlightened self-interest, but not consciously. It is maintained and realized through a better insight into collective institutions, even against the will of those involved if necessary. Yet we must remember that even such deviations from the classical individualistic position are achieved in the interest of the individuals who form society. They do not arise with the imposition of aims or interests of an autonomous "society as a person," represented through collective organs.

B. Private Initiative

The Western economic constitutions which have grown from liberal soil insure the individual's freedom to choose his occupation according to his inclination and abilities. Everyone shall, on his own responsibility, work without restriction in the occupation he has selected, or change it by his own free will. This also includes the right to work wherever he wishes to. The abolition of the feudal system and of the obligation to belong to a guild (accomplished with the development of bourgeois economy) were necessary steps toward the realization of such goals. The principle of complete freedom of action had its greatest influence upon

220

those who were considered the real bearers of liberalism, the bourgeois entrepreneurs.[106] The role they took over after mercantilism disappeared is still central in the economic order in the West.

In economic theory, the socio-philosophical importance of the entrepreneurs in the economy was diminished in order to make room for a more functional view. Nevertheless we must see this move as, first of all, not a purposeful decentralization of economic decisions but rather an essential step toward human liberty.[107] At the same time, the special conditions for realization of that liberty require it to serve economic purposes. Since decisions depend on the possibility of making a profit and on the need for efficient use of the available means and methods of production, they are also meant to satisfy the needs of the greatest number.[108] The thesis of optimal self-regulation of private enterprise connects here the emphasis on economic freedom as a meta-economic demand with the strictly economic task of organizing that process in the best way possible.

A mutual relationship of these two aspects has made it possible for the economy to be based on free competition without deliberate co-ordination by a central institution. Western economies are therefore characterized by theories concerning the market, in which there is a more or less instinctive, positivistic identification of the privately organized economy and an ideal of maximum welfare. Indeed, such ideas in the specific area of economics are benefited by the problems created by the conscious co-ordination of many economically relevant factors and, on the other hand, by the necessary competition among dependent enterprises. So far there is no convincing argument, no proof for abolition of either the co-ordinating function of the market or of the incentive to compete.[109] The various related factors lead to a great number of problems, which cannot be fully solved, not even with computers or planning concepts based on cybernetics. From the point of view of economics, enterpreneurs on the free market must favor decentralized management; this is necessary for rational use of productive factors. Recently such views have been widely supported by economic reorganization in the highly centralized system of planning and guidance in the U.S.S.R. and in the "people's republics" that are modeled after it.[110] After Stalin's death such experiments have dealt with the problem of "centralization or decentralization of economic organization," and the decision has been in favor of Western market methods. Here is a vast formal equality of aims that is remarkable.

In view of this fact the question arises as to whether we understand the problem properly by identifying, in the West, the decentralization of

221

decisions and market co-ordination with free enterprise. In the East we see at least the attempt to evade the ultimate conclusion and to distribute authority without resorting to private enterprise, as is considered ideal in the West. In this case the solution would lie in management directed by the employees. Western critics of the market system, sometimes referring to the trend toward the entrepreneur-manager type of organization (a tendency which exists anyhow), have sketched similar blueprints of economic systems which have more or less strong authoritarian overtones.[111] Usually their primary aim is the dissolution of the predominant identification of a rational, decentralized economic system with private enterprise. Under the influence of such theories, extensive similarity has thus been achieved for these hypothetical economies. The original socio-ethical foundation of private enterprise as an arena of human freedom has here become secondary to the instrumentalization of the economic order, which is measured solely by the yardstick of purposefulness and greatest output.[112] But even such considerations often contain a meta-economic core, although this is not always emphasized.

When meeting such arguments, the defenders of unlimited free enterprise usually seek to support their arguments with a description of the function of the entrepreneur as defined by Schumpeter. The possibility of making a profit and taking a risk is considered superior to management on a socialized base.[113] Although an over-all economic dynamics can develop without entrepreneurs, they argue that in practice there is greater flexibility and incentive under private enterprise.

Nevertheless, even the modern market economy in the West is characterized by many restrictions on free enterprise. Such restrictions have to do with the discrepancies between the ideal form and the reality of an economy left to itself. Government intervention may arise from the effort to prevent an increase in and an exploitation of market power gained by limiting or eliminating competition. The influence monopolistic or oligopolistic market factors have on the distribution of income and the availability of goods and services is often considered detrimental to the economy as a whole.[114] As early as the nineteenth century, the obvious discrepancy between such phenomena and the acceptance of classical economic doctrine led to corrective legislation. Such measures were taken in the United States in particular where, traditionally, free enterprise has seldom been restricted. Eventually these measures were also applied to many other institutions in the West. The use of the state to secure free competition in private enterprise is therefore an important part of neoliberal economic policy, which emphasizes private enterprise as an essential element, whether the point of view is an economic or a socio-philosophical one.

While such intervention in the market deals mostly with the undesirable side effects of unlimited free enterprise, other interference is based on the experiences of the Great Depression in the thirties. On the basis of the insights made then and also of Keynes's theories, securing economic stability and proper growth is increasingly felt to be a public concern.[115] In order to do this a certain measure of government planning must be taken in stride. With its help, defects which arise under the influence of societal changes and technical development and which impede smooth and steady economic growth will be counteracted.[116] * This might apply to measures in harmony with the market, such as tax policy, and to direct intervention in enterprise. Thus controls on prohibition of investment might result. We should remember the growing activity of international institutions and also the government's power of "moral suasion." On the Western market, the free play of private enterprise thus becomes more and more restricted, and we see the emphasis on long-term guidance of the economy as the common task of economic policy and private initiative. This new outlook is clearly expressed in the concept of a social market economy. Its main element is a social tightening of free initiative and, particularly within the frame of economic and social policy data, a restriction of enterprises which affect the entire economy. Here the influence of the state leads to a promotion of the original socio-philosophical concepts.[117]

These ideas must be guided by the ideal of equality and justice and at the same time they should improve the practicality of the system by offsetting the imbalance which results from the economic process. Here we must take the cumulative effect into consideration, which, in an increasingly dynamic economy, is the consequence of the power of capital and technology. The classical concept notwithstanding, an advantage once attained will lead to more advantages, such as more competitive costs and accumulated profit for further investment. This in turn strengthens the competitive power of capital and technology.[118] This means that inequalities in the economy are not solely due to differences in productivity. On the other hand, there is greater incentive for private economic efforts and growth of the entire economy. But such an advantage for certain individuals or particular groups results in economic gains bought at the expense of others.[119] Therefore, intervention by the state

* A contributing factor is the increasing dependence of the producer on sales potential, made necessary by greater output, which in turn is a consequence of technological advance.

aims at a compromise, which, assisted by clearly directed social policies, lessens the negative effects and more or less resolves the conflict between concern for productivity and social justice.

C. Private Property

Another essential characteristic of economic organization in the West is that its attitude toward property is fundamental. All such systems stress not only the private aspects of personal goods but also of the means of production. While in the East the latter may be a means for exploiting man and depriving him of his freedom, in the West it tends to be the economic foundation of the individual's struggle for liberty and also an important goal in itself. While everybody can obtain property through personal achievement, control by the individual of the means of production is also economically necessary. What we have said in connection with other features of the economy is valid here too: socio-philosophical ideas, related to the concept of human freedom and self-realization, are intertwined with economic considerations which aim for the beneficial utilization of the resources at hand.

From the point of view of economics, properly speaking, what counts mainly is the relationship of private property with purposeful, meaningful action.[120] Here observers stress the experiences that other economic systems (those without private property) have had concerning the means of production, and these are mostly less favorable. In this connection, private property, no matter what kind, is considered a secure basis of existence for the individual, and this basis gains in importance with increasing division of labor and social interdependence, allowing room for personal decisions and also strengthening his market position.[121] The latter effort is also evident in attempts to have the employee, too, share in ownership of the entire economy. Such a form of property ownership, carried out by non-entrepreneurs, must be seen in connection with the significance capital formation has in the economic process. There is to some extent a relationship between private property itself and ownership of the means of production.

While economic arguments favor private enterprise, we cannot deny that modern developments have increasingly led to an undermining of the traditional concept of property and to a separation of ownership and control of the means of production.[122] For technological reasons, modern industry is in need of more and more funds, and thus more and more owners share in the capital. For the same reason we find, in many areas of industry, a blocking of free access to the market and less readi-

224

ness to take a risk, unless it is in line with management policy. There is certainly a common trend toward separating the economic function of the classical entrepreneur from the ownership of property, which had been typical in Western economics.[123]

The rise of large conglomerates, where such a separation is best seen, has facilitated, on the other hand, a democratization in ownership of the means of production. Here, America is a case in point. The efforts of society to encourage private ownership are basic, since the demands for capital formation have to be taken into consideration. In several Western countries such efforts are mainly directed at the promotion of employee ownership of stocks and other shares in production capital.

Along with economic and social developments in the West there has also occurred a weakening in the formerly strict dogma of the inviolability of private property. In spite of basic guarantees, the constitutions of most countries allow for intervention by the state or other social institutions in support of joint goals, and this includes expropriation. More or less extensive limitations on the free use of individual property are therefore a feature of modern economic constitutions. The separation of ownership and control of industry leads also to a change of thinking in the field of meta-economics, where private property is regarded less as an aspect of function than as one of human freedom.[124] We may see in this a new emphasis on the individual and his interests as far as ownership is concerned, although social obligations are more evident than they were in the nineteenth century.

XV. EASTERN SOCIALISM AND COMMUNISM

1. THE BOLSHEVIK BACKGROUND

A. Theory of Revolution

The Western bourgeois world of the past two hundred years and the Eastern antibourgeois world of the last fifty years may be considered as practical examples in the history of human freedom. Marxism relates the origin of freedom, not to the individual, but to the species and particularly to the institutional forms that have evolved for living and working together.

The problem in question is the origin and the present development of the Eastern planned economy. The causative factors of its beginning and of its changes are many: ideology, economic structure, Russian social structure and mentality, party dictatorship, foreign policy, and, lately, the pressures of a partly developed industrial society. First and most noticeable are the effects of the fundamental meta-economic causes.

Eastern or, in this case, Russian socialism and communism are a variety of Marxism founded by Lenin and frequently called Bolshevism.[1] * Lenin (see chapter VI) was a disciple of the Marxian orthodoxy taught by Plechanov and Kautsky.[2] He transformed into reality

* A definition of Bolshevism is given by J. P. Plamenatz in *German Marxism and Russian Communism* (London–New York, Longmans–Green, 1954), pp. 317–322.

Marx's philosophy of revolution, which called for action without defining what was meant by "action." A genius at political strategy and the tactics of conspiracy, Lenin gave practical form and aggressive force to Marx's doctrine of the overthrow of society.[3] This made possible and effected the first dissemination of the new image of man.[4]

An examination of Leninism shows its peculiar nature in that it bridged such dualities as means and ends and the ideal and the pragmatic. Lenin united in his personality both the enthusiastic idealist looking to a future society of perfect humanity and the pragmatist of the revolution, the first form of which had little similarity to the final goal.[5] In other words, it is problematic whether the means followed by the Bolshevist regime should be considered necessary conditions for the realization of freedom.

The socio-philosophical trademark of Lenin's version of Marxism was a practical model for the transitional period into socialism and thereafter into communism. The phase called the "dictatorship of the proletariat" was drafted in detail. In this phase the doctrine of revolution was given prime importance in two ways: it opposed the reformism of the revisionists and the evolutionary methods advocated by orthodox Marxists.[6] The carrying out of revolution was no longer thought of as a spontaneous uprising of the masses. It was the task of a cadre or syndicate—a party composed of professional revolutionaries, an intellectual elite, the proletarian aristocracy. It is only too evident that in this new type of party, the subsequent totalitarian dictatorship was outlined.[7] A social-democratic (revisionist) pact and any contract with the existing powers which looked to "a gradual development of capitalism into socialism" was condemned as "trade unionism".[8] *

Institutionally, a strict centralist state form of organization was sanctioned for the transitional period, the duration of which was uncertain. The "withering away of the state" was postponed to the future. For the time being, it was still necessary, first, to suppress the bourgeoise and, secondly, because the masses had up to then neither adequate self-consciousness as a class nor sufficient education to shape their own destiny.

Against the purism of those who did not want to have the "genuine and proper" humanity of utopian communism adulterated, the doctrine of temporary class alliance was advanced.[9] † According to this doctrine the proletarian movement could temporarily ally itself with other class interests if they had some aspects in common. Revolutionary policy

* The principal advocate of this attitude, which was later victorious in the Western social democracies, was E. Bernstein.

† Later Trotsky turned against the idea of a preliminary alliance.

was, however, not to deviate from the path toward its more distant goal. This kind of practical mobility was supplemented by Lenin with a decided rejection of all efforts toward theoretical conciliation between Bolshevik doctrine and opposing points of view. Here he insisted on strict party discipline. "The Party" holds and knows the objective truth of history. Therefore, that which is truly humane and progressive is that which conforms to the Party, that is, to the doctrines and intentions of its leaders.[10]

Finally, the collapse of capitalism was no longer expected to occur first in the most industrialized nations. Instead, Lenin's theory of imperialism was advanced. Its starting point was the transformation of capitalism into "international monopoly capitalism," whereby capitalism also took underdeveloped regions into its sphere of influence.[11] * In this way, concluded Lenin, it might be possible that capitalism would break down first, not at its center, but at the weakest link of the chain. Besides, capitalism itself had developed into centrally administered combines, which showed that it had already taken an essential step toward socialism which would facilitate the transition. Thus, Lenin could rationalize why the revolution could first take hold in Russia. Marx had already proposed this idea in his correspondence with Zasulič. This made it possible for Stalin to replace Marx's expectation of international revolution, which was still maintained by Lenin, with the doctrine of "revolution in one country" and finally with nationalistic thinking.[12] †

B. The Influence of History

This program of action and its theoretical underpinning were evidently shaped to fit the conditions in Russia at the time. It considered the retarded industrial status, the social-revolutionary élan of the Russian intelligentsia,[13] and finally the spiritual incapability of the masses in general. In this way Marx's "scientific socialism" was, from the very beginning of its realization, the ideological generator for the industrialization of underdeveloped areas.[14] ‡ In addition, it became the socio-eth-

* Lenin explains that because of their corruption the social-democratic working class came to accept the legitimacy of the capitalist state.

† For an elaboration of the theory of the historical possibility and legitimacy of a Russian revolution as advocated by Trotsky and Lenin (1905), see Plamenatz, *German Marxism and Russian Communism*, pp. 283 ff.

‡ The crisis of communism might therefore always occur when the need for catching up in the industrialization is less urgent.

ical program succeeding the reform-directed ideas of justice held by the Russian intelligentsia.

Reference is made here to what was said in the beginning about the polarity of Lenin's thinking. It will not do to think of him as a pure pragmatist [15] * of "Soviet power and electrification." [16] The social philosophy of Marx, ontologically founded and ethically accentuated, is based on the anti-liberal thought—inspired by Hegel—[17] † of a universal solidarity of all men and a social method of production consistent with the current point in history. This thought was fully retained by Lenin.[18] He did not abandon his conviction of an imminent communist utopia of perfect freedom and equality and of its revolutionary beginning. Only his conception of the evolutionary steps to this goal was changed. Above all, Lenin broke loose from Marx's theory that only a fully industrialized bourgeois country could achieve the leap into communism.

In this connection the revolution was "premature" and did not arise out of historical consequence. Rather it came about from revolutionary fervor, social idealism, and the opportunity provided by the political situation. Accordingly, the deterministic tinge of Marx's historical materialism—although it did not make light of activism—was repressed.[19] ‡ The professional revolutionaries came increasingly to the fore.[20] § The theory of imperialism, however, supports this to an extent. It shows the beginning of the revolution in Russia—rather willed than automatic—as an outgrowth of the development of capitalism, thus conforming with the law of history. Whether this is adequate remains questionable.

At the same moment that Marx's communism was first actually realized by revolution, changes were made in his doctrine which were required by the actual situation. In Marx's historical materialism the spontaneous proletarian revolution by the masses was conceived so that it should originally and of necessity result from a discrepancy between the method of ownership of the means of production and the method of

* For Lenin, of course, "Soviet power" did not, or at least not finally, mean what we connect with it and what became of it, all too soon, that is, strictly centralistic regulation. He thought in terms of a federated self-government of the factory soviets.

† This is true even if his concept of community was turned from its head (the idea, the national and universal spirit) to its feet (the proletariat).

‡ Marx's synthesis of theory and practice is too often minimized; it may happen that the evolutionary socialization of the West will prove him right.

§ It would not be correct to consider Lenin a mere instrument. He saw himself —as have many active great persons—to be the executor of a historic mission.

production in advanced capitalism. Out of this came the theorem of a "revolution from above," which seems to be only barely supported by the theory of imperialism and which leads to the foundation of state capitalism.[21] * Marx's hope and expectation degenerated into mere words and the Bolshevik state began—charged with all of the problems of an insufficiently prepared planned centralism—to install itself as a budding industrial nation in the world.

From the principle of revolt in a highly industrialized country resulted the revolution of a nation which was at that time still preponderantly agrarian. This gave to the program of the October Revolution its strange, Janus-like face: it carried the day by demanding the socialization of the meager industry and at the same time promising the partition and private ownership of the land.[22]

Marx had thought of a short-term phase of proletarian dictatorship, serving only for the rapid elimination of the bourgeois power establishment. It was now reinterpreted into a phase of longer duration for centrally guided work by the state to build socialism. This deviation from Marxism was forced by prevailing conditions: the Western status of industrial development which he had assumed did not exist in Russia. Instead, an authoritarian intelligentsia, the nucleus of the Party, determined the steps to be taken. The Party, represented by its leadership, could not be criticized. It would know, by scientific rationalization, what to do and how to do it, because it was the knowledgeable avant-garde of the proletariat, the class which was called upon to solve all problems of history.[23] †

All this was by no means meant to be the final solution, but only a necessary step toward it. The goal itself was taken fully from Marx's social philosophy. It was a communistic association of free and autonomous men who were concerned about the common well-being and would seek it in their own sovereignty and spontaneity. In this association the disparity among men would disappear. The allegedly demoralizing evil of private property, of the market economy, of the monetary system, and of other forms of the desire for goods among men and the resulting "materialization" of men are nonexistant in Marx's goal. Consequently, in the communistic association there would be neither a political hierarchy nor a planning bureaucracy because they are no longer needed.

* On the other hand, this revolution from above is not an absolute break with Marx's teachings. Marx had already emphasized that the proletariat needed the guidance of philosophy in order to awaken its revolutionary self-consciousness.

† It is remarkable in this connection how Lenin goes back farther than Marx and Hegel.

This enlightened, optimistic, and joyfully progressive vision of the ultimate perfection of the human race was never abandoned by Lenin, even though it receded into the background. The theorem of "scientifically" demonstrable progress obviated the need to search for ethical duty. A considerably dangerous situation arose when Lenin started to prepare the way for perfect human self-realization by the severe methods of the Revolution. Did not the means threaten to become rigidified, and the goal to collapse into mere talk of mythical ritual? This danger became a reality and reached its peak during the Stalinist terror. It is the danger of all the absolutist, close-ended social remedies that they coerce man to their own advantage and liquidate the opposition.[24] *

C. Bolshevik Practice

Lenin had changed the emphasis in the theory of the dictatorship of the proletariat. His approach gave substance to the suspicion that the allegedly temporary means might destroy the desired goal. From the idea of collective self-administration the threat of a bureaucratic state capitalism arose which would be difficult to abolish.[25] †

Lenin imagined the progress from dictatorship of the proletariat to communism, socially as well as economically, in two stages. First of all, formal legal equality is the rule in socialism. Equal wages are paid for equal work (incentive wages). Socialism differs from the Western system by the "socialization" of ownership of the means of production. Private economic exploitation is thus abolished. There is no longer a capitalist who withholds surplus value from the workers. Since, however, distribution of consumer goods is still maintained by the principle

* The question as it is posed today is whether the danger of forces immanent in the system can be surmounted. Marxism itself stands in the midst of history. Would its superstructure not therefore have to change also when special conditions change? What will be the ideology of a Soviet industrial humanism? Now particularly, when the construction of a socialist economy is supposed to be essentially completed, the Marxian idea of humanism may turn virulent, destroy its leaders, and correct the system.

† The setting-up of the central administrative state and of the central administrative economy was, from a pragmatic point of view, the answer to the difficulties of the initial Russian position. Soon after the Soviet system of factory administration collapsed, centralism became the sole form of organization. Today's reality, however, is still far from the ideal of a collective of men who are all equal. New "liberalizing" traits in Eastern society remain ambiguous. Are they the consequence of economic constraints; do they mean a slackening of communistic ardor or an approximation to the West; or are they—as maintained by the new Party program of 1962—an effective breakthrough toward the realization of the Marxist ideal of the future?

of productivity—which is not just, if need is supposed to be the basis of distribution—the state is still necessary as a regulatory institution. In socialist society men are no longer led by the leash of blind material laws of the capitalist system but freely and consciously plan for the future. The interests of the still existing classes of workers, peasants, and intellectuals already coincide. There is no need for competing parties.[26] Moreover, communism is imagined as it always was in utopian socialism. In it every one is paid according to his needs. The economy which is geared for supplying necessities rather than for gain turns into collective self-administration. The working hours are greatly reduced. The state withers away. People live in almost paradisiacal fulfillment of their wishes. To be sure there are still "nonantagonistic" differences, but only in the matter of differing views on details among people who are principally in agreement.[27]

During the early stages of militant communism the attempt to build a genuine self-administration failed. The village and factory soviets proved unable to function [28] * and were soon replaced by a tight centralism. Lenin was resigned and reconciled to the fact that many more developments in the economy and in education were necessary before the state could wither away.[29] † Lenin, even as tribune of the people, was not a secluded dictator and lord of the Kremlin. Intraparty discussion was still relatively free. Nevertheless, the fact that the idea of a communistic social order in a very short time changed into a centrally planned economy and society, with a resultant lack of freedom, requires an examination of its causes. An important cause may be psychological in nature. The dogmatic faith in genuine Marxist progress, which is true because necessary and because it can be proven that it will bring about perfect humanity, demands of its advocates a total centralized plan. Furthermore, it demands dictatorial planning of the path to the final phase. Voluntarism in practice and in formation of consciousness has replaced the original orthodox Marxist way of following the objective course of events.

In discussing the related social-anthropological problems it is important to understand honestly the obvious in the enlightened, humanistic vision of the future in Marxism. The question remains, as previously stated, why in the course of its realization did this ideal turn out contrary to its original concept? Collectivism, understood as an all-inclusive

* The causes may be found in such aspects as the lack of knowledge and ability, residual private interest, and nepotism.

† Shortly before his death, he is supposed to have described the Soviet Union as a "bureaucratic utopia."

community, does not of itself equal centralistic dictatorship.[30] In principle it is rather the opposite. In order to find an answer which transcends the psychological causes, let us compare it with the basic ideas of the West.[31] * Here, individuals are primarily considered as unique. Ideally, equality and justice are valid, but they are not codified, in their actual practice, by absolute dogma. They are, rather, brought about or protected, or both, according to the circumstances by administrative measures. These give latitude to the course of production and marketing carried out on the initiative of the individual and refer at best cautiously and only rarely to an absolute and final knowledge of the true common good for mankind. On the contrary, under collectivism the one-sided concept of man as a unit of society shows an evident connection with totalitarianism. It is hardly possible to unite individuals each of whom is unique [32] into a collectivism that is free of friction unless there is coercion and dictation by the few of the many.[33] † For justification it is said that this would be a disagreeable transitory phenomenon which would neither touch nor diminish the final goal. Still, such factors as incomplete re-education, lack of collective consciousness, bourgeois residues, and belated industrialization (as a foundation for progress toward communism) would stand in the way of an immediate beginning of the communistic social order.

Present-day social philosophy, taught by experiences like those in the U.S.S.R., leads us to another possibility. This could be expressed in a dialectic theory of structure as follows. It is now a philosophically and anthropologically well-founded hypothesis that man, an indivisible unity of contradictory tendencies, is simultaneously an individual and a member of a community.[34] ‡ Man, who exists both privately and publicly, is determined by self-interest and socialization.[35] § Consequently, totalitarian programs which attribute absolute validity to one of the poles can never do justice to these dynamic relations, which cannot be completely fixed in any system.

The Bolshevik revolution led by Lenin was soon criticized from the Marxist camp. Kautsky and Luxemburg feared that it would definitely do away with the liberal and democratic co-operation espoused in

* It does not mean that there is a Western ideology in the sense of the one in the East.

† Just as—vice versa—the individualism of Western origin turned into the "social ethos" of an organized humanism.

‡ In the East there also arose a corresponding trend of anthropological thinking.

§ Political development shows that, also in the East, man may autonomously act in a socially responsible way.

233

Marx's writings. They foresaw that the revolutionary dictatorial "means" would destroy the communistic ends by outliving their alleged temporary necessity and solidifying into bureaucracy.[36] In their opinion the tightly knit, doctrinarily immobilized, and autocratically led Party cadre would destroy liberty. Trotsky said that the coercive state, once it came into being, would defraud the revolution and would demand to be made permanent. He brought his objections first against Stalin, but they applied to the statements of Lenin as well. Another point of attack was the principle of Party discipline. This was rationalized by Lenin, following Marx's ideas. His reasons were, first, that the proletariat was the class whose emancipation would liberate all mankind and, secondly, that the Communist party was the head of the proletariat. The Party was the representative of the proletariat and, for this reason, its interests were the highest interests of mankind at large. Simultaneously, it would dictate the materially substantiated laws of historic development to which all human action is subject. "Marx's teachings are omnipotent because they are true," declared Lenin. Kautsky, however, objected that this was dogmatic priggishness from which reality and science might escape. The correct point of view would be "to remain above all class struggle and class controversies." [37] *

The socio-philosophical basis of the Eastern planned economy was not designed for an authoritarian regime. It did not encompass the idea of eternal domination by the elite and submission of the masses. It proposed a future solidarity of all mankind, conscious joint control of all social and economic affairs, and unrestricted consumption freed of private ownership. It was Lenin's achievement to realize the Revolution; his failing, to have begun the falsification of its ideas.

2. THE COMMUNIST IMAGE OF MAN

A. The Social Philosophy of Marx

The principal socio-anthropological idea of communism originated with Marx and Hegel.[38] † Man, essentially man among men (a member of a

---

* The original long-held condemnation of political science as a superstructure of interests is at present suspended. The turning point was Stalin's writings on the philosophy of language.

† Lenin describes this origin: "Marx's teaching . . . is the rightful heir to the best that nineteenth-century man has created in the form of German philosophy, English political economy, and French socialism."

species)[39] * and interacting with them, provides and prepares his means of living in conscious adjustment to the conditions of nature.[40] In the course of this work of "natural origin," men contract certain social relations with one another. These arise from the historic nature of their productive powers. The social conditions again are mirrored in political and legal ideas as well as in man's view of the world.

In producing his living, according to this view, social man produces, at the same time, the conditions for the distinct historical evolution of his entire self-concept, his culture. Finally, he produces, out of his economic activity, himself as a historic being; that is, as one immanent in history and the making of history. He himself produces all the various ideas of history by which he then determines his philosophical existence.[41] † In practice, he shapes himself by social labor using the material of nature under prevailing conditions into what he conceives himself to be.[42] ‡ According to Marxian anthropology man is a living being who can be shaped and reshaped indefinitely. All his qualities are derived from his economic and social relations. Therefore, there are no eternal, meta-historical characteristics of man, such as a primordial need for private property or, conversely, the need to merge into a collective.

The need to assert one's existence is characteristic behavior for reactionary classes. Accordingly, man shapes his own existence in the historical context of his living conditions. In this way, first socialistic and then communistic man would be, respectively, the man of the present and of the future. His ascendancy would be inescapably marked by the industrial evolution of human productive forces.

This total historification of man with its emphasis on progress is an essential trait of Marx's and Marxist thought.[43] § Today, there would be few who would pay more than lip service to any assertion about the eternal, unchanging nature of man.[44] || According to the concept sketched above, the individualist of liberal philosophy is the product of a society of private ownership. This again is based on the historically

* This means further that man is never primarily an individual but above all a member of a class.

† In this (atheistic) philosophy of the unlimited egoism of man, L. Landgrebe sees the essential point of Marx.

‡ The young Marx took this theory over from Hegel.

§ This is the romantic heritage of Marx which is also noticeable in his social theory.

|| Man is both a social and a working creature. Plurality and activity are the two forces that shape man's condition in history and which evolve with changing conditions.

necessary stage of an early capitalistic economy in which the bourgeois class liberates itself from feudalistic suppression.

Meanwhile, capitalism would have progressed to such an extent that private ownership of the means of production, interaction of all society, and mutual dependency of the productive forces would no longer coincide. This would be manifested in strikes, stock market crashes, business crises, and their consequences.[45] * Man would be alienated, first, from the products of his work; second, from his work altogether; third, from himself; and fourth, from his fellow men.[46] According to this way of thinking, the products of his labor become merely merchandise and even his labor becomes merchandise on the labor market. The acquisitive world, regulated by money, subjects man to its own laws. The capitalistic production system—as "scientific (Marxian) socialism" tries to prove —will bring about its own demise by raising within itself the very powers which will destroy it.

It should be about this time that the entire society, represented by the proletariat as a class, takes over the means of production which had long ago in fact become a function of society as a whole; surplus value becomes of benefit to all, and man "regains" himself.[47] The development of industry makes a life of widely spread affluence possible.[48] † But capitalistic methods prevent the enjoyment of it because of crises and wars. The cause of this is the struggle for profit with all its consequences, such as accumulation of capital and pauperization of the working class. In addition, the extreme division of labor under capitalism is dehumanizing, according to Marx. The critical state of capitalism is not due to a fault in the system which could be corrected but to the faultiness of the system itself. Therefore, there is only one solution, revolution of the conditions of production, that is of the social and political structure of the capitalist order.[49] ‡ Communism is the societal structure of the future postulated by the evolution of productive forces.[50] § Marx visual-

* Marx's explanations are not so much a realistic description of conditions in early capitalism, although they are this, too; they are especially an idealized typical pattern of unlimited capitalism and its own dynamics. One can therefore say that Marx is just as much a "Ricardo in reverse" as he is—in his own words—"a Hegel in reverse."

† Here there appears an ambiguity in Marx's thought which lays the foundation for the later neglect of the humanity principle in favor of economic progress.

‡ Later this led to an interim stage of state capitalism in the U.S.S.R. which was introduced in order to create this economic foundation for communism.

§ It is remarkable how much the entire economic doctrine and social philosophy of Marxism remained attached to liberalism, its opponent, just because Marxism originated as its dialectical reverse.

236

ized himself at a critical point in history, at the dividing line between pre-history and the history of human emancipation. There, it became evident that primary importance, socially and economically, be given to fulfillment of man's present-day destiny; that is, the realization of a co-operative community of free, equal, and fraternal man. But, private ownership and division of labor are the two great stumbling blocks on the path to universal development of the forces of human essence. They make impossible this wholeness of personality, which is limited by the self-seeking ego of man or his special work. Only in perfect solidarity with others is it possible for man to live his life freely in unhindered exchange with a humanized nature.[51]

This is the "realm of freedom" of which young Marx writes. His perspective into this realm reached as far as the thought of abolition of labor altogether, not only of its alienated aspects,[52] as well as a perfect community of universal mankind identifying with the common will.[53] * Later on, Marx uses the "realm of freedom" to mean leisure time outside the shorter working day which could be devoted to culture or perhaps even contemplation.[54]

The social philosophy of the East is understood to be a scientific theory of the law of the development of human society. This law of development is supposed to result in the fulfillment of the demands of humanist enlightenment—liberty, equality, and fraternity. In Marxist terms, the scientifically necessary state of perfection of the present social and economic processes signifies also the realization of man as a universal being of one species.

To achieve the realization of this being by force and to coerce men, if necessary, against their erroneous opinion or their vague or misled will, for their own good serves to justify all concrete dictatorial actions. The actual status of knowledge in social philosophy, however, rather seems to support Hegel's conviction that man does not possess such singular harmonious qualities. His existence arises, rather, from the tension between individual and social qualities of equality and nonequality, from a shifting framework of unreconcilable contradictory tendencies. But then, a dogmatic fixation and the creation by despotic means of an imagined ideal and harmonious final stage would have to be understood as a priori inhuman.[55]

Total harmony brought about dictatorially is as far from the actual

* It is a realm in which humanism has become equal to communism and equal to naturalism. But whether this dream of universal harmony of interests and identity of individuals is realizable in even an optimal human society may well be doubted.

structure that Marx envisioned in socio-philosophical terms as its anti-pode which Marx opposed. This antipode was the extremely liberal, ideological doctrine of the automatically self-regulating harmony of private interests as they interact without intervention. In each case allegedly incontestable, objective, social and economic laws are asserted to which the individual is supposed to be subject. In each case, however, the objective course of events is left to the interests of a ruling group of individuals. In each case a final state without friction and without conflict is suggested as possible. This state, however, does not conform to the actual quality of human co-operation. On the contrary, this would be defined by the mobile, unstable, and nebulous floating of human relations between all too patent solutions and by the dialectic unity of the subjective and the objective.[56] *

B. Controversial Problems

Now, the question arises, whether the approach to future harmony could not succeed by way of the democratic advances of the West rather than by the one-party dictatorship of the East which seeks to achieve perfection through force.

Caution should, however, be used against rash judgments stemming from conditioning in the Western way of living and against an easy "black-or-white" approach. Instead, an honest discussion of the socio-philosophical as well as the economic risks and dangers, possibilities and impossibilities, of each method is necessary.[57]

Meanwhile, each system neglects one aspect of the tensile framework of human social existence.[58] † The West overlooks the solidarity which permeates all individuality, of the universality of brotherhood, sometimes referred to as a "matter in common" or an "overlapping universality" (Hegel), without which there is no spiritual, expressly human, existence. Spirit is the "being with oneself in the other person," said Hegel. The West mostly refers apologetically to plurality and the beauty of diversity and also contends that the "common cause" means curtailment of the free play of liberty. Reality offers different experiences. The consumer, unconsciously led, is not free. The "organization man" and "role actor" in the "lonely crowd" loses sovereignty over himself.[59] The partner in the common cause, on the contrary, develops himself as

---

* There are indications that a new, more mature humanism is arising in the East and West: communism without coercion and individual freedom without arbitrary rule by a private individual over others.

† The common basis is the humanism of enlightenment.

a person through working with others, and becomes a definite, noninterchangeable self, standing on his own.[60]

The East, however, fails to recognize that the overlapping common cause is only real in the individual sense given it by the autonomous individual. When only a few individuals of a centralized power dictate the course, the common good is robbed of its fullness because its varied realization in different formulations by many individuals is prevented.

The imaginary idol of the Eastern views is "the society." [61] * It is almost identified with the liberty of all individuals. What is more, were the state to wither away, there would remain "society itself, represented by its central guiding economic agency." [62] Meanwhile, it has become clear that, philosophically and anthropologically, it is not realistic to declare "society" to be the last resort of human relations. Society is always a web of individual experiences and actions as well as a framework of institutions, norms, rules, and hierarchies, which stem from the interchange between individuals.[63] It is real only insofar as it acts in each case through individuals. If, now, society is made a court of last resort over the intentions and actions of men, only two results are possible. The first is that society will be distinct from the multitude of individuals and seen as "something higher." Then, it must manifest itself somewhere and personify itself. It does this, for instance, in an elite which establishes the guidelines for the action of all others.[64] In the second possibility, society is understood actually to be "all individuals." Then results a universal democracy with equal rights for all, disposition of everything by everybody, and eventually a leveling.

A social philosophy equal to the conditions of today's world can no longer be satisfied with the antitheses of individualism and socialism. Rather, it must look for the common root in the basic nature of men out of which the faults and the advantages of each must be understandably deducible. Such a basic structure might well be that of a dialectical (which could be termed "tensional") unity of opposing tendencies. On the one hand would be the striving for private well-being, individual detachment, and the pre-eminence of private interests. Opposed to this is the tendency toward socialization, interaction with others, and a sense of community. Therefore, it is not practicable to comprehend man as essentially singular and as only in superficial touch with others, which is, for most intents and purposes, what extreme liberalism does. Likewise, man is not to be considered as just a link in an imaginary, complete organism to which he has to subordinate himself, disregarding his

* Even this idea distinguishes between society as a purposeful association of privately interested parties and society in the sense of Toennies's "community."

239

own judgment. A one-sided solution to this knotty problem is the philosophical equivalent of the socio-philosophic "isms."

This paradoxical unity of individual freedom and collective integration may be deduced from the nature of man generally.[65] * It may also be that it is only a mark of Western man. In any case, Soviet thought treats it as the motivating force in its order; indeed it is the very foundation of Marxist philosophy.

How did the ideal of a comprehensive solidarity of universally free individuals become inverted? Was it caused by the interests and prejudices of the men who carried on and led the Revolution, by the special conditions of Russia, or by its underdeveloped industrial base? All this was certainly of importance and will be discussed later. The comprehensive substantiation of this development may, however, be looked for in the socio-philosophical presuppositions. The question becomes whether social philosophy must today decide either to suppose the existence of well-defined, eternal characteristics of the individual or the species or to surrender all traits of man's being to historical growth and change.

The East presumes to know, on the one hand, the essential destiny of men and, on the other, to be able to subject man to total bondage by history. Human nature, however, may be such that it can transform its historic realizations into a realm of open possibilities which cannot be calculated in advance. At the same time, there is a well-founded hypothesis in which active man is integrated in a way which is fundamentally indivisible and which resolves the conflicts of the two opposing tendencies here discussed: individualism and socialization.[66] † Man lives in a basic tension from which other tensions result: domination and subordination, autonomy and dependence, revolt and conformity, free planning and functional adaptation, isolation and integration. Because such dichotomous combinations of opposing tendencies are in a tension which constitutionally cannot be compromised they spontaneously release an infinite plurality of "schemes for solution," of which there are—including all minute variations—probably as many as there are individuals.

---

* It is exactly this paradox which determines today's socio-philosophical thinking on the various origins and shadings of human nature.

† The deliberations made here are guided by the thoughts of writers who take seriously the interdependence—the "unity of unity and non-unity" of Hegel—of these two tendencies in human existence.

240

C. The East-West Tensions
as a Socio-Philosophical Experience

In the Eastern realization of Marx's ideas "society" was raised to an imaginary objectivity. This did not remain hidden from the founders of Bolshevism, not to mention its critics—Plechanov, Trotsky, and Luxemburg.[67] * In the final resort the return of joint rule to sovereign individuals was deferred to the future for which the East was preparing. In this way Marxist humanism became a mythical ritual superimposed upon a practice obedient to the necessities of gaining political and economic power.

In the West the reverse happened. The principle of private interest and individual autonomy threatens here, as a consequence of absolutism, to lead to the growth of a mass society in which every one functions according to his "role." [68] † On one hand, the result was a change of society into a coercive state governed by selected individuals; on the other, a reversal of individualism into the formation of an anonymous society which compels the individual into universal dependence.[69] ‡ The search for a way out has to begin with a critical understanding of the metamorphesis of extreme viewpoints into their opposites.

This is why only today can the socio-philosophical question of Enlightenment be appreciated with full consciousness, in all its complexity, in the setting of a threatening world situation: how can the two facts of the individual and the community be reconciled so that freedom of the individual and optimal functioning of the economic society can exist together.[70] §

Observed from another point of view, both systems appear to be primarily economic systems.[71] Whether under Eastern bureaucracy, where private initiative and consumer choice are strictly guided, or whether under the private entrepreneurial market economy of the West, which

* Perroux gives an independent introduction to the complexity and uncertainty of the East-West contrast. He emphasizes above all the intertwining of the economy and total "culture" as well as the common origins of both systems.

† This contrast is pointed, but for this very reason it may effectively show noteworthy contemporary trends.

‡ "The egoistic purpose in its realization, if universally required, establishes a system of universal dependence . . ." (Hegel).

§ To look for possible solutions here seems to be the foremost task of a social philosophy which seeks to keep pace with the current world situation.

241

takes heed of the economy for survival's sake,[72] * philosophy poses the question in terms of man in the economy. Marx's political economy may in this respect be regarded as classical political economy in reverse.[73] † Even the state of things after the revolution, when surplus value created by labor is to revert to the common good, is a variant of the liberal doctrine of the furthering of the common good by industrious economic activity on the part of all individuals. The East today is in this state of rigorously enforced productivity. Communism is still only a distant vision. Whether the economic and social power of disposition is in the hands of a few private persons or a few officials creates differences in ideology but hardly in fact.[74] ‡

Affluence, centrally imposed, differs from the ideal of free society just as much as the consumers' tendency to mass conformity deviates from free self-realization of the individual. In both cases there is danger of alienation. The possible, better world which Marx expected would have to combine the two forms so that a real "socialist humanism" would result. In this world the public concern would no longer be dictated by the few and private matters would no longer be limited to their respective narrow confines.[75] § In such a world individual existence and public life could interact and yet preserve their respective special rights.[76]

The Western social order might have a head start toward the society as outlined above. It even realizes some traits of Marx's ideal more than the Eastern, such as social wages, joint control, and reduction of class differences.[77] It is just as evident that it has also acquired simultaneously along the way some disadvantages, for example, influence of private interests on public policy, lobbying power, policy decisions based

* This remark is not supposed to put the self-endangerment of the West on the same level as the inhumanities of the East. But it does put forth for discussion the question of whether the barely functioning consumer-citizen is not an acute danger for the humanity of man.

† Marx's political economy may be understood as the reversal of classical social philosophy. For Smith, private egoism, because it is always formed by ethical sympathy, works for the good of all. For Marx, however, the communist association, because the source of individual welfare is immanent in it, helps the individual to develop fully.

‡ A mushrooming of consumption in the more advanced Western economies, priority of capital industry in the developing Eastern economies: here man is materialized by a world of goods; there, dehumanized as labor for development. Where is the Eastern world headed?

§ The purpose is the optimal adaptation of productive forces and means of production so that the best possible satisfaction of the material and cultural needs of the greatest possible number is achieved.

on public opinion polls, political lethargy, and slavery to consumption.[78] Even so, considering these dangers and the impossibility of perfection, here may lie a more humane and successful way toward progress. This would-be progress toward a future society is not to be achieved just by taking one side or the other in the East-West question.[79] *

3. SOCIO-PHILOSOPHICAL HISTORY OF THE EAST [80]

A. In Stalin's Shadow

The history of the realization of Marxism is the history of the continuous leveling of a highly speculative social and historical philosophy. Certainly, the image of the future, even if in a faded or "Westernized" picture, was retained. Its realization, however, was deferred further and further into the future, while it became increasingly difficult to reconcile a utopian goal with present reality.[81] It was not until the 1950s that things once more began to ferment. Economic and technological necessities forced a loosening of the Party's reins. Political changes in the Eastern bloc destroyed the ideological monopoly of the Kremlin. The social philosophy of the young Marx seemed to have become the source of strong reformist currents within the system. The development of Soviet society is, therefore, to an important extent, determined by problems in its economic policy, if one disregards the power struggles of the ruling group. These pragmatic problems and measures caused some ideological shifting of emphasis.

While the economic changes are described more fully elsewhere, their ideological rationale or their reflections in the changes of Soviet social philosophy shall be examined here. The central problem is the determination of the duration and content of the phase between the October Revolution and the predicted final stage of a communist society.[82] By reason of the centralistic structure of the system, the doctrine of control by the Party is here placed in the foreground, although there also exists a Soviet sociology.[83] Even a new "linguistic philosophy" [84] and the rise of cybernetics were officially approved only after the Party decreed that these innovations were in agreement with Marxist teachings.[85] †

Today—unlike the time up to Stalin—the rulers are under the pres-

---

* An interesting development in this direction in the East may be found in Poland at the beginning of the 1960s.

† In this case the problem of reform and orthodoxy arises from the Party's claim to possess the true knowledge of nature and man.

243

sure of material requirements and revisionistic ideas which they can no longer counter with dogma but which, on the contrary, create pressures toward reform of the social framework and theories.[86] * It should be emphasized, however, that changes of this kind by no means necessarily take the course of mere "Westernization." [87]

After the Bolshevik Revolution, Eastern social and economic policies immediately began to work toward socialistic self-administration by the working masses. The hope for the speedy establishment of a communist society was still high. It showed itself first in the setting up of an immediate and comprehensive democracy of the village and factory soviets. But they were soon replaced by dictation and regulation by central state authorities. They proved to be unable to build a well-functioning—much less a prospering—economy. Besides, central distribution, independent of efficiency, proved to be a brake on individual initiative in production. In 1921 Lenin liberalized the economy by introducing price determination and production planning according to market demand.[88] The New Economic Policy, however, constituted only a partial reversion to a private economy. "State capitalism," as Lenin himself called it, came into being in which the leaders of the economy were permitted extensive sovereignty. Lenin conceived of this phase only as a short transitory stage.[89] † After it appeared that hope for an early proletarian revolution in the Western industrialized countries was deceptive, Stalin began his policy of "building socialism in one country." [90] By ingenious manipulation of the Party machine, Stalin transformed the Party, which up to then resembled a religious order, into a totalitarian ruling apparatus. A precise hierarchy of power existed. The chain of identification led from persons deputized for the proletariat in the Communist party and its organizational forms in the Central Committee and Politbureau up to Stalin.

Between 1924 and 1930, Stalin enforced his policy against the "deviationists to the right and to the left." [91] ‡ The struggle which ended in

* That a loosening of the autocratic system was initiated while Stalin was still living is shown by Meissner.

† Lenin decided very soon after 1905, starting from the theory that the Russian Revolution would be followed by Western revolutions, for a revolution in his country. His faction, the Bolsheviks, who followed him in this respect, won out over the Mensheviks, who preserved the original internationalism. Still, Lenin expected the immediate spread of the revolutionary spark. This changed only under Stalin.

‡ This controversy is primarily ontological and is therefore treated in detail in chapter VI. Here, only one aspect is relevant, the question of the legitimacy of the evolution of socialism-communism.

244

his victory was intimately connected with the questions of the First Five Year Plan. Stalin advocated intervention which was to advance industrialization and the *kolkhoz* system. His opponents were in favor of slowing down the reform movement and awaiting the "objective" development of economic conditions. These were the antiphilosophically oriented rightists or "mechanists," [92] * who insisted on basing the progress of socialism on the development of productive forces. Out of this, automatically, rather by evolution, the new society would grow. Opposed to this point of view were the Deborinists, who were Hegel-oriented. They accentuated the role of the tensions immanent in the system as the generating force of the movement. [93] †

Stalin at first supported Deborin. In 1929, simultaneously with the collectivization of agriculture, the formation of the *kolkhozy,* and the setting-up of machine-tractor centers, mechanism was condemned and Bucharin's group was eliminated. In 1931 followed the condemnation of the Deborinists. [94] This dual-front position, which assured a useful vagueness to the "party line" itself, shows Stalin's mixture of realistic political sense and support for the revolutionary movement. The contemplative, expectant, positivist evolutionism of the right-wing deviationists put a brake on the momentum of revolutionary activity. The strict historical concept of the left, however, did not recognize the necessities of politically logical tactics. [95]

Later, Stalin gave as reason for his dictatorial procedure in "collectivizing" agriculture his theory of "revolution from above." Since the Communist party, in its position of power, should itself be the vanguard of progress, its domination should not be weakened by progressive upheaval. On the contrary, it is the Party which was to lead the way to communism. [96] These questionable propositions of Stalinism are summarized in Trotsky's criticisms. He feared that Stalin's procedures would create a new class system under the rule of officials and the formation of a coercive state. He was conscious of the seductive force of power and foresaw the stabilization of a totalitarian system in which the privileges of the bureaucrats would grow to "capitalistic" dimensions. [97] His opinion proved correct. In 1936, Stalin, in his speech on the new constitution, declared the building of socialism to be essentially completed. His comprehensive, retrospective view on the socialistic achievements culminated in the prediction of an early beginning to the communistic

* Their concept, which was in opposition to planned economy, was derived from the idea of an equilibrium of forces.

† Both groups could refer to Marx, in whose writings appear the theory of evolution as subject to natural law as well as the doctrine of dialectic leaps.

245

phase. The level of industrial production at that time had risen seven-fold compared with the 1913 figures. Now, announced Stalin, there were no longer hostile classes, but only two, allied in a united party, of workers and peasants. Led by an intelligentsia which had equal interests with both, society, already harmonized, would start on its way to communism. The projected constitution, as submitted, was to institutionalize democracy, not of the parlamentarian kind, which separates the people from the government, but "democracy of the working class" where only the one and true will of all would exist.[98] At the same time, with the increasing strength of the "dictatorship of the proletariat" and advancing socialism, the class struggle would intensify.[99] *

For this, on one hand, the education of each person into a generally efficient individual was called for. This individual could then, exercising real autonomy and, at the same time, collective responsibility, in alliance with the progressive forces of history, participate in the administration of society by society. But, on the other hand, these ideas led to an optimal adaptation of man to the material needs of society, that is, to the strengthening of the Soviet empire's power politics, as desired by the new ruling class of functionaries.[100] †

According to Marxist teachings, men had up to now been incited to their actions and productivity by exclusively material motivations—as if without a will of their own.[101] ‡ Against this, there would be a new phase of history in which such motivations—originating from class antagonism—no longer exist and new stimulants would be required.[102] They were "consciousness of solidarity," "socialist competition," and, finally, the more or less nationalistically oriented "Soviet patriotism." [103] The latter was brought forward partly by the necessities of World War II and was an evident regression from the internationalism of Marx's doctrine.[104]

Stalin's last writings set forth which changes of the economy were to be expected during the transition to communism.[105] The starting point was the theory of the historical variability of economic laws. These changes, declared Stalin, would not take place automatically but would require active intervention by man.[106] §

The goal of socialism would be optimal satisfaction of the continu-

---

* Today these theories of Stalin are rejected.

† On this nationalistic line, Stalin, in 1939, promulgated his theory of "building communism in one country."

‡ In capitalism the material laws of production have the effect of natural laws even though they are man-made.

§ Here is manifested the theory of "revolution from above."

ously growing material and cultural needs of the total society. Contemporary Soviet society had not yet reached such a final stage. It would, for the time being, still be determined by the production of goods for the market, at least in the exchange between city and country. This would be the difference—despite the disappearance of class antagonisms and exploitation—between the socialistic society and communism. Another defect would be the remaining separation between manual and intellectual labor.

According to Stalin, in the transitory stage to communism, the contrast of industry under state administration and agriculture under collectivism must be abolished in an "all-inclusive production sector." In this, the "general property of the people" would be realized and administered by a "central guiding economic agency of the entire population." Here also the money economy and with it the goods-money relationship could be replaced by a simple exchange of products. It was emphasized that the prerequisites for this would be an enormous increase in production, a broad technical education for all, the attainment of a higher cultural level, a reduction in working hours, and the doubling of real wages. One year later, Stalin died. Thus ended a process which, out of the hope for a universal community of fully educated free men, created a state which rather resembled a tsarist, feudal structure.[107] *

The enlightener, Marx, was theoretically in error with his statement that the proletarian private-interest collective was or could be more than a liberal, purposeful association. The consequence of this error was, on the one hand, the coercive shaping of a monolithic society by the controlling state and, on the other, the justification for this, which was that this would lead to a community of freemen in a utopian, affluent society. Marx's concept of the "realm of freedom" was twofold: first, democratic and universal rule over the processes of a society in which everyone is sovereign and in which the will of all converges into Rousseau's common will, and second, a realm of leisure time beyond labor. This kind of thought, preponderant with the later Marx, only repeats the anti-public ideal of education in the German classical period as formulated by Humboldt. This idol has also been discarded by Bolshevism. Instead, the importance of the individual, autonomously taking a socially concerned stand, was to be stressed. In fact, however, this goal disappeared in the strictly planned development of industry.

* New class stratifications had hardened between the bureaucratic ruling caste, on one hand, and workers and peasants, on the other. The fact that the political and economic top strata looked at state property as being more social than co-operative shows again a scantily disguised reneging on original ideals.

The following observations are concerned with whether there are noticeable tendencies in the post-Stalinist period which may resolve this contradiction in the system.

Tito's Marxist criticism of Russian state socialism was simultaneously of a theoretical and practical nature. Because Tito could prove the feasibility of a different way, no objection of "being secluded from the world" could be raised against him. For this reason his reforms had an impact reaching beyond the confines of Yugoslavia. He took issue with Stalin and asserted that the Soviet Union had developed into a new imperialist state. According to Tito, its centralistic despotism represented the exact opposite of what Marx, and even Lenin, had imagined to be the society of the future.[108] There could be no question of "socializing" state property. Tito, on the contrary, established the general agricultural cooperative and tried, in industry also, a transition to managerial autonomy by means of workers' collectives.[109] This experiment has not yet been carried through to its conclusion. However, the Yugoslav economy does seem to be developing toward a "market economy without private enterprise." [110]

B. Party Congresses

Soon after Stalin's death it became evident that power was coming into the hands of the second generation [111] of Bolshevists who had already, at the Nineteenth Party Congress of 1952, made themselves heard.[112] While the final goal of communism was maintained, the social and economic methods began to change. The joint leadership which took the place of Stalin's autocracy started an ideological "thaw" and in the economic sphere a "New Course." Despite several opposing movements, this has since then determined the proceedings of events in the U.S.S.R. and the various people's republics.[113] Under the cover of ideological controversies which cloaked the power struggles among the new masters of the Kremlin, the intentions of all who animated the New Course were directed toward rather similar reform goals: increase of consumer goods production, democratic loosening of dictatorial planning, liberalization in science and art, and turning away from exaggerated Russian nationalism and imperialism.[114] Certainly, these climatic improvements did not take from the ruling monopoly its central decision-making political authority and nor did it do away with the omnipotent Party. The system remained as it was, but it has tried to eliminate its shortcomings, which are only too evident, by its own dynamics. The Western observer must here avoid two kinds of errors. He must not conclude from such

248

aspects of change which on first glance seem to indicate liberalization that this is "Westernization." Nor should he, in his disappointment that "Westernization," seen at close range, is simply not there, consider the inner changes in the system as unimportant.

The economic rise of the U.S.S.R. continued under Stalin's successors. For the further development of the Russian social and economic policy, Khrushchev set the motto "to catch up with and overtake" the West.[115] This created a problem which may be characterized as follows. Does the desired communism mean an affluent dictatorship with Western levels of consumption instead of the non-alienated self? Will the measures taken for a higher level of economic well-being bring about a reversion from planning to market orientation and the free play of prices? Will the Party permit such a development, and what are its limits?

The new tendencies reached their first climax in the condemnation of the "personality cult" in Khrushchev's secret speech before the Twentieth Party Congress of 1956. In his report, Soviet imperialism was sharply rejected. To each country was conceded its particular way to socialism. A somewhat enlightened despotism was to take the place of Stalin's dictatorship. Its intention was to "convince and educate," even though its beginning remained within rather narrow limits, to effect decentralization and partial managerial adjustments, as, for instance, profit calculation in economic planning.[116] The most important motivation of the new dynamic activity in the Soviet system may be found in a divergence of interests—specific to the system—of the "elite." The Party leadership aims at an early change of the centralist-dictatorial apparatus by resumption of the ideal of a communist utopia.[117] The technocratic leaders, however, tend rather toward conservation of the previous class hierarchy, which assures it of privileges.[118] On the other hand, it is the technocrats and economists who demand a loosening of centralistic restrictions, whereas the Party, fearing a concomitant tendency toward a "bourgeois system," seeks to maintain hierarchical guidance. From this double dilemma arise the peculiarities of present Soviet economic policy.

Despite the resultant dampening and channeling of all reform tendencies, the movement, once begun, could no longer be stopped, as shown by the revolts in Poznan and Budapest in 1956. The conflict of idea and reality—or, in Marxist thought, the tension of forces—was once more heard and spoken of and resulted in spontaneous actions. Khrushchev and the Party, which under him gained increased influence relative to the economic leadership and army, knew how to curb and direct this ac-

249

tivity. A vigorous course was set for attaining communism, now interpreted as an affluent dictatorship.

Increasingly, functions of political and social administration on the district level were given over to the large *kolkhozy,* which had been merged with the machine-tractor stations. The system of incentive wages—in money—for agricultural labor was intended to reconcile the wages of *kolkhoz* peasants and industrial workers.[119] A tendency toward the dissolution of farms was noticeable. After Khrushchev's fall from power, some of these tendencies were reversed.

In industry, an experiment was initiated in which the labor unions were given tasks which the state had previously managed.[120] This decentralization and delegation of power to the economic districts have since been partly reversed. It is only too clear that merely some vascilating shifts in the continuing dictatorial power were achieved. However, the intent was to bring about the widest possible effective co-operation among people of all walks of life in the administration of matters of common interest by increasingly reducing the difference between manual and intellectual labor. The "classless society" will be possible and finally the state will gradually be abolished, which, by the way, was originally a goal of liberalism. The latest tendencies toward managing enterprises through profit and systematic determination of prices point in the same direction.[121]

At the Twenty-First Party Congress in 1959, the New Course, which was to accelerate the achievement of communism by emphasizing economic development, was established.[122] Khrushchev, particularly under pressure from the controversy with China [123] and the growing self-assertion of the Soviet citizen because of economic and technological successes, confirmed the principle of "peaceful coexistence" of West and East. In this way he stressed a program of nonbelligerent but ideologically antithetic competition between the two systems, in which victory, he hoped, would fall to the East.[124] In opposition to self-administrating bodies not confined to one enterprise, as exemplified by the Yugoslavian "general co-operatives" and the Chinese "people's communes," the transition of *kolkhoz* property to "general people's property" was propagandized.[125] This brought to the foreground the problem of reconciliating actual possession of property by society—under joint control of all—with an optimally functioning economy, simultaneously totally collective and yet offering material incentives to the individual. As early as 1957, in Poland, calculation of an enterprise's profits in market terms as well as sharing of the profits among the workers were demanded and, since then, partially carried out.[126]

The socio-philosophically decisive contrast [127] * which dominated the Eastern discussions at this time and which united Russia with Yugoslavia and the European people's republics in a front against China represented the tension between, on one hand, a total denial of private and national individual existence by China and, on the other, tendencies toward a liberation of personal judgment and decision as well as toward a nationalistic approach to socialism and communism and more frankness in the settlement of differences.[128] † The COMECON arrangement of 1949 had been criticized as a Soviet instrument of domination. Now, co-operation on a genuinely mutual basis was tried. At first, the conflict with China was officially denied, but it broke into the open when Khrushchev's coexistence theories were stigmatized as revisionistic by a more militant and aggressive Chinese doctrine.[129]

The Twenty-Second Party Congress of 1961 was particularly important. Looking back on past achievements, Khrushchev committed the Party to attaining full communism by 1980 when it accepted his new Party program. The central problem and point of socio-philosophical interest at this congress became the gradual development of the new socialist man (which can only remind one of a test-tube baby). This new man would be willing and able to function independently, on his own (but, take note, Party-inspired) responsibility and initiative in equal co-operation with others and would have the largest possible share in a social and economic development, the outline of which would be determined by the Secretariat of the Central Committee of the Communist party.[130]

The new Party program—the third, after the first of 1903 and the second of 1919—was the theoretical foundation for Khrushchev's new domestic and foreign policies and also for those of his successors. It has, ever since, been considered the standard for Eastern preparation for the future. Much of what was contained in the second Party program—such as "withering away of the state" and reduction of working hours—returned as a hope for the future, even though it had been stated that the previous program had been fulfilled.[131] Furthermore, the unrealistic polemic contention of the early collapse of capitalism was maintained. At the same time it was admitted that the first stage in the building of communism (up to 1970) was the singular task of drawing

* Besides the socio-philosophical contrast, there is the contrast in external policy between the theory of coexistence and the Chinese doctrine of revolution by force.

† China also, for a short time (1957), experimented with liberalization; this soon ended.

even with and overtaking the per capita productivity of the United States.[132] In the second phase an excess of material and cultural goods should be achieved which would then be the basis for awakening a new type of human being in a new stateless society.[133] In this better world, universally educated, intellectually and socially equalized, and autonomous men (who are at the same time sworn to the truth of the party) [134] * will take over the administration of a highly organized society.

The economic goal of the plan presupposes an annual rate of growth in total production of about 10 percent. Furthermore an attempt will be made to raise the rate of investment with a simultaneous increase in the standard of living and an approximately fourfold increase in output. This is the ambitious program [135] which is prophesized to win out universally within this century in the competitive "class struggle" with the West.[136] †

The ideal of a centrally directed, planned economy on the soviet pattern [137] is socio-philosophically based on the illusory idea of the one true (that is, Marxist) knowledge of the future course of events, and "therefore" of the absolute common good of the human species, against which any opposition must be egoistic and erroneous.[138] It is correspondingly based, so far as economic theory is concerned, on the questionable doctrine that economic and social processes under strict central dictation and control will be more effective than liberalism in bringing about improvements in the general welfare.[139] Actual developments, however, show an obvious wave-like loosening of rigid doctrine. These may arise from human nature as well as the vitality of Marxian humanitarian socialism, which still respects the individual, and finally, the requirements of industrial society.

It remains uncertain whether the tendencies which can be observed at present will endure or whether these are only periodic fluctuations. It may also be that the fluctuations of "liberalization" and "Party dictatorship" are not oscillating around a static center but move along a stable line of development. At the same time it is clear that no change in the system can be connected with them.[140] The importance of the Party has even increased. According to Stalin, it was supposed to wither away with the state. According to Khrushchev, it will be, in the perfect fu-

* Despite withdrawal from terrorism, the system of a standardized view of the world will remain. But, is "freedom within the Party line" really freedom?

† Finally, the question poses itself whether all this is "only" about an American standard of living.

ture, "the guide and leader of the self-administration transferred from the state to organizations of the society." But a freedom in which the individuals must necessarily think and act according to the Party line is no freedom.

XVI. THE EASTERN PLANNED ECONOMY

1. REVISIONISM

While the market economies, in their diversity of approaches to economic reality, are able to follow, to some extent, its changes, the fundamental economic concepts of the East are frequently less flexible. An ideologically determined course of action is faced by a not quite congruent economic theory, which aims, as necessity requires, to provide suggestions for solutions of economic problems as they arise, while observing the basic dogmas. Economic theory cannot be separated from its concrete tasks. It is significant for this situation that laissez faire and the planned economy move on different tracks.

When the Eastern planned economy is analyzed, it is particularly advisable to examine the changes relating to the present situation. Out of them the real future chances of the Eastern economy may best be recognized. The background of such an analysis is furnished by the goals fixed for the course of developments in Soviet economics: building of industry, with the emphasis on heavy industry, thorough collectivization, and relatively equal distribution of income. The post-World War II era initially brought about an extension of the Soviet concept to the entire Eastern satellite bloc. Then in the 1960s, there appeared hints of changes which are very informative.

At a full session of the Central Committee of the Communist party of the U.S.S.R. in Moscow in September 1965, plans submitted by Pre-

254

mier Kosygin amounting to extensive changes in the Soviet planning system were unanimously approved.[1] Even if it cannot yet be foreseen when and to what extent these intentions will be realized, the first steps are already recognizable. As an example, about three weeks after the speech a regulation was issued pertaining to the position of state enterprises in the U.S.S.R. which may be considered to be the Soviet enterprise regulatory law.[2] Further steps were announced, particularly the comprehensive reform of the Soviet pricing system, which had been envisaged for several years. These were closely related to the plans reported by Kosygin.

In the West these new developments are frequently welcomed as the adoption of market economy elements by Eastern planned economies. Reference is made to the detailed argument to which the so-called plan was subjected. In fact, present-day Soviet planning is based to a great extent on the numerous suggestions for reform published in the Soviet trade and party press. It is well known that this was started by Liberman's first article in *Pravda*.[3]

In most people's republics and other Eastern economies, similar developments occurred. Czechoslovakia and East Germany might be mentioned here.[4] Both started several years ago on the path which the U.S.S.R. is now following. The economic changes made by Czechoslovakia are in some respects very radical, even more so than those made by East Germany and, above all, by the Soviet Union.[5]

A. Goals and Plans for Reform

In all Eastern economies, plans for improvement center around the problem of how control of the economy can be adapted to the requirements of an economic structure which is undergoing changes during the build-up of industry. For example, reforms in pricing procedure were suggested or put into effect which should make efficient economic calculation possible. Deliberations and measures of this kind are particularly intended to bring about a rationalization of the economy which had previously often been lacking. Reformers also stimulated changes in the role of the consumer in the Eastern economy. General developments in this area are marked by the 1961 program of the Communist party for the Soviet Union. The people's republics have also recently emphasized the importance of better satisfaction of the consumer needs.[6] There is an additional problem common to the entire Eastern bloc which is closely connected with freedom of choice in consumer goods. A stagnation of sales, which had already begun during the late 1950s, led to an unexpected accumulation of inventories in trade and industry.[7] In production, also, many managerial mistakes, partly due to incorrectly planned prices, resulted in an excessive use of scarce materials, such as imported goods. Shortcomings of this kind in planning are a waste of productive resources which cannot be tolerated.[8]

On this basis the economic reforms above all indicate a new regulation of the relations between central planning and management decisions as well as market developments. Increasingly differentiated industrial production makes it more and more difficult for the planning and control agencies to regulate the course of the economy as successfully as in the past. Therefore, necessarily, methods which give the plant managers more authority gain in importance. Logically, efforts are made to tie central planning, with its hitherto valid principle of fixed quotas "from above," to financial guidelines. These are to be used by plant managers in the detailed planning of production, which is now left much more to their discretion. Instead of administrative pressure, automatic controls are to be used, by which the conditions of the plan are enforced "from below." [9] *

In a similar way the attitude of plant managers as well as workers is influenced by a differential wage and incentives policy. Graduated wage scales with marked differences in income, already previously practiced, are to be increasingly applied to production to promote quality and satisfaction of market demands. By offering differential wage incentives, an effort is made to furnish stimulants which are considered important to a socialist economy.[10] †

According to such ideas, profit becomes the principal indicator of success of a plant and simultaneously measures the degree to which the plan is met. Thus the nature of profit changes considerably and becomes more variable, rather than being set by the plan. Profit was also chosen because of the necessity to standardize the criteria of success, which had heretofore been numerous, and to eliminate mutually contradictory criteria. These had frequently been very annoying in the past. The change from quantitatively determined to financial criteria of success was brought particularly by the change in purpose with which the economic control agencies were confronted. During the building-up phase of Soviet economics the establishment of "norms" for fulfilling the plan was

---

* Here the starting points are generally the goods-money relationship and material incentives, the use of which was expressly mentioned in the 1961 program of the Russian Communist party.

† To support this practice the "socialistic law of distribution according to productivity" is used.

frequently predominant. They were geared to maximum production of all planned items. Surpassing these norms—overfulfilling plan requirements—was rewarded by a bonus. With progressing industrialization, the necessity of qualitative "norms" as the basis of plan-fulfillment was now recognized.[11] Traditional planning methods, however, often cannot keep pace with well-balanced production of goods of high quality. By de-emphasizing quantity in favor of quality, the frequently uneconomical use of scarce means of production will also be reduced.

Finally, the role of capital in the modern production process is central in Eastern economic discussions.[12] On the one hand, it is assumed that industries will be forced to introduce the most modern production methods by appropriate measures in pricing policy. On the other hand, it was recognized that past investment policy has lost its meaning. The practice of financing investments from the state budget and giving the funds to plants free of charge, as well as the practice of underpricing capital goods, led to an erroneous combination of factors and an excessive emphasis on investment capital. In addition, both procedures often tempted plants to use their basic capital in an uneconomical way. Overextended construction or investment projects, less than maximum utilization of machinery on hand, sometimes also long periods of non-use of existing installations, and similar situations gradually became typical in all Eastern economies.[13] *

The criterion of profit for determination of investments was first used to eliminate these uneconomical practices. By the use of profit results, it was thought that a correct formula for the assignment of investments could be made. In the course of discussion of the Liberman plan, attention increasingly focused on the question of interest on capital.[14] Numerous theoretical efforts were made to assess production funds as a part of the disposition of profits. But this, no doubt, only disguised the fact that capital is also of—incremental—importance in the production process, a reality which must be adequately acknowledged.

B. The Ambivalent Nature of Reforms

The reforms, which have occurred in varying degrees throughout the Eastern bloc, have led Western observers—particularly in connection with the Liberman plan in the Soviet Union—into much discussion and many attempts at interpretation. Two theories have emerged. On the

* In 1963 the percentage of incomplete to total investments was almost 45 percent (as compared to approximately 16 percent in 1950–1954 and 28 percent in 1955–1957).

one hand, it has often been said that this is a "Westernization" of the Soviet economic system. It is taken as a sign of increasing convergence of the world's two major economic principles. This was the line taken, e.g., in the publications of the Geneva Economic Commission for Europe, in which the problem of co-ordination of the market economy and planning—a problem common to East and West—was analyzed. However, there is far too much wishful thinking regarding the convergence hypothesis.[15] In view of the more conservative opinion maintained by other Western analysts on the nature of these changes, it is questionable whether these are indeed fundamental changes in the system.[16]

An examination of the reforms realized up to now as well as of the projects still under discussion shows that the innovations have obvious characteristics of a market economy. This is particularly true for the fundamental design of the reforms. Simultaneously with the partial replacement of quantitative planning methods based on financial criteria, direct orders to the executing agencies are no longer always given, rather, there is a movement toward decisions at the industry level. The analogy to the market economy in this respect is evident. Ideally, the micro-economic units regulate themselves under market conditions according to independent and objective data.[17] * The emphasis on profit, which is presently increasing, as the principle measure of plant activity and efficiency also constitutes an essential innovation. Even though "profit" *sui generis* existed previously as a category in Soviet economics, the changes mentioned here indicate a fundamental redefinition.[18] † Finally, the increasing consideration of consumer demands may also be interpreted as a move toward a market economy. One result of meeting such demands might indeed be a movement away from an economy in which there is a chronic scarcity of consumer goods.

As judged from these views, an adaptation of market economy elements could indeed be observed for the 1960s. Necessarily, this is a long-term process, which leads immediately to the question of future developments, particularly as concerns the theory that changes in the Eastern economy would continue and lead to increasing convergence of the

* This is exactly what Adam Smith had in mind when he spoke of the "invisible hand."

† This kind of "profit" has only part of the function of its market-economy counterpart. Missing in it particularly is the function of co-ordination and guidance of investment; such macro-economic tasks of profit in the market economy are reserved for planning by public authority in the East.

258

economic systems of the East and the West. May present events be interpreted in this way?

An analysis of questions of this kind must take stock of total developments in the Soviet economic system. From this analysis it may be concluded that these developments are not necessarily moving toward a market economy. They should, rather, be considered as a new phase of a long-term wavelike movement.

This movement, which is structural rather than tied to business cycles in the Eastern economy, has been noticeable for several decades.[19] It embodies the principle of flexibility in the pursuit of economic goals. Retaining the basic tenet of a progressing transition to communism, Soviet-type economic policy endeavors to take optimal steps toward its realization. It is, however, prepared to undertake short-term deviations from the straight line as soon as the economic situation requires it. The New Economic Policy under Lenin's guidance is the first example of this and the most impressive, because it was openly rationalized.[20] * Undisputably, this turn-about in Soviet economic policy, which was forced on him by unfavorable economic developments, did not cause Lenin to lose sight of the distant goal of communism. Indeed, subsequent events prove that the previous general course was immediately resumed as soon as the economic situation showed some improvement.[21]

The New Economic Policy, however, is not the only example on which the theory advocated here can be based. In his time Stalin strictly followed the principle that the building of socialism was the way to communism, yet several reforms were started in which Western observers found elements of a market economy. Nevertheless, they proved to be only temporary; some of them never emerged beyond discussion and postulates. Particular mention should be made of the reorganization of the Soviet pricing system at the end of the 1940s which took supply and demand into account. This also was necessitated by a change in economic conditions.[22] Still, because of his very modest suggestions for reform in this respect, the then chairman of the *Gosplan,* Voznesensky, was removed from office by Stalin. Finally, the latest wave of this movement in the entire Eastern bloc was the "New Course," which lasted from 1953 to 1955. It was marked by increased consideration of consumer needs. It is well known that this was a relatively short-termed deviation from the basic line of a "transition economy," which was soon followed by partial regression.[23] Similar but more limited tendencies

* The outline of the New Economic Policy and the basic lines of the present reforms show informative similarities.

259

can be recognized in more recent investment policies of the individual people's republics. Contrary to the supposition that these tendencies indicate Westernization, there has been a general resumption of the communist course as soon as conditions warrant.

It is particularly evident that one cannot place a great deal of weight on the reforms if they are almost exclusively mere instruments of economic policy. A reorganization of the relationship between central planning and the position of industry, changes in pricing regulations, and similar measures are brought about principally to facilitate the execution of directives from the economic planning agencies. Increased consideration of the consumers and, particularly, better adaptation of production to meet their demands may indicate some philosophic adjustments. Nevertheless, in this respect also, it should be remembered that the quantity made available to consumers is centrally determined as heretofore. The aggregate amount of consumption and with it the relationship between agriculture and industry remain subordinated to industrialization, which is to be accelerated as much as possible. In view of the increasing productivity of the economy, it is quite probable that aggregate consumption may be extended further; a permanent de-emphasis of heavy industry is not immediately likely, despite an interest in more balanced growth.[24] *

The use of reforms as mere instruments of economic policy is further underlined by the fact that Eastern sources always point out expressly that the pre-eminence of planning by the state is unchanged. In this respect, also, it is necessary to distinguish carefully between facts, on the one hand, and demands or suggestions, on the other, if the picture is to be complete. Therefore, observations should not only be directed toward external, superficial, and consequently short-term changes but also toward the long-term goals which constitute their basis. As much as ever, these goals are the nucleus of the Soviet economic system; an analysis of them must begin with the socio-philosophical and social-ethical roots of the system, that is, beyond the purely economic goals, among which industrialization and socialization of the means of production and the pre-eminence of collective over individual needs are most conspicuous. Only on this wider foundation is it possible to form a cautiously balanced judgment, as free as possible from speculative elements, of the past and future character of the visible changes.

* Attempts in this direction have been undertaken repeatedly since Stalin's death; they were an essential mark of the "New Course" in 1953. Since then they have been more or less abandoned after a short time in all Eastern bloc countries.

2. COLLECTIVE PROPERTY

In the reform of Soviet-type economies, two distinctive characteristics have been left unchanged: (1) collective ownership of the means of production and (2) collective planning of the economic process. This first feature is even rather explicit, although it may vary qualitatively (for example, state property as opposed to co-operative property) as well as quantitatively (total as opposed to partial socialization). Because collective ownership of the means of production is a basic element of the system, it is hardly likely that private ownership will be introduced in the future. As for the second characteristic, there immediately arises the question of who controls what and how? [25] Since there are no private owners to direct the use of the means of production, some other agency will have to assume this function. Planning the course of the economy can be done either on a co-operative or on a collective basis, i.e., by a decentralized method or by a central state agency.

Discussions of these questions, some of which cover a wide range, and of the measures for economic rationalization generally presuppose collective ownership of the means of production. It is an essential link between the economic domain and the socio-philosophical and socio-ethical ideas on which it is based. Indeed, the creation of common ownership was considered a major task of economic policy and practiced in all countries which copied the pattern of the Soviet Union after World War II. Finally, the goal of a special, fundamental, and comprehensive integration of the individual into the community constitutes a fundamental difference between Eastern and Western economic systems.

The collectivization of property as a central premise in the Eastern system was intimately connected with the emancipation of the worker.[26] In the East, capitalism is seen to be the main obstacle to this emancipation, to the self-realization of man, and to the rebirth of man's personality. The demand for abolition of private property follows logically from this idea. Besides, the point is not merely a demand but is an integral part of the industrial development itself. Thus, the accumulation of private property in modern Western industrial economies is seen as a preliminary stage in the socialization of property because of the power structure of the productive forces.

As heretofore, collective property is the enduring fundamental pillar of Eastern economic systems which has not been touched by any reform. It is not considered as an end in itself but as the basis for the realization of the image of man that is the goal of human development.

261

Particular attention should be given this image of man since it is the declared final goal that the East is striving for.[27] Its basic concept is, as previously mentioned, that man has no "existence" given by nature but that he creates himself in his works. According to this theory, man creates, in the process of earning a living, his own social patterns and, coincidentally, the historic conditions for his total self-image.[28] In a highly industrialized economic system it is said that each person becomes dependent on every other person as well as on the course of the economy as a whole. This state of things, according to the Eastern concept, necessitates a communist society in which the Enlightenment ideal of humaneness shall be realized.[29] Collective property is, of course, not state property in which the individual has no part but the property of all. The entire economy is considered here as a single large co-operative. Accordingly, the means of production in the community are seen to be regulated on a similar basis, so that men organize production voluntarily, in mutual consideration, and with a common goal.[30]

3. COLLECTIVE NEEDS

The idea of collective property is supplemented by the concept of the pre-eminence of collective needs of the group as provided for by social institutions.[31] This idea is reinforced by the traditional Russian attitude which saw man less as a free individual and more as belonging to an absolutist society.[32] The modern world is well acquainted with motives which are independent of the system and which can nevertheless be used for the extension of community tasks. These may result from growth of population, technological progress, or social movements. Their cumulative effect has generally contributed to an increase in the kind of economic problems which may often be best solved by collective measures. In the market-oriented Western economies, meta-economic categories such as security, social equality, and freedom of choice aim at collective institutions for the satisfaction of the needs of individuals and of groups. Economic categories such as full employment and control of business cycles work in the same direction.[33] In the Soviet-type economies the plan has priority. It treats the entire economy as a household to which individuals are subordinated.[34] The satisfaction of individual needs must take second place to the satisfaction of collective needs.

Communal ownership of the means of production should guarantee, according to the "fundamental economic law of socialism," the greatest possible satisfaction of the needs of all members of society. "Proportional development according to plan" (the so-called second law of socialism) "comprises the entire socialist economy: production, distribution, exchange, and use." [35] In an economic society which is in this way controlled by a plan, most needs will have to be those which are socially determined and satisfied through collective enterprises. The socialist state guarantees not only the supply of goods necessary for existence (food, clothing, and housing) and services on a level commensurate with the current level of production and calculated according to "reasonable norms" but also "real concern for such vital rights as the right to work, recreation, education, and material provision in the case of disability and old age." [36]

Social affluence, optimal satisfaction of needs (at first, those of the largest possible number, later of all), has been the central concern of the economy since the beginning of bourgeois society. While maximization of the social product is a goal with material and technological benefits, in optimalization the question of distribution comes to the foreground. The liberal theorems tend toward a pre-ponderantly material-technological solution of such problems. In this, the commonweal is evaluated as the sum of all individuals' well-being or utility. In planned societies of the Soviet type, standardization of the structure of individual needs is attempted [37] while the concept of individual utility is circumvented. From this follows logically the elimination of difficulties in the comparison of interpersonal utility. Centrally established regulation of needs replaces the market orientation. In practice the maximization of social welfare in Soviet-type economies is not left to an anonymous market but put into the hands of selected representatives. These, therefore, take over the role of the entrepreneur as far as economic decisions are concerned.[38] *

Because of pragmatic interests in the calculation and planning of consumption and in the pursuit of the final communist goal, state funds are transferred to a social consumption fund in each factory. The gradual increase in this fund means a consistent approach to the communistic distribution of goods.[39] Its rationale is that in the final communistic society, individual needs will be fully satisfied if individual and social welfare have become sufficiently identical. It appears to be a particular characteristic of the first stage of communistic development that the proportion of income distributed on a communistic basis grows faster than individual remuneration according to productivity.[40] For the time

* According to communist views, an economy oriented to individualistic maxims leads to the concentration of power in the hands of a few; that is, to formation of monopolies and exploitation of the masses.

being, the latter is being encouraged in the interest of economic growth. Under the title of "material concern," this encouragement has even increased lately. It does, however, in this way, come into conflict with the ideological goal.

4. SOCIALIST PLANNING

The communist society of the future has been the goal of Soviet-type countries since the October Revolution. Beginning with the Program of the Communist party of the Soviet Union in 1961, it has been stressed even more than during the previous decades.[41] For the first time it was more closely defined as to its contents and the time of its advent. This program showed great similarities to the developments and trends in Western industrial countries.

Primarily because of unfavorable experiences during the October Revolution, which was directed toward immediate realization of the communist order, and during the ensuing phase of war communism,[42] Lenin saw the attainment of communism as a long-term process.[43] According to his concept, which is still respected, the transition period will lead through several stages of socialism and finally to communism. Based on the philosophical discussions of the 1920s (which were commented upon in chapters VI and XV), the conviction prevails in the East that, although this goal will result of historic necessity, it can be accelerated by human action.[44] Here arises the task of making conscious use of "historical principles" to hasten this development. In this connection the Party has a particular role, which is, from its understanding of history, to lead society along the right path.

It is on this basis, during the transition phase, that the economy is to be guided. The desired goal of economic policy is the creation of the material-technological basis for a communist society. This should mean maximum productivity and an "abundance" of food and other necessities of life. Man's needs will be satisfied insofar as they are not considered (by the Party) unreasonable.[45] * At the same time conditions will be created so that man can largely escape from the "realm of necessity" and realize the "realm of freedom." The realm of necessity consists of the functional compulsions of the industrial world. The realm of freedom is the independent organization of his life by every individual. This is a thread that runs through the entire complex of communist thought, starting from the chiliastic sketches of the young Marx. Marx

* "The demands and wishes of men, with all their variety, shall be the expression of the healthy, reasonable needs of the universally developed man."

264

went so far as to envision the abolition of labor altogether as well as a perfect community of men sharing a universal identity with a common will. Later, however, the realm of freedom was seen as a reduction in working hours which would give man opportunity to "organize his leisure time." The realm of freedom changed into a realm of free time, which, in the East, is predominantly understood as political activity outside working hours in the interests of the Party. In this polarity is seen the dilemma in which communism finds itself. It is, to a great extent, the reason for the relaxation and tightening of planning and control in the economy and society. The realm of economic necessity demands periodic revisions which sometimes resemble elements of Western systems. The idea of freedom in relation to the collective tends to maintain the central direction.

The most important prerequisite for the system was instituted immediately after the October Revolution by collectivization of the means of production. In the people's republics of southeast Europe and elsewhere this was done after the Soviet model had been introduced.[46] * Collectivization is the necessary condition if exploitation is to be eliminated. According to this, the Party, during the transition to communism, must prevent a strengthening or resurgence of "antisocialistic" attitudes among men. It should not permit deviations from the set course. In a similar way it is necessary to secure, as far as the economy is concerned, a logical transition to communist society.

With respect to this requirement the principle of central planning and guidance became a pre-eminent means of economic policy. With its help the goals of the Party are to be realized. The principle of comprehensive planning corresponds to entrepreneurial freedom in the market economy, which it is intended to cancel out along with other mechanisms of the market economy. In their place is the statist, collective, "conscious" guidance of the economy based on the "law of planned proportional development of the economy" and appeals to growing socialist consciousness as man transforms himself into the "new man." According to Eastern ideas planning takes the place of the anarchy of the capitalist system, its spontaneity, and that attitude which allows men to be dictated to by competition and eagerness for profit.[47] Planning is supposed to prevent undesirable disturbances during the transitory phase. On the other hand, the plan is supposed to lead gradually toward communism until finally this stage, because of the development of produc-

* For example, Hungary first nationalized mining, steel and iron industry, power plants, and banks in 1947. Rumania and Bulgaria proceeded in a manner similar to Hungary's, where the process of collectivization has continued.

tive forces, can be realized—in a dialectic leap or by gradual transition.[48]

Therefore, collectivization of the means of production and centralized planning and guidance of the economy are measures by which the basic socio-philosophical ideas which determine the goal shall be realized. They have to be taken as necessary conditions; without them the conditions for exploitation would continue to exist. Also, the transition to communism would be endangered by continued influence by "remnants of the capitalist attitude" among men. The elimination of private ownership of the means of production, already effected in the U.S.S.R. and in several people's republics, may not fully correspond to the orthodox idea of communism as a process developing out of a fixed law. Control of the means of production by the collective permits, according to Eastern ideas, the early conscious use of the law of transition, which is at the same time under scientific investigation. In this way the destructive side effects of capitalistic development should be avoided.[49]

This preponderantly instrumental character of the principle of the planned economy, as well as of economics in general, has lost importance in the course of development of Eastern economies because of the increasing importance of allowing more independence for economic policies. Goals, as, for instance, accelerated industrialization, are essentially founded on the claim that a high rate of growth would be possible only by means of more or less strict central planning.[50] These measures are mostly justified on the grounds that the envisaged goal must be realized as soon as possible.

5. DIRECTIONS OF REFORM

Central to present-day reforms in Eastern economies are two areas which are closely connected. Some of the changes are aimed at the distribution of economic control, which previously was strictly centralized, among a greater number of decision-makers. It must be observed, however, that only a limited amount of decision-making power is to be given to decentralized agencies; they are then supposed to execute the plans established by the state. Only the manner of execution but not the intent or the plan itself is to be changed. On the other hand, material incentives are to be increasingly granted in order to influence the agents executing decentralized economic authority in the desired direction. The preferred measures to further this policy are the profit motive and differentiation of incomes by productivity bonuses.

Essentially similar measures are also found in the Western market

266

economy. Their foundations show the marks of individual psychology. Their appeal is chiefly to the self-interest of the individual, limited in most cases only by a real or hypothetical community consciousness. The image of man on which they are based still shows marked traits of previous classical and neoclassical economic ideas. The Party's intention, however, is to do away with the desire for personal advantage, an attitude which hardly reflects a desire to "conform to the system" with dialectical skill.

To this end, for instance, "profit" is reinterpreted to serve to accelerate the building of communism. Whereas in the West, profit accrues to the capitalist, in the East it is not individual income but the "net income" of society. Profit does not bear the mark of exploitation, and it is, therefore, legitimate in the sense of Marx's teachings and a suitable economic policy for the attainment of certain goals of communism. Similarly, "interest from capital" is explained as different from "capitalism." [51] It is, in fact, because of collective ownership of the means of production, not an independent category of income. Its only function is the expression of the scarcity of capital. From the point of view of value theory such an interpretation presents some difficulties especially in the denial of capital productivity by the adherents of the labor theory of value. Therefore it is necessary to define interest as a kind of tax. It is called "anticipation of additional production." [52] A dialectical turnabout has to be assumed when a transitory economy must employ highly rationalized and, to a great extent, quasi-capitalistic methods to achieve perfect communism.

A comparison of this development with the socio-philosophical and socio-ethical aims of the East presents one of the most enduring and effective reasons for the assumption that the present reformist movement is part of a wavelike movement. A conflict is apparent between increasing socialistic consciousness which is said to be necessary for the development of communism and the actual developments in the economy during the period of transition.

Lenin's first conception of the economy after the Revolution proceeded more or less from his utopian hope of economically effective self-administration by industry. Not ideological, but pragmatic reasons caused Lenin, in his New Economic Policy, to return, under state rule, greater autonomy and rights to private initiative and to guarantee freedom of trade and marketing.[53] From his experiences Lenin thought that an extended period of education in permitted private interests and desired socialist consciousness was necessary. This mixture of voluntarism and determinism, utopia and pragmatism, was primarily directed toward

267

acceleration of the growth of productive forces and the attainment of economic autonomy.

The problems of Bolshevik economy may be recognized from the planning activities of Lenin. At first glance, central planning and Marxism are hardly identical. Ideologically, communism is founded on the co-operation of free individuals under collective ownership—in fact without the concept of property altogether. After the Revolution had abolished private property, a fluctuation began among communist self-administration, dictatorship of the Party, and "capitalistic" concessions. Lenin's justification for a temporary return to the individualistic desire for gain was that socialism in Russia could not be realized directly but only via an intermediate step of state-regulated capitalism. It would, finally, be up to the cultural forces of the proletariat and its avant-garde to bring the ideal of Marxist goals to victory.[54] The ideal goal, however, would remain the transformation of the economy into a gigantic machine, the central steering organism of which would be controlled by all citizens.[55]

In order to avoid disturbances and deviations from the right-wing, the principle of a planned economy seemed to be the most practical means of implementing the collective concept. Lenin here interpreted the predominance of collective needs as a necessary element in the development toward communism, which would come about of historic necessity. According to this idea, central planning takes care of the "well-understood interests" of all members of society. From what has been achieved in economic development after fifty years of socialism, there are evidently new kinds of material demands on the persons active in the economy and on the organization of the economic process. The maintenance of a strict planned economy is no longer viable.[56] This is because, among other reasons, of the increasing complexity of the total economic structure and the diversified growth of industry. The growing interdependence made it necessary to react in certain parts of the system faster and closer to the goal than heretofore. Rapid transmission of information and expert decisions are becoming increasingly basic conditions for a satisfactory functioning of the economy.[57] *

On the other hand, the expectation that individuals will more and more live up to their social obligations has, up to now, not taken place. Material stimulants are now used more than previously to assure that they behave in the desired way.[58] Socialist competition and similar

* From this postulate has evolved the increased attention to mathematical methods of planning and guidance. For some time now cybernetics has been much emphasized.

forms of moral incentive to work for the collective good are declining in importance. The much too hesitant progress, if progress there is, in the reformation of man into a being integrated into and responsible to the community and the economic requirement that individuals perform responsibly both aim in the same direction. They indicate a fundamental discord in the present economies of the entire Eastern bloc which may greatly influence its future.

The relaxation of central planning and the concurrent transfer of decentralized functions of decision-making to subordinate agencies is limited.[59] Nevertheless the question is whether this limitation can be maintained for any length of time. This would be an essential if the pattern used up to now, according to which a logical development toward communism is taking place, is to be valid. Therefore, the most important problem is whether the limited concession of free choice independent of ideology and based on noncollective motives (such as an appeal to individual interests) might not spread and increasingly hinder the realization of the Soviet image of man? Would not this process of development itself, if it is a continuous progress, disprove Soviet theory?

Man's behavior can be categorized into relatively separate spheres only with difficulty. The sphere of materialism and the sphere of ideology—that is, the sphere of individual interests and of community interests—should be harmoniously united. The final result should be the desired future ideal of a communist society in the sense outlined above. If this assumption is disproved, there is a schism which endangers the system. Since there has been no indication up to now that the schism can be eliminated, Soviet leadership is confronted by a dilemma: the real value of its dialectical structure is uncertain.

Unless Soviet leaders want to give up the basic principle of the system and defer the utopian communist society more and more into the future, they will be forced to revoke the present relaxations as soon as the immediate economic difficulties have been conquered. Neither is it a principle of communism to admit an increasing inequality in the distribution of income. This is, however, unavoidable while the awarding of bonuses and incentive wages continues.

From a purely economic point of view it may appear as though the increased relaxation and liberalization of the Eastern system is irreversible and will lead to an approximation to the Western system; however, there are reasons to expect, in the long run, a revocation of the economic concessions. Finally, there is the question of to what extent the Soviets, in the future, will give more emphasis to the guidance of their economic processes by the consumer?[60] Consideration of consumers' wishes in the planning of these processes requires the introduction of greater price flexibility. Flexible prices, however, are a hindrance to planning techniques and economic calculation. Another possibility lies in consumer research. It would have the advantage that consumer polls could indicate the structure of their needs. If effective cost analysis were made, planning could be carried out on the basis of firm prices.[61] Also, a reduction in the extent of planning would not necessarily destroy the system. If the framework of the plan is fixed by the central planning agency, taking into consideration the demands of households, foreign trade, and pricing policy, the share of the entire economy devoted to consumption and savings could be fixed and with it the amount of net investment. Within these limits it would then be left to the plants which products and in what quantities—within set limits—should be manufactured. Thus, consumers would also determine in which branches of the consumer goods industry investment should be made. But the total extent of investment in consumer goods would remain subject to the goals of the plan. By fixing the proportion of investment the pattern of economic growth would remain within the decision-making power of the planning agency. Improvements in consumer planning have definitely and irrevocably become a part of the program.[62] *

6. SOUTHEAST EUROPEAN TYPES OF REFORM

Revisionist developments are not limited to the Soviet Union,[63] † Czechoslovakia, East Germany, and Poland. Similar tendencies, which are very instructive, have appeared, for example, in the people's republics of southeast Europe. The picture here becomes quite varied compared to the economies which have already proceeded rather far on the way to a comprehensive reorganization of total planning and control systems and partly also compared to the larger reforms which actually were realized in the Soviet Union. But systematic economic changes, which up to now belonged only to the realm of possibility, and effective but more or less limited measures in general conform to the general Soviet pattern. Particularly, the same causes are argued for the necessity of introducing changes in economic policy. The measures to carry them out

* "The Party is determined to fight against dogmatism in planning, in planning methods, and in adherence to formulas which once were correct but are now clearly obsolete."

† After several people's republics had shown interest in the development of capital, partly as an experiment and under various names, a similar step was resolved in the Soviet Union.

also conform to the methods of the Soviet type. Previously there was a one-sided adoption of the Soviet pattern of planned economy with collectivization and industrialization; now there is also an obvious mutual influence. The Soviet Union may have been hesitant to relax central planning as long as no tangible results of similar reforms in other Eastern economies were available.

The diversity of economic policies in pursuance of goals set in the different southeast European countries is apparent. This displays itself in varied emphasis on the necessity of reform as well as in other ways. In Rumania in particular it is evident that the traditional goals of economic policy are maintained, and rapid industrialization is still a primary concern there.[64] Occasionally the requirements of more productive use of available facilities are given some weight. But, in general, the respective economic policy programs often differ considerably among the other people's republics. The detailed discussions on economic planning at the Ninth Party Convention of the Rumanian Communist party in July 1965 show, for example, at best marginal and departmentally limited amendments to the former line.[65] The principal goal is, as ever, to establish industrialization on as diversified a basis as possible in order to make the country economically self-sufficient.[66] *

On the other hand, in Hungary and Bulgaria tendencies similar to those in the Soviet Union have been apparent for some time. The reform measures started or realized up to now in both countries differ in detail. In Hungary the new problems were recognized early, particularly because of the special circumstances in the country after the events of October 1956; solutions were also discussed and proposed. In these, consideration was given to better quality consumer goods, raising of the standard of living, and increased production in light manufacturing industries.[67] A really comprehensive reform of the economy was not achieved. It was envisaged for some later time.[68] † However, beginning in 1962, several organizational changes in industry were carried out; industries were structured according to category and factories were given increased independence.[69]

Also, in respect to production planning some shift in emphasis has resulted. A purely quantitative, maximum fulfillment of plans and, if possible, overfulfillment has not been advocated for some time. Instead, it was seen fit to remedy disproportions in economic planning, which

---

* Rumania's policy of industrialization is still visibly influenced by the earlier pattern of the most autarchic economy possible for any socialist country.

† Here the bonus system in industry was also reorganized in order to make increasing use of "material interest" in developing the economy.

had become manifest repeatedly, by quantitative curtailment of planned goals. A noticeable decrease in the planned rate of industrial growth since about 1963 is the visible result of this policy.[70] In Hungary also, economic policy is supposed to be increasingly directed toward international standards of quality. In addition, the Hungarian economy is burdened with large involuntary inventories.[71] Supposedly this will be remedied by increased scrutiny of the production of consumer goods by adapting to consumer demand, by correct pricing, and by better consumer research.

Various steps have been taken in order to further the introduction of highly productive modern manufacturing methods. For example, factories are reimbursed for technological development and for the manufacture of new products. Obsolete products are subject to a special tax, in order to discourage the manufacture of these goods. Finally, there are also premium payments to the plants for export. These payments are not given for domestic sales but are a necessary consequence of domestic prices which are often not realistic compared to the world market.[72]

In the same category of financially effective "levers" which are intended to encourage factories to support planning goals is the practice of paying interest on capital, which was introduced in Hungary at the beginning of 1964. Interest as a cost item was previously almost unknown in Soviet-type countries. With this reform Hungary was considerably ahead of other members of the Eastern bloc which had tried only isolated experiments.[73] * But not all kinds of capital investment were subjected to this special control tax. Only industrial and commercial capital is taxed (with an interest rate of 5%).[74] It was hoped that this would lead to better utilization of existing plants and equipment as well as new investments.

The fundamental reorganization of relations between the central economic control agency and industry is still mainly in the planning stage; factories are mostly tied to a plan at present. Increased independence of industry is considered an inevitable necessity if a rational economic process is to be achieved. An output "geared to the market" is often mentioned here as important.[75]

In Bulgaria, some additional progress has been made. As resolved by the Central Committee of the Bulgarian Communist party in May 1963, a new system of planning and control was designed and put in force.[76] This, however, was at first valid only for selected industries. In this re-

* In East Germany, for instance, a "production fund tax" was experimentally introduced for several groups of publicly owned plants and also for private enterprises.

spect, the picture in Bulgaria is similar to the Soviet experiments, which were at first also limited to a certain number of industries and were only gradually extended. In the meantime, a general extension of the factories' power of decision and the formation of "production committees" were instituted; the purpose of these committees was to improve the planning of the industries and they were soon installed in a considerable number of factories. It was further intended to revise the relation between central planning and industry as had already been done in East Germany.[77] * In Bulgaria, also, planning is to be more or less limited to guidelines for all economically important units; in execution of the plan, the factories are to have considerably more freedom in decision-making. Although attention was centered on "modernized" profit, in order to encourage genuine participation, wages were also made dependent on net profit.[78] Industries providing consumer goods were granted complete freedom in July 1964. Their payments to the state budget out of their profits, however, are still subject to planning.[79]

* In Bulgaria, the problem of bonuses for exceeding the plan is felt on the national as well as the plant level. In order to increase profitability and managerial efficiency by emphasizing "material interest," the major strategy in Bulgaria has been through tax policy. The forms of taxation are a tax for regulating profits, a production fund tax, and, to some extent, a progressive income tax.

XVII. THE SOCIO-PHILOSOPHICAL OVERLAP OF EAST AND WEST

1. AN APPRAISAL OF THE ANTITHESIS

The two social systems that create the East-West schism can be used to explain each other. The importance of this for understanding the intellectual history of the present cannot be overestimated. Each of the two contradictory intellectual worlds is able to explain the opposing one as a faulty and special case of its total picture of "reality" and "goal" in the human sense.

The West, viewing itself as a democracy with legal and political equality, sees the East as a picture of state omnipotence and intellectual slavery. Marxism appears to be a form of illusory and utopian coercion for the enforced attainment of total equality and fraternity; that is, two values which have already been realized in the West to the desired degree or, at least, are being increasingly realized. The East sees the West as an imperialistic, monopolistic capitalism that suffers perpetual crises. The Eastern world considers itself to be a classless society of universal men who, without domination of man over man, work together for the common good. The West considers its social order to be a system of equilibrium among free producers and free consumers. In the West, the Eastern social order is generally seen as an inhumane system of individual enslavement. In the judgment of the East, the West is ruled by mutual exploitation.

274

Denials by the respective sides that this is no longer so—that oppression or, on the other hand, that crises have abated—are usually ignored with the statement that this is negligible or only temporary. In both cases the opponent is denied the possibility of real upward development or of doing away with previous evils. It would be commensurate with the progressive status of today's socio-philosophical knowledge and economic theory to consider liberal market principles, on one hand, and planning, on the other, as alternative means to certain ideal goals, not as absolute ends in themselves. In this way it should be possible ultimately to develop a human image and reconciliable economic goals which could be realized.

The fundamental socio-philosophical uncertainty remains: Is not, after all, private property the best guarantee of real freedom? Are not all other theories of freedom—from the city-state and the social contract of Rousseau to the propertyless communism of Marx in continuous danger of changing into non-freedom? The Western mixed systems (for instance, Sweden and England under the Labour party) are perhaps the laboratory in which this question could be more closely examined.[1]

Reality, since it is so difficult to obtain an objective picture of it, can hardly conform to ideological images. Intellectual history shows that it may be reasonably represented in very different ways. There are several guidelines. Nevertheless, some facts hardly admit more than one interpretation. The totalitarian system, with its economic planning, finds itself in the 1960s once again forced toward "liberalization" and "decentralization." The proposed future changes in control and planning of the economic process have mainly been suggested by economists (Liberman, Nemchinov, and Trapeznikov). To them may be attributed the current inclination toward instrumental economic thinking.

The bureaucrat, who is more bound by ideology and may, for instance, see an element of capitalism in the introduction of the profit motive as a means of control, must, under the pressure of the economic forces, re-interpret the nature of profit. Since in the East, profit would not benefit individual capitalists but would go to society, it would accelerate the building of communism. The capitalist system in which individuals strive for self-sufficiency is, against its will, confronted with an economy of conglomerates, unions, and management which it has, to a great extent, created for itself. This state of affairs must be faced squarely when similarities and differences in East-West relations are discussed.

In the West, economic rationality is accompanied by a gradual decrease of individual voice in the economic leadership. A system of "universal interdependence" (Hegel) of the members of the economy has arisen, which is expressed in the social conditioning that comes from consumption and production. A market economy based on the cooperation of many consumers and producers in some cases actually limits their individual decisions. The introduction of elements of a market economy into Soviet-type economies cannot be interpreted simply as an adaptation of Western economic systems. Nor must increasing activity by the state in Western economic systems be taken simply as a conversion to Eastern economic philosophy. It is rather a measure intended to guarantee or improve the functioning of the market economy under changed conditions.

The East is dominated by the struggle between a centralist doctrine and an expanding technological-economic pragmatism which requires "freer" conditions. Early Marxism was an impetuous countermovement, intended to achieve absolute social harmony, against the pointedly liberal system.[2] Originally derived from Rousseau's ideal democratic society and Hegel's principle of subservience to history, the "materialistic" philosophy of the enlightenment rose against the Anglo-Saxon enlightenment.[3] The radical centralist revolution, however, spoiled the diagnosis and the prognosis by creating a coercive state.[4] The individual of the West, free in his personal life, and subject only to the demand that the economy may make on his labor, is indeed "on his own." But this liberty threatens to turn into a private void which must be filled by the activity of the consumer goods industry.[5] * Despite different ideological and historical contexts, there is detectable in the West a threat to personal "freedom" corresponding to the danger of the collective apparatus characteristic of the East. Soviet social philosophy, of course, acknowledges no such parallel. Claims that it exists are denied vehemently as a befogging of the truth.[6] In several people's republics, however, extensive ideological revisions have made themselves felt in the reception of Western philosophical, anthropological, and existential-philosophical concepts.[7]

The present, if one abstains from ideologies, may mainly be seen as consisting of an old and a new industrial society. Both are, for the time being, still materialistically oriented and look to a future in which "new man," that is one whose purpose is more than merely materialistic, is foreseen.[8] † Economically and technologically the so-called second in-

* Sociology as cultural criticism emphasizes this dangerous tendency, in contrast to role sociology which uses an exact methodology that justifies conditions as they are.

† But the totality of the claims on man are determined independently (by "the Party"); this concept was meant to be a revolutionary answer to the Western

dustrial revolution corresponds to this. Automation has changed considerably such aspects as the conditions for full employment, division of labor, job organization, affluence, concept of work, and image of life. In this connection it is of importance to mention the progress of cybernetic thinking in East and West.[9] In the West classical liberalism becomes a cybernetically understandable and calculable society [10] of role-players,[11] functionally categorized according to interests. In the East, an authoritarian regime is gradually giving increased consideration to the "material interests" of the private individual.[12]

It may be easy to assume that two convergent movements are necessitated by modern industrial society. The base-superstructure pattern may perhaps be applicable here. The "overlapping" or practical "approximation" of East and West may have a base in the challenges both face in industrial society as well as in human nature in general.[13] * Both societies are influenced by them, each in its specific way, particularly since the answers offered by the respective ideologies—in theory at least—are different.

The facts of human communities can be understood only in a defined context. It seems, however, that a socio-philosophical interpretation of the present situation may be based on some statements which are, comparatively speaking, objectively secure. An industrial society in the twentieth century, whether defined by a liberal-individualistic or a communistic image of man, demands of both systems attitudes that conform to contemporary reality. Industrial society presents requirements and contains forces which refer equally to East and West. Both must face them, each in its own way. The shaping forces of history are not known. The continued development of both "worlds" and their mutual relations cannot be predicted.[14] The result of an analysis—as free from bias as possible—confirms that the two opposed socio-philosophical positions might converge into an economic policy that is not devoid of hope. Perhaps mankind is actually in an "era of adjustment"—an adjustment, however, which does not consist in an assimilation of one or another set of economic and philosophical principles, but in a convergence of two economic structures and images of man which oppose each other only on the question of property.[15] †

Yet similarity in appearance does not mean similarity of cause. A

"alienation" symptoms and is even more conclusive proof of the exclusion of independent personality.

* This means the dialectical unity of individual freedom and social determinism, of material and spiritual interests, and related concepts.

† This opinion of the situation mediates between a theory of assimilation and emphasis on an irreconcilable dualism.

market economy, welfare state is not the same system as a Marxist state-centralized collectivism adapted to modern requirements. This latter created—by force—the restricted operations of "secondary systems," [16] a threat which also menaces the West.[17] * The controversy, in the West as well as the East, is not about present-day conditions and the resulting questions for the future; but rather each sees its own traits in the light of its ideals, and its opponent in terms of its worst, and already partly outmoded, traits.

On the other hand, within the modern period (that is, within the last two hundred years) each system seems to be one-sided. The two systems represent the conflict between private property and collective property, self-interest and communal interests, individual freedom and conformist regulation.[18] These are, so to speak, contradictions for which it cannot be said at present which side might offer better prospects of resolution.[19] As long as both sides remain intransigent, they fail to recognize the facts of human action in which each impulse is faced by its opposite. Since both are rationally and humanely directed social orders, West and East each have the possibility of surmounting this dichotomy. The West does not need to descend to an idealized image of itself and a caricature of the other side. The West possesses a unique freedom, the creative power of which is the final source of all social "necessity." [20] †

The dangers of the East—autocracy of party leadership, ideological dictatorship, and economic despotism—are known. It is the danger of the West that its much-vaunted freedom becomes a meaningless expression. In fact, individuals, urged by the necessity of guaranteeing their advancement by conforming roles, are easy prey to the "pressures" of an anonymous system. This appears clearly in the area of consumption, among others, and is called "conspicuous consumption" (Veblen). Individual concepts of needs correspond to an increasing extent with social ones by association. In this way individual consumption threatens to meld with collective consumption and into attempts to work out rational, scientific norms for consumption as in the Soviet Union, although by a different path.

Placing the blame for deficiencies in coping with formal freedom on

* The theory that the allegedly nihilistic "lack of ideals" of the West could open the market for communism as an "idea of salvation" may be correct for some moralists but may be disregarded here.

† The West indeed needs a philosophical anthropology which makes clear the advantages of its image of man compared to that of the East's. The first steps toward such an anthropology, which could reach Marx's level, may be found in the widely divergent works of A. Gehlen, H. Plessner, H. Freyer, J.-P. Sartre, H. Marcuse, T. Adorno, J. Habermas, and others.

human fallibility is often defended by the proponents of liberalism, in reference to its greater economic rationality, by objecting to the economic results of centrally planned systems in which Western freedom has been eliminated. Eastern economists, on the other hand, still maintain a picture of the West as an incorrigible system of exploitation of imperialistic character, shaken by crises and chronic unemployment. This caricature only demonstrates that they do not have any valid arguments against the Western economic structure as it really is.[21] *

Marx, according to his image of man as a species subject to the laws of history, began by giving functional precedence to social welfare. His successors erected a planned economy on this foundation. Smith imagined the functional precedence of unadulterated individual welfare according to the puritanical and individualistic image of man of his time. The Manchester liberalists succeeding him created from this the doctrine and practice of unfettered private capitalism. The legacy of this past is the East-West conflict. There is an unmistakable discrepancy between what is claimed by each of these one-sided anthropologies and what actually occurs. A Rousseau-type community did not arise in one instance nor was the felicitous commonality of completely free man realized in the other.[22] † A vacuum of rational values, marked by talk of "pluralism" here and a petrified world of utopian and deterministic values there, demand that the observer understand both sides in terms of intellectual history. This would lead to a dialectical treatment of the fundamental socio-philosophical antitheses, individualism and communism.

2. A SOCIO-PHILOSOPHICAL RESOLUTION OF THE CONFLICT

The cardinal point in the humanitarian problems existing today may be approached in another way. An intellectual-historical synthesis of liberalism and Marxism surpasses both isms, which appear to be obsolete and spurious solutions. The historical challenges of today can only be seen correctly from a view radically severed from the stereotyped formulas in which obsolete theoretical principles are overemphasized. Observation must, beyond this, turn to the common origin of both philosophies.

* Certainly after the world depression, but even before, liberalism was increasingly influenced by a tendency toward government social policy.

† In both cases the failure of extreme "pre-fabricated solutions" to all problems of human society was shown. Instead, the idea that there are dialectically opposed tendencies in human behavior imposed itself.

An appropriate starting point for this is not offered by any particular concept of the nature of man nor by declaring any statement about nature as bankrupt in the total setting of human history (which would be to threaten nihilism). Neither total re-organization of the social world by communist revolution nor mere acceptance of the status quo seems credible. As already mentioned, Scheler called the present an "era of adjustment." It seems that self-understanding in our times should above all be directed toward a synthesis of the seemingly opposed anthropological concepts discussed here.[23] Out of this could originate a social philosophy which is more progressive than the allegedly most progressive Marxism. It would correspond to a reality no longer divisible into planning and laissez faire, freedom and equality, or the individual and the collective. The obviously dialectical structure of human existence, which makes possible and substantiates such extreme historical positions, would have to be worked out. It would no longer have much in common with the stereotypes of the two "blocs" as described above. The current economic and social effects of this philosophical situation may be seen in the fact that in the East the sphere of private property is again hesitatingly expanding. The existing collective ownership of the means of production may not be disturbed by this development. Furthermore, even the individual personal interests of socialist man may again gain some strength. In the West, however, an increase in government control is becoming evident.[24]

In the meantime, West and East have further developed into industrial blocs which are confronted by the same problem: how to encourage human pride to manifest itself, subject to the requirements of technology and economics, in the form of free, responsible co-operation. For this it would be necessary to resolve the contradictions between labor and humanity.[25]

The dividing lines between economics, society, and politics that appeared in the middle of the eighteenth century are being blurred by philosophically vague opinions in which the issue is naively simplified by statements that there is a little more individualism in the West and a little more socialism in the East. The impression is created that a quantitative equilibrium between the two opposites of human existence (the individual and society) is about to be achieved. This approach does not take into consideration that the question is not one of a calculated parallel existence of two elements, which have an objective reality. The reality resides in a dialectical penetration of autonomous individuality by socio-economic demands and vice versa. Today, both spheres threaten to become dehumanized. This is shown, not least, in the antagonistic and increasing independence and isolation of each. In the end, each concept is turned into its contrary. The private sphere in the West becomes the object of outside forces, for instance, the production apparatus and compulsive consumption. Social action in the communal process of living becomes in the East an area for the individual's search for profit, success, and power.

3. THE COMMON ORIGIN OF THE TWO PHILOSOPHIES

The most uncertainty, in socio-anthropological respects, may lie in the area where East and West overlap most significantly. Since the time of Locke and Rousseau, this area has been the battle field of enlightened occidental social philosophies. The East-West contrast, therefore, appears to be a consequence of the opposite directions taken by these two ways of thinking since their common origin in the idea of harmony of individual and society.[26] Hegel, Goethe, and others who sought to interpret man as a unit of society and as a private individual contributed to the idea. As ever, both the East and the West are confronted by this task. An analysis of their solutions and their experiences with advantages and disadvantages of their methods could enrich modern thinking in detail and in scope. A person who combined within himself both positions would contain the extremes of liberalism and totalitarianism. This antithesis could reconcile Smith and Marx with one another and lead to an integrated person, because each of these philosophers intended the opposite of the one-sided isms that eventually grew out of his thinking. In fact, what was originally an individualistic striving for welfare in the West became an economic order that also directed communal and public policy. Out of the effort to prepare for communism by enforced socialization and the dictatorship of the proletariat originates an industrial combine in which materialism becomes the incentive to the individual and allows him to seek a private sphere of his own.

The free market often left masses of men in misery, at a time when liberalism was already older than Bolshevism is now. It remains an open question whether another period of Stalinist terror is possible in the Soviet Union of the present. But speculations on the future will have to take second place to discussion of the present situation. The Marxists paid for the supposed creation of universal man by forcing every one into a monolithic, uniform, and universal mold. The West paid for the variations of individuality and freely chosen styles of living by leading men as if they were on a leash, using a thoroughly organized labor market and mass consumption that was hardly likely to create liberated personalities. A reconciliation and pragmatically effective mediation between individual autonomy and humanistic empathy ought to be the goal for both sides. It may be, however, that the radical "either-or" of ideologists and power politicians hides the point that the goal of both factions is one; that is, after attaining adequate affluence, the individual is responsible both to the society as a whole and to himself, as one among many essentially equal individuals.[27]

XVIII. EPILOGUE: THE FUTURE COURSE

1. FREEDOM AND PROSPERITY FOR ALL

In their current opposition to each other, both the Western and Eastern social and economic orders manifest the contemporary problems of humanism. With constant progress in the mastery of nature and the shaping of society, this humanism attempts to create free and full self-realization for each individual.

The dissolution of the medieval human image manifested itself first as the physiocratic and then as the liberal image of a new order of nature, in which the free, "autonomous" activity of each person, guided by self-interest, should generate the maximum common welfare. The concept of equality expressed itself here as a demand for equal opportunity for all and hence as a rejection of class privilege. The safeguard against degeneration of self-interest into antisocial egoism seemed in the original concept to be guaranteed by the idea that private interests balance each other in the open marketplace and that in any case they are tempered by the affinity for brotherhood inherent in man.

Marxism is a countermovement that grew out of liberal social economics at a time when that philosophy was already in a very advanced stage, and Marxism developed along the guidelines of the same fundamental humanist idea. It was preceded by utopian socialism. The root of both was the experience that unlimited liberalism did not bring the expected freedom for all but rather humiliation of the worker and a deepening of social differences. The right of all workers to an equal share of the social product became the key principle of both socialism and Marxism. The institutional basis for this—supposedly a historical necessity—was seen in a socialist or communist societal structure that was devoid of private property and whose economic activity was not related to individuality but was to be directed by all and for all. In past experience, this meant economic planning by an authoritative administration acting in the interest of common welfare.

Since then, two opposite principles for the ordering of human relationships, both with the same humanitarian goal, have been competing with each other. One allows a community to develop through the co-operation of self-motivated individuals. The other presumes to have the right to subjugate individuals to the dictate of a supposedly definite common interest, which is understood as universally binding. The shortcomings in each of these one-sided systems are known. During early capitalism, insufficient social security, considerable inequalities, and, at best, an imperfect realization of the goal of freedom and prosperity for all prevailed. Bolshevism exhibited lack of individual autonomy, a coercive regime, neglect in production of consumer goods, and therefore also failure to reach the humanitarian goal.

Such a structural confrontation does, however, suffer from a neglect of historical factors. The time span in which the liberal order has been functioning is many times longer than that of Eastern socialism. The objection could be made that the West has largely overcome the deficiencies which may have been acceptable for Manchesterism and that the market economy is being changed through social progress and intervention. By the same token Marxism, which implemented the social countermovement through absolutism while in the West it was integrated into the liberal system, may in the future also experience internal changes that will at least weaken its shortcomings. It has often been debated whether it is realistic to expect that the extremes in these two systems might eventually be resolved in a Hegelian synthesis.

Instead, modern ideas on comparative economics point toward a compromise solution of problems. In reference to the East, both sides occasionally express the complementary opinion that relaxation of control in favor of quasi-market techniques, which are already observable, could eventually change the entire planning system.

In contrast to such argumentation, one must remember that time and time again in history socio-economic forms have arisen that were not previously conceivable; Titoism is just one example. According to its own interpretation, the Soviet system is in the process of transition into

284

communism; in fact, a highly advanced communism. Because of the advanced socialist consciousness of the population (which under the dictatorship developed various ways of profiting from loopholes in the plan), greater economic opportunities, and extensive withering away of class differences, the end of the strict "plan-and-dictate" hierarchy is near. Henceforth, the perspective is open to economic management that is still centralistic, to be sure, but in an ascending as well as descending direction with responsible co-operation on the part of all citizens.

In contrast, Western students of Eastern economic policy, possibilities, and limitations argue that either a "New Class" of authoritarian economic functionaries or the Party leadership—or both—will not permit a true democratization of the social and economic order. The ambitious programs, which are to enable the economies to at least catch up with the American economy by 1980, also speak against a general relaxation in the direction of greater consumer freedom and consumer orientation. These programs require continued emphasis on heavy industry. Specialists in Eastern economics do, however, acknowledge that greater material incentives and competition for plant profits can increase the general economic productivity.

The year 1980 has been predicted as the time for the introduction of full communism. This does not mean freedom of private property but rather voluntary co-operation in the interest of the social whole. Greater consideration for needs and interests of the individual will come about through expanded "participation" in "societal consumption," that is, gratuitous support. This is already emphasized today, and it is intended to prevent privileges that would otherwise develop from differences which arise from the practice of incentive wages. Incentive wages, partial decentralization, and other measures are consequently intended primarily to increase productivity. To be sure, they pose a double-edged problem for the Soviet regime and its economic and social order because they can easily lead to a simple oscillation between "bourgeoisation" and centralist coercion. But now, as ever, there is the basic ideological hypothesis that the Soviet system will, by shaping the consciousness and raising the educational level of its members, lead to a communistic society of free and willing workers who co-operate for the welfare of all. Thus even in Western arguments, reference is frequently made—appearances to the contrary—to an existing continuity in Eastern development in terms of "model realization" and "ideological stability."

The situation thus contains a multi-sided conflict of interest between the Party and the economy. The Party cannot permit an increase in productivity at the price of bourgeoisation. It would lose its claim to existence. Conversely—in the interest of Party power—Khrushchev attempted, through regional decentralization, to counteract the efforts of economic leaders to be independent from the centralism of the branch ministries. This move regained a stronger influence in individual economic districts for the Party. But Khrushchev's successors rescinded this decentralization.

Profit calculation by plants—a method that, according to present information, is gaining ground—would promote the tendency to a true market economy only if the state abandoned its practice of price setting. This practice links the general central management with the potential and needs of plants and consumers by means of plan establishment and price determination. However, information and suggestions from "below" are apparently increasingly considered in this phase. Centralism thus becomes more collectivized, more accessible to peripheral influences.

It becomes evident that the affairs of the Soviet economic system are in a state of flux, first from internal sources, and secondly through the challenges of global political competition. What is more, this situation could lead to a humanization of the old planning dictatorship. This does not mean that the basic concepts that separate East from West (central direction and collective ownership of the means of production) would be relinquished or even weakened. But if central management veers from government omnipotence, which was often rather economically inefficient, toward a "socialist democracy," in which self-administration and autonomy receive stronger emphasis, then it is not impossible that a compromise between consumption and investment as well as centralist and democratic co-determination could be worked out. A marriage of the interests of personal income with those of increased social prosperity, as well as modern cybernetics as a means of information, could be of help in this.

If this assumption is correct, then one is confronted by the fact that developments could prove that some of the suggestions of Marxism and its idealist critics are about equally valid. For one sees, on one hand, that the necessities of modern industrial society force changes on the Eastern economic system and its social, political, and ideological structure. But, on the other hand, one also sees that the changed basis does not lead to a superstructure analogous to the West, but something quite different.

The concepts "de-ideologizing" and "re-ideologizing" used in the West for analysis of Eastern development are both true, but only if con-

286

sidered together. For renunciation of the narrowness and rigidity of the old ideology is to no small degree necessary in order to make productive co-operation with Western economies possible.

2. TRENDS IN ECONOMIC EVOLUTION

A summary of fundamental positions indicates the possibility of a future accord between the two opposing socio-philosophical concepts. There is evidence for an optimistic evaluation of future developments if less attention is paid to the abstractly formulated and thus antithetical principles of the systems and more is given to economic and social facts. From this point of view numerous trends are discernable which clearly express a surrender of traditionally accepted, intellectually sharply defined opinions. This holds true for the West as well as for the East. In both systems, "signs of softening" below the surface of apparently unchanged ideologies—at times quite undisguised—have become evident. Moreover, various attempts by Soviet economic management to bring about improved functional capability have especially increased lately.

Ideas that originate from the most diverse motives and which, in part, are of a more instrumental kind have also emerged in the West. They can hardly be expected to reflect fundamental changes in economic-philosophical concepts. In the final analysis, however, they express numerous deviations from the model and the spirit of a liberal market economy. Western economic systems today are a mixture of absolute individual freedom and a centrally planned economy. This economy is still often not recognized in theoretical economy concepts. The dethroning of economic laissez-faire, which was especially emphasized from the liberal point of view, by an increasing number of governmental interventions in the economic sector is only one indication of this.

A multitude of more superficial changes that arise from the confrontation of the organizational mechanics of a functional economy by fundamental concepts offer insight on the philosophical questions involved. Some of these concepts pertain to the individual's position in the economy, his role as consumer, and, consequently, to the "final goal" of all economic processes as such, and the role played by free enterprise. This last factor refers particularly to the principles of use by the members of economic society of the income which they produce. To be sure, no quick conclusion must be drawn that there is a clean-cut division between intellectual and technological causes. Rather a reciprocal effect must be assumed so that under certain circumstances changes in the in-

287

tellectual climate represent only a reflex of economic development, just as remodeling of the economic structure can result from new ideas.

In the West, a whole complex of phenomena can be observed which are labeled as social or socio-political and which stand, or at least are seen as standing, in opposition to the market mechanism as well as laissez-faire thinking. At the same time commitments by the individual to society are emphasized, which in effect means a considerable step away from freedom of the individual as emphasized in liberal concepts. Of course, this is often only a reaction to economically caused changes in the structure of society. Thus, the advent of government old age insurance was partly caused by dissolution of the large family, which in the past had to a great extent been able to take care of its economically weak members. Nevertheless, the new tendencies developed out of the ideological reorientation required by new conditions. This reorientation leads to an ever-increasing expansion of anti-individualistic measures and therefore seems to be simultaneously cure and cause for the weakening of the individual's economic position. The development of governmentally guaranteed social security and economic measures introduced for this purpose, such as progressive taxation and compulsory contributions to social insurance in the broadest sense, may be viewed both as a reaction to economic realities as well as their actual cause.

Answers to this dilemma, coming from several sides, are correspondingly varied. In the sense of an orthodox liberal viewpoint, it is indisputable that the measures mentioned, which are currently gaining in scope for Western economies, indicate a partial departure from the basic concepts of liberalism. This is particularly important since economic productivity is far advanced compared with the nineteenth century and the possibilities for the individual to take responsibility for his security in life should have increased. In addition, the abundance of "measures to equalize social burdens" must also be viewed in the sense of a social policy oriented toward the ideal of equality. These measures are less adjusted to the "productivity" of the beneficiary and his contribution to the common social product than to other criteria such as need.

Similar shifts have made themselves felt in the area of income and property distribution in the West. Beginning with the classical liberal doctrine of equality of opportunity, the attitudes on this point have experienced considerable change. A generally increased emphasis upon more equality in distribution has also considerably affected the relationship among individual income shares. This is especially true in respect to income from property. In contrast to earlier, more statically oriented concepts of a "natural" distribution of property and wealth, inequalities

288

in the dynamic formation of wealth have become more and more apparent. As social movements progressed, emphasis on the contribution of labor to the production process has become predominant. In present distribution policies, labor has therefore been accorded the number one position. The leveling tendency which goes hand in hand with this is related to the rising standard of living and the above-mentioned socio-political measures indicate a significant deviation from earlier opinions that stressed productivity.

A further empirical basis for such a view of the problem is also provided by the micro-economic formation of wages. The methods which management has developed to ascertain the fairest productivity wage parity, on the one hand, are offset by an increasingly significant number of wage elements not dependent upon productivity, on the other. To be sure, there are still major regional and international differences in the amount of consideration given factors which promote equality, as the examples used in the present analysis clearly demonstrate. Without doubt, economies that are politically oriented to the left have made the greatest progress in this respect. This is further reinforced through the more or less essential role of the state in wage structuring. The frequent tendency to link the general determination of economic goals with the structuring of incomes just as often entails a disadvantage with regard to productivity. It also expresses the growing influence of planning elements in shaping the over-all course of the economy, whose goals are, above all, elimination of both economic fluctuations and currency devaluation as well as securement of full employment and steady, balanced economic growth. In respect to private ownership of the means of production, the West shows little inclination to undertake drastic changes. Nevertheless, a growing expansion of government influence can also be noted in various production sectors, such as recent discussions on nationalization of basic industries by the Labour government in Great Britain. Such discussions promote the idea of more or less rigid planning of the economy.

In consideration of this situation, a transformation in Western habits of economic thought is quite probable. Moreover, in economic practice the increasing importance given to the principle of equality is demonstrable. To be sure, economic and intellectual motives intermingle in the causal background of these developments so as to preclude a clear labeling of these interdependencies. Within the relative inflexibility of basic Eastern ideologies, the Soviet Union, too, is moving toward a reduction of the contrasts. Economic facts are forcing this development.

In recent years, an increasing emphasis on economic necessity has been noticeable in Western comments about the Soviet economy. This is primarily based on the assumption that the determining role of the Marxist ethic and its social philosophy has receded into the background in favor of a more pragmatically aligned, flexible, and fact-oriented economic policy. Nevertheless, this hypothesis should not be carried too far. There are also ethical and socio-philosophical considerations. Examples from history can be drawn from the U.S.S.R. as well as from the people's republics that follow its economic system, even though their earlier ties with the West and its ideas still exert some influence. A number of phenomena can be pointed out which, in principle, though perhaps with opposite intent, are similar to those of the West.

To begin with, the basic organization of the Soviet economy may be considered. An increasing complexity of the economy can lead to repeated and often extensive changes, which at times even contradict one another. The steady relaxation of the formerly strictly centralized economic administrative apparatus is noteworthy even though the policy has suffered periodic reversals. A demand that decisions be based on the facts of production also involves moderation in applying the plan in concept as well as in execution.

The tendency toward pragmatic and regional differentiation in the economic system is not new, but had already manifested itself—even though sometimes less obviously—in earlier stages of development in the Soviet Union. This applies especially to the managerial system and profit and loss accounting, which has led many observers to speak of the growth of "market economy elements." On the other hand, increasing public and quasi-public ownership of certain types of property and units of production is quite generally observable in the West. Besides a sometimes extensive formalization of the ownership concept (namely in regard to ownership of the means of production), there has been a growing willingness to interfere with private property in favor of "common welfare." At the same time, this also affects the relationship of the income shares. In the East, ownership of capital and acquisition of income from landed property are not considered as contributing to the social product. Yet the possibility cannot be excluded that in the future, as more Western elements are incorporated into the economic system, changes may occur also in this area. Agricultural policies in Poland could be an indication of this.

The considerable variation in incomes in the East offers, in addition, varying possibilities for private savings, which can lead to formation of wealth. The acquisition of income from such sources, at least to a limited extent (such as apartment ownership), is absolutely within the

290

realm of possibility. Developments in the consumer goods sector still seem to be oriented toward influencing the consumption choices of the population. Here, too, there is some evidence of greater consideration of individual consumer wishes. The market research institutes, which have existed for some time, concern themselves with research on consumer desires as do corresponding institutions in Western market economies. In this respect differences between the two systems are obviously diminishing. Continuation of this trend in the East could lead to a gradual end to planning in the area of "consumer goods markets." However, this would require emendation of the principle of economic planning to allow for the needs of the consumer, that is, planning could become "precalculation" of real consumer needs. Thus the differences between planning and freedom to shape the market could be more apparent than real. Interesting parallels offer themselves here also when one considers the increasing "manipulation" of consumer wishes in the West through advertising. The differences here seem to be mostly a matter of degree.

To be sure, these tendencies in the East, which to a limited degree take individual consumer freedom into consideration, are countered by a number of other phenomena of income and consumption formation in which collectivist-egalitarian symptoms are visible. This refers particularly to supplying the population with free goods, which has been strongly emphasized even in the latest program of the Russian Communist party. In addition to planned control of consumption, this has obvious ideological motives. The increased national income is not to be subjected to bourgeois-individualistic consumption but to moneyless allocation.

The success of planning in the area of consumer goods requires that these goods provide collective need satisfaction insofar as they must be consumed if production costs are to be covered. It may be assumed that in the East part of the labor product can more easily be held back, whereas in the Western economy it is passed on to the workers in the form of wage increases and consequently is controlled by individual decisions (as to spending or saving as well as to the allocation of spending among various types of goods). The returns from excess production could also be paid to the state in an appropriate form, for example, as a "profit tax" or "product for the society" to cover costs of goods to be distributed to the population.

The consumer, therefore, loses in part the possibility of making his own choice. The planning aspects of this also relate to the question of investment decisions. In addition to the "buying power excesses," which have appeared repeatedly in the monetary sector and have severely disturbed the consistency of the planning and which, of course, are a result of individual decisions by consumers, other grave planning problems may also develop from consumer freedom. The hypothesis of a "communistic" people with a relatively uniform need structure seems to have little real significance in this connection, at least in the forseeable future.

Changes in the U.S.S.R. and in the people's republics that have been visible for a relatively short time may be considered to indicate a move toward the realization of the ultimate communist state only to a limited extent. With increasing attempts to raise profitability and efficiency in the economic system, a greater measure of market freedom seems, in general, to be unavoidable. Rigid planning, as was typical of the earlier five year plans, may have little chance in the future. Hence, the economies of the Eastern bloc seem to exhibit a tendency to incorporate elements of the Western system and possibly also elements of its socio-ethical foundation similar to that which can already be observed for the West and its market economies in adapting elements from the East.

3. THE CONVERGENCE QUESTION

The multitude of governmental interventions in the West as well as relaxation of the central dictatorship and greater consideration for the consumer in the East are not conclusive evidence of a "convergence" of systems. However, it is possible to speak of an approach in appearances, although basic differences still exist, at least according to present indications. Just the same, it is doubtful whether or not changes solely in the "peripheral zones" of a more pragmatic and, in the short run, flexible economic policy are of as great an importance if the ideological "nucleus" is retained as some Western observers assume. Of course, elements of the opposing system can be incorporated but they will, however, in the new context change in character and consequently accommodate and integrate themselves without much trouble. Even this hypothesis is not sufficient for the facts, because they contain the additional possibility that many of the so-called peripheral corrections will turn the nucleus of the system itself into a meaningless formula in the end. Socially responsible individualism and a socialism or communism in which there is individual initiative could, in the ideal case (that is, if both sides realize their ideals), differ in label only. But the ideal lies far in the indefinite future, in the West as well as in the East.

For the time being then, the fact remains that the differences between the one-sided images of man (the creation of social identity in the individual and of individual autonomy in society) as well as the opposing ownership and planning concepts originating from this also lead to differences in the actual shaping of existence. These differences can only be moderated by more or less extensive revisions in the philosophic approaches of both sides.

A simple convergence simply cannot be expected. However, the contrary opinion that the Eastern (like the Western) system is incapable of decisive change is equally questionable. A collapse of the Soviet system is hardly postulated by Sovietologists today. "Westernization" is wishful thinking and the claim that everything has remained as it was under the dictatorship of the 1930s would be blindness to the facts. There are visible changes that weaken much past criticism. That the changes also often seem to be only poorly co-ordinated attempts to hasten the final goal of a communist society which actually threaten the functional efficiency of the present system is a newly evolved problem.

Just as the Western socially oriented market economies threaten to turn the principle of the common welfare into governmental satisfaction of group egoism by means of a seductive consumer ideology, so in the East a new ethos of free Soviet citizens, acting with social responsibility, could be misused to impose new regimentation of behavior and conformity of thought. Allowing for the unpredictability of human behavior, the following points will probably have a major influence on future developments.

A. Modern, complex, and highly technical industrial society challenges both systems to compromise the "purity" of their respective, one-sided philosophies. The changed forces of production demand new forms of economic organization. Neither central planning nor laissez-faire competition by a large number of small- and medium-sized entrepreneurs seems able to cope with it. Thus in the East, there is promotion of individual initiative and increased use of expert guidance; and in the West, there is a sensibly discreet economic guidance by means of overlapping policies, such as growth, full employment, and stability. In the interest of productivity, the Eastern economies are allowing increasing license for the individual, while the West develops policies that are more responsible to the total economy than has been the case in the past.

B. World economic competition, to no small degree in the area of foreign aid for development, points in a similar direction. In this area, the Western order is being pressured, in the interest of social goals, to reduce its emphasis on rising income and shorter hours. The Eastern order must increasingly place a higher value upon a comprehensive balanced growth and cannot much longer risk isolated programs that duplicate efforts.

C. Finally then, under conditions imposed by the industrial age, the original ethos of a modern functional society is once more relevant. A leading role in this is played by the concept of society as a collective unit made up of the achievements of free and equal individuals with divergent character, productivity status, and opportunities. Modern economic growth and its accompanying organizational requirements cannot be mastered by slaves to the state nor by those who behave purely egoistically.

When considered from the point of view of economic philosophy, the philosophical fundamentals and the economic reality of modern society substantiate each other in surprising harmony. At its practical and theoretical source lies the principle of rational activity by autonomous human beings. The oversimplified, one-sided "isms" and the practices derived from them retreated in favor of an uninhibited and soberly realistic economic practice and a synthetic format of ethical ideals. At times the goal of society must be equal freedom and equal prosperity for all within the framework of a national society; at other times it must be self-motivated action by equals in a community of equals. A further advance in this direction would be in accordance with the image of man —overlooked by the one-sided ideological "solutions"—toward which both orders actually strive. As an interim goal, the schism in the world's economy must be bridged.

FOOTNOTES FROM THE GERMAN EDITION

The footnotes printed here are taken from the German edition with corrections demanded by the revised English text. All substantive footnotes also
appear in English translation in the text.

Abbreviations of Journals Cited

Abhdlg. Inst. Sowjetol.	Abhandlungen des Instituts für Sowjetologie
Amer. Econ. R.	American Economic Review
Amer. Hist. R.	American Historical Review
Archiv Sozwiss. Sozpol.	Archiv für Sozialwissenschaft und Sozialpolitik
Dtsche Z. Philos.	Deutsche Zeitschrift für Philosophie
Econ. J.	Economic Journal
Eth. Nic.	Nicomachische Ethik (ARISTOTELES)
Frankfurter Wirtsch. Sozwiss. Stud.	Frankfurter Wirtschafts- und Sozialwissenschaftliche Studien
Hamburger Jb. Wirt. Gesellpol.	Hamburger Jahrbuch für Wirtschafts- und Gesellschaftspolitik
HdSW	Handwörterbuch der Sozialwissenschaften
HdStW	Handwörterbuch der Staatswissenschaften
H. Ostk.	Hefte zur Ostkunde
Inform. pol. Bild.	Informationen zur politischen Bildung
Jb. Nat. Ökon. Statist.	Jahrbücher für Nationalökonomie und Statistik
Jb. Sozwiss.	Jahrbuch für Sozialwissenschaft
Jogtud. Közl.	Jogtudományi Közlöny
J. Philos.	The Journal of Philosophy

Kölner Z. Soz. Sozpsychol.	Kölner Zeitschrift für Soziologie und Sozialpsychologie
Közgazd. Szle	Közgazdasági Szemle
Konjunk.pol.	Konjunkturpolitik
MEGA	MARX, K. und ENGELS, F., «Historisch-kritische Gesamtausgabe. Werke, Schriften, Briefe»
Mitt. Wirtsch. Inst. Gewerk.	Mitteilungen des Wirtschaftswissenschaftlichen Instituts der Gewerkschaften
NWB	Neue Wissenschaftliche Bibliothek
Ordo	Jahrbuch für die Ordnung von Wirtschaft und Gesellschaft
Osteuropa Wirtsch.	Osteuropa Wirtschaft
Ost-Prob.	Ost-Probleme
Pénzügyi Szle	Pénzügyi Szemle
Phil. Bibl.	Philosophische Bibliothek
Phil. Soz. Veröff. Osteuropa-Inst. Berlin	Philosophische und Soziologische Veröffentlichungen des Osteuropa-Instituts an der Freien Universität Berlin
Presse Sowjet.	Die Presse der Sowjetunion
Prob. Comm.	Problems of Communism
R. Econ. Statist.	The Review of Economics and Statistics
RGG	Religion in Geschichte und Gegenwart
Schmollers Jb.	Schmollers Jahrbuch
Schr. ev. Stud.gem.	Schriften der evangelischen Studiengemeinschaft
Schr. Inst. Handwerk.	Schriftenreihe des Instituts für Handwerkswirtschaft
Schr. Österr. Gewerk.	Schriftenreihe des Österreichischen Gewerkschaftsbundes
Schr. Stud.gem. ev. Akad.	Schriften der Studiengemeinschaft der evangelischen Akademien
Schr. Ver. Socpol.	Schriften des Vereins für Socialpolitik
Schweizer Z. Volkswirtsch. Statist.	Schweizerische Zeitschrift für Volkswirtschaft und Statistik
Social. Trud	Socialističeskij Trud
Sov. Stud.	Soviet Studies
Társad. Szle	Társadalmi Szemle
Veröff. Akad. Gemeinw.	Veröffentlichungen der Akademie für Gemeinwirtschaft
Veröff. Akad. Wirt. Pol.	Veröffentlichungen der Akademie für Wirtschaft und Politik
Volksw. Schr.	Volkswirtschaftliche Schriften
Vopr. Écon.	Voprosy Économiki
Vopr. Filos.	Voprosy Filosofii
Wirtsch.wiss.	Wirtschaftswissenschaft
Wirtsch.wiss. Abhdlg. Freie Univ. Berlin	Wirtschaftswissenschaftliche Abhandlungen. Volks- und betriebswirtschaftliche Schriftenreihe der Wirtschafts- und Sozialwissenschaftlichen Fakultät der Freien Universität Berlin
Wiss. D. Südosteuropa	Wissenschaftlicher Dienst Südosteuropa
Wiss. Z. Univ. Leipzig	Wissenschaftliche Zeitschrift der Karl-Marx-Universität Leipzig
World Aff. Quart.	World Affairs Quarterly
WWA	Weltwirtschaftliches Archiv
Z. ges. Staatswiss.	Zeitschrift für die gesamte Staatswissenschaft
Z. Nat. Ökon.	Zeitschrift für Nationalökonomie

Notes to Chapter I

[1] AMMON, A., «Nationalökonomie und Philosophie», Berlin, Duncker und Humblot, 1961, S. 11 ff.

[2] BRECHT, F. J., «Die Wirtschaft, das Geld und das Denken. Zwei wirtschaftsphilosophische Rektoratsreden», Stuttgart, Kohlhammer, 1961, S. 8, 11.

[3] KRAUS, O., «Grundfragen der Wirtschaftsphilosophie. Eine analytische Einführung», Berlin, Duncker und Humblot, 1962, S. 22–33, passim.

[4] AMMON, «Nationalökonomie und Philosophie», a. a. O., S. 17 f.

[5] Ebd., S. 24.

[6] Ähnliches gilt für die liberale Wirtschaftsauffassung, die den Ideen der klassischen Nationalökonomie entspricht.

[7] POPPER, K. R., «Naturgesetze und theoretische Systeme», ALBERT, H. (Hrsg.), Theorie und Realität. Ausgewählte Aufsätze zur Wissenschaftslehre der Sozialwissenschaften, Tübingen, Mohr (Siebeck), 1964, S. 84–102.

[8] LÖWITH, K., «Max Weber und Karl Marx», ders., Gesammelte Abhandlungen. Zur Kritik der geschichtlichen Existenz, Stuttgart, Kohlhammer, 1960, passim.

[9] Vgl. v. KROCKOW, C., «Soziologie des Friedens. Drei Abhandlungen zur Problematik des Ost-West-Konfliktes», Gütersloh, Bertelsmann, 1962, vor allem die dritte Abhandlung. Auch die Renaissance des Humanismus-Begriffs in der neueren revisionistischen Literatur des Ostens weist in diese Richtung.

[10] Das Werttheorem der Wiener Schule ist ein anderes Beispiel.

[11] POPPER, K. R., «Die Zielsetzung der Erfahrungswissenschaft», ALBERT (Hrsg.), Theorie und Realität usw., a. a. O., S. 74 ff. – Ferner POPPER, ALBERT u. a., in: TOPITSCH, E. (Hrsg.), Logik der Sozialwissenschaften, Köln-Berlin, Kiepenheuer und Witsch, 1965 (NWB, Bd. 6).

[12] Vgl. in diesem Sinne der Anklage der rationalen Wirtschaftstheorie durch E. HEIMANN.

[13] KAUFMANN, F., «Methodenlehre der Sozialwissenschaften», Wien, Springer, 1936, S. 129 ff.

[14] AUSTEDA, F., «Axiomatische Philosophie. Ein Beitrag zur Selbstkritik der Philosophie», Berlin, Duncker und Humblot, 1962, S. 95–108, 170 ff.

[15] HOLZER, K., «Theorie des Datenrahmens. Ökonomische Theorie ‹meta-ökonomischer› Faktoren», Berlin, Duncker und Humblot, 1964, S. 5.

[16] Vgl. v. KEMPSKI, J., «Brechungen. Kritische Versuche zur Philosophie der Gegenwart», Hamburg, Rowohlt, 1964, S. 223–231, 310–327. – DAHRENDORF, R., «Pfade aus Utopia. Zu einer Neuorientierung der soziologischen Analyse», ALBERT (Hrsg.), Theorie und Realität usw., a. a. O., S. 331–350.

[17] HABERMAS, J., «Kritische und konservative Aufgaben der Soziologie», ders., Theorie und Praxis. Sozialphilosophische Studien, Neuwied, Luchterhand, 1963, S. 215–230.

[18] LANGE, O., «Kritik der subjektivistischen Ökonomik», ALBERT (Hrsg.), Theorie und Realität usw., a. a. O., S. 287–304. – Ferner v. KEMPSKI, «Brechungen usw.», a. a. O., S. 231. – Ders., «Handlung, Maxime und Situation. Zur logischen Analyse der mathematischen Wirtschaftstheorie», ALBERT (Hrsg.), Theorie und Realität usw., a. a. O., S. 232–247. – JONAS, F., «Das Selbstverständnis der ökonomischen Theorie», Berlin, Duncker und Humblot, 1964 (Volksw. Schr., Nr. 73), S. 157–168, 217–226. – KRAUS, «Grundfragen der Wirtschaftsphilosophie usw.», a. a. O., S. 55 ff. – SCHACK, H., «Wirtschaftsleben und Wirtschaftsgestaltung. Die Grundlagen der Wirtschafts- und Sozialphilosophie», Berlin, Duncker und Humblot, 1963, S. 115 f., 167 f. – GADAMER, H.-G., «Wahrheit und Methode. Grundzüge einer philosophischen Hermeneutik», Tübingen, Mohr (Siebeck), 1960, S. 1–7.

[19] Alles Beweisen einer größeren oder geringeren Leistungsfähigkeit etwa in bezug auf Wohlstand des einen oder anderen Systems gerät von daher in die Schwebe. Ebenso zeigt sich manche normative Forderung als ratlose Illusion, sei sie nun retrospektiven oder utopischen Charakters.

[20] Eine Ausschließlichkeit oder Alleingeltung dieser drei Alternativen wird hier nicht be-

hauptet. Noch weniger eine Trefflichkeit der zu ihrer Kennzeichnung verwendeten Ausdrücke. Doch stehen sie im Zentrum der Sache.

21 Vgl. v. KEMPSKI, «Brechungen usw.», a. a. O., S. 231.

22 DAHRENDORF, «Pfade aus Utopia usw.», a. a. O., S. 331–350.

23 FREYER, H., «Das soziale Ganze und die Freiheit der Einzelnen unter den Bedingungen des industriellen Zeitalters», Göttingen, Musterschmidt, 1957, passim.

24 Wirtschaftsphilosophie ist demnach wenigstens nicht primär Logik und Erkenntnistheorie der Einzelwissenschaft(en) von der Wirtschaft. Sie ist vor allem eine anthropologisch umgreifende Erörterung des tätigen Umgangs des Menschen mit seiner Welt und so auch des wirtschaftenden Tuns. Anschließend kann sie dann auch Überprüfung der wirtschaftswissenschaftlichen Erkenntnisweise sein. BRECHT, «Die Wirtschaft, das Geld und das Denken usw.», a. a. O., S. 15 f.

25 WANNENMACHER, W., «Der geduldete Kapitalismus. Wesen und Wege der Wirtschaft in West und Ost», Düsseldorf, Droste, 1964, S. 12–18, passim. Zu erwähnen sind hier auch R. ARON, W. W. ROSTOW, A. GEHLEN, H. FREYER und D. HOROWITZ.

26 BRECHT, «Die Wirtschaft, das Geld und das Denken usw.», a. a. O., S. 17–20.

27 Vgl. v. ZWIEDINECK-SÜDENHORST, O., «Mensch und Wirtschaft. Aufsätze und Abhandlungen zur Wirtschaftstheorie und Wirtschaftspolitik», Bd. 1, Berlin, Duncker und Humblot, 1955, S. 232.

28 Vgl. v. KEMPSKI, J., «Zur Logik der Ordnungsbegriffe, besonders in den Sozialwissenschaften», ALBERT (Hrsg.), Theorie und Realität usw., a. a. O., S. 232, passim.

29 Reine «Ismen» metaphysischer Art, solche also, die sich als Letztbegründungen der Weltwirklichkeit im ganzen verstehen, werden heute kaum noch vertreten.

30 Dieser Satz bedeutet nicht eine «Interdependenz der Ordnungen». Ob eine solche hier besteht, ist problematisch.

31 HEIMANN, E., «Soziale Theorie der Wirtschaftssysteme», Tübingen, Mohr (Siebeck), 1963 (Veröff. Akad. Wirt. Pol., Hamburg), S. 293.

32 Die Problematik dieser Verbindung zwischen Seins- und Sollensurteil wird noch weiter unten diskutiert.

33 Inzwischen gibt es eine explizite kommunistische Ethik und marxistische Moral. Diese wird im Vierten Teil erörtert.

34 Ausdrücklich lehnt K. MARX, der historischen Art aller menschlichen Dinge bewußt, eine «Wesensbestimmung» des Menschen ab.

35 BOHNEN, A., «Die utilitaristische Ethik als Grundlage der modernen Wohlfahrtsökonomik», Göttingen, Schwartz, 1964, passim.

36 ALBERT, H., «Ökonomische Ideologie und politische Theorie. Das ökonomische Argument in der ordnungspolitischen Debatte», Göttingen, Schwartz, 1954, S. 15 ff., passim.

37 Vgl. v. ZWIEDINECK-SÜDENHORST, «Mensch und Wirtschaft usw.», a. a. O., S. 381 f., 387 ff.

38 HORKHEIMER, M., «Philosophie und Soziologie», Kölner Z. Soz. Sozpsychol., Jg. 11, Köln, 1959, S. 155–164. – JÖHR, W. A. und SINGER, H. W., «Die Nationalökonomie im Dienste der Wirtschaftspolitik», 2. Aufl., Göttingen, Vandenhoeck und Ruprecht, 1964 (Kleine Vandenhoeck-Reihe 176/177/178), S. 48 f., 86 f.

39 MESSNER, J., «Das Gemeinwohl. Idee, Wirklichkeit, Aufgaben», Osnabrück, Fromm, 1962, S. 123. – WILPERT, P., «Sachlichkeit und Sittlichkeit in der Wirtschaft», SPITALER, A. (Hrsg.), Sachlichkeit und Sittlichkeit in der Wirtschaft, Graz-Wien-Köln, Styria, 1962, S. 15 bis 38. – TOPITSCH, E., «Sozialphilosophie zwischen Ideologie und Wissenschaft», Neuwied, Luchterhand, 1961, S. 53–70, passim.

40 Vgl. dazu den Aufsatz des Verfassers «Über die Ausgangspunkte der Volkswirtschaftspolitik», Schmollers Jb., Jg. 52, 2. Halbbd., München-Leipzig, 1928, S. 823–848.

41 RÖPKE, W., HÜNERMANN, J., MÜLLER, E., «Wirtschaftsethik heute», Hamburg, Furche, 1956, S. 4 f., 8 f., 24 ff., 36 f., passim.

42 TOPITSCH, «Sozialphilosophie zwischen Ideologie und Wissenschaft», a. a. O., S. 107 bis 153. – BRECHT, A., «Politische Theorie. Die Grundlagen politischen Denkens im 20. Jahrhundert» (aus dem Engl.), Tübingen, Mohr (Siebeck), 1961, S. 3–15, 200 ff., 313–362. – Vgl.

auch v. FERBER, C., «Der Werturteilsstreit 1909–1959. Versuch einer wissenschaftsgeschichtlichen Interpretation», Kölner Z. Soz. Sozpsychol., Jg. 11, a. a. O., S. 21–37. – MÜLLER-ARMACK, A., «Wandlungen des Wissenschaftsideals im Blick auf Max Weber», KLOTEN, N., KRELLE, W., MÜLLER, H. und NEUMARK, F. (Hrsg.), Systeme und Methoden in den Wirtschafts- und Sozialwissenschaften. Erwin von Beckerath zum 75. Geburtstag, Tübingen, Mohr (Siebeck), 1964, S. 305–319.

⁴³ Vgl. v. MISES, L., «Human Action. A Treatise in Economics», New Haven, Yale University Press, 1949. – Ferner v. KEMPSKI, «Zur Logik der Ordnungsbegriffe usw.», sowie DERS., «Handlung, Maxime und Situation usw.», ALBERT (Hrsg.), Theorie und Realität usw., a. a. O., S. 209–247, vor allem S. 232 ff.

⁴⁴ VITO, F., «Der ‹Methodenstreit› in der wissenschaftlichen Atmosphäre des 20. Jahrhunderts», KRUSE, A. (Hrsg.), Wirtschaftstheorie und Wirtschaftspolitik, Berlin, Duncker und Humblot, 1951, S. 323–341. – TAYLOR, O. H., «Philosophies and Economic Theories in Modern Occidental Culture», DERS., Economics and Liberalism, Collected Papers, Cambridge/Mass., Harvard University Press, 1955, S. 191–223, vor allem S. 198 f.

⁴⁵ SALIN, E., «Geschichte der Volkswirtschaftslehre», 3. erw. Aufl. Bern, Francke, 1944, S. 210, 212. – FREYER, H., «Die Bewertung der Wirtschaft im philosophischen Denken des 19. Jahrhunderts», KRUEGER, F. (Hrsg.), Arbeiten zur Entwicklungspsychologie, Leipzig, Engelmann, 1921, Nr. 5, vor allem die methodologische Einleitung, S. 90 ff.

⁴⁶ Ebd., S. 100 f., 112 f., 128, 131.

⁴⁷ JÖHR und SINGER, «Die Nationalökonomie im Dienste der Wirtschaftspolitik», a. a. O., S. 86 ff. – ACHINGER, H., «Sozialpolitik und Wissenschaft», Stuttgart, Enke, 1963, S. 27–77. – TOPITSCH, E., «Sozialtheorie und Gesellschaftsgestaltung» sowie «Konventionalismus und Wertproblem in den Sozialwissenschaften», ders., Sozialphilosophie zwischen Ideologie und Wissenschaft, a. a. O., passim.

⁴⁸ SCHACK, «Wirtschaftsleben und Wirtschaftsgestaltung usw.», a. a. O., S. 23, 161–186. – KERIMOV, D. A., «Freiheit, Recht und Gesetzlichkeit in der sozialistischen Gesellschaftsordnung» (aus dem Russ.), Berlin, Deutscher Zentralverlag, o. J. (1962), S. 42–62. – ILJITSCHOW (IL'IČEV), L. F., «Methodologische Probleme der Naturwissenschaften und der Gesellschaftswissenschaften», Sowj. wiss. Ges. wiss. Beitr., Berlin, 1964, Nr. 3, S. 217–268. – STARK, W., «Die Geschichte der Volkswirtschaftslehre in ihrer Beziehung zur sozialen Entwicklung» (aus dem Engl.), Dordrecht/Holland, Rydell, 1960, passim. – KAUFMANN, «Methodenlehre der Sozialwissenschaften», a. a. O., passim. – MORGENSTERN, O., «Logistik und Sozialwissenschaften», Z. Nat. Ökon., Bd. 7, Wien, 1936, S. 1–24. – BACK, J., «Nationalökonomie und phänomenologische Philosophie», Jb. Nat. Ökon. Statist., Bd. 126, 3. Folge, Bd. 71, Jena, 1927, S. 225–257.

Notes to Chapter II

¹ Vgl. vom Verfasser ferner «Geschichte der Wirtschaftsphilosophie», MOOG, W. (Hrsg.), Geschichte der Philosophie in Längsschnitten, Nr. 1, Berlin, Junker und Dünnhaupt, 1931. – «Die Entwicklung der theoretischen Volkswirtschaftslehre im ersten Viertel des 20. Jahrhunderts», Jena, Fischer, 1927. – «Die philosophischen Grundlagen wirtschaftspolitischer Zielsetzungen», SERAPHIM, H.-J. (Hrsg.), Zur Grundlegung wirtschaftspolitischer Konzeptionen, Berlin, Duncker und Humblot, 1960 (Schr. Ver. Socpol., N.F., Bd. 18), S. 96–113. – «Scope and Problems of Economic Philosophy», Z. ges. Staatswiss., Bd. 116, Tübingen, 1960, S. 385–401. – «Wirtschaftsethik», HdSW, Bd. 12, Stuttgart-Tübingen-Göttingen, Fischer-Mohr (Siebeck)-Vandenhoeck und Ruprecht, 1962, S. 83–103. – «American Economic Theory Comes of Age», Z. ges. Staatswiss., Bd. 112, Tübingen, 1956, S. 440–463.

² MARCUSE, H., «Vernunft und Revolution. Hegel und die Entstehung der Gesellschaftstheorie» (aus dem Engl.), 2. Aufl., Neuwied, Luchterhand, 1962, S. 229 ff., passim. – HEISS, R., «Die großen Dialektiker des 19. Jahrhunderts, Hegel, Kierkegaard, Marx», Köln-Berlin, Kiepenheuer und Witsch, 1963, S. 327, 330, 336.

3 MYRDAL, G., «Das politische Element in der nationalökonomischen Doktrinbildung» (aus dem Schwed.), Berlin, Junker und Dünnhaupt, 1932, S. 112, 123 f., 161, 198 f., 288 f.

4 LENIN schreibt: «Die Lehre von Marx ... ist die rechtmäßige Erbin des Besten, was die Menschheit im 19. Jahrhundert in Gestalt der deutschen Philosophie, der englischen politischen Ökonomie und des französischen Sozialismus geschaffen hat.» LENIN, W. I., «Drei Quellen und drei Bestandteile des Marxismus», ders., Werke, Bd. 19, Berlin, Dietz, 1962, S. 63 f. – Die Reihenfolge der Meinungen dürfte wichtig sein. ENGELS bezeichnet «die deutsche Arbeiterbewegung» direkt als «Erbin der deutschen klassischen Philosophie» und nennt die drei Namen KANT, FICHTE und HEGEL. ENGELS, F., «Ludwig Feuerbach und der Ausgang der klassischen deutschen Philosophie», Leipzig, Meiner, o.J. (1946), S. 51, 91 (Artikel «Fichte»). – SAGE, P., «Die theoretischen Grundlagen des Stalinismus und ihre Auswirkungen auf die Wirtschaftspolitik der Sowjetunion», Bern, Haupt, 1953, S. 14. – METZKE, E., «Mensch und Geschichte im ursprünglichen Ansatz des Marx'schen Denkens», FETSCHER, I. (Hrsg.), Marxismusstudien, 2. Folge, Tübingen, Mohr (Siebeck), 1957 (Schr. ev. Stud.gem., 5), S. 1 ff., betont, daß auch der heutige Marxismus nicht ohne den Rückgang auf MARX eingehend und kritisch zu würdigen sei; eine Meinung, der beispielsweise G. A. WETTER widerspricht. Er bestreitet die Möglichkeit, durch Bezugnahme auf MARX ein vertieftes Verständnis des derzeitigen Sowjetsystems zu fördern.

5 METZKE, «Mensch und Geschichte usw.», a. a. O., S. 12 f. – HENRICH, D., «Karl Marx als Schüler Hegels», Universitätstage 1961, Marxismus-Leninismus, Geschichte und Gestalt, Veröffentlichungen der Freien Universität Berlin, Berlin, de Gruyter, 1961, S. 5–19.

6 FROMM, E., «Das Menschenbild bei Marx», Frankfurt/M., Europäische Verlagsanstalt, 1963, S. 34–37.

7 WETTER, G. A., «Der dialektische Materialismus. Seine Geschichte und sein System in der Sowjetunion», 4. Aufl., Wien, Herder, 1958, S. 27 f.

8 KWANT, «Philosophy of Labor», a. a. O., S. 84 ff. – DAHRENDORF, R., «Marx in Perspektive. Die Idee des Gerechten im Denken von Karl Marx», Hannover, Dietz, 1953, S. 48.

9 RAMM, T. (Hrsg.), «Der Frühsozialismus. Ausgewählte Quellentexte», Stuttgart, Kröner, o.J. (Kröners Taschenbuchausgabe, Bd. 223), passim.

10 Auch der englische Frühsozialismus setzte hier ein; er machte die von den Klassikern vernachlässigten ethischen Aspekte des Distributionsproblems zum Angelpunkt seiner Überlegungen. – MYRDAL, «Das politische Element usw.», a. a. O., S. 169 ff., 188 ff.

11 RAMM, T., «Die künftige Gesellschaftsordnung nach der Theorie von Marx und Engels», FETSCHER (Hrsg.), Marxismusstudien, 2. Folge, a. a. O., S. 77 f., 103 f., 117 f. – TALMON, J. L., «Die Geschichte der totalitären Demokratie», Bd. 2: Politischer Messianismus. Die romantische Phase (aus dem Engl.), Köln, Westdeutscher Verlag, 1963, passim. – STOLLBERG, R., «Geschichte der bürgerlichen politischen Ökonomie. Eine allgemeinverständliche Einführung», Berlin, Die Wirtschaft, 1960, S. 123–139.

12 RAMM, «Die künftige Gesellschaftsordnung usw.», a. a. O., S. 104–110, 116 f.

13 KWANT, «Philosophy of Labor», a. a. O., S. 59–84. – FRIEDRICH, M., «Philosophie und Ökonomie beim jungen Marx», Berlin, Duncker und Humblot, 1960 (Frankfurter Wirtsch. Sozwiss. Stud., Nr. 8), S. 123–142. – JONAS, F., «Sozialphilosophie der industriellen Arbeitswelt», Stuttgart, Enke, 1960, S. 9–68. – LAUTH, R., «Die ‹verwirtschaftete› Humanität», Neue Deutsche Hefte, Bd. 2, Gütersloh, 1955, Nr. 17, S. 334–346.

14 MEGA, Abt. I, Bd. 3, Frankfurt/M.-Moskau, Marx-Engels-Institut, 1927 ff., S. 125, passim. – FROMM, «Das Menschenbild bei Marx», a. a. O., S. 32 ff., 37 ff.

15 STAVENHAGEN, G., «Geschichte der Wirtschaftstheorie», 2. Aufl., Göttingen, Vandenhoeck und Ruprecht, 1957, S. 139 ff., betont, daß erstmals MARX – in der Nachfolge HEGELS – die Wirtschaft streng historisch begriff: «Sein ökonomisches System ist der erste größere Versuch, der mit der Konzeption einer *dynamischen* Theorie Ernst macht» (ebd., S. 141).

16 METZKE, «Mensch und Geschichte usw.», a. a. O., S. 10 f. – RAMM, «Die künftige Gesellschaftsordnung usw.», a. a. O., S. 99–103.

17 THIER, E., «Über den Klassenbegriff bei Marx», FETSCHER, I. (Hrsg.), Marxismusstudien, 3. Folge, Tübingen, Mohr (Siebeck), 1960 (Schr. ev. Stud.gem., Bd. 6), S. 170–184.

[18] Die Entwicklung und Ausformulierung des historischen Materialismus von MARX ist in den folgenden Schriften enthalten: 1. «Die heilige Familie» und «Die deutsche Ideologie» (1844/45), 2. «Das kommunistische Manifest» (1847/48), zusammen mit ENGELS verfaßt und 3. Vorwort der Schrift «Zur Kritik der politischen Ökonomie» (1859). – Vgl. CORNFORTH, M., «Dialectical Materialism. An Introduction», Bd. 2: Historical Materialism, 2. Aufl., London, Lawrence and Wishart, 1962, passim. – CORNU, A., «Karl Marx. Die ökonomisch-philosophischen Manuskripte», Vortrag vor der Deutschen Akademie der Wissenschaften, Berlin, Akademie Verlag, 1955, passim. – KOFLER, L., «Geschichte und Dialektik. Zur Methodenlehre der dialektischen Geschichtsbetrachtung», Hamburg, Kogge Verlag, 1955, passim. – FRIEDRICH, «Philosophie und Ökonomie beim jungen Marx», a. a. O., vor allem S. 181 bis Schluß.

[19] MOORE, S. W., «The Critique of Capitalist Democracy. An Introduction to the Theory of the State in Marx, Engels and Lenin», New York, Paine-Whitman Publishers, 1957, S. 124–134, ferner S. 58 ff.

[20] TOPITSCH, «Sozialphilosophie zwischen Ideologie und Wissenschaft», a. a. O., S. 54, 188 f., 268, passim. – TUCKER, R., «Karl Marx. Die Entwicklung seines Denkens von der Philosophie zum Mythos» (aus dem Engl.), München, Beck, 1963, passim.

[21] HEISS, «Die großen Dialektiker des 19. Jahrhunderts usw.», a. a. O., S. 309 f., 320, 332 f., 340 f. – Die Umbiegung der MARXschen Philosophie in naturwissenschaftliches Entwicklungsdenken war schon das Werk von ENGELS. – BOLLNOW, H., «Engels' Auffassung von Revolution und Entwicklung in seinen ‹Grundsätzen des Kommunismus› (1847)», Marxismusstudien, 1. Folge, Tübingen, Mohr (Siebeck), 1954 (Schr. Stud. gem. ev. Akad., Bd. 3), S. 77–144.

[22] TAUBES, J., «Abendländische Eschatologie», Bern, Francke, 1947, S. 149 bis Schluß.

[23] MÄRZ, E., «Die Marxsche Wirtschaftslehre im Widerstreit der Meinungen: Ist sie heute noch gültig?», Wien, Verlag des Österreichischen Gewerkschaftsbundes, 1959 (Schr. Öster. Gewerk., Nr. 76), passim.

[24] MOORE, «The Critique of Capitalist Democracy», a. a. O., S. 58–83. – HOFMANN, W., «Ideengeschichte der sozialen Bewegung des 19. und 20. Jahrhunderts», Berlin, de Gruyter, 1962 (Sammlung Göschen 1205/1205a), S. 98–151.

[25] MARX selbst war alles andere als ein Darwinist. Vgl. MARX' Brief vom 18. 6. 1862 an F. ENGELS in MARX, K. und ENGELS, F., «Ausgewählte Briefe», Berlin, Dietz, 1953. – Vor allem K. KAUTSKY vertrat diese Richtung; vgl. MATTHIAS, E., «Kautsky und der Kautskyanismus. Die Funktion der Ideologie in der deutschen Sozialdemokratie vor dem Ersten Weltkrieg», FETSCHER (Hrsg.), Marxismusstudien, 2. Folge, a. a. O., S. 151 ff.

[26] Als wichtige Vertreter des Revisionismus sind zu nennen: E. BERNSTEIN, R. CALWER, A. SCHULTZ, E. FISCHER und E. DAVID. – HOFMANN, «Ideengeschichte der sozialen Bewegung usw.», a. a. O., S. 172–174. – GNEUSS, C., «Um den Einklang von Theorie und Praxis. Eduard Bernstein und der Revisionismus, FETSCHER (Hrsg.), Marxismusstudien, 2. Folge, a. a. O., S. 198–226. – FICKENSCHER, W. (Hrsg.), «Die UdSSR. Enzyklopädie der Union der Sozialistischen Sowjetrepubliken» (aus dem Russ.), Leipzig, Verlag Enzyklopädie, 1959, Bd. 50, S. 664 f., Spalte 1328 f.

[27] FETSCHER, I., «Das Verhältnis des Marxismus zu Hegel», ders. (Hrsg.), Marxismusstudien, 3. Folge, a. a. O., S. 66–169. – Zur Entwicklung des russischen Bolschewismus: WAGENLEHNER, G., «Das sowjetische Wirtschaftssystem und Karl Marx», Köln-Berlin, Kiepenheuer und Witsch, 1960, passim. – v. MARTIN, A., «Ordnung und Freiheit. Materialien und Reflexionen zu Grundfragen des Soziallebens», Frankfurt/M., Knecht, 1956, S. 43 ff., 65, 68. – LANDSHUT, S., «Die Gegenwart im Lichte der Marxschen Lehre», Hamburger Jb. Wirt. Gesellpol., Jg. 1, Tübingen, 1956, S. 42 ff. – Als östliche Version vgl. SCHULZ, G., «Der Prozeß der Vergesellschaftung der Produktion und seine Hauptbestandteile», Dtsche Z. Philos., Jg. 9, Berlin, Verlag der Wissenschaften, 1961, Nr. 8, S. 970 ff., vor allem S. 975 f.

[28] FLECHTHEIM, O. K., «Marx und die Sozialdemokratie», Universitätstage 1961, Marxismus-Leninismus, Geschichte und Gestalt, Veröffentlichung der Freien Universität Berlin, Berlin, de Gruyter, 1961, S. 20–31.

Notes to Chapter III

1 HÖLZLE, E., «Die Revolution der zweigeteilten Welt. Eine Geschichte der Mächte 1905–1929», Hamburg, Rowohlt, 1963, S. 63–76. – JASPERS, K., «Die geistige Situation der Zeit», Berlin-Leipzig, de Gruyter, 1931, S. 135–144.

2 FREYER, «Das soziale Ganze usw.», a. a. O., passim.

3 ELIOT, T. S., «Zum Begriff der Kultur», Hamburg, Rowohlt, 1961, S. 89.

4 KARRENBERG, F., «Verantwortung und Möglichkeiten des einzelnen in der modernen Gesellschaft», ders., ALBERT, H. (Hrsg.), Sozialwissenschaft und Gesellschaftsgestaltung. Festschrift für Gerhard Weisser, Berlin, Duncker und Humblot, 1963, S. 229–248.

5 LE BON, G., «Psychologie der Massen», Hamburg, Rowohlt, 1956, S. 85–92.

6 CASSOU, J., «Politik, Gesellschaft, geistiges Leben», ders., PEVSNER, N., LANGUI, E. (Hrsg.), Durchbruch zum 20. Jahrhundert. Kunst und Kultur der Jahrhundertwende, München, Callwey, 1962, S. 5–115.

7 GITERMANN, V., «Die russische Revolution», Propyläen Weltgeschichte. Eine Universalgeschichte, Bd. 9: Das 20. Jahrhundert, Berlin-Frankfurt-Wien, Propyläen-Verlag, 1960, S. 131.

8 TSCHIŽEWSKIJ, D., «Rußland zwischen Ost und West. Russische Geistesgeschichte, Bd. 2, 18.–20. Jahrhundert», Hamburg, Rowohlt, 1961, S. 160.

9 Vgl. das Buch des Verfassers «Weltwirtschaftspolitik im Entstehen. Ein Beitrag zur Lehre v. d. Gemeinbedürfnissen», Jena, Fischer, 1933, S. 55 ff., 98–133, 158–220, 227 ff.

10 HEILBRONER, R. L., «Wirtschaft und Wissen. Zwei Jahrhunderte Nationalökonomie» (aus dem Engl.), Köln, Bund Verlag, 1960, S. 273.

11 Die Gründe für diese Tendenz liegen nicht allein in der nationalsozialistischen Ideologie, die sich z. B. auf FICHTES «Geschlossenen Handelsstaat» stützte, sondern auch in der allgemeinen politischen Situation.

12 COCHRAN, T. C., «Wirtschaft und Gesellschaft in Amerika. Von der Jahrhundertwende bis zur Gegenwart», Stuttgart, Fischer, 1964, S. 152–160.

13 Noch 1940 gab es über 8 Millionen Arbeitslose.

14 KEYNES, J. M., «The General Theory of Employment, Interest, and Money», London, Macmillan, 1946 (Abdruck der ersten Ausgabe von 1936).

15 PREDÖHL, A., «Das Ende der Weltwirtschaftskrise. Eine Einführung in die Probleme der Weltwirtschaft», Hamburg, Rowohlt, 1962, S. 40 ff.

16 COCHRAN, «Wirtschaft und Gesellschaft in Amerika usw.», a. a. O., S. 4 ff. – BENDIX, R., «Herrschaft und Industriearbeit. Untersuchungen über Liberalismus und Autokratie in der Geschichte der Industrialisierung», Frankfurt/M., Europäische Verlagsanstalt, 1960, S. 382 ff.

17 STRUMILIN, S. G., «Problemy ekonomiki truda» (Die Probleme der Arbeitsökonomik), Moskau, Gosudarstvennoe Izdatel'stvo Političeskoj Literatury (Staatsverlag für politische Literatur), 1957, S. 50. – POGREBINSKIJ, A. P., MOTYLEV, V. E., PAŽITNOVA, T. K., und PODKOLZIN, A. M., «Istorija narodnogo chozjajstva SSSR – 1917–1963 gg.» (Die Geschichte der Volkswirtschaft der UdSSR – 1917–1963), 2., verb. und erg. Aufl., Moskau, Izdatel'stvo «Vysšaja Škola» (Verlag «Höhere Schule»), 1964, S. 96, 119.

18 RAUPACH, H., «Geschichte der Sowjetwirtschaft», Reinbek, Rowohlt, 1964 (Rowohlts Deutsche Enzyklopädie, Bd. 203/204), S. 47 ff.

19 MYRDAL, G., «Das politische Element usw.», a. a. O., S. 6–42. – ROBINSON, J., «Doktrinen der Wirtschaftswissenschaft» (aus dem Engl.), München, Beck, 1965 (Beck'sche Schwarze Reihe, Bd. 33), S. 7–35. – Ferner v. MERING, O., «Social Ideals and Economic Theory», Kyklos, Bd. 4, Basel, 1950, S. 172–195.

20 Zur geistesgeschichtlichen Herkunft der materialistischen und idealistischen Wirtschaftsbetrachtung vgl. auch infra, Abschnitte IV und V im Zweiten Teil.

²¹ Vgl. v. FERBER, «Der Werturteilsstreit 1909–1959 usw.», a. a. O., S. 21–37. – DAHRENDORF, R., «Sozialwissenschaft und Werturteil», ders., Gesellschaft und Freiheit. Zur soziologischen Analyse der Gegenwart, München, Piper, 1961, S. 27–48.

²² EUCKEN, W., «Die Grundlagen der Nationalökonomie», 5. Aufl., Bad Godesberg, Küpper vorm. Bondi, 1947, S. 243 f.

²³ WEISSER, G., «Die Überwindung des Ökonomismus in der Wirtschaftswissenschaft», in: Grundsatzfragen der Wirtschaftsordnung. Ein Vortragszyklus veranstaltet von der Wirtschafts- und Sozialwissenschaftlichen Fakultät der Freien Universität Berlin, SommerSemester 1953, Berlin, Duncker und Humblot, 1954 (Wirtschwiss. Abhdlg. Freie Univ. Berlin, Nr. 2), S. 9–40. – NAWROTH, «Die Sozial- und Wirtschaftsphilosophie des Neoliberalismus», a. a. O., passim. – ALBERT, H., «Zur Problematik der ökonomischen Perspektive», Z. ges. Staatswiss., Bd. 117, Tübingen, 1961, S. 439, passim.

²⁴ Vgl. den Aufsatz des Verfassers «Die philosophischen Grundlagen wirtschaftspolitische. ᵀᵉᵉlsetzungen», SERAPHIM, H. J. (Hrsg.), Zur Grundlegung wirtschaftspolitischer Konzeptionen, Berlin, Duncker und Humblot, 1960 (Schr. Ver. Socpol., N.F., Bd. 18), S. 95–113.

²⁵ Zum Utilitarismus in der Nationalökonomie vgl. MYRDAL, «Das politische Element usw.», a. a. O., S. 13 ff.

²⁶ ALBERT, «Zur Problematik der ökonomischen Perspektive», a. a. O., S. 453.

²⁷ MÜLLER-ARMACK, A., «Wirtschaftslenkung und Marktwirtschaft», Hamburg, Verlag für Wirtschaft und Sozialpolitik, 1947, S. 58.

²⁸ NAWROTH, «Die Sozial- und Wirtschaftsphilosophie des Neoliberalismus», a. a. O., passim, besonders S. 328 ff.

²⁹ Das Freiheitspostulat, das beispielsweise in der neoliberalen Theorie so zentral ist und durchaus idealistisch konzipiert ist, wird unter der ökonomischen Perspektive zur ökonomisch formulierten Freiheit, die mit Freiheit schlechthin gleichgesetzt wird.

³⁰ Vgl. das Buch des Verfassers «Geschichte der Wirtschaftsphilosophie», a. a. O., S. 23.

³¹ MORGENSTERN, O., «Vollkommene Voraussicht und wirtschaftliches Gleichgewicht», Albert (Hrsg.), Theorie und Realität usw., a. a. O., S. 251–271.

³² HOFMANN, W., «Rationalismus und Irrationalismus im ökonomischen Denken der Gegenwart», Jb. Sozwiss., Göttingen, 1959, S. 268 ff.

³³ HOLZER, «Theorie des Datenrahmens usw.», a. a. O., S. 14.

³⁴ PAULSEN, A., «Neue Wirtschaftslehre. Einführung in die Wirtschaftstheorie von John Maynard Keynes und die Wirtschaftspolitik der Vollbeschäftigung», Berlin-Frankfurt/M., Verlag für Rechtswissenschaft, 1950, S. 36.

³⁵ SERAPHIM, H.-J., «Theorie der allgemeinen Volkswirtschaftspolitik», Göttingen, Vandenhoeck und Ruprecht, 1963, S. 64–111.

³⁶ MORGENSTERN, «Spieltheorie und Wirtschaftswissenschaft», Wien-München, Oldenbourg, 1963, S. 76. – DAHRENDORF, R., «Gesellschaft und Freiheit. Zur soziologischen Analyse der Gegenwart», München, Piper, 1961, S. 112.

³⁷ DAHRENDORF, R., «Zu einer Theorie des sozialen Konflikts», Hamburger Jb. Wirt. Gesellpol., 3. Jahr, Tübingen, 1958, S. 76. – PARSONS, T., «Toward a General Theory of Action», Cambridge/Mass., Harvard University Press, 1952, S. 25, 35, 242 f. – DAHRENDORF, R., «Homo sociologicus. Ein Versuch zur Geschichte, Bedeutung und Kritik der Kategorie der sozialen Rolle», Köln-Opladen, Westdeutscher Verlag, 1960, S. 24 ff.

³⁸ MYRDAL, G., «Das Zweck-Mittel-Denken in der Nationalökonomie», Z. Nat. Ökon., Bd. 4, Wien, 1933, Nr. 4, S. 327, Anm. 1.

³⁹ DAHRENDORF, «Homo sociologicus usw.», a. a. O., S. 17 ff.

⁴⁰ PARSONS und SMELSER, «Economy and Society usw.», a. a. O., S. 69.

⁴¹ GEYER, H. und OPPELT, W. (Hrsg.), «Volkswirtschaftliche Regelungsvorgänge in der Technik», München, Oldenbourg, 1957 (Beihefte zur Regelungstechnik), passim.

⁴² RIESMAN, D., «Die einsame Masse. Eine Untersuchung der Wandlungen des amerikanischen Charakters» (aus dem Engl.), Hamburg, Rowohlt, 1958, passim. – WHYTE, W. H. jr., «Herr und Opfer der Organisation» (aus dem Engl.), Düsseldorf, Econ, 1958, S. 69–106, 175–204.

43 LUNDBERG, G. A., «Foundations of Sociology», New York, Macmillan, 1939, S. 5.

44 SCHELSKY, H., «Demokratie und moderne Technik», in: Atomzeitalter, Jg. 1, Frankfurt/M., 1961, Nr. 5, S. 99 ff. – BAHRDT, H. P., «Fiktiver Zentralismus in den Großunternehmungen», Kyklos, Bd. 9, Basel, 1956, S. 483–491. – POPITZ, H., «Technik und Industriearbeit», Tübingen, Mohr (Siebeck), 1957 (Soziale Forschung und Praxis, Bd. 16), passim.

45 WEIPPERT, G., «Instrumentale und kulturtheoretische Wirtschaftsbetrachtung», Jb. Sozwiss., Bd. 1, Göttingen, 1950, S. 30–64. – DERS., «Zur Theorie der zeitlosen Wirtschaft», ebd., Bd. 12, 1961, S. 270–338.

46 WEISSER, «Die Überwindung des Ökonomismus in der Wirtschaftswissenschaft», a. a. O., passim.

47 HEIDEGGER, M., «Sein und Zeit», 7. Aufl., Tübingen, Niemeyer, 1953, S. 15 ff., 45 ff., passim.

48 LANDMANN, M., «Die absolute Dichtung», Stuttgart, Klett, 1963, S. 176.

49 Dabei enthält HEIDEGGERS Ontologie mit der Kategorie des menschlichen In-der-Welt-Seins, der «Sorge», einen fruchtbaren Ansatzpunkt für eine philosophische Erklärung der Wirtschaft. Einen Ansatz in dieser Richtung unternimmt BRECHT, «Die Wirtschaft, das Geld und das Denken usw.», a. a. O., S. 18 f., passim.

50 GEHLEN, A., «Anthropologische Forschung», Reinbek, Rowohlt, 1961, S. 7–25. – ROTHACKER, E., «Probleme der Kulturanthropologie», Bonn, Bouvier, 1948, S. 63–70.

51 LANDMANN, M., «Der Mensch als Schöpfer und Geschöpf der Kultur», München-Basel, Reinhardt, 1961, S. 13–27, passim.

52 WEIPPERT, G., «Jenseits von Individualismus und Kollektivismus. Studien zum gegenwärtigen Zeitalter», Düsseldorf, Schilling, 1964, S. 15–37, passim.

53 «Die Sozialpolitik und die Freiheit des Menschen», Vorträge von A. PAULSEN, E. SALIN und T. BLANK, Berlin, Duncker und Humblot, 1959 (Schriften der Gesellschaft für sozialen Fortschritt, Bd. 9), S. 54 f., passim. – FEDOSSEJEW, P. N., «Sozialismus und Humanismus», Berlin, Deutscher Verlag der Wissenschaften, 1960, S. 10 f., 26 f., passim.

54 RÜSTOW, A., «Das Versagen des Wirtschaftsliberalismus», 2. Aufl., Düsseldorf, Küpper vorm. Bondi, 1950, S. 90 ff., passim.

55 ALBERT, «Ökonomische Ideologie und politische Theologie usw.», a. a. O., S. 21–31, 79 ff.

56 HOLZER, «Theorie des Datenrahmens usw.», a. a. O., S. 11 ff., passim.

57 ARNDT, E., «Wirtschaftlicher Liberalismus und Wirklichkeit», ORTLIEB, H. D. (Hrsg.), Wirtschaftsordnung und Wirtschaftspolitik ohne Dogma, Hamburg, Selbstverlag der Akademie für Gemeinwirtschaft, 1954, S. 33–52, passim.

58 HOROWITZ, D., «Anatomie unserer Zeit. Kapitalismus und Sozialismus im Schmelztiegel», Wien-Köln-Stuttgart-Zürich, Europa Verlag, 1964, S. 54–65, passim.

59 Zur Entwicklung in den USA vgl. HEILBRONER, «Wirtschaft und Wissen usw.», a. a. O., S. 323–362.

60 KRENGEL, R., «Ähnlichkeiten zwischen der sowjetischen und der westdeutschen Wirtschaftsentwicklung nach dem Kriege», in: Vergleich zwischen den Wirtschaftssystemen in der Welt, Berlin, Duncker und Humblot, 1961 (Beihefte der Konjunkturpolitik, Nr. 8), S. 34, passim.

61 Im Marxismus wird Freiheit als persönlichkeitsbildsame Mitarbeit an den öffentlichen Geschicken definiert, während im Liberalismus der private Raum (die eigenen vier Wände) Residuum der Freiheit ist.

62 SOMBART, W., «Sozialismus und soziale Bewegung», 8. Aufl., Jena, Fischer, 1919, S. 34 ff. – MICHEL, E., «Der Prozeß ‹Gesellschaft contra Person›. Soziologische Strukturwandlungen im nachgoetheschen Zeitalter, 2. Teil», Stuttgart, Klett, 1959, S. 106. – ALBERT, H., «Nationalökonomie als Soziologie», Kyklos, Bd. 13, Basel, 1960, S. 24 ff. – MULLER, H. J., «Issues of Freedom. Paradoxes and Promises», New York, Harper and Brothers, 1960 (World Perspectives, Bd. 23), S. 134–143.

63 Vgl. ARISTOTELES, «Nic. Eth.», 1129b.

64 Vgl. ARISTOTELES, «Nic. Eth.», 1130b.

[65] Ebd., 1130b, 1131a.

[66] Vgl. das Buch des Verfassers «Philosophie in der Volkswirtschaftslehre. Ein Beitrag zur Geschichte der Volkswirtschaftslehre», Bd. 1, Jena, Fischer, 1923, S. 94.

[67] ARISTOTELES, «Nic. Eth.», 1130b, 1131b.

[68] Ebd., 1131a 27 f.

[69] Ebd., 1131b, 1132a.

[70] Ebd., 1133a.

[71] Ebd., 1132a, 1132b, 1133a.

[72] BRECHT, «Politische Theorie usw.», a. a. O., S. 176.

[73] Vgl. infra, Abschnitte VII und XI.

[74] DAHRENDORF, R., «Reflexionen über Freiheit und Gleichheit», Zur Ordnung von Wirtschaft und Gesellschaft. Festgabe für E. Heimann, Tübingen, Mohr (Siebeck), 1959 (Hamburger Jb. Wirt. Gesellpol., 4. Jahr), S. 67.

[75] DÖRGE, F.-W., «Menschenbild und Institution in der Idee des Wirtschaftsliberalismus», Zur Ordnung von Wirtschaft und Gesellschaft. Festgabe für E. Heimann, a. a. O., S. 83.

[76] Eine Sammlung der wichtigsten Äußerungen über den Gedanken der Gleichheit in der geschichtlichen Reihenfolge gibt ABERNETHY, G. L., «The Idea of Equality. An Anthology», Richmond/Virg., Knox Press, 1959, passim.

[77] Vgl. v. KÜHNELT-LEDDIHN, E., «Freiheit oder Gleichheit? Die Schicksalsfrage des Abendlandes» (aus dem Engl.), Salzburg, Müller, 1953, S. 33–111.

[78] DÖRGE, «Menschenbild und Institution in der Idee des Wirtschaftsliberalismus», a. a. O., S. 99.

[79] BICKERMANN, J., «Freiheit und Gleichheit. Eine soziologische Untersuchung über das Grundproblem der menschlichen Gesellschaft», Berlin, Collignon, 1934, S. 34–63.

[80] Vgl. v. MISES, «Die Wurzeln des Antikapitalismus» (aus dem Engl.), Frankfurt/M., Knapp, 1958, S. 102.

[81] Vgl. v. KÜHNELT-LEDDIHN, «Freiheit oder Gleichheit? usw.», a. a. O., S. 96–108.

Notes to Chapter IV

[1] Vgl. den Aufsatz des Verfassers «Die philosophischen Grundlagen wirtschaftspolitischer Zielsetzungen», SERAPHIM (Hrsg.), Zur Grundlegung wirtschaftspolitischer Konzeptionen, a. a. O., S. 104–107.

[2] BRECHT, «Die Wirtschaft, das Geld und das Denken usw.», a. a. O., S. 17–20. – ACHINGER, «Sozialpolitik und Wissenschaft», a. a. O., S. 67–78.

[3] BENDIX, R., «Work and Authority in Industry. Ideologies of Management in the Course of Industrialization», New York, Wiley and Sons, 1956, passim.

[4] PRELLER, L., «Sozialpolitik. Theoretische Ortung», Tübingen-Zürich, Mohr (Siebeck)-Polygraphischer Verlag, 1962, S. 78–89.

[5] Fast völlig anderer Provenienz ist der Wirtschaftsmaterialismus von MARX. Vgl. infra, Abschnitt V.

[6] Vgl. v. ZWIEDINECK-SÜDENHORST, O., «Der Begriff homo oeconomicus und sein Lehrwert», ders., Mensch und Wirtschaft. Aufsätze und Abhandlungen zur Wirtschaftstheorie und Wirtschaftspolitik, Bd. 1, Berlin, Duncker und Humblot, 1955, S. 276–295.

[7] Die Wirtschaft wird hier als ein Rückkopplungssystem aufgefaßt, in dem die homines oeconomici auf befriedigende bzw. frustrierende Fakten mit Ja- bzw. Nein-Antworten reagieren.

[8] Hier ist ein Unterschied zwischen östlichem und westlichem Materialismus zu beachten: MARX betont die vom westlichen Idealismus geltend gemachten Zusammenhänge ebenfalls,

aber mit umgekehrter Ursachbehauptung. Der westliche Materialismus hingegen ist eher geneigt, diese Zusammenhänge ganz und gar außer acht zu lassen.

9 HEIMANN, «Soziale Theorie der Wirtschaftssysteme», a. a. O., S. 38–40.

10 Die komplizierte Spannungseinheit von Materialismus und Idealismus im kommunistischen Denken ist in dem Ausgangspunkt von MARX begründet, nämlich dem aus freier Selbst-Produktion sich verwirklichenden Menschen, dessen fundamentaler und alles weitere bestimmender Tätigkeitsbereich der ökonomische «Stoffwechsel mit der Natur» ist. (Vgl. infra, Abschnitt VI).

11 Vgl. v. NELL-BREUNING, O., «Wirtschaft und Gesellschaft. I. Grundfrage», Freiburg, Herder, 1956, S. 198–207.

12 STEINBERG, «Der Einzelne und die Gemeinschaft usw.», a. a. O., S. 142–148. HEGEL und MARX führten den gemeinschaftsbetonten Idealismus fort. KIERKEGAARDS Subjektivismus betonte dagegen den einzelnen. Heute treten Existentialismus (SARTRE) und Marxismus (SCHAFF) in Auseinandersetzung miteinander.

13 Auch hier kann gezeigt werden, daß MARX in gewisser Weise der letzte Klassiker gewesen ist. Sein «Materialismus» ist die Gegenthese zu HEGELs Vorzugsstellung der Idee und Staatsüberschätzung.

14 HIRSCHBERGER, J., «Geschichte der Philosophie», Bd. 2, Freiburg, Herder, 1952, S. 49, 62–80.

15 HAHN, L. A., «Merkantilismus und Keynesianismus», v. BECKERATH, E., MEYER, F. W., MÜLLER-ARMACK, A. (Hrsg.), Wirtschaftsfragen der freien Welt. Ludwig Erhard zum 60. Geburtstag, Frankfurt/M., Knapp, o. J. (1957), S. 140–150.

16 TREUE, «Wirtschaftsgeschichte der Neuzeit usw.», a. a. O., S. 14.

17 BRECHT, «Die Wirtschaft, das Geld und das Denken usw.», a. a. O., S. 16 f. – LÖWITH, K., «Gesammelte Abhandlungen. Zur Kritik der geschichtlichen Existenz», Stuttgart, Kohlhammer, 1960, S. 74, 164, 168, 211, 250 f.

18 JASPERS, «Plato-Augustin-Kant usw.», a. a. O., passim.

19 R. KRONER («Von Kant bis Hegel», Bd. 1, 2. Aufl., Tübingen, Mohr (Siebeck), 1961, passim) ist der Ansicht, daß HEGEL die Philosophie von KANT konsequent weitergedacht hat. – Vgl. auch HEIMSOETH, «Die sechs großen Themen der abendländischen Metaphysik usw.», a. a. O., Abschnitt «Verstand und Wille».

20 Es ist allerdings fraglich, ob bei KANT überhaupt von einer Metaphysik die Rede sein kann.

21 SCHMÖLDERS, G., «Das Bild vom Menschen in der neuen Sozialpolitik», Wirtschaftsordnung und Menschenbild. Geburtstagsgabe für A. Rüstow, Köln, Verlag für Politik und Wirtschaft, 1960, S. 115–127.

22 HIRSCHBERGER, «Geschichte der Philosophie», Bd. 2, a. a. O., S. 340 f. – Vgl. auch v. ZWIEDINECK-SÜDENHORST, «Mensch und Wirtschaft usw.», Bd. 1, a. a. O., S. 323–327. – KRAUSE, W., «Die ökonomischen Ansichten Fichtes in seinem ‹Geschlossenen Handelsstaat›», Wirtsch.wiss., Jg. 10, Berlin, 1962, Nr. 6, S. 815–824.

23 MARX, K., «Zur Judenfrage (1843)», MARX und ENGELS, Die Heilige Familie und andere philosophische Frühschriften, Berlin, Dietz, 1953, S. 56 f.

24 DAHRENDORF, «Homo Sociologicus usw.», a. a. O., S. 52–63.

25 LITT, T., «Das Bildungsideal der deutschen Klassik und die moderne Arbeitswelt», 5. Aufl., Bonn, Bundeszentrale für Heimatdienst, 1958, S. 54–63.

26 BRECHT, «Die Wirtschaft, das Geld und das Denken usw.», a. a. O., S. 16 ff.

27 ROSENTAL, M., «Materialistische und idealistische Weltanschauung» (aus dem Russ.), 2. Aufl., Berlin, Dietz, 1947, passim. – SCHISCHKIN (ŠIŠKIN), A. F., «Grundlagen der marxistischen Ethik» (aus dem Russ.), Berlin, Dietz, 1964, S. 21–48. – WETTER, G. A., «Sowjetideologie heute. I. Dialektischer und historischer Materialismus», Frankfurt/M., Fischer, 1962, S. 24–27.

28 Hier können freilich allerlei Modifikationen und Mischformen auftreten.

29 PRELLER, «Sozialpolitik usw.», a. a. O., S. 34 f., 195–202. – SCHMÖLDERS, «Das Bild

vom Menschen usw.», a. a. O., S. 115–127. – SCHACK, «Wirtschaftsleben und Wirtschaftsgestaltung usw.», a. a. O., S. 103–160. – HEIMANN, «Soziale Theorie der Wirtschaftssysteme», a. a. O., S. 323–328. – RAPOLD, M. U., «Demokratie und Wirtschaftsordnung. Ein Beitrag zur sozialwissenschaftlichen Grundlagenforschung», Zürich, Polygraphischer Verlag, o. J. (1958), S. 75 f., 127 f.

[30] Eine bedeutsame kritische Erörterung des Problemkreises modernen Geschichtlichkeitsdenkens bietet LÖWITH, «Gesammelte Abhandlungen usw.», a. a. O., S. 156–163, 167–174. – Zu SCHELER vgl. LENK, K., «Von der Ohnmacht des Geistes. Darstellung der Spätphilosophie Max Schelers», Tübingen, Hopfer, 1959, S. 62 f., passim.

[31] BRECHT, «Die Wirtschaft, das Geld und das Denken usw.», a. a. O., S. 23. – PRELLER, «Sozialpolitik usw.», a. a. O., S. 6–36. – SCHMÖLDERS, «Das Bild vom Menschen usw.», a. a. O., S. 115–127. – RAPOLD, «Demokratie und Wirtschaftsordnung usw.», a. a. O., S. 122–128.

Notes to Chapter V

[1] Vgl.v. ZWIEDINECK-SÜDENHORST, «Mensch und Wirtschaft usw.», a. a. O., S. 319–325. – SCHMÖLDERS, «Das Bild vom Menschen usw.», a. a. O., S. 115–127. – SCHACK, «Wirtschaftsleben und Wirtschaftsgestaltung usw.», a. a. O., S. 103–160. – HEIMANN, «Soziale Theorie der Wirtschaftssysteme», a. a. O., S. 323–328. – RAPOLD, «Demokratie und Wirtschaftsordnung usw.», a. a. O., S. 75 f., 127 f.

[2] HIRSCHBERGER, «Geschichte der Philosophie», Bd. 2, a. a. O., S. 7, 33.

[3] Ebd., S. 78 f., 171–174.

[4] Daß demgegenüber die Einflüsse der schottischen Moralphilosophie und des idealistisch begründeten Naturrechts standen, wurde bereits in Abschnitt IV dargelegt.

[5] Zu der Problematik, die darin liegt, daß diese Vorstellungen nur in der Produktionssphäre einigen Halt an den Tatsachen finden, siehe SCHMÖLDERS, «Das Bild vom Menschen usw.», a. a. O., S. 117.

[6] KRAUS, «Grundfragen der Wirtschaftsphilosophie usw.», a. a. O., S. 16, 56.

[7] Auch als Unabhängigkeit von äußerer Nötigung und als ausschließliche Befolgung der inneren Antriebe, also im umgangssprachlichen Sinne, wird sie gelegentlich aufgefaßt.

[8] KRAUS, «Grundfragen der Wirtschaftsphilosophie usw.», a. a. O., S. 23 ff.

[9] Falsch wäre es, den praktischen Materialismus vulgären Menschentums oder das rein materielle Wohlstandsinteresse mit dem marxistischen Materialismus in Affinität zu setzen.

[10] BEHRENS, F., «Grundriß der Geschichte der politischen Ökonomie», Bd. 1: Die politische Ökonomie bis zur bürgerlichen Klassik, Berlin, Akademie Verlag, 1962, S. 12. – STOLLBERG, «Geschichte der bürgerlichen politischen Ökonomie usw.», a. a. O., S. 13.

[11] Vgl. den Aufsatz des Verfassers «Über die Ausgangspunkte der Volkswirtschaftspolitik», a. a. O., S. 823–848.

[12] Dieser Punkt bedarf vorsichtiger Erörterung. Wie weit materialistische Lebenseinstellung und materialistische Metaphysik zusammengehören, darf nicht durch eine falsche Gleichsetzung beider vorentschieden werden.

[13] Vgl. v. NEUMANN, J. und MORGENSTERN, O., «Spieltheorie und wirtschaftliches Verhalten» (aus dem Engl.), 3. Aufl., Würzburg, Physica Verlag, 1961, S. 1. – COURNOT, A., «Untersuchungen über die mathematischen Grundlagen der Theorie des Reichtums» (aus dem Franz.), Jena, Fischer, 1924, S. X.

[14] STEINBUCH, K., «Automat und Mensch. Kybernetische Tatsachen und Hypothesen», 2. Aufl., Berlin-Göttingen-Heidelberg, Springer, 1963, S. VII f., 10, 242, 287, 338, 352. – KLAUS, G. und THIEL, R., «Über die Existenz kybernetischer Systeme in der Gesellschaft», Dtsche Z. Philos., Jg. 10, Berlin, Deutscher Verlag der Wissenschaften, 1962, Nr. 1, S. 22–57.

15 Vgl. v. NEUMANN und MORGENSTERN, «Spieltheorie und wirtschaftliches Verhalten», a. a. O., S. 1–8, 40 ff.

16 Ebd., S. 12, 31 f., 40 ff.

17 JONAS, «Sozialphilosophie der industriellen Arbeitswelt», a. a. O., S. 206–215, passim. – Typisch für die Allianz von Soziologie und kybernetischem Denken: PARSONS und SMELSER, «Economy and Society usw.», a. a. O., S. 69, passim.

18 Zur Darstellung dieser Situation in modernen Romanen vgl. ZELTNER-NEUKOMM, G., «Das Wagnis des französischen Gegenwartsromans. Die neue Welterfahrung in der Literatur», Reinbek, Rowohlt, 1960 (Rowohlts Deutsche Enzyklopädie, Bd. 109), passim. – MUSIL, R., «Der Mann ohne Eigenschaften», Hamburg, Rowohlt, 1952, S. 35.

19 Diese Unterscheidung soll keine Wiederaufnahme der Abbild- und Widerspiegelungstheorie von K. MARX sein.

20 DAHRENDORF, «Gesellschaft und Freiheit», a. a. O., S. 73 ff., 355 ff., vertritt die These, daß die Rollen-Soziologie von PARSONS das genaue Abbild einer heute mindestens tendenziell herrschenden Gesellschaftsform sei. – PARSONS und SMELSER, «Economy and Society», a. a. O., S. 69 f.

21 Das wirtschaftstheoretische Pendant dieser Entwicklungsstufe der Praxis war die rationale und kausalanalytische Vorstellung vom rational und also kalkulierbar handelnden homo oeconomicus.

22 PARSONS, T. und SHILS, E. (Hrsg.), «Toward a General Theory of Action», Cambridge/Mass., Harvard University Press, 1952, S. 3–29.

23 Das war Wirklichkeit der Zeit, in der die Theorien von G. SOREL bis C. SCHMITT Geltung hatten.

24 PLESSNER, H., «Das Problem der Öffentlichkeit und die Idee der Entfremdung», Göttinger Rektoratsrede, Göttingen, Vandenhoeck und Ruprecht, 1961, passim.

25 Vgl. die Ausführungen von PIEPLOW, R., KRAUSE, W., SCHMELING, S., DOMDEY, K.-H., SONNTAG, H., BEHRENS, F., THIEL, R., Wirtsch.wiss., Jg. 10, Berlin, 1962, Nr. 6, S. 801–905.

26 WHYTE, «Herr und Opfer der Organisation», a. a. O., S. 29–38, 175–185. – STEINBUCH, «Automat und Mensch», a. a. O., S. 316–355.

27 Für die Vereinbarkeit der Freiheit mit kybernetischen Prozessen sprechen hingegen auf westlicher Seite STEINBUCH, «Automat und Mensch», a. a. O., S. 10, 242, 286 f., und auf östlicher Seite THIEL, R., «Zur mathematisch-kybernetischen Erfassung ökonomischer Gesetzmäßigkeiten», Wirtsch.wiss., Jg. 10, Berlin, 1962, Nr. 6, S. 905.

28 Dies gilt für den Westen. Neuerdings zeigen sich aber auch im Osten philosophische Neuansätze, die sich zwar weiterhin parteitreu marxistisch verhalten, in Wahrheit aber einer Idealismus und Materialismus übersteigenden Lehre vom handelnden Menschen zuneigen (A. SCHAFF).

Notes to Chapter VI

1 BOCHENSKI, I. M., «Der sowjetrussische dialektische Materialismus (Diamat)», Bern-München, Francke, 1962 (Dalp-Taschenbücher, Bd. 325 D), S. 47 f.

2 BAUER, R. A., «Der neue Mensch in der sowjetischen Psychologie», Bad Nauheim, Christian, 1955, S. 23. – HUNT, R. N. C., «The Importance of Doctrine», BRUMBERG, A. (Hrsg.), Russia under Khrushchev. An Anthology from Problems of Communism, New York, Praeger, 1962, S. 5–14. – ARMSTRONG, J. A., «Ideology, Politics, and Government in the Soviet Union. An Introduction», New York, Praeger, 1962, S. 26–34. – BOETTCHER, E., «Die sowjetische Wirtschaftspolitik am Scheidewege», Tübingen, Mohr (Siebeck), 1959, S. 205–296, bes. S. 270 ff.

³ STALIN, J. W., «Marksizm i voprosy jazykoznanija» (Marxismus und die Fragen der Sprachwissenschaft), Moskau, Gospolitizdat (Staatsverlag für politische Literatur), 1950, S. 114. Zur späteren Problematik vgl. WETTER, «Der dialektische Materialismus usw.», a. a. O., S. 309 ff.

⁴ BOCHENSKI, «Der sowjetrussische dialektische Materialismus (Diamat)», a. a. O., S. 53. Zu der Sonderentwicklung in Polen vgl. JORDAN, Z. A., «Philosophy and Ideology. The Development of Philosophy and Marxism-Leninism in Poland since the Second World War», Dordrecht/Holland, Reidel, 1963, S. 480–501. – BRZEZINSKI, Z. K., «Ideology and Power in Soviet Politics», New York, Praeger, 1962, S. 97–134.

⁵ WETTER, «Der dialektische Materialismus usw.», a. a. O., S. 627. – BAUMGARTEN, A., «Bemerkungen zur Erkenntnistheorie des dialektischen und historischen Materialismus», Berlin, Akademie-Verlag, 1957, S. 48 ff.

⁶ BOCHENSKI, «Der sowjetrussische dialektische Materialismus (Diamat)», a. a. O., S. 54.

⁷ «Bol'šaja Sovetskaja Ènciklopedija» (Große Sowjetische Enzyklopädie), Bd. 50: Sojuz Sovetskich Socialističeskich Respublik (Union der Sozialistischen Sowjetrepubliken), 2. Aufl., Moskau, Gosudarstvennoe Naučnoe Izdatel'stvo «Bol'šaja Sovetskaja Ènciklopedija» (Wissenschaftlicher Staatsverlag «Große Sowjetische Enzyklopädie»), 1957, S. 521.

⁸ «Filosofskij Slovar'» (Philosophisches Wörterbuch), M. M. ROZENTAL' und P. F. JUDIN (Hrsg.), Moskau, Izdatel'stvo Političeskoj Literatury (Verlag für politische Literatur), 1963, S. 128–130, 177–179.

⁹ Vgl. das Buch des Verfassers «Philosophie in der Volkswirtschaftslehre. Ein Beitrag zur Geschichte der Volkswirtschaftslehre», Bd. 2, Jena, Fischer, 1926, S. 484 ff.

¹⁰ DAHRENDORF, «Marx in Perspektive usw.», a. a. O., S. 143. – KAMENKA, E., «The Ethical Foundations of Marxism», New York, Praeger, 1962, S. 127 ff.

¹¹ Seit der Entstalinisierung ist die STALINsche Formulierung der Dialektik zurückgetreten und die ursprüngliche Ausarbeitung durch ENGELS wieder mehr in den Vordergrund gerückt. – BOCHENSKI, J. M., «Die dogmatischen Grundlagen der sowjetischen Philosophie (Stand 1958)», Dordrecht/Holland, Reidel, 1959 (Sovietica. Veröffentlichungen des Ost-Europa-Instituts der Universität Freiburg/Schweiz), S. 17–19.

¹² DERS., «Der sowjetrussische dialektische Materialismus (Diamat)», a. a. O., S. 33.

¹³ Die Narodniki waren Anhänger eines vormarxistischen Sozialismus, der überwiegend auf einer ethischen Grundlage aufbaute.

¹⁴ WETTER, «Der dialektische Materialismus usw.», a. a. O., S. 69 f.

¹⁵ MARX, K., «Vorwort zur Kritik der politischen Ökonomie», MARX, K. und ENGELS, F., Ausgewählte Schriften in zwei Bänden, Bd. 1, Berlin, Dietz, 1958, S. 337 f.

¹⁶ Vgl. die Ausführung bezügl. MARX bei WETTER, «Der dialektische Materialismus usw.», a. a. O., S. 47 f.

¹⁷ Vgl. dazu den Brief F. ENGELS an J. BLOCH vom 21./22. 9. 1890, MARX, K. und ENGELS, F., «Ausgewählte Briefe», Berlin, Dietz, 1953, S. 502 f.

¹⁸ Neuerdings wird der Ökonomismus verworfen. – WETTER, «Der dialektische Materialismus usw.», a. a. O., S. 90 f.

¹⁹ «Perepiska K. Marksa i F. Engel'sa s russkimi političeskimi dejateljami» (Korrespondenz von K. Marx und F. Engels mit russischen Politikern), Leningrad, Gospolitizdat (Staatsverlag für politische Literatur), 1947, S. 240–242.

²⁰ WETTER, «Der dialektische Materialismus usw.», a. a. O., S. 101.

²¹ PLECHANOW, G. W., «Über materialistische Geschichtsauffassung» (aus dem Russ.), Moskau, Verlag für fremdsprachige Literatur, 1946, S. 10–14.

²² Ebd., S. 17 f.

²³ WETTER, «Der dialektische Materialismus usw.», a. a. O., S. 450.

²⁴ PLECHANOW, G. W., «Über die Rolle der Persönlichkeit in der Geschichte, 1896» (aus dem Russ.), Moskau, Verlag für fremdsprachige Literatur, 1946, S. 12 f. – BOCHENSKI, «Die dogmatischen Grundlagen der sowjetischen Philosophie (Stand 1958)», a. a. O., S. 32 (11.42).

²⁵ PLECHANOW, «Über die Rolle der Persönlichkeit in der Geschichte, 1896», a. a. O., S. 44 f.

26 WETTER, «Der dialektische Materialismus usw.», a. a. O., S. 91, Fußnote 7.

27 Ebd., S. 456.

28 Ebd., S. 102.

29 LANGE, M. G., «Marxismus, Leninismus, Stalinismus. Zur Kritik des dialektischen Materialismus», Stuttgart, Klett, 1955, S. 93.

30 WETTER, «Der dialektische Materialismus usw.», a. a. O., S. 147. – «Filosofskaja Ènciklopedija» (Philosophische Enzyklopädie), Moskau, Gosudarstvennoe Naučnoe Izdatel'-stvo Sovetskaja Ènciklopedija (Wissenschaftlicher Staatsverlag «Sowjetische Enzyklopädie»), 1960, S. 478. – Die Bedeutung der Realpolitik bei LENIN würdigt: LABEDZ, L., «Ideology: The Fourth Stage», BRUMBERG (Hrsg.), Russia under Khrushchev usw.», a. a. O., S. 49 ff.

31 FETSCHER, I., «Von Marx zur Sowjetideologie», 10. Aufl., Frankfurt/M.-Berlin-Bonn, Diesterweg, 1963 (Staat und Gesellschaft, Bd. 4), S. 73 f.

32 BOGDANOV war der Hauptvertreter des Empiriomonismus. Dieser Ansatz stellte eine erhebliche Gefährdung des materialistischen Grundsatzes der Philosophie dar und wurde entsprechend scharf bekämpft.

33 LENIN, W. I., «Materialismus und Empiriokritizismus. Kritische Bemerkungen über eine reaktionäre Philosophie», ders., Werke, Bd. 14, Berlin, Dietz, 1962, S. 7–366.

34 FETSCHER, «Von Marx zur Sowjetideologie», a. a. O., S. 74.

35 WETTER, «Der dialektische Materialismus usw.», a. a. O., S. 338.

36 Ebd., S. 345, 561 f.

37 FETSCHER, «Von Marx zur Sowjetideologie», a. a. O., S. 76.

38 LENIN, «Materialismus und Empiriokritizismus usw.», Bd. 14, a. a. O., S. 42.

39 LENIN, W. I., «Konspekt knigi Gegelja ‹Nauka Logiki›. Tret'ja kniga. Sub-ektivnaja logika·ili učenie o ponatii. O ponatii voobšče» (Zur Kritik des Buches von Hegel, Wissenschaft der Logik. Drittes Buch. Die subjektive Logik oder die Lehre vom Begriff. Vom Begriff im allgemeinen), ders., Sočinenija (Werke), Bd. 38, Moskau, Gosudarstvennoe Izdatel'stvo Političeskoj Literatury (Staatsverlag für politische Literatur), 1958, S. 157. Ein Teil der philosophischen Arbeiten von LENIN ist in deutscher Sprache erschienen. Vgl. infra, Fußnote 61.

40 FETSCHER, «Von Marx zur Sowjetideologie», a. a. O., S. 77.

41 Die Frage, ob dem menschlichen Denken gegenständliche Wahrheit zukomme, ist keine Frage der Theorie, sondern eine praktische Frage. In der Praxis muß der Mensch die Wahrheit, d. h. die Wirklichkeit und Macht, die Diesseitigkeit seines Denkens beweisen.

42 BAUMGARTEN, «Bemerkungen zur Erkenntnistheorie usw.», a. a. O., S. 124.

43 LENIN, «Konspekt knigi Gegelja ‹Nauka Logiki› usw.», a. a. O., S. 160 f.

44 WETTER, «Der dialektische Materialismus usw.», a. a. O., S. 585.

45 FETSCHER, «Von Marx zur Sowjetideologie», a. a. O., S. 88.

46 LENIN, W. I., «Wie soll man den Wettbewerb organisieren?», ders., Werke, Bd. 26, Berlin, Dietz, 1961, S. 411 f. – DERS., «Materialismus und Empiriokritizismus usw.», a. a. O., S. 103, insbes. S. 137 f., 166.

47 An diesem Dogma wird noch heute unbeirrbar festgehalten. – Vgl. Pravda vom 15. 10. 1964, S. 1: «Slava gerojam!» (Heil den Helden!).

48 DEBORIN wurde wegen dieser richtigen Folgerung aus dem undialektischen Ansatz LENINS angegriffen. – WETTER, «Der dialektische Materialismus usw.», a. a. O., S. 588 und Fußnote ebd.

49 LENIN, W. I., «K voprosu o dialektike» (Zur Frage der Dialektik), ders., Sočinenija (Werke), Bd. 38, a. a. O., S. 358. – JORDAN, «Philosophy and Ideology usw.», a. a. O., S. 368 f.

50 KONSTANTINOV, F. V., «Osnovy marksistskoj filosofii» (Die Grundlagen der marxistischen Philosophie), 2. Aufl., Moskau, Gosudarstvennoe Izdatel'stvo Političeskoj Literatury (Staatsverlag für politische Literatur), 1963, S. 289 ff., 322 ff.

51 LÖWENTHAL, R., «The Logic of One-Party Rule», BRUMBERG (Hrsg.), «Russia under Khrushchev usw.», a. a. O., S. 27–45.

52 RUTKEVIČ, M. N., «Praktika – osnova poznanija i kriterij istiny» (Die Praxis als

Grundlage der Erkenntnis und als Kriterium der Wahrheit), Moskau, Gosudarstvennoe Izdatel'stvo Političeskoj Literatury (Staatsverlag für politische Literatur), 1952, S. 167–191.

[53] BOCHENSKI, «Die dogmatischen Grundlagen der sowjetischen Philosophie (Stand 1958)», a. a. O., S. 47 f. (15.54; 15.55).

[54] DERS., S. 27, insbes. die Nummern 10.54, 10.55. – FETSCHER, «Von Marx zur Sowjetideologie», a. a. O., S. 88.

[55] FETSCHER, I., «Stalin. Über dialektischen und historischen Materialismus», Frankfurt/M.-Berlin-Bonn, Diesterweg, 1956, passim.

[56] ČESNOKOV, D. I., «Istoričeskij materializm» (Der historische Materialismus), Moskau, Izdatel'stvo social'no-ekonomičeskoj literatury (Verlag für Sozialwesen und Ökonomik), 1964, S. 3–20. – «Filosofskij Slovar'», a. a. O., S. 128–130, 257–259. – Vgl. auch MEHNERT, K., «Der Sowjetmensch. Versuch eines Porträts nach zwölf Reisen in die Sowjetunion, 1929 bis 1957», 3. Aufl., Stuttgart, Deutsche Verlags-Anstalt, 1958, S. 269 ff.

[57] «Geschichte der Kommunistischen Partei der Sowjetunion (Bolschewiki)», Kurzer Lehrgang, 10. Aufl., Berlin, Dietz, 1952 (Bücherei des Marxismus-Leninismus, Bd. 12), S. 131–166.

[58] ROSTOW, W. W., LEVIN, A., u. a., «The Dynamics of Soviet Society», New York, The New American Library, 1954, S. 49–59.

[59] AHLBERG, R., «‹Dialektische Philosophie› und Gesellschaft in der Sowjetunion», Wiesbaden-Berlin, Harrassowitz, 1960 (Philosophische und Soziologische Veröffentlichungen des Osteuropa-Instituts an der Freien Universität Berlin, Bd. 2), S. 11.

[60] Ebd., S. 12.

[61] LENIN, W. I., «Aus dem philosophischen Nachlaß. Exzerpte und Randglossen», Berlin, Dietz, 1949 (Bücherei des Marxismus-Leninismus, Bd. 4).

[62] AHLBERG, «‹Dialektische Philosophie› und Gesellschaft in der Sowjetunion», a. a. O., S. 18.

[63] Über den allgemeinen Zusammenhang von Natur und Gesellschaft in der heutigen Sowjetgesellschaft vgl. ROZENTAL', M., «Marksistskij dialektičeskij metod» (Die marxistische dialektische Methode), Moskau, Gosudarstvennoe izdatel'stvo političeskoj literatury (Staatsverlag für politische Literatur), 1951, S. 52–111.

[64] AHLBERG, «‹Dialektische Philosophie› und Gesellschaft in der Sowjetunion», a. a. O., S. 46–61.

[65] Zu den ökonomischen Theorien vgl. KNIRSCH, P., «Die ökonomischen Anschauungen Nikolaj I. Bucharins», Berlin, Duncker und Humblot, 1959 (Wirtschaftswissenschaftliche Veröffentlichungen des Osteuropa-Instituts an der Freien Universität Berlin, Bd. 9), passim.

[66] AHLBERG, «‹Dialektische Philosophie› und Gesellschaft in der Sowjetunion», a. a. O., S. 80. – BUCHARIN, N. I., «Ökonomik der Transformationsperiode», 1. Teil, Allgemeine Theorie des Transformationsprozesses, Hamburg, Verlag der Kommunistischen Internationale, 1922, passim.

[67] LANGE, «Marxismus, Leninismus, Stalinismus usw.», a. a. O., S. 107.

[68] STALIN, J. W., «Über die rechte Abweichung in der KPdSU (B)», Rede auf dem Plenum des ZK und der ZKK der KPdSU (B) im April 1929, in: ders., Werke, Bd. 12, Berlin, Dietz, 1954, S. 1–95, insbes. S. 50–60.

[69] MITRANY, D., «Marx Against the Peasant. A Study in Social Dogmatism», 2. Aufl., London, Wiedenfeld and Nicolson, 1952, S. 67–99.

[70] WETTER, «Sowjetideologie heute usw.», a. a. O., S. 98–121. – BOCHENSKI, «Der sowjetrussische dialektische Materialismus (Diamat)», a. a. O., S. 86–98. – INGENSAND, H., «Die Ideologie des Sowjetkommunismus. Philosophische Lehre», Hannover, Verlag für Literatur und Zeitgeschehen, 1962 (H. Ostk., Nr. 1), S. 32–45. – DAHM, H., «Die Dialektik im Wandel der Sowjetphilosophie», Köln, Verlag für Wissenschaft und Politik, 1963, passim.

[71] HOOVER, E. J., «A Study of Communism», New York, Holt, Rinehart, and Winston, 1962, S. 34.

[72] Ebd., S. 35 f.

[73] WETTER, «Der dialektische Materialismus usw.», a. a. O., S. 379.

[74] Ebd., S. 397.

75 AHLBERG, «‹Dialektische Philosophie› und Gesellschaft in der Sowjetunion», a. a. O., S. 84.
76 Ebd., S. 80.
77 Ebd.
78 «Geschichte der Kommunistischen Partei der Sowjetunion (Bolschewiki)», a. a. O., S. 449.
79 AHLBERG, «‹Dialektische Philosophie› und Gesellschaft in der Sowjetunion», a. a. O., S. 86.
80 STALIN, «Über die rechte Abweichung in der KPdSU (B)», a. a. O., S. 1 ff. – MITIN, M., RAL'CEVIČ, V., JUDIN, P., «O novych zadačach marksistsko-leninskoj filosofii» (Über die neuen Aufgaben der marxistisch-leninistischen Philosophie), in: Pravda vom 7. 6. 1930, S. 3 f.
81 AHLBERG, «‹Dialektische Philosophie› und Gesellschaft in der Sowjetunion», a. a. O., S. 81 f.
82 «Geschichte der Kommunistischen Partei der Sowjetunion (Bolschewiki)», a. a. O., S. 363–372.
83 AHLBERG, «‹Dialektische Philosophie› und Gesellschaft in der Sowjetunion», a. a. O., S. 98.
84 MITIN, RAL'CEVIČ, JUDIN, «O novych zadačach marksistsko-leninskoj filosofii», a. a. O., S. 3 f.
85 Ebd.
86 AHLBERG, «‹Dialektische Philosophie› und Gesellschaft in der Sowjetunion», a. a. O., S. 94. – DALLIN, D. J., «The Changing World of Soviet Russia», 3. Aufl., New Haven/Conn., Yale University Press, 1956, S. 171 ff., bes. S. 181.
87 LANGE, «Marxismus, Leninismus, Stalinismus usw.», a. a. O., S. 110.
88 BAUERMEISTER, M., «Die russische kommunistische Theorie und ihre Auswirkungen in den Planwirtschaftsversuchen der Sowjetunion», Jena, Fischer, 1930, S. 86–117.
89 «Voprosy političeskoj ekonomii» (Fragen der politischen Ökonomie), Leningrad, Izdatel'stvo Leningradskogo universiteta (Verlag der Leningrader Universität), 1957 (Učenye zapiski leningradskogo ordena Lenina gosudarstvennogo universiteta imeni A. A. Ždanova; Wissenschaftliche Schriften der mit d. Lenin-Orden ausgezeichneten Leningrader A. A. Ždanov-Staatsuniversität, Nr. 241), S. 70–71, 183 ff., 208 ff. – KARATAEV, N., STEPANOV, I., «Istorija ekonomičeskich učenij Zapadnoj Evropy i Rossii» (Die Geschichte der ökonomischen Lehren in Westeuropa und Rußland), Moskau, Izdatel'stvo social'no ekonomičeskoj literatury (Verlag für Sozialwesen und Ökonomik), 1959, S. 5–7. – ARZUMANJAN, A. A., LEMIN, I. M., CHMEL'NICKAJA, E. L. (Hrsg.), «Problemy sovremennogo kapitalizma. K 80-letiju akademika E. S. Varga» (Die Probleme des gegenwärtigen Kapitalismus. Zum 80. Geburtstag des Akademikers E. S. Varga), Moskau, Izdatel'stvo Akademii Nauk SSSR (Verlag der Akademie der Wissenschaften der UdSSR), 1959, S. 13–15.
90 «Političeskaja ekonomija» (Politische Ökonomie), tret'e, pererabotannoe i dopolnennoe izdanie (3. überarb. und erg. Aufl.), Moskau, Gosudarstvennoe Izdatel'stvo političeskoj literatury (Staatsverlag für politische Literatur), 1959, S. 697–703.
91 BOCHENSKI, I. M., «Kommunistische Ideologie I», Bonn, Bundeszentrale für politische Bildung, 1964 (Informationen zur politischen Bildung, Folge 106), S. 6a.
92 BELZ, H. G., «Marxismus-Leninismus. Ein Leitfaden durch die marxistisch-leninistische Philosophie-Soziologie-Ökonomie», Bremen, Schünemann, 1962, S. 59–66.
93 SALTER, E. J., THOMAS, S., «Taschenbuch des Kommunismus in These und Gegenthese», Bad Godesberg, Hohwacht-Verlag, 1963, S. 168.
94 MEISSNER, B., «Rußland im Umbruch. Der Wandel in der Herrschaftsordnung und sozialen Struktur der Sowjetunion», Frankfurt/M., Verlag für Geschichte und Politik, 1951 (Dokumente und Berichte des Europa-Archivs, Bd. 9), S. 19.
95 LANGE, «Marxismus, Leninismus, Stalinismus usw.», a. a. O., S. 112–115.
96 GROTTIAN, W., «Das sowjetische Regierungssystem. Die Grundlagen der Macht der kommunistischen Parteiführung», 2. Aufl., Köln-Opladen, Westdeutscher Verlag, 1965, S. 95–113, 489–511.
97 «Geschichte der Kommunistischen Partei der Sowjetunion (Bolschewiki)», a. a. O., S. 131–166 (Über dialektischen und historischen Materialismus).
98 BOCHENSKI, «Der sowjetrussische dialektische Materialismus (Diamat)», a. a. O., S. 50, Fußnote 24, S. 40–42.

⁹⁹ BOCHENSKI rechnet diese Zeit zu einer Periode der «Liberalisierung».

¹⁰⁰ WETTER, «Der dialektische Materialismus usw.», a. a. O., S. 224.

¹⁰¹ Ebd., S. 226, 228.

¹⁰² FETSCHER, «Von Marx zur Sowjetideologie», a. a. O., S. 136, 169. – LÖWENTHAL, R., «Das kommunistische Experiment. Theorie und Praxis des Marxismus-Leninismus», Köln, Markus-Verlag, 1957, S. 225 f.

¹⁰³ WETTER, «Der dialektische Materialismus usw.», a. a. O., S. 225.

¹⁰⁴ Ebd., S. 254.

¹⁰⁵ I. FETSCHER weist mit Recht auf den geistigen Zusammenhalt mit HEGELschen und ROUSSEAUschen Theorien hin. – FETSCHER, «Von Marx zur Sowjetideologie», a. a. O., S. 132.

¹⁰⁶ STALIN, J. W., «Ekonomičeskie problemy socializma v SSSR» (Ökonomische Probleme des Sozialismus in der UdSSR), Moskau, Gosudarstvennoe izdatel'stvo političeskoj literatury (Staatsverlag für politische Literatur), 1952.

¹⁰⁷ LÖWENTHAL, «Das kommunistische Experiment usw.», a. a. O., S. 227.

¹⁰⁸ FETSCHER, «Von Marx zur Sowjetideologie», a. a. O., S. 138.

¹⁰⁹ WETTER, «Der dialektische Materialismus usw.», a. a. O., S. 265.

¹¹⁰ LÖWENTHAL, «Das kommunistische Experiment usw.», a. a. O., S. 228.

¹¹¹ SCHISCHKIN, «Grundlagen der marxistischen Ethik», a. a. O., S. 496 ff.

¹¹² STALIN, «Ekonomičeskie problemy socializma v SSSR», a. a. O., S. 40 f.

¹¹³ Ebd., S. 40.

¹¹⁴ GALLUS, W., «Zur Kritik der sowjetischen Wirtschaftslehre (Polit-Ökonomie)», 2. Aufl., Pfaffenhofen, Ilmgau Verlag, 1959 (Sonderausgabe für das Bundesministerium für Gesamtdeutsche Fragen), S. 67.

¹¹⁵ STALIN, Ekonomičeskie problemy socializma v SSSR», a. a. O., S. 87 f. – MEISSNER, B., «Das Ende des Stalin-Mythos. Die Ergebnisse des XX. Parteikongresses der Kommunistischen Partei der Sowjetunion. Parteiführung, Parteiorganisation, Parteiideologie», Frankfurt/M., Europäischer Austauschdienst, 1956 (Dokumente und Berichte des Europa-Archivs, Bd. 13), S. 32 f.

¹¹⁶ FAINSOD, M., «What Happened to ‹Collective Leadership›?», BRUMBERG (Hrsg.), Russia under Krushchev usw., a. a. O., S. 1–10, 97–113.

¹¹⁷ Vgl. die drei Aufsätze von DEGRAS, J., DALLIN, A., LYND, G. E. unter dem gemeinsamen Obertitel «The Fruits of Destalinization», Prob. Comm., Bd. 11, Washington, 1962, Nr. 2, S. 1–23.

¹¹⁸ LÖWENTHAL, «Das kommunistische Experiment usw.», a. a. O., S. 234, 258.

¹¹⁹ Vgl. z. B. CHRUŠČEV, N. S., «Stroitel'stvo kommunizma v SSSR i razvitie sel'skogo chozjajstva» (Der Aufbau des Kommunismus in der UdSSR und die Entwicklung der Landwirtschaft), Bd. 2, Moskau, Gosudarstvennoe izdatel'stvo političeskoj literatury (Staatsverlag für politische Literatur), 1962, S. 192.

¹²⁰ GROSSMAN, G., «Economic Rationalism and Political ‹Thaw›», Prob. Comm., Bd. 6, Washington, 1957, Nr. 2, S. 22–26.

¹²¹ THALHEIM, K. C., «Grundzüge des sowjetischen Wirtschaftssystems», Köln, Verlag für Wissenschaft und Politik, 1962 (Abhandlungen des Bundesinstituts zur Erforschung des Marxismus-Leninismus, Institut für Sowjetologie), Bd. 1, S. 41.

¹²² NOVE, A., «Problems of Economic Destalinization», Prob. Comm., Bd. 6, a. a. O., Nr. 2, S. 15–21. – THALHEIM, «Grundzüge des sowjetischen Wirtschaftssystems», a. a. O., S. 41.

¹²³ Ebd., S. 218–225.

¹²⁴ FETSCHER, «Von Marx zur Sowjetideologie», a. a. O., S. 141–150.

¹²⁵ LÖWENTHAL, «Das kommunistische Experiment usw.», a. a. O., S. 248.

¹²⁶ MEISSNER, «Das Ende des Stalin-Mythos usw.», a. a. O., S. 175–198.

¹²⁷ DEGRAS, J., «Anatomy of Tyranny: Krushchev's Attack on Stalin», BRUMBERG (Hrsg.), Russia under Krushchev usw., a. a. O., S. 77–84.

¹²⁸ CHRUSCHTSCHOW (CHRUŠČEV), N. S., «Rechenschaftsbericht des Zentralkomitees der KPdSU an den XX. Parteitag. Referat vom Genossen N. S. Chruschtschow, dem Ersten

Sekretär des ZK der KPdSU, gehalten am 14. Februar 1956», Berlin, Dietz, 1956, S. 43–49, 112–128.

129 SWEARER, H. R., «Decentralization in Recent Soviet Administrative Practice», Slav. R., Bd. 21, Washington, 1962, Nr. 3, S. 456–470, insbes. S. 458. – FETSCHER, «Von Marx zur Sowjetideologie», a. a. O., S. 148. – LEVINE, H. S., «The Centralized Planning of Supply in Soviet Industry», und BASAN, P. A., «National Economic Planning: The Soviet Experience», BORNSTEIN, M. und FUSFELD, D. R. (Hrsg.), The Soviet Economy. A Book of Readings, Homewood/Ill., Irwin, 1962, S. 69–111. – SPULBER, N., «The Soviet Economy. Structure, Principles, Problems», New York, Norton, 1962, S. 227–242. – WILES, P. J. D., «The Political Economy of Communism», Oxford, Blackwell, 1962, S. 131–146.

130 ULAM, A. B., «Expansion and Coexistence: Counterpoint on Soviet Foreign Policy», Prob. Comm., Bd. 8, Washington, 1959, Nr. 5, S. 1–6. – MEISSNER, «Das Ende des Stalin-Mythos usw.», a. a. O., S. 56.

131 KOONER, M., «The Challenge of Co-Existence. A Study of Soviet Economic Diplomacy», Washington, Public Affairs Press, 1961, S. 21–42, 52–79. – ULAM, A. B., «The New Face of Soviet Totalitarianism», Cambridge/Mass., Harvard University Press, 1963 (Russian Research Studies, 47), S. 91–118.

132 SHAFFER, H. G. (Hrsg.), «The Soviet Economy. A Collection of Western and Soviet Views», London, Methuen, 1964, S. 297–339.

133 LÖWENTHAL, «Das kommunistische Experiment usw.», a. a. O., S. 248.

134 WETTER, «Der dialektische Materialismus usw.», a. a. O., S. 383.

135 THALHEIM, «Grundzüge des sowjetischen Wirtschaftssystems», a. a. O., S. 45.

136 LÖWENTHAL, «Das kommunistische Experiment usw.», a. a. O., S. 234.

137 FETSCHER, «Von Marx zur Sowjetideologie», a. a. O., S. 149 f.

138 Ebd., S. 152.

139 MEISSNER, B., «Rußland unter Chruschtschow», München, Oldenbourg, 1960, S. 13, 19–22.

140 Ebd., S. 103–105, 111, 114.

141 Ebd., S. 255. – GREENSLADE, R. V., «Forward to Communism?», Prob. Comm., Bd. 11, Washington, 1962, Nr. 1, S. 36–42.

142 GREENSLADE, R. V., «Khrushchev and the Economists», Prob. Comm., Bd. 12, Washington, 1963, Nr. 3, S. 27–32.

143 FETSCHER, «Von Marx zur Sowjetideologie», a. a. O., S. 156. – NEMCHINOV (NEMČINOV), N. S., «The Use of Mathematical Methods in Economic Research and Planning», und CAMPBELL, R. W., «Marxian Analysis, Mathematical Methods and Scientific Economic Planning: Can Soviet Economists Combine Them?», SHAFFER (Hrsg.), The Soviet Economy usw., a. a. O., S. 350–367, 397–402.

144 BRONSKA-PAMPUCH, W., «Kommunismus, gibt es das überhaupt?», GAITANIDES, J. (Hrsg.), Die Zukunft des Kommunismus, München, List, 1963, S. 62–72. – JASNY, N., «Plan and Superplan», – BALINKY, A. S., «The Proclaimed Emergence of Communism in the USSR», – DOBB, M., «Transition from Socialism to Communism: Economic Aspects» und ANCHISHKIN, I., «The Problem of Abundance and the Transition to Communist Distribution», in: SHAFFER (Hrsg.), «The Soviet Economy usw.», a. a. O., S. 90–105, 105–121, 122 bis 133, 133–138. – CORNFORTH, «Dialectical Materialism usw.», a. a. O., S. 130–147.

145 MEISSNER, «Rußland unter Chruschtschow», a. a. O., S. 141–260. – GASTEYGER, C. W. (Hrsg.), «Perspektiven der sowjetischen Politik. Der XXII. Parteitag und das neue Parteiprogramm. Eine Dokumentation», Köln-Berlin, Kiepenheuer und Witsch, 1962, S. 28–75. – FETSCHER, «Von Marx zur Sowjetideologie», a. a. O., S. 153–165. – FAINSOD, M., «The XXII. Party Congress», BRUMBERG (Hrsg.), Russia under Krushchev usw., a. a. O., S. 127–149.

146 WETTER, «Der dialektische Materialismus usw.», a. a. O., S. 400.

147 Ebd., S. 256.

148 BEZUGLOV, A., «The Moral Code of the Builders of Communism», SHAFFER (Hrsg.), The Soviet Economy usw., a. a. O., S. 139 ff.

[149] PÁLÓCZI HORVÁTH, G., «Chruschtschow», Hamburg, Fischer, 1961, S. 44 f. – MEHNERT, «Der Sowjetmensch usw.», a. a. O., S. 311.

[150] FLEMING, D. F., «The Cold War and its Origins, 1917–1960», Bd. 2: 1950–1960, New York, Doubleday, 1961, S. 791–803. – HARTMANN, K., «Polens Geist zwischen Ost und West. Eine Betrachtung zur geistigen Lage in Polen nach dem Zweiten Weltkrieg», Hannover, Niedersächsische Landeszentrale für Politische Bildung, 1962 (Schriftenreihe der Niedersächsischen Landeszentrale für Politische Bildung, Ost-Probleme, Nr. 6), passim, bes. S. 53, 101 bis 106. – MEISSNER, «Rußland unter Chruschtschow», a. a. O., S. 265.

[151] HERMENS, F. A., «Der Ost-West-Konflikt. Gründe und Scheingründe», Frankfurt/M.-Bonn, Athenäum Verlag, 1961 (Demokratische Existenz heute. Schriften des Forschungsinstituts für Politische Wissenschaft an der Universität Köln, Nr. 5), S. 13.

[152] ARON, R., «Soviet Society in Transition», WILES, P., «The Consumer and the System», und NOVE, A., «Social Welfare in the USSR», BRUMBERG (Hrsg.), Russia under Khrushchev usw.», a. a. O., S. 539–553, 571–590, 606–609.

[153] MEISSNER, «Rußland unter Chruschtschow», a. a. O., S. 268.

[154] NOLLAU, G., «Der Zerfall des Weltkommunismus. Einheit oder Polyzentrismus», Köln-Berlin, Kiepenheuer und Witsch, 1963, passim, bes. S. 75–92. – LABEDZ, «Ideology. The Fourth Stage», HOOK, S., «The Import of Ideological Diversity», DE JOUVENEL, B., «The Logic of Economics», BRUMBERG (Hrsg.), Russia under Khrushchev usw., a. a. O., S. 51–66, 554–570, 599–605. – Vgl. die Abhandlungen unter dem Sammeltitel «The Future of Communist Society», Survey, New York, 1961, Nr. 38, S. 3–196.

Notes to Chapter VII

[1] Vgl. das Buch des Verfassers «Comparative Economic Systems», a. a. O., S. 132–137. – DERS., «Wirtschaftsethik», a. a. O., S. 83–103.

[2] ZIEGENFUSS, W., «Gesellschaftsphilosophie. Grundzüge der Theorie von Wesen und Erkenntnis der Gesellschaft», Stuttgart, Enke, 1954, S. 2–16.

[3] WEBER, W., ALBERT, H., KADE, G., «Wert», HdSW, Bd. 11, a. a. O., 1961, S. 637–658.

[4] REHFELDT, B., «Wertnihilismus? Bemerkungen zu Theodor Geiger. Vorstudien zu einer Soziologie des Rechts», Kölner Z. Soz. Sozpsych., Jg. 6, a. a. O., S. 278 f.

[5] Diese Tatsache muß besonders gegenüber häufig geäußerten gegenteiligen Ansichten östlicher Autoren beachtet werden.

[6] Vgl. den Artikel des Verfassers «Wirtschaftsethik», a. a. O., S. 86–89.

[7] WEIPPERT, G., «Vom Werturteilsstreit zur politischen Theorie», WWA, Bd. 49, Jena, 1939, S. 1–17. – Vgl. auch v. MARTIN, «Ordnung und Freiheit usw.», a. a. O., S. 70–77.

[8] Vgl. den Artikel des Verfassers «Wirtschaftsethik», a. a. O., S. 88. – LEVI, J., «Must the Scientist Make Value Judgements?», J. Philos., Bd. 57, Lancaster, 1960, Nr. 11, S. 357.

[9] Vgl. supra, Abschnitt I, V.

[10] WEISSER, G., «Zur Erkenntniskritik der Urteile über den Wert sozialer Gebilde und Prozesse. Weiterführung der ‹Werturteilsdebatte›», Kölner Z. Soz. Sozpsychol., Jg. 6, a. a. O., S. 16–30, bes. S. 23 ff. – WEIPPERT, «Vom Werturteilsstreit zur politischen Theorie», a. a. O., S. 90–97.

[11] Vgl. v. NELL-BREUNING, «Wirtschaftsethik. Zum gleichnamigen Buch von Walter Weddigen», a. a. O., S. 62–69.

[12] WILPERT, P., «Sachlichkeit und Sittlichkeit in der Wirtschaft», SPITALER (Hrsg.), Sachlichkeit und Sittlichkeit in der Wirtschaft, a. a. O., S. 21.

[13] HÜNERMANN, J., «Freiheit und sittliche Bindung im Wirtschaftsleben», in: RÖPKE, W.,

HÜNERMANN, J., MÜLLER, E., Wirtschaftsethik heute. Drei Reden an jeden, der produziert, kauft und verkauft, Hamburg, Furche, 1956, S. 28–40, bes. S. 30.

14 Vgl. den Aufsatz des Verfassers «Über die Ausgangspunkte der Volkswirtschaftspolitik», a. a. O., S. 56–61.

15 PFISTER, A., «Die Wirtschaftsethik Antonius' von Florenz (1389–1459)», Diss. Freiburg, 1946, S. 19–48.

16 Vgl. das Buch des Verfassers «Comparative Economic Systems», a. a. O., S. 132–137.

17 DERS., «Wirtschaftsethik», a. a. O., S. 86.

18 SCHACK, «Wirtschaftsleben und Wirtschaftsgestaltung usw.», a. a. O., S. 46 f.

19 Vgl. supra, Abschnitt VI.

20 Vgl. das Buch des Verfassers «Comparative Economic Systems», a. a. O., S. 137.

21 WEIPPERT, «Jenseits von Individualismus und Kollektivismus usw.», a. a. O., S. 15 ff., passim. – DERS., «Vom Werturteilsstreit zur politischen Theorie», a. a. O., S. 29–90.

22 SCHACK, «Wirtschaftsleben und Wirtschaftsgestaltung usw.», a. a. O., S. 100.

23 MÖBUS, G., «Das Menschenbild des Ostens und die Menschen im Westen», Bonn, Deutscher Bundesverlag, 1955, S. 3–39.

24 HÜNERMANN, «Freiheit und sittliche Bindung im Wirtschaftsleben», a. a. O., S. 35 f.

25 MÜLLER, E., «Redlichkeit und Wirklichkeit im heutigen Wirtschaftsleben», in: RÖPKE, HÜNERMANN, MÜLLER, Wirtschaftsethik heute usw., a. a. O., S. 46 ff.

26 WIENER, N., «Mensch und Menschmaschine» (aus dem Engl.), Frankfurt/M.-Berlin, Metzner, 1952, S. 102.

27 Vgl. supra, Abschnitt III.

28 Vgl. v. MARTIN, «Ordnung und Freiheit usw.», a. a. O., S. 29–50.

29 Wie die Ereignisse seit 1961 in der DDR zeigen, kann eine fremde Gesetzlichkeit dieser Art zu extremer Unfreiheit für die Gesellschaftsmitglieder führen.

30 Vgl. das Buch des Verfassers «Comparative Economic Systems», a. a. O., S. 141.

31 SALIN, «Geschichte der Volkswirtschaftslehre», a. a. O., S. 122. – SCHÖNFELD, W., «Über die Gerechtigkeit. Ein Triptychon», Göttingen, Vandenhoeck und Ruprecht, 1952, S. 63–79, 93–105.

32 Vgl. den Artikel des Verfassers «Wirtschaftsethik», a. a. O., S. 90.

33 Vgl. Vortrag «Wettkampf der Systeme» von GREIFFENHAGEN im Westdeutschen Rundfunk am 8. 4. 1964 (Vortragsmanuskript).

34 Vgl. infra, Abschnitt XI.

35 Vgl. den Artikel des Verfassers «Wirtschaftsethik», a. a. O., S. 90.

36 HEIMANN, E., Soziale Theorie des Kapitalismus. Theorie der Sozialpolitik», Tübingen, Mohr (Siebeck), 1929, S. 3–13.

37 DAHRENDORF, «Reflexionen über Freiheit und Gleichheit», a. a. O., S. 79.

38 SALIN, «Geschichte der Volkswirtschaftslehre», a. a. O., S. 121–128, 134 f., 138. – JANTKE, C., «Der vierte Stand. Die gestaltenden Kräfte der deutschen Arbeiterbewegung im XIX. Jahrhundert», Freiburg, Herder, 1955, S. 1–95. – SOMBART, «Sozialismus und soziale Bewegung», a. a. O., S. 21–46, 195–244.

39 DAHRENDORF, «Reflexionen über Freiheit und Gleichheit», a. a. O., S. 59–62. – Vgl. ferner v. KUEHNELT-LEDDIHN, «Freiheit oder Gleichheit? usw.», a. a. O., S. 15–29.

40 DAHRENDORF, «Reflexionen über Freiheit und Gleichheit», a. a. O., S. 62.

41 Ebd., S. 64. – BICKERMANN, «Freiheit und Gleichheit usw.», a. a. O., S. 15–63.

42 GALLIE, «Liberal Morality and Socialist Morality», a. a. O., S. 116–128, 132.

43 UTZ, A.-F., «Sozialethik mit internationaler Bibliographie. 1. Teil: Die Prinzipien der Gesellschaftslehre», Löwen-Heidelberg, Nauwelaerts-Kerle, 1958, S. 192, 218–226.

44 DAHRENDORF, «Reflexionen über Freiheit und Gleichheit», a. a. O., S. 79.

45 WEDDIGEN, W., «Wirtschaftsethik. System humanitärer Wirtschaftsmoral», Berlin, Duncker und Humblot, 1951, S. 45, 94 f., 148 ff.

[46] Vgl. v. KUEHNELT-LEDDIHN, «Freiheit oder Gleichheit? usw.», a. a. O., S. 45, 47. – DAHRENDORF, «Reflexionen über Freiheit und Gleichheit», a. a. O., S. 74–77.

Notes to Chapter VIII

[1] KWANT, «Philosophy of Labour», a. a. O., S. 1–27, 125–159. – FÜRSTENBERG, F., «Arbeit, soziologisch», RGG, 3. Aufl., Bd. 1, Tübingen, Mohr (Siebeck), 1957, Sp. 535. – SCHELER, M., «Die Wissensformen und die Gesellschaft», 2. Aufl., Bern-München, Francke, 1960, S. 447–458.

[2] COX, C. O., «The Foundations of Capitalism», New York, Philosophical Library, 1959, S. 374–476. – HEIMANN, «Soziale Theorie der Wirtschaftssysteme», a. a. O., S. 86–94.

[3] CRONIN, «Social Principles and Economic Life», a. a. O., S. 165–196. – HALLER, H., «Arbeit, wirtschaftlich», RGG, Bd. 1, a. a. O., Sp. 537.

[4] HEIMANN, E., «Kapitalismus», RGG, Bd. 3, a. a. O., 1959, Sp. 1139. – EXNER, H. K., «Return to the Family in Community-Oriented Social Work», DIXON (Hrsg.), Social Welfare and the Preservation of Human Values, a. a. O., S. 164–172.

[5] FÜRSTENBERG, «Arbeit, soziologisch», a. a. O., Sp. 536.

[6] Vgl. den Artikel des Verfassers «Wirtschaftsethik», a. a. O., S. 100. – PETER, H., «Über gerechte Verteilung des Einkommens und Eigentums», Z. ges. Staatswiss., Bd. 112, Tübingen, 1956, S. 218–230.

[7] JANTKE, «Der vierte Stand usw.», a. a. O., S. 40–95.

[8] WOLF, W., «Freiheit, kirchengeschichtlich», RGG, Bd. 2, a. a. O., 1958, Sp. 1105 f.

[9] FETSCHER, I., «Freiheit, systematisch», RGG, Bd. 2, a. a. O., Sp. 1110.

[10] BENDISCIOLI, M. und LOUSSE, M., «Neueste Zeit», in: Grundbegriffe der Geschichte. 50 Beiträge zum europäischen Geschichtsbild, Gütersloh, Bertelsmann, 1964, S. 270.

[11] RÜSTOW, A., «Zwischen Kapitalismus und Kommunismus», Ordo, Bd. 2, Bad Godesberg, 1949, S. 100–169, bes. S. 138 f.

[12] DÖRGE, «Menschenbild und Institution in der Idee des Wirtschaftsliberalismus», a. a. O., S. 84.

[13] NAWROTH, «Die Sozial- und Wirtschaftsphilosophie des Neoliberalismus», a. a. O., S. 13.

[14] EUCKEN, W., «Grundsätze der Wirtschaftspolitik», Bern-Tübingen, Francke-Mohr (Siebeck), 1952, S. 179. – NAWROTH, «Die Sozial- und Wirtschaftsphilosophie des Neoliberalismus», a. a. O., S. 16, 83 f.

[15] DERS., «Die wirtschaftspolitischen Ordnungsvorstellungen des Neoliberalismus», a. a. O., S. 21.

[16] DERS., «Die Sozial- und Wirtschaftsphilosophie des Neoliberalismus», a. a. O., S. 162 f., 347 ff.

[17] HEIMANN, «Soziale Theorie der Wirtschaftssysteme», a. a. O., S. 140. – SUNDBOM, J., «Über das Gleichheitsprinzip als politisches und ökonomisches Problem», Berlin, de Gruyter, 1962, S. 18–23.

[18] LANDAUER, C., «Sozialismus und sozialistische Bewegung», in: Grundbegriffe der Geschichte usw.», a. a. O., S. 346 ff.

[19] Vgl. supra, Abschnitt VII.

[20] JANTKE, «Der vierte Stand usw.», a. a. O., S. 105–110.

[21] Vgl. infra, Abschnitt IX.

[22] Vgl. den Artikel des Verfassers «Wirtschaftsethik», a. a. O., S. 98.

[23] SCHÜDDEKOPF, O.-E., «Konservativismus», in: Grundbegriffe der Geschichte usw.», a. a. O., S. 175–181.

[24] SCHWEITZER, W., «Sozialethik», RGG, Bd. 6, a. a. O., 1962, Sp. 162 ff.

Notes to Chapter IX

1 WEISSER, G., «Vermögen und Vermögenspolitik», HdSW, Bd. 11, a. a. O., 1961, S. 175.
2 EUCKEN, «Grundsätze der Wirtschaftspolitik», a. a. O., S. 249.
3 Programm und Statut der Kommunistischen Partei der Sowjetunion. Angenommen auf dem XXII. Parteitag der KPdSU, 17. bis 23. Oktober 1961», Berlin, Dietz, 1961, S. 84 f.
4 Für den Neo-Liberalismus vgl. EUCKEN, «Grundsätze der Wirtschaftspolitik», a. a. O., S. 247. – Für den freiheitlichen Sozialismus vgl. SCHILLER, «Sozialismus und Wettbewerb», a. a. O., S. 28.
5 OHM, H., «Definitionen des Leistungswettbewerbs und ihre Verwendungsfähigkeit für die praktische Wirtschaftspolitik», SERAPHIM (Hrsg.), Zur Grundlegung wirtschaftspolitischer Konzeptionen, a. a. O., S. 239.
6 MÜLLER-ARMACK, A., «Soziale Marktwirtschaft», HdSW, Bd. 9, a. a. O., 1956, S. 390.
7 MOLL, B., «Gerechtigkeit in der Wirtschaft? Kritische Analyse der volkswirtschaftlichen Verteilung. Eine theoretisch-soziologische Studie», 2. Aufl., Bonn, Bouvier, 1961, S. 24.
8 RÖPKE, W., «Die Gesellschaftskrisis der Gegenwart», 5. Aufl., Erlenbach-Zürich, Rentsch, 1948, S. 364.
9 Bei oligopolistischen Marktformen ist aufgrund der Kapitalakkumulation, der beschleunigten Einführung des technischen Fortschritts und der Ausnutzung betriebsinterner Ersparnisse eine stärkere Kostendegression wahrscheinlich.
10 Die Parallelität der Leistungsanstrengungen zwischen den Produzenten wurde von EUCKEN hervorgehoben. – EUCKEN, «Grundsätze der Wirtschaftspolitik», a. a. O., S. 42.
11 Das Abweichen vom Leistungsprinzip besagt jedoch nicht, daß damit eine weniger «gerechte» Verteilung erfolgt.
12 LIEFMANN-KEIL, E., «Ökonomische Theorie der Sozialpolitik», Berlin-Göttingen-Heidelberg, Springer, 1961, S. 15.
13 WEBER, M., «Wirtschaft und Gesellschaft. Grundriß der verstehenden Soziologie», 1. Halbband, Köln-Berlin, Kiepenheuer und Witsch, 1964, S. 38.
14 PRELLER, «Sozialpolitik usw.», a. a. O., S. 14.
15 «Düsseldorfer Leitsätze der CDU/CSU vom 15. Juli 1949», in: Die Christlich-Demokratische Union Deutschlands. Geschichte. Idee, Programm, Statut (hrsg. von der Bundesgeschäftsstelle der Christlich-Demokratischen Union Deutschlands), Bonn, 1960, S. 22 f. – «Grundsatzprogramm der Sozialdemokratischen Partei Deutschlands. Beschlossen vom Außerordentlichen Parteitag der Sozialdemokratischen Partei Deutschlands in Bad Godesberg vom 13. bis 15. November 1959» (hrsg. vom Vorstand der Sozialdemokratischen Partei Deutschlands), Köln, 1959, S. 21 ff.
16 RÖPKE, «Jenseits von Angebot und Nachfrage», a. a. O., S. 134 f.
17 Ebd., S. 34.
18 Nach liberaler Auffassung ist die Sicherung des Erbrechts ein notwendiger Bestandteil des Privateigentums. – Ebd., S. 135.
19 Hinsichtlich der Begriffe vgl. EUCKEN, «Grundsätze der Wirtschaftspolitik», a. a. O., S. 42.
20 KISKER, K. P., «Die Erbschaftsteuer als Mittel der Vermögensredistribution», Berlin, Duncker und Humblot, 1964 (Volkswirtschaftliche Schriften, Nr. 79), S. 36 f., 43.
21 Ebd., S. 96.
22 Ebd., S. 37, 75, 113.
23 Vermögensverteilungseffekte können auch durch Kriege, Einkommensteuergestaltung und testamentarische Bestimmungen bewirkt sein.
24 KISKER, «Die Erbschaftsteuer als Mittel der Vermögensredistribution», a. a. O., S. 90, 120.

[25] Schon SMITH und RICARDO lehnten die Erbschaftsteuer aus diesem Grunde ab.

[26] KATONA, G., «Das Verhalten der Verbraucher und der Unternehmer» (aus dem Engl.), Tübingen, Mohr (Siebeck), 1960, S. 83 f.

[27] Liquiditätsschwierigkeiten bei Personengesellschaften, die mit der Zahlung von Erbschaftsteuern auftreten können, werden in Großbritannien und den Vereinigten Staaten durch Steuerstundung und Ratenzahlung zu mildern versucht.

[28] Beispielsweise Form des Steuertarifs, zeitnahe Bewertung, Freigrenzen, Berücksichtigung von Härtefällen, Ratenzahlung der Steuerbeträge usw.

[29] KISKER, «Die Erbschaftsteuer als Mittel der Vermögensredistribution», a. a. O., S. 189.

[30] RAPOLD, «Demokratie und Wirtschaftsordnung usw.», a. a. O., S. 141.

[31] RÖPKE, «Jenseits von Angebot und Nachfrage», a. a. O., S. 18.

[32] Vgl. v. HAYEK, «Der Weg zur Knechtschaft», a. a. O., S. 109.

[33] Ebd., S. 110.

[34] Die Steuergesetzgebung steht dazu nicht im Widerspruch. Z. B. erfaßt die Einkommensteuer mit ihren progressiven Sätzen die Spitzeneinkommen, wirkt jedoch nicht nivellierend im materiell egalitären Sinne.

[35] PREISER, E., «Wachstum und Einkommensverteilung», Heidelberg, Winter-Universitätsverlag, 1961 (Sitzungsberichte der Heidelberger Akademie der Wissenschaften. Philosophischhistorische Klasse, Jg. 1961, 5. Abhdlg.), S. 7 f.

[36] Diese Annahme hat den Vorzug größerer Realitätsnähe. – PREISER, E., «Erkenntniswert und Grenzen der Grenzproduktivitätstheorie», Schweizer Z. Volkswirtsch. Statist., Jg. 89, Bern, 1953, S. 37.

[37] BOMBACH, G., «Die verschiedenen Ansätze der Verteilungstheorie», SCHNEIDER, E. (Hrsg.), Einkommensverteilung und technischer Fortschritt, Berlin, Duncker und Humblot, 1959 (Schr. Ver. Socpol., N.F., Bd. 17), S. 98 f.

[38] PREISER, «Erkenntniswert und Grenzen der Grenzproduktivitätstheorie», a. a. O., S. 44.

[39] KRELLE, W., «Bestimmungsgründe und Einkommensverteilung in der modernen Wirtschaft», in: Einkommensbildung und Einkommensverteilung. Verhandlungen auf der Tagung des Vereins für Socialpolitik in Köln 1956, Berlin, Duncker und Humblot, 1957 (Schr. Ver. Socpol., N.F., Bd. 13), S. 55–109.

[40] KUZNETS, S., «Shares of Upper Income Groups in Income and Savings», New York, National Bureau of Economic Research, 1953 (Publications of the National Bureau of Economic Research, Nr. 55), S. 46.

[41] GERBER, E., «Veränderungen der Einkommensverteilung in England 1938–1948», Bern, Francke, 1952, S. 77.

[42] Es geht hier in erster Linie nicht um die Umverteilung von vorhandenem Vermögen, sondern vielmehr darum, wie das zuwachsende Vermögen den einzelnen Wirtschaftsteilnehmern zuzuordnen ist. – WEISSER, «Vermögen und Vermögenspolitik», a. a. O., S. 175.

[43] Als Beispiel für die Bundesrepublik Deutschland sei hier nur der ‹Leber-Plan› erwähnt.

[44] So u. a. die Maßnahmen der Eigenheimbauförderung, das Gesetz zur Förderung der Vermögensbildung der Arbeitnehmer (312-DM-Gesetz) und die Steuerbegünstigung gemäß § 10 EStG, die das Sparen in Form von Versicherungen steuerlich begünstigt.

[45] Die Gesamtersparnis in der Bundesrepublik Deutschland verteilte sich im Jahre 1963 zu 57,7 v.H. auf die privaten und zu 43,4 v.H. auf die öffentlichen Ersparnisse. (Saldo der Vermögensübertragungen mit der übrigen Welt: –1,1 v.H.) – Berechnet aus: «Monatsberichte der Deutschen Bundesbank», Jg. 16, o. O., 1964, Nr. 4, S. 6.

[46] Diese Unterschiede erscheinen letztlich nur als Ausfluß der bestehenden Eigentumsverfassungen.

[47] Vgl. das Buch des Verfassers «Comparative Economic Systems», a. a. O., S. 462.

[48] Es sei besonders auf die «Reichtumsmacht» hingewiesen, die leicht in politische Macht ummünzbar ist. – ORTLIEB, H.-D., «Das Ende des Wirtschaftswunders. Unsere Wirtschafts- und Gesellschaftsordnung in der Wandlung», Wiesbaden, Steiner, 1962 (Veröff. Akad. Wirt. Pol., Hamburg), S. 41. – EUCKEN, W., «Die Wettbewerbsordnung und ihre Verwirklichung», Ordo, Bd. 2, a. a. O., 1949, S. 12.

49 Ebd., S. 51.

50 Vgl. v. NELL-BREUNING, «Wirtschaft und Gesellschaft usw.», a. a. O., S. 61 f.

51 NEMITZ, «Sozialistische Marktwirtschaft usw.», a. a. O., S. 164.

52 Ebd., S. 224.

53 ROTHSCHILD, K., «Der Lohnanteil am Gesamteinkommen. Einige Bemerkungen zu einem umstrittenen Problem», WWA, Bd. 78, a. a. O., 1957, S. 160 ff.

54 HÖFFNER, J., «Die Funktionen des Privateigentums in der freien Welt», v. BECKERATH, MEYER, MÜLLER-ARMACK (Hrsg.), Wirtschaftsfragen der freien Welt usw., a. a. O., S. 127.

55 Den Zusammenhang zwischen Einkommenshöhe und Möglichkeiten der Vermögensbildung durch Sparen zeigen deutlich die von S. KUZNETS angegebenen Relationen für Sparen und Einkommen. – KUZNETS, «Shares of Upper Income Groups in Income and Savings», a. a. O., S. 224.

56 LITTMANN, K., «Über einige Zwangsläufigkeiten der Vermögensverteilung in der Marktwirtschaft. Wirtschaftstheoretische Bemerkungen zur neueren sozialpolitischen Diskussion», Z. ges. Staatswiss., Bd. 113, a. a. O., S. 215 f.

57 Ebd., S. 217.

58 KLUG, O., «Volkskapitalismus durch Eigentumsstreuung. Illusion oder Wirklichkeit?», Stuttgart, Fischer, 1962, S. 373.

59 «Statistisches Jahrbuch für die Bundesrepublik Deutschland 1965», hrsg. vom Statistischen Bundesamt Wiesbaden, Mainz, Kohlhammer, 1965, S. 552 sowie «Monatsberichte der Deutschen Bundesbank», Jg. 16, o. O., 1964, Nr. 4, S. 6.

60 WEISSER, G., «Eigentumspolitik als Ausweg aus zunehmender sozialer Abhängigkeit», in: Eigentum in der industrialisierten Gesellschaft (hrsg. vom ständigen Ausschuß für Selbsthilfe, anläßlich des dritten deutschen Selbsthilfetages 1958), Göttingen, Schwartz, o. J., S. 38.

61 SPIEGELHALTER, F., «Eigentum und Wirtschaftsordnung», Paderborn, Bonifacius Verlag, o. J. (Schriftenreihe der Arbeitsgemeinschaft katholisch-sozialer Bildungswerke in der Bundesrepublik Deutschland, IV. Eigentum, Nr. 1), S. 23.

62 ACHINGER, «Sozialpolitik und Wissenschaft», a. a. O., S. 60. – LIEFMANN-KEIL, «Ökonomische Theorie der Sozialpolitik», a. a. O., S. 226 f.

63 WEISSER, «Eigentumspolitik als Ausweg aus zunehmender sozialer Abhängigkeit», a. a. O., S. 56.

64 ERHARD, L., «Über den ‹Lebensstandard›», ders., Deutsche Wirtschaftspolitik. Der Weg der sozialen Marktwirtschaft, Düsseldorf-Wien, Econ, 1962, S. 392.

65 In vielen unterentwickelten Ländern zeichnen sich noch heute ähnliche Tendenzen ab, wo «gehorteter Wohlstand» sichtbares Zeichen des Prestiges ist. – WOLF, C. und SUFRIN, S. C., «Capital Formation and Foreign Investment in Underdeveloped Areas. An Analysis of Research Needs and Program Possibilities. Prepared from a Study Supported by the Ford Foundation», verb. Aufl., Syracuse, Syracuse University Press, 1958, S. 16.

66 Auch bei einer bewußt auf Vollbeschäftigung ausgerichteten Wirtschaftspolitik lassen sich starke Schwankungen der Aktienkurse nachweisen. So fiel in der Bundesrepublik Deutschland der Index der Aktienkurse im Zeitraum vom Januar 1962 bis Januar 1963 um 25,2 v.H. Hierbei war der Rückgang der Aktienkurse in einzelnen Industriebranchen noch beträchtlich höher. (Papierindustrie: Abnahme um 52,6 v.H.; Steinkohlenbergbau: Abnahme um 36,4 v.H.). – Berechnet aus: «Monatsberichte der Deutschen Bundesbank», Jg. 16, o. O., 1964, Nr. 12, S. 70 f.

67 KISKER, «Die Erbschaftsteuer als Mittel der Vermögensredistribution», a. a. O., S. 166.

Notes to Chapter X

1 Vgl. das Buch des Verfassers «Comparative Economic Systems», a. a. O., S. 492.

2 Gewisse Lockerungen zeichneten sich allerdings mit dem Sturz CHRUŠČEVs im Oktober

1964 ab. Der Nationale Wirtschaftsrat der Sowjetunion zeigte sich schon kurz danach den Vorschlägen des Reformers LIBERMAN geneigt, die eine staatlich prämiierte Gewinnerzielung und eine Ausrichtung der Produktion an der Nachfrage beinhalten. – E. LIBERMAN veröffentlichte seine Vorstellungen zuerst in der Pravda vom 9. 9. 1962. Deutsche Übersetzung unter dem Titel: «Plan, Gewinn, Prämie», Presse Sowjet., a. a. O., S. 2331–2335.

3 KEIRSTEAD, B. S., «Capital, Interest and Profits», Oxford, Basil Blackwell, 1959, S. 30 ff.

4 Vgl. das Buch des Verfassers «Comparative Economic Systems», a. a. O., S. 492 f.

5 In den Volkswirtschaften planwirtschaftlicher Prägung wurde der Gewinn lange Zeit als kapitalistische Erscheinung abgelehnt. Im Rahmen der Maßnahmen für eine Erhöhung der Effektivität der Planwirtschaften fand er jetzt jedoch auch Eingang in die Wirtschaftspraxis, wobei hauptsächlich der Instrumentalcharakter des Gewinns als Lenkungsmechanismus entscheidend gewesen sein dürfte. – In westlichen Volkswirtschaften wurde der Unternehmergewinn in der Vergangenheit als solcher und auch in seiner jeweiligen Höhe moralisch sanktioniert. Seit einigen Jahrzehnten vollzieht sich hingegen ein Wandel in Richtung auf eine Beschneidung der als zu hoch angesehenen Gewinne mittels der redistributiven Einkommens- und Gewinnbesteuerung sowie über die Besteuerung der aus Mangellagen (Kriege) entstandenen Gewinne.

6 Größere Anlagen ermöglichen neben einer Kostensenkung auch – sofern sie an den Markt weitergegeben wird – eine Preissenkung.

7 HENZLER, R., «Konzentrationsprobleme in der Unternehmersphäre», NEUMARK, F. (Hrsg.), Die Konzentration in der Wirtschaft, Berlin, Duncker und Humblot, 1961 (Schr. Ver. Socpol., N.F., Bd. 22), S. 326.

8 MÜLLER, J. H., «Konzentration und Wettbewerb», NEUMARK (Hrsg.), Die Konzentration in der Wirtschaft, a. a. O., S. 119.

9 WESSELS, T., «Über wirtschaftspolitische Konzeptionen des Wettbewerbs», GREISS, F. und MEYER, F. W. (Hrsg.), Wirtschaft, Gesellschaft und Kultur. Festgabe für Alfred Müller-Armack, Berlin, Duncker und Humblot, 1961, S. 26.

10 Vgl. «Sieg im Aluminium-Krieg», Handelsblatt, Düsseldorf, 1965, Nr. 220, S. 5.

11 KOZLOV, G. A. und PERVUŠIN, S. P. (Hrsg.), «Közgazdasági Kislexikon» (Volkswirtschaftliches Kleinlexikon), Budapest, Kossuth-Verlag, 1960, S. 193.

12 WICKSELL, K., «Vorlesungen über Nationalökonomie auf der Grundlage des Marginalprinzips. Theoretischer Teil, Bd. 2: Geld und Kredit», Jena, Fischer, 1922, S. 220.

13 FISHER, I., «The Theory of Interest. As Determined by Impatience to Spend Income and Opportunity to Invest It» (Wiederabdruck), New York, Kelley, 1961, S. 62.

14 HARROD, R., «Second Essay in Dynamic Theory», Econ. J., Bd. 70, London, 1960, Nr. 278, S. 277–293.

15 Vgl. v. STACKELBERG, «Grundlagen der theoretischen Volkswirtschaftslehre», a. a. O., S. 318.

16 Die dabei aufgetretenen Schwierigkeiten sollen hier nicht weiter untersucht werden.

17 Vgl. v. BÖHM-BAWERK, E., «Geschichte und Kritik der Kapitalzinstheorie», 4. Aufl., Jena, Fischer, 1921, S. 2 f.

18 PREISER, «Erkenntniswert und Grenzen der Grenzproduktivitätstheorie», a. a. O., S. 38 f.

19 FORSTMANN, A., «Geld und Kredit. 2. Teil: Die Anwendung der Geld- und Kredittheorie», Göttingen, Vandenhoeck und Ruprecht, 1952, S. 323.

20 MYRDAL, G., «Der Gleichgewichtsbegriff als Instrument der geldtheoretischen Analyse», v. HAYEK, F. A. (Hrsg.), Beiträge zur Geldtheorie, Wien, Springer, 1933, S. 415.

21 MEANS, G. C., «Collective Enterprise and Economic Theory», ARNDT, H. (Hrsg.), Die Konzentration in der Wirtschaft, Bd. 3, Wirkungen und Probleme der Konzentration, Berlin, Duncker und Humblot, 1960 (Schr. Ver. Socpol., N.F., Bd. 20/III), S. 1534 f.

22 Vgl. das Buch des Verfassers «Comparative Economic Systems», a. a. O., S. 474 f.

23 Ebd., S. 517.

24 Ebd., S. 509.

25 PAULSEN, A., «Allgemeine Volkswirtschaftslehre. Bd. 3: Produktionsfaktoren», Berlin, de Gruyter, 1961 (Sammlung Göschen, Bd. 1171), S. 72.

26 Vgl. auch den Anteil der Grundsteuern an dem Realsteueraufkommen. In der Bundesrepublik Deutschland belief sich der Anteil der Grundsteuern A und B im Jahre 1963 auf 17,1 v.H. des gesamten Realsteueraufkommens. Hingegen betrug der Anteil der Gewerbesteuer nach Ertrag und Kapital 75,7 v.H. – «Finanzen und Steuern», hrsg. vom Statistischen Bundesamt Wiesbaden, Stuttgart-Mainz, Kohlhammer, 1963 (Reihe 9, Realsteuern, I. Realsteuervergleich), S. 5.

27 Vgl. v. STACKELBERG, «Grundlagen der theoretischen Volkswirtschaftslehre», a. a. O., S. 278.

28 Vgl. das Buch des Verfassers «Comparative Economic Systems», a. a. O., S. 486.

29 ARNDT, E., «Theoretische Grundlagen der Lohnpolitik», Tübingen, Mohr (Siebeck), 1957, S. 80.

30 Lehner, M., «Die kurzfristigen Lohnbestimmungsfaktoren in der modernen Volkswirtschaft», Winterthur, Keller, 1962, S. 17.

31 ZIMMERMAN, L. J., «Geschichte der theoretischen Volkswirtschaftslehre», Köln-Deutz, Bund Verlag, 1954, S. 68.

32 Vgl. supra, Abschnitte III, VIII.

33 Vgl. den Aufsatz des Verfassers «Die philosophischen Grundlagen wirtschaftspolitischer Zielsetzungen», a. a. O., S. 99.

34 Vgl. das Buch des Verfassers «Comparative Economic Systems», a. a. O., S. 463.

35 PFISTER, B., «Sozialpolitik als Krisenpolitik», Stuttgart-Berlin, Kohlhammer, 1936, S. 149 ff.

36 MÜLLER-ARMACK, «Soziale Marktwirtschaft», a. a. O., S. 390.

37 Ebd., S. 391.

38 Ebd.

39 LEHNER, «Die kurzfristigen Lohnbestimmungsfaktoren in der modernen Volkswirtschaft», a. a. O., S. 50.

40 Ebd., S. 53.

41 WEDDIGEN, W., «Die wirtschaftlichen Folgen des Investivlohnes», Berlin, Duncker und Humblot, 1964 (Sozialpolitische Schriften, Nr. 17), S. 12.

42 Ebd., S. 13.

43 SWEERTS-SPORCK, P., «Investivlohn – ein Irrweg», Der Volkswirt, Jg. 18, Frankfurt/M., 1964, Nr. 37, S. 2049.

44 ARNDT, E., «Die Lohnpolitik in einzel- und gesamtwirtschaftlicher Sicht», ORTLIEB (Hrsg.), Wirtschaftsordnung und Wirtschaftspolitik ohne Dogma, a. a. O., S. 286.

45 DERS., «Theoretische Grundlagen der Lohnpolitik», a. a. O., S. 90.

46 Ebd., S. 107.

47 Besondere Formen des Leistungslohnes zeigen sich im Akkordlohn, Prämienlohn und Zeitlohn einschließlich Leistungszuschlägen. Alle diese Modifizierungen orientieren sich an der Produktivität.

48 Besonders stark wirkt sich dieser Effekt bei Gütern aus, deren Nachfrage relativ preisunelastisch ist.

49 LIEFMANN-KEIL, E., «Produktivitätsorientierte Lohnpolitik», WWA, Bd. 76, a. a. O., 1956, S. 245.

50 Ebd., S. 262.

51 OTT, A. E., «Lohnhöhe und Produktivität», Volkswirtschaftliche Korrespondenz der Adolf-Weber-Stiftung, Nr. 10, Frankfurt/M., 1963, passim.

52 LIEFMANN-KEIL, «Produktivitätsorientierte Lohnpolitik», a. a. O., S. 240.

53 Ebd., S. 248. – ROTHSCHILD, «Der Lohnanteil am Gesamteinkommen. Einige Bemerkungen zu einem umstrittenen Problem», a. a. O., S. 157 ff.

54 LIEFMANN-KEIL, «Produktivitätsorientierte Lohnpolitik», a. a. O., S. 245.

55 CLARK, J. M., «Criteria of Sound Wage Adjustment, with Emphasis on the Question of Inflationary Effects», McCORD WRIGHT, D. (Hrsg.), The Impact of the Union. Eight Economic Theorists Evaluate the Labor Union Movement, New York, Kelley and Millman, 1956, S. 14.

[56] SPIEGELHALTER, F., «Lohnpolitik vom Standpunkt der Arbeitgeber», BAYER, H. (Hrsg.), Lohnpolitik und Lohntechnik heute, Berlin, Duncker und Humblot, 1962, S. 39.

[57] LIEFMANN-KEIL, «Produktivitätsorientierte Lohnpolitik», a.. a. O., S. 242.

[58] LEHNER, «Die kurzfristigen Lohnbestimmungsfaktoren in der modernen Volkswirtschaft», a. a. O., S. 101.

[59] Manchen gewerkschaftlichen Kreisen erscheint jedoch der Mitbesitz an den Produktionsmitteln geradezu als Verrat an der Klassensolidarität.

[60] LIEFMANN-KEIL, «Produktivitätsorientierte Lohnpolitik», a. a. O., S. 256.

[61] ARNDT, «Theoretische Grundlagen der Lohnpolitik», a. a. O., S. 274.

[62] GESTRICH, H., «Kredit und Sparen», 2. durchges. Aufl., Bad Godesberg, Küpper vorm. Bondi, 1947, S. 158. – ROBINSON, J., «Essays in the Theory of Employment», Oxford, Basil Blackwell, 1953, S. 14 ff.

[63] JACK, T., «Full Employment in Retrospect», Econ. J., Bd. 62, London, 1952, Nr. 248, S. 744.

[64] SCHUPP, W., «Die Sicherung der Vollbeschäftigung nach der neoliberalen Theorie», Zürich, Polygraphischer Verlag, 1958 (Schriften des Schweizerischen Wirtschaftsarchivs, Bd. 12), S. 93.

[65] LIEFMANN-KEIL, «Produktivitätsorientierte Lohnpolitik», a. a. O., S. 257.

[66] HANSEN, A. H., «Monetary Theory and Fiscal Policy», New York-Toronto-London, McGraw-Hill, 1949, S. 126.

[67] ARNDT, «Theoretische Grundlagen der Lohnpolitik», a. a. O., S. 127.

[68] EHRENBERG, H. und SPIEGELHALTER, F., «Lohnpolitik heute», Stuttgart, Kohlhammer, 1963, S. 143.

[69] ARNDT, «Theoretische Grundlagen der Lohnpolitik», a. a. O., S. 283.

[70] BOMBACH, G., «Preisstabilität, wirtschaftliches Wachstum und Einkommensverteilung», Schweizer. Z. Volkswirtsch. Statist., Jg. 95, Basel, 1959, S. 1.

[71] Ebd., S. 17 f.

[72] ARNDT, «Theoretische Grundlagen der Lohnpolitik», a. a. O., S. 228.

[73] OTT, «Lohnhöhe und Produktivität», a. a. O., S. 4.

[74] LIEFMANN-KEIL, «Produktivitätsorientierte Lohnpolitik», a. a. O., S. 254.

[75] Ebd., S. 262.

[76] FUNCK, R., «Möglichkeiten einer verteilungsaktiven Lohnpolitik», JÜRGENSEN (Hrsg.), Gestaltungsprobleme der Weltwirtschaft usw., a. a. O., S. 586.

[77] AGARTZ, V., «Expansive Lohnpolitik», Mitt. Wirtsch. Inst. Gewerk., Jg. 6, Köln, 1953, Nr. 12, S. 245 ff.

[78] WEDDIGEN, «Die wirtschaftlichen Folgen des Investivlohnes», a. a. O., S. 58.

[79] KLAUS, J., «Lohnquote und Gewerkschaften. Über die Möglichkeiten einer Beeinflussung der Einkommensverteilung durch das kollektive Arbeitsangebot», Konjunk. pol., Jg. 5, Berlin, 1959, Nr. 4, S. 247 f.

[80] DIECKOW, J., «Die Wirkungen von Lohnerhöhungen auf Beschäftigung und Preisniveau» (Diss.), Berlin, 1960, S. 80.

Notes to Chapter XI

[1] KAMENKA, «The Ethical Foundations of Marxism», a. a. O., S. VII ff., 151 f.

[2] RAMM, «Die künftige Gesellschaftsordnung usw.», a. a. O., S. 110 ff. – DAHRENDORF, «Marx in Perspektive usw.», a. a. O., S. 70.

[3] KAMENKA, «The Ethical Foundations of Marxism», a. a. O., S. 70 f.

[4] Ebd., S. 43.

[5] FRIEDRICH, «Philosophie und Ökonomie beim jungen Marx», a. a. O., S. 91.

6 MEGA, Abt. I, Bd. 1, erster Halbband, a. a. O., S. 614. – KAMENKA, «The Ethical Foundations of Marxism», a. a. O., S. 51 ff.

7 FRIEDRICH, «Philosophie und Ökonomie beim jungen Marx», a. a. O., S. 138 ff.

8 HOFMANN, «Ideengeschichte der sozialen Bewegung des 19. und 20. Jahrhunderts», a. a. O., S. 120.

9 FALK, W., «Hegels Freiheitsidee in der Marxschen Dialektik», Archiv Sozwiss. Sozpol., Bd. 68, Tübingen, 1933, S. 16.

10 Vgl. infra, Abschnitt XV.

11 MARX legt seine Ansichten zu diesem Thema vornehmlich in seiner Dissertation dar. – MEGA, Abt. I, Bd. 1, erster Halbband, a. a. O., S. 41–44. – ADAMS, H. P., «Karl Marx and His Earlier Writings», London, Allen and Unwin, 1940, S. 27–41.

12 MARX meinte, HEGEL habe die begriffliche Auflösung der richtig erkannten Widersprüche mit ihrer realen Auflösung identifiziert. – BOCHEŃSKI, J. M., «Die kommunistische Ideologie und die Würde und Freiheit der Menschen», Bonn, Bundeszentrale für Heimatdienst, 1957 (Schriftenreihe der Bundeszentrale für Heimatdienst, Nr. 21), passim.

13 DAHRENDORF, «Marx in Perspektive usw.», a. a. O., S. 14 f.

14 In den Jahren 1957/58 wuchs die Literatur, die sich mit marxistischer Ethik befaßt, spürbar an. Siehe die Angaben in: «Eżegodnik. Knigi SSSR» (Jahrbuch. Bücher der UdSSR), 1957, 1958, 1959, Moskau, Izdatel'stvo Vsesojuznoj Knižnoj palaty (Verlag des Allunionsbibliographischen Instituts), 1959, 1960, 1961.

15 HEISS, «Die großen Dialektiker des 19. Jahrhunderts usw.», a. a. O., S. 338 ff. – BOLLNOW, «Engels' Auffassung von Revolution usw.», a. a. O., S. 77–144. – NÜRNBERGER, «Lenins Revolutionstheorie usw.», a. a. O., S. 161–172.

16 MARX, K., «Kritik des Gothaer Programms», Berlin, Dietz, 1946, S. 21.

17 TOPITSCH, E., «Marxismus und Gnosis», ders., Sozialphilosophie zwischen Ideologie und Wissenschaft, a. a. O., S. 235–270.

18 DAHRENDORF, «Marx in Perspektive usw.», a. a. O., S. 136.

19 MARX, K., «Das Elend der Philosophie» (aus dem Franz.), Berlin, Dietz, 1947, S. 73. – MEGA, Abt. I, Bd. 3, a. a. O., S. 209.

20 BIRNBAUM, N., «Ideologie», RGG, 3. Aufl., Bd. 3, a. a. O., 1959, Sp. 567–572. – GRIMM, T., «Kommunismus», ebd., Sp. 1733–1744.

21 Vgl. supra, Abschnitt VI.

22 WETTER, «Der dialektische Materialismus usw.», a. a. O., S. 634 ff.

23 «Politische Ökonomie. Lehrbuch», a. a. O., S. 339 ff.

24 THALHEIM, «Grundzüge des sowjetischen Wirtschaftssystems», a. a. O., S. 21.

25 WETTER, «Der dialektische Materialismus usw.», a. a. O., S. 72.

26 Ebd., S. 87 f.

27 Ebd., S. 90.

28 Vgl. supra, Abschnitt VI.

29 HOFMANN, «Ideengeschichte der sozialen Bewegung des 19. und 20. Jahrhunderts», a. a. O., S. 21.

30 LENIN, W. I., «Proletariat und Bauernschaft», ders., Werke, Bd. 8, a. a. O., 1958, S. 224 f.

31 FETSCHER, «Von Marx zur Sowjetideologie», a. a. O., S. 58–62, 79–81.

32 TREUE, «Wirtschaftsgeschichte der Neuzeit usw.», a. a. O., S. 701–704.

33 SCHELER, «Philosophische Probleme des Übergangs vom Kapitalismus zum Kommunismus», a. a. O., S. 31–48.

34 LENIN, W. I., «Staat und Revolution. Die Lehre des Marxismus vom Staat und die Aufgaben des Proletariats in der Revolution», ders., Werke, Bd. 25, a. a. O., 1960, S. 393–507.

35 MARX, «Kritik des Gothaer Programms», a. a. O., S. 19.

36 LENIN, W. I., «Die Aufgaben der Jugendverbände», Rede auf dem III. Gesamtrussischen Kongreß des Kommunistischen Jugendverbandes Rußlands vom 2. Oktober 1920, ders., Werke, Bd. 31, a. a. O., 1959, S. 281, 283.

³⁷ PRUDENSKIJ, G. A. (Hrsg.), «Voprosy truda v SSSR» (Fragen der Arbeit in der UdSSR), Moskau, Gosudarstvennoe izdatel'stvo političeskoj literatury (Staatsverlag für politische Literatur), 1958, S. 322 ff. – Vgl. ferner «Konstitucija (osnovnoj zakon) Sojuza Sovetskich Socialističeskich Respublik» (Verfassung (Grundgesetz) der Union der Sozialistischen Sowjetrepubliken), Moskau, Gosudarstvennoe izdatel'stvo juridičeskoj literatury (Staatsverlag für juristische Literatur), 1952, S. 5, 28.

³⁸ In sowjetischen Quellen wird dieser Widerstand als Rebellion bezeichnet, die von den Kulaken und anderen Konterrevolutionären organisiert wurde. – PANKRATOVA, A. M. (Hrsg.), «Istorija SSSR» (Die Geschichte der UdSSR), 3. Teil, 11. Aufl., Moskau, Gosudarstvennoe učebno-pedagogičeskoe izdatel'stvo Ministerstva Prosveščenija RSFSR (Staatsverlag des Kultusministeriums der RSFSR für Schul- und Lehrbücher und für pädagogische Literatur), 1952, S. 279. – «Geschichte der Kommunistischen Partei der Sowjetunion», a. a. O., S. 372, 423 f.

³⁹ STALIN, J. W., «Voprosy leninizma» (Fragen des Leninismus), 11. Aufl., Moskau, Gosudarstvennoe izdatel'stvo političeskoj literatury (Staatsverlag für politische Literatur), 1947, S. 136 ff. – ŽDANOVSKAJA, Z. V., ŽIBAREV, P. B., MASLOVA, A. T., ŠIROKOV, A. I. und ŠPYNOV, A. G., «Obzor istočnikov istorii KPSS. Kurs lekcij» (Eine Quellenübersicht zur Geschichte der KPdSU. Vortragsreihe), Moskau, Izdatel'stvo Moskovskogo Universiteta (Verlag der Moskauer Universität), 1961, S. 314 f.

⁴⁰ Denn Moralforderungen lassen sich nach der kommunistischen Theorie des Materialismus nicht aus frei gesetzten Moralanschauungen, sondern einzig aus den gesellschaftlichen Verhältnissen ableiten.

⁴¹ Vgl. das Buch des Verfassers «Studien zum Wirtschaftswachstum Südosteuropas», a. a. O., S. 56.

⁴² STALIN, J. W., «O proekte konstitucii Sojuza SSR», Doklad na črezvyčajnom VIII s-ezde sovetov 25 nojabrja 1936 g. (Über den Entwurf der Verfassung der Union der SSR. – Referat auf dem Außerordentlichen VIII. Allunions-Sowjetkongreß vom 25. November 1936), Moskau, Partizdat CK VKP (B) (Parteiverlag des ZK der KPdSU (B)), 1936, S. 17.

⁴³ STALIN, J. W., «Neue Verhältnisse – neue Aufgaben des wirtschaftlichen Aufbaus», Rede auf der Beratung der Wirtschaftler, 23. Juni 1931, ders., Werke, Bd. 13, a. a. O., 1955, S. 51 f.

⁴⁴ BOECK, H., «Zur marxistischen Ethik und sozialistischen Moral», Berlin, Akademie Verlag, 1959, S. 113.

⁴⁵ «Kontrol'nye cifry razvitija narodnogo chozjajstva SSSR na 1959–1965 gody» (Kontrollziffern der Entwicklung der Volkswirtschaft der UdSSR für die Jahre 1959–1965), Tezisy doklada tovarišča N. S. Chruščeva na XXI s-ezde KPSS (Thesen in dem Bericht des Genossen N. S. Chruščev auf dem XXI. Kongreß der KPdSU), Moskau, Gosudarstvennoe Izdatel'stvo Političeskoj Literatury (Staatsverlag für politische Literatur), 1958, S. 29 ff., 60 ff.

⁴⁶ Beschluß des ZK der KPdSU: «O pedologičeskich izvraščenijach v sisteme narkomprosov (Über die pädologischen Entartungen im Bereich der Volkskommissariate für Bildungswesen), Bol'šaja Sovetskaja Ènciklopedija, Bd. 32, a. a. O., S. 279.

⁴⁷ BAUER, «Der neue Mensch in der sowjetischen Psychologie», a. a. O., S. 107, 120.

⁴⁸ Ebd., S. 113.

⁴⁹ BOECK, «Zur marxistischen Ethik und sozialistischen Moral», a. a. O., S. 79 ff.

⁵⁰ BAUER, «Der neue Mensch in der sowjetischen Psychologie», a. a. O., S. 110, Fußnote 13.

⁵¹ Ebd., S. 111.

⁵² MARCUSE, H., «Die Gesellschaftslehre des sowjetischen Marxismus», Neuwied, Luchterhand, 1964, S. 185–247.

⁵³ BAUER, «Der neue Mensch in der sowjetischen Psychologie», a. a. O., S. 115.

⁵⁴ FEDOSSEJEW, «Sozialismus und Humanismus», a. a. O., S. 8.

⁵⁵ BOECK, «Zur marxistischen Ethik und sozialistischen Moral», a. a. O., S. 79–98.

⁵⁶ Vgl. infra, Abschnitte XII, XIII.

Notes to Chapter XII

1 MEISSNER, «Das Parteiprogramm der KPdSU 1903–1961», a. a. O., S. 132.

2 Über die Bedingungen für die Verwirklichung des kommunistischen Prinzips «Jeder nach seinen Fähigkeiten, jedem nach seinen Bedürfnissen» vgl. «Politische Ökonomie. Lehrbuch», a. a. O., S. 695.

3 Bauermeister, «Die russische kommunistische Theorie usw.», a. a. O., S. 54. – Zur Stellung des Arbeitslohnes im Sozialismus vgl. «Politische Ökonomie. Lehrbuch», a. a. O., S. 617.

4 LENIN, W. I., «Die Aufgaben des Proletariats in unserer Revolution (Entwurf einer Plattform der proletarischen Partei)», ders., Werke, Bd. 24, a. a. O., 1959, S. 70.

5 THALHEIM, K. C., «Wandlungen der Sowjetwirtschaft im Zeichen des Übergangs zum Kommunismus», Osteuropa Wirtsch., Jg. 7, a. a. O., Nr. 1, S. 3. – «Kontrol'nye cifry razvitija narodnogo chozjajstva SSSR na 1959–1965 gody. (Tezisy doklada tovarišča N. S. Chruščeva na XXI. s-ezde KPSS)» (Kontrollziffern der Entwicklung der Volkswirtschaft der UdSSR für die Jahre 1959–1965. (Thesen der Rede des Genossen N. S. Chruščev auf dem XXI. Parteitag der KPdSU)), Pravda, Jg. 47, Moskau, 1958, Nr. 318 (14712), S. 1 f., 9.

6 LENIN, «Staat und Revolution. Die Lehre des Marxismus und die Aufgaben des Proletariats in der Revolution», a. a. O., S. 480.

7 THALHEIM, «Wandlungen der Sowjetwirtschaft usw.», a. a. O., S. 3.

8 «Politische Ökonomie. Lehrbuch», a. a. O., S. 612 f. – MARX, K., und ENGELS, F., «Werke», Bd. 20, Berlin, Dietz, 1962, S. 186.

9 «Politische Ökonomie. Lehrbuch», a. a. O., S. 617. Als Grundbedingung wird eine rasche und stetig steigende Arbeitsproduktivität angegeben. Nur so erscheint es möglich, wirtschaftliches Wachstum zu sichern, um die Stufe des Übergangs vom Sozialismus zum Kommunismus zu ermöglichen.

10 MEISSNER, «Das Parteiprogramm der KPdSU 1903–1961», a. a. O., S. 135.

11 Ebd., S. 118.

12 Ebd., S. 187.

13 MEGA, Abt. I, Bd. 3, a. a. O., S. 118.

14 Vgl. v. BISSING, W. M., «Theorie der sozialistischen (sowjetischen) Wirtschaft», JAHN, G. und v. BISSING, W. M. (Hrsg.), Die Wirtschaftssysteme der Staaten Osteuropas und der Volksrepublik China. Untersuchungen der Entstehung, Entfaltung und Wandlung sozialistischer Wirtschaftssysteme, Berlin, Duncker und Humblot, 1961 (Schr. Ver. Socpol., N.F., Bd. 23/I), S. 39. – STALIN, J. W., «Fragen des Leninismus», 11. Aufl., Moskau, Verlag für fremdsprachige Literatur, 1947, S. 604 f.

15 «Politische Ökonomie. Lehrbuch», a. a. O., S. 695.

16 Vgl. supra, Abschnitt XI und Abhandlung des Verfassers Die philosophischen Grundlagen wirtschaftspolitischer Zielsetzungen, a.a.O., S. 112 f.

17 LENIN, W. I., «Dritter gesamtrussischer Kongreß der Sowjets der Arbeiter-, Soldaten- und Bauerndeputierten, 10.–18. (23.–31.) Januar 1918», ders., Werke, Bd. 26, a. a. O., S. 474.

18 «Politische Ökonomie. Lehrbuch», a. a. O., S. 718.

19 Ebd., S. 696.

20 SCHELER, «Philosophische Probleme des Übergangs vom Kapitalismus zum Kommunismus», a. a. O., S. 43. – LENIN, «Die Aufgaben des Proletariats in unserer Revolution usw.», ders., Werke, Bd. 24, a. a. O., S. 62. – Vgl. insbesondere auch CHRUSTSCHOW, «Die Kontrollziffern für die Entwicklung der Volkswirtschaft der UdSSR in den Jahren 1959–1965», a. a. O., S. 127 ff.

21 Ebd., S. 129.

22 «Politische Ökonomie. Lehrbuch», a. a. O., S. 613.

23 Zum Problem der notwendigen Steigerung der Arbeitsproduktivität siehe (o. Verf.),

«Chrestomathie zur politischen Ökonomie. Ein Nachschlagewerk» (aus dem Russ.), Berlin, Verlag Die Wirtschaft, 1964, S. 505. – «Plenum des Zentral-Komitees der KPdSU, 24. bis 29. Juni 1959: Beschluß über die Arbeit der Parteiorganisationen und Sowjets sowie der Volkswirtschaftsräte zur Erfüllung der Beschlüsse des XXI. Parteitages der KPdSU über die Beschleunigung des technischen Fortschritts in der Industrie und im Bauwesen», Presse Sowjet., a. a. O., 1959, Nr. 79, S. 1830.

[24] KNIRSCH, P., «Produktion und Distribution im Kommunismus», Osteuropa, Jg. 11, a. a. O., Nr. 7/8, S. 482.

[25] CHRUSTSCHOW, «Die Kontrollziffern für die Entwicklung der Volkswirtschaft der UdSSR in den Jahren 1959–1965», a. a. O., S. 130 f.

[26] POL'ŠČIKOV, A., «Rost narodnogo blagosostojanija» (Wachstum des Volkswohlstandes), Kommunist, Jg. 36, Moskau, 1959, Nr. 15, S. 78, 80.

[27] «Grundlagen des Marxismus-Leninismus. Lehrbuch», 5. Aufl., Berlin, Dietz, 1960, S. 814.

[28] Ebd., S. 775. – CHRUSTSCHOW, «Die Kontrollziffern für die Entwicklung der Volkswirtschaft der UdSSR in den Jahren 1959–1965», a. a. O., S. 134 f.

[29] BECKER, «Die kommunistische Verteilung als Ideal und Wirklichkeit», a. a. O., S. 10.

[30] CHRUSTSCHOW, «Die Kontrollziffern für die Entwicklung der Volkswirtschaft der UdSSR in den Jahren 1959–1965», a. a. O., S. 62 f.

[31] «Grundlagen des Marxismus-Leninismus. Lehrbuch», a. a. O., S. 806.

[32] CHRUSTSCHOW, «Die Kontrollziffern für die Entwicklung der Volkswirtschaft der UdSSR in den Jahren 1959–1965», a. a. O., S. 130 f.

[33] Die von sowjetischer Seite für den Übergang zum Kommunismus erwartete Zunahme des «gesellschaftlichen Konsums» ist jedoch keineswegs auf das östliche Wirtschaftssystem beschränkt – die in der westlichen Welt mit dem Entstehen des Wohlfahrtsstaates verbundenen Erscheinungen sind ein ähnlicher Vorgang.

[34] Schon 1959 gebrauchte KANTOROVIČ in der UdSSR für den Begriff «Zinsfuß» den Ausdruck «Nutzeffekt-Norm», und 1960 sprach CHOLMOGOROV von ihm als einer «Art Belastung für die Zeit». In seiner Linearprogrammierung verwendet KANTOROVIČ Preise für den Gebrauch von Kapital und Boden sowie Gewinne. In der jüngsten Diskussion in Mitteldeutschland werden sowohl die Begriffe Zins als Produktionsfondsabgabe verwendet. Letzterer entspricht dem «Zins», während der erste Begriff eher einer Gewinnsteuer nahekommt. Die Bulgaren nennen Zinsen «Steuer auf Produktionsfonds», während man in Ungarn «Abgabe» oder «Gebühr» vorzieht. Nur in Polen und Jugoslawien spricht man vom «Zinsfuß». In Ungarn besteht seit dem 1. 1. 1964 eine Jahresabgabe und in Jugoslawien wird die Verzinsung seit 1961 angewendet.

[35] «Vor Neuerungen im sowjetischen Planungssystem», Ost-Prob., Jg. 14, a. a. O., Nr. 21, S. 662.

[36] Ebd., S. 662.

[37] CHRUSTSCHOW, «Die Kontrollziffern für die Entwicklung der Volkswirtschaft der UdSSR in den Jahren 1959–1965», a. a. O., S. 134.

[38] Ebd., S. 131.

[39] GOLDSMITH, S. F., «Changes in the Size Distribution of Income», Amer. Econ. R., Bd. 47 (Papers and Proceedings), Menasha, 1957, Nr. 2, S. 517.

[40] YANOWITCH, M., «The Soviet Income Revolution», Slav. R., Bd. 22, Washington, 1963, Nr. 4, S. 692.

[41] CHRUSTSCHOW, «Die Kontrollziffern für die Entwicklung der Volkswirtschaft der UdSSR in den Jahren 1959–1965», a. a. O., S. 59. – YANOWITCH, «The Soviet Income Revolution», a. a. O., S. 692.

[42] YANOWITCH, «The Soviet Income Revolution», a. a. O., S. 692. – BERGSON, A., «The Structure of Soviet Wages», 3. Aufl., Cambridge (Mass.), Harvard University Press, 1954, S. 123.

[43] YANOWITCH, «The Soviet Income Revolution», a. a. O., S. 692.

[44] Ebd., S. 689.

[45] GOLDSMITH, «Changes in the Size Distribution of Income», a. a. O., S. 527.

[46] Vernachlässigt wurden bei der Analyse der östlichen Einkommensverteilung die Ge-

327

währung von Prämien und die Bevorzugung der Mitglieder der Parteispitzen bei der unentgeltlichen Verteilung. Ihre Berücksichtigung dürfte wohl eine faktisch stärkere Einkommensdifferenzierung hervortreten lassen als es die angeführten Zahlen tun.

Notes to Chapter XIII

[1] HOFMANN, W., «Die Arbeitsverfassung der Sowjetunion», Berlin, Duncker und Humblot, 1956, S. 358.

[2] KOSTIN, L., «Löhne und Gehälter in der sowjetischen Industrie», Moskau, Verlag für fremdsprachige Literatur, 1960, S. 11.

[3] So weisen die für eine weitere Industrialisierung wichtigsten Industriezweige (Kohlenind., NE-Metallurgie, E-Metallurgie, Erdölindustrie, Chem. Ind., Maschinenbau und Kraftwerke) auch das höchste Durchschnittslohnniveau auf. – KOSTIN, «Löhne und Gehälter in der sowjetischen Industrie», a. a. O., S. 16.

[4] MANEWITSCH, J. L., «Der Arbeitslohn und seine Formen in der sowjetischen Industrie» (aus dem Russ.), Berlin, Verlag Die Wirtschaft, 1954, S. 137.

[5] BERGSON, «The Structure of Soviet Wages», a. a. O., S. 201. – HOFMANN, «Die Arbeitsverfassung der Sowjetunion», a. a. O., S. 372, passim.

[6] Darunter fallen auch Lohnerhöhungen für solche Personen, die in erster Linie für die Volksbildung, im Gesundheitswesen, im Handel und anderen Dienstleistungsbereichen tätig sind. – «O merach po vypolneniju programmy KPSS v oblasti povyšenija blagosostojanija naroda – Doklad tovarišča N. S. Chruščeva na sessii Verchovnogo Soveta SSSR 13 ijulja 1964 goda» (Über die Maßnahmen zur Erfüllung des Programms der KPdSU auf dem Gebiete der Hebung des Volkswohlstandes. Bericht des Genossen N. S. Chruščev auf der Sitzung des Obersten Sowjets der UdSSR am 13. Juli 1964), Pravda, Moskau, Nr. 196 (16782), 14. Juli 1964, S. 3 f.

[7] Vgl. v. BISSING, «Theorie der sozialistischen (sowjetischen) Wirtschaft», a. a. O., S. 41. – KOSTIN, «Löhne und Gehälter in der sowjetischen Industrie», a. a. O., S. 30–54.

[8] STALIN, «Voprosy leninizma», a. a. O., S. 502.

[9] MANEWITSCH, «Der Arbeitslohn und seine Formen in der sowjetischen Industrie», a. a. O., S. 143.

[10] ŠKURKO, S., «Material'noe stimulirovanie i formy oplaty truda v promyšlennosti» (Materieller Anreiz und die Formen der Arbeitsentlohnung in der Industrie), Vopr. Ėkon. (Fragen der Ökonomie), Jg. 15, Moskau, 1962, Nr. 5, S. 40 ff.

[11] YANOWITCH, «The Soviet Income Revolution», a. a. O., S. 689.

[12] MEERZON, D., «Techničeskij progress i soveršenstvovanie form i sistem zarabotnoj platy» (Der technische Fortschritt und die Vervollkommnung der Form und der Systeme des Arbeitslohnes), Vopr. Ėkon., Jg. 12, a. a. O., 1959, Nr. 4, S. 49.

[13] KOSTIN, «Löhne und Gehälter in der sowjetischen Industrie», a. a. O., S. 56.

[14] Der Reallohn aller Arbeiter und Angestellten stieg von 1950 (= 100) bis 1955 auf 141 und bis 1959 auf 156. – «Narodnoe chozjajstvo RSFSR v 1959. Statističeskij ežegodnik» (Die Volkswirtschaft der RSFSR im Jahre 1959. Statistisches Jahrbuch), Moskau, Gosstatizdat CSU SSSR (Statistischer Staatsverlag der Zentralverwaltung für Statistik der UdSSR), 1960, S. 23.

[15] TULEBAEV, A., «Oplata truda i rezervy sel'skochozjajstvennogo proizvodstva» (Arbeitsentlohnung und die Reserven der landwirtschaftlichen Produktion), Socialističeskij Trud (Die sozialistische Arbeit), Jg. 9, Moskau, 1964, Nr. 2, S. 45, 50–56.

[16] Vgl. v. BISSING, «Theorie der sozialistischen (sowjetischen) Wirtschaft», a. a. O., S. 48.

[17] VOLIN, L., «Agricultural Policy of the Soviet Union», BORNSTEIN, FUSFELD (Hrsg.), The Soviet Economy usw., a. a. O., S. 271.

¹⁸ Vgl. v. BISSING, «Theorie der sozialistischen (sowjetischen) Wirtschaft», a. a. O., S. 50.

¹⁹ TERJAEVA, A., «Pod-em obščestvennogo proizvodstva i soveršenstvovanie form oplaty truda v kolchozach» (Aufschwung der gesellschaftlichen Produktion und Vervollkommnung der Formen der Arbeitsentlohnung in den Kolchosen), Vopr. Ėkon., Jg. 12, a. a. O., Nr. 1, S. 110. – NOVE, A., «Die sowjetische Wirtschaft», Wiesbaden, Rheinische Verlagsanstalt, o. J., S. 139.

²⁰ Vgl. das Buch des Verfassers «Studien zum Wirtschaftswachstum Südosteuropas», a. a. O., passim. – DERS., «Arbeit und Produktivität in Südosteuropa», Schmollers Jb., Jg. 82, a. a. O., Nr. 1, S. 41–70.

²¹ JOÓ, F., «Entstehung und Entfaltung des sozialistischen Wirtschaftssystems in Ungarn» (aus dem Ungar.), JAHN, G. (Hrsg.), Die Wirtschaftssysteme der Staaten Osteuropas und der Volksrepublik China. Untersuchungen der Entstehung, Entfaltung und Wandlung sozialistischer Wirtschaftssysteme, Berlin, Duncker und Humblot, 1962 (Schr. Ver. Socpol., N.F., Bd. 23/II), S. 23.

²² Der Reallohnindex für Arbeiter und Angestellte (1949 = 100) sank zwar bis 1952 auf 82,3. Für die nachfolgenden Jahre liegt jedoch eine ständige Zunahme vor (1954: 102,3; 1956: 118,3; 1958: 145,4; 1960: 156,0; 1961: 156,3; 1962: 158,6; 1963: 165,7 und 1964: 170,0).
Der Index des Netto-Nominaleinkommens (1949 = 100) stieg von 147,4 (1952) bis auf 293,3 (1964). «Statisztikai Évkönyv 1964» (Statistisches Jahrbuch 1964), hrsg. v. Központi Statisztikai Hivatal (Statistisches Zentralamt), Budapest, 1965, S. 279, Tab. 1.10.

²³ LIESS, O. R., «Planwirtschaft und Sozialismus in Rumänien», JAHN (Hrsg.), Die Wirtschaftssysteme der Staaten Osteuropas und der Volksrepublik China usw.», a. a. O., Bd. 23/II, S. 161.

²⁴ Vgl. den Aufsatz des Verfassers «Einkommensverteilung in Südosteuropa», Jb. Nat. Ökon. Statist., Bd. 174, Stuttgart, 1962, Nr. 6, S. 534 f.

²⁵ Zuwachs des Reallohnes der Arbeiter (1950 = 100) in den Jahren 1955–1963:

1955: 128   1958: 161   1961: 193
1956: 138   1959: 172   1962: 201
1957: 153   1960: 189   1963: 213

«Anuarul Statistic al R.P.R. 1964» (Statistisches Jahrbuch der Volksrepublik Rumänien 1964), Bukarest, Direcţia Centrală de Statistică (Zentraldirektion für Statistik), 1964, S. 120, Tab. 40.

²⁶ DEVEDŽIEV, M., «Sŭčetavane na vŭtrešnata stopanska smetka s premialnite sistemi» (Die Koordination der innerbetrieblichen wirtschaftlichen Rechnungsführung mit dem Prämiensystem), Planovo stopanstvo i statistika (Planwirtschaft und Statistik), Jg. 18, Sofia, 1963, Nr. 4, S. 39–50.

²⁷ Vgl. den Aufsatz des Verfassers «Einkommensverteilung in Südosteuropa», a. a. O., S. 537.

²⁸ Jahres-Durchschnittslöhne und Gehälter (in Lewa) der Arbeiter und Angestellten nach Produktionszweigen (ohne landwirtschaftl. Produktionsgen.) in Bulgarien:

Jahr	Volkswirtschaft insgesamt	Industrie	Bauindustrie	Landwirtschaft
1948	485 (= 100)	457 (= 100)	640 (= 100)	383 (= 100)
1952	646 (133)	663 (145)	812 (127)	472 (123)
1955	754 (155)	793 (174)	946 (148)	623 (163)
1959	864 (178)	895 (196)	1029 (161)	844 (220)
1962	1020 (210)	1040 (228)	1206 (188)	907 (237)
1963	1051 (217)	1075 (235)	1263 (197)	930 (243)

Quelle: «Statističeski Godišnik na Narodna republika Bŭlgarija 1963» (Statistisches Jahrbuch der Volksrepublik Bulgarien 1964), Sofia, Centralno Statističeski Upravlenie pri Ministerskija Sŭvet (Statistisches Zentralamt beim Ministerrat), 1964, S. 80.

FOOTNOTES PP. 186–90

²⁹ KISS, T., «A szocialista országok gazdasági együttmüködése» (Die wirtschaftliche Zusammenarbeit der sozialistischen Länder), Budapest, Kossuth Könyvkiadó (Kossuth Buchverlag), 1961, S. 293.
³⁰ Vgl. den Aufsatz des Verfassers «Arbeit und Produktivität in Südosteuropa», a. a. O., S. 68 f.
³¹ SCHWANKE, R., «Die Verwirklichung der Sowjetwirtschaft in Albanien», JAHN (Hrsg.), Die Wirtschaftssysteme der Staaten Osteuropas und der Volksrepublik China usw., a. a. O., Bd. 23/II, S. 276–280.
³² MAMPEL, S., HAUCK, K., «Sozialpolitik in Mitteldeutschland», Stuttgart, Kohlhammer, 1962, S. 46 f.
³³ HAAS, G., LEUTWEIN, A., «Die rechtliche und soziale Lage der Arbeitnehmer in der sowjetischen Besatzungszone», Bonn-Berlin, Deutscher Bundesverlag, 1960, S. 67 f.
³⁴ Der Index des Reallohns (1958 = 100) für vollbeschäftigte Arbeiter und Angestellte (ohne Lehrlinge) in den sozialistischen Betrieben der Bereiche der materiellen Produktion stieg von 81,0 (1955) auf 122,3 (1963). – «Statistisches Jahrbuch der Deutschen Demokratischen Republik 1964», Jg. 9, Berlin, Staatsverlag der Deutschen Demokratischen Republik, 1964, S. 55. – Vgl. hierzu auch die Zahlenangaben in den Fußnoten 14, 22.
³⁵ GÜNZEL, K., «Die Wirtschaftspolitik der Volksrepubliken», MARKERT, W. (Hrsg.), Osteuropa-Handbuch. Polen, Köln-Graz, Böhlau, 1959, S. 392 ff.
³⁶ Vgl. auch die neueren Untersuchungen über moderne Aspekte der Organisation von Arbeitsplätzen: CHOLUJ, E., «Die komplexe Organisation der Arbeitsplätze», Presse Sowjet., a. a. O., 1964, Nr. 68, S. 1525 f. – «A lengyel munkapiac helyzete» (Die Lage des polnischen Arbeitsmarktes), Figyelö, a. a. O., 1964, Nr. 21, S. 6.
³⁷ TUREČEK, O., «Die Verwirklichung des Sozialismus in der Tschechoslowakei», JAHN und v. BISSING (Hrsg.), Die Wirtschaftssysteme der Staaten Osteuropas und der Volksrepublik China usw., a. a. O., Bd. 23/I, S. 392.
³⁸ STROBEL, G.W., «Probleme und Ziele der tschechoslowakischen Industrieplanung für die Jahre 1961–1965», Osteuropa, Jg. 10, a. a. O., Nr. 9, S. 597.
³⁹ HANDKE, W., «China auf dem Wege zum Sozialismus und Kommunismus», JAHN (Hrsg.), Die Wirtschaftssysteme der Staaten Osteuropas und der Volksrepublik China usw., a. a. O., Bd. 23/II, S. 481.
⁴⁰ GROSSMANN, B., «Die wirtschaftliche Entwicklung der Volksrepublik China», Stuttgart, Fischer, 1960 (Ökonomische Studien, hrsg. vom Institut für Außenhandel und Überseewirtschaft der Universität Hamburg), S. 366 ff.
⁴¹ Ebd.
⁴² BAUERMEISTER, «Die russische kommunistische Theorie usw.», a. a. O., S. 129 ff.
⁴³ MANEWITSCH, «Der Arbeitslohn und seine Formen in der sowjetischen Industrie», a. a. O., S. 90.
⁴⁴ Zur Heraufsetzung der Mindestlöhne lt. Beschluß vom 8. 9. 1956 vgl. Izvestija vom 9. 9. 1956, Moskau, S. 1. – Zum Erlaß des Rentengesetzes vom 14. 7. 1956 vgl. Pravda vom 15. 7. 1956, a. a. O., S. 2. – Über Preissenkungen vgl. Pravda vom 1. 3. 1960, a. a. O., S. 2.
⁴⁵ «Az adózás alapkérdései» (Grundfragen der Besteuerung), Budapest, Közgazdasági és Jogi Könyvkiadó (Buchverlag für Volkswirtschaft und Recht), 1959, S. 287 ff., 321–330. – NAGY, T., «A szövetkezetek jövedelemadói» (Einkommensteuern der Genossenschaften), Jogtudományi Közlöny (Rechtswissenschaftliches Mitteilungsblatt), Jg. 2, Budapest, 1952, S. 544 ff.
⁴⁶ «Az adózás alapkérdései», a. a. O., S. 322, 324.
⁴⁷ Ebd., S. 91.
⁴⁸ NAGY, «A szövetkezetek jövedelemadói», a. a. O., S. 544 ff.
⁴⁹ POLÓNYI SZÜCS, L., «A lakosság adóztatása különös tekintettel a mezögazdasági lakosság általános jövedelemadójára» (Die Besteuerung der Bevölkerung mit besonderer Rücksicht auf die allgemeine Einkommensteuer der landwirtschaftlichen Bevölkerung), Pénzügyi Szle (Finanzwirtschaftliche Rundschau), Jg. 3, Budapest, 1956, Nr. 5, S. 193 f.
⁵⁰ CHRUSTSCHOW, N. S., «Rede vor dem Obersten Sowjet am 5. 5. 1960», Presse Sowjet.,

a. a. O., 1960, Nr. 55, S. 1199–1212. – NEWTH, J. A., «Income Distribution in the USSR», Sov.. Stud., Bd. 12, Oxford, 1960, Nr. 2, S. 193 ff.

[51] CHRUSTSCHOW, «Rede vor dem Obersten Sowjet am 5. 5. 1960», a. a. O., S. 1203.

[52] Beispielsweise die Senkung der Landwirtschaftsteuer für Kolchosbauern um 60 v.H. im Jahre 1953. – Ebd., S. 1204.

[53] NEWTH, «Income Distribution in the USSR», a. a. O., S. 194.

[54] CHRUSTSCHOW, «Rede vor dem Obersten Sowjet der UdSSR am 5. 5. 1960», a. a. O., S. 1204.

[55] Ebd., S. 1205.

[56] MOŽINA, M., «Izmenenija v raspredelenii promyšlennych rabočich SSSR po razmeram zarabotnoj platy» (Änderungen der Lohnstruktur der Industriearbeiter in der UdSSR), Bjulleten' naučnoj informacii, trud i zarabotnaja plata (Bulletin für wissenschaftliche Information, Arbeit und Lohn), Moskau, 1961, Nr. 10, S. 24.

[57] YANOWITCH, «The Soviet Income Revolution», a. a. O., S. 686.

[58] Ebd., S. 687.

[59] MOŽINA, «Izmenenija v raspredelenii promyšlennych rabočich SSSR po razmeram zarabotnoj platy», a. a. O., S. 24.

[60] YANOWITCH, «The Soviet Income Revolution», a. a. O., S. 687.

[61] Ebd., S. 688.

[62] Ebd., S. 690. – KOMAROV, V. E., «Ekonomičeskie osnovy podgotovki specialistov dlja narodnogo chozjajstva» (Die ökonomischen Grundlagen der Heranbildung von Spezialisten für die Volkswirtschaft), Moskau, Izdatel'stvo Akademii Nauk SSSR (Verlag der Akademie der Wissenschaften der UdSSR), 1959, S. 156.

[63] RUBAN, E., «Die Entwicklung des Lebensstandards in der Sowjetunion unter dem Einfluß der sowjetischen Wirtschaftsplanung», Berlin, Duncker und Humblot, 1965 (Wirtschaftswissenschaftliche Veröffentlichungen des Osteuropa-Instituts an der Freien Universität Berlin, Bd. 23), S. 56.

[64] Nach Ansicht CHRUŠČEVS ist es weitaus wichtiger, Mindestlöhne, Mindestrenten und Löhne anzuheben anstelle der weiteren Befürwortung allgemeiner Preissenkungen. Auch hier tritt wieder der Gedanke einer mehr gleichmäßigen Form in der Entlohnung in den Vordergrund.

[65] CHRUSTSCHOW, «Die Kontrollziffern für die Entwicklung der Volkswirtschaft der UdSSR in den Jahren 1959–1965», a. a. O., S. 59.

[66] «Trud v SSSR. Statističeskij spravočnik» (Die Arbeit in der UdSSR. Statistisches Handbuch), Moskau, 1936, S. 32–48.

[67] CHAPMAN, J. G., «Real Wages in the Soviet Union 1928–1952», R. Econ. Statist., Bd. 36, Cambridge/Mass., 1954, S. 134–156. – BERGSON, «The Structure of Soviet Wages», a. a. O., S. 201.

[68] KASSIROV, L., «Material'nye stimuli i proizvodstvo» (Materielle Anreize und Produktion), Pravda, a. a. O., 1965, Nr. 22 (16974), S. 2.

[69] Ebd.

[70] RUBINČIK, S., «Soveščanie po voprosam soveršenstvovanija form oplaty truda v kolchozach» (Beratung über die Fragen der Vervollkommnung der Formen der Arbeitsentlohnung in den Kolchosen), Vopr. Ėkon., Jg. 12, a. a. O., Nr. 2, S. 150–155.

[71] «Kredite, Preise, Steuern», Ost-Prob., Jg. 17, a. a. O., Nr. 5, S. 152 f.

[72] TERJAEVA, «Pod-em obščestvennogo proizvodstva i soveršenstvovanie form oplaty truda v kolchozach», a. a. O., S. 108.

[73] «Politische Ökonomie. Lehrbuch», a. a. O., S. 449.

[74] HOFMANN, «Die Arbeitsverfassung der Sowjetunion», a. a. O., S. 500.

[75] LIBERMAN, E., «Noch einmal über Plan, Gewinn und Prämie», a. a. O., S. 2525–2527.

[76] Vgl. das Buch des Verfassers «Studien zum Wirtschaftswachstum Südosteuropas», a. a. O., S. 56.

[77] STROBEL, G., «Krise und Veränderungen im Wirtschaftssystem 1955–1958», MARKERT (Hrsg.), Osteuropa Handbuch. Polen, a. a. O., S. 521.

331

78 «Die Lage der Handwerkswirtschaft in der sowjetisch besetzten Zone Deutschlands unter besonderer Berücksichtigung der letzten Steuergesetzänderung vom 12. 3. 1958», Berlin, 1959 (Schr. Inst. Handwerk. Berlin, Nr. 14), S. 7.

79 LIESS, «Planwirtschaft und Sozialismus in Rumänien», a. a. O., S. 143 f.

80 «Politische Ökonomie. Lehrbuch», a. a. O., S. 449.

81 TERJAEVA, «Pod-em obščestvennogo proizvodstva i soveršenstvovanie form oplaty truda v kolchozach», a. a. O., S. 106.

82 MANEVIČ, E. L., «Aktual'nye voprosy teorii i organizacii zarabotnoj platy v SSSR» (Die aktuellen Fragen der Theorie und Organisation des Arbeitslohnes in der UdSSR), Problemy političeskoj ekonomii socializma. Sbornik statej (Die Probleme der politischen Ökonomie des Sozialismus. Aufsatzsammlung), Moskau, Gosudarstvennoe izdatel'stvo političeskoj literatury (Staatsverlag für politische Literatur), 1959, S. 181.

83 «Privatinitiative verhindert Versorgungskrisen. Die Hoflandwirtschaft in Ungarn», Wiss. D. Südosteurop., Jg. 13, München, 1964, Nr. 1/2, S. 17–19.

84 SZABÓ, F., «A háztáji gazdaságok helyzete és megítélése» (Die Lage und Beurteilung der Rolle der Hauswirtschaften), Társad. Szle, Jg. 19, a. a. O., Nr. 1, S. 21 f.

85 KOLESOV, N. D., und KOLESOVA, K. J., «O razvitii i sbliženii dvuch form socialističeskoj sobstvennosti» (Über die Entwicklung und Annäherung der beiden Formen des sozialistischen Eigentums), Vopr. Filos., Jg. 14, a. a. O., Nr. 1, S. 17.

86 Ebd.

87 «Vor Neuerungen im sowjetischen Planungssystem», Ost-Prob., Jg. 14, a. a. O., Nr. 21, S. 662.

88 GRUZINOV, V., «Premirovanie inženerno-techničeskich rabotnikov i služaščich v nekotorych socialističeskich stranach» (Prämiierung der ingenieur-technischen Arbeiter und Angestellten in einigen sozialistischen Ländern), Social. Trud, Jg. 8, a. a. O., Nr. 9, S. 122 ff.

89 WOLKOW, A., «Arbeit und Prämie», Presse Sowjet., a. a. O., 1965, Nr. 1, S. 10.

90 Ebd., S. 9 f.

91 GRUZINOV, «Premirovanie inženerno-techničeskich rabotnikov i služaščich v nekotorych socialističeskich stranach», a. a. O., S. 127 f.

92 WOLKOW, «Arbeit und Prämie», a. a. O., S. 9 f.

93 GRUZINOV, «Premirovanie inženerno-techničeskich rabotnikov i služaščich v nekotorych socialističeskich stranach», a. a. O., S. 125 f.

94 In der ČSSR darf die maximale Prämienhöhe in der Schwerindustrie nicht 60–75 v.H. des Gehaltes überschreiten und in anderen Zweigen nicht 45–50 v.H. Die Prämierungsspanne in Bulgarien liegt ebenfalls zwischen 40 und 60 v.H. des Gehalts. Während früher der Prozentsatz der Prämiengewährung mit wachsendem Gehalt anstieg, bleibt er jetzt gleich. Dadurch wurde eine gewisse Nivellierung erreicht.

95 GRUZINOV, «Premirovanie inženerno-techničeskich rabotnikov i služaščich v nekotorych socialističeskich stranach», a. a. O., S. 126.

96 Zuweisungen an den zusätzlichen Prämienfonds in v.H. des geplanten Lohnfonds: Schwerindustrie 3 v.H., Chemische Industrie 2,5 v.H., Leichtindustrie 2 v.H., Bergbau und Energie 1,9 v.H. – Ebd., S. 127.

97 KUSNEZOWA, M., «Nachfrage – Qualität – Plan», Presse Sowjet., a. a. O., 1964, Nr. 121, S. 2669.

98 Im Zusammenhang mit den ökonomischen Experimenten in der Sowjetunion gelten ab 1965 für einige Betriebe als Hauptbewertungsmaßstab die Produktion in Naturalform und der Gewinn. – «Ein Experiment beginnt», Presse Sowjet., a. a. O., 1965, Nr. 5, S. 9.

99 In den Jahren 1964 und 1965 sollten diese Gewinnabführungen an den Staatshaushalt 74 v.H. erreichen. – RJUMIN, S., «Pribyl'» (Gewinn), Ekonomičeskaja Gazeta. Eženedel'nik Central'nogo Komiteta KPSS (Wirtschaftszeitung. Wochenzeitung des Zentralkomitees der KPdSU), Moskau, 1964, Nr. 14, S. 10.

[100] Daneben bestanden noch sogenannte Massenbedarfs- und Prämienfonds, aus denen nur teilweise individuelle Prämien gezahlt wurden.

[101] RJUMIN, «Pribyl'», a. a. O., S. 10.

[102] Ebd.

[103] NOVE, A., «Social Welfare in the USSR», BORNSTEIN und FUSFELD (Hrsg.), The Soviet Economy usw., a. a. O., S. 338.

[104] «Über Maßnahmen zur weiteren Verbesserung der medizinischen Betreuung und des Gesundheitsschutzes der Bevölkerung der UdSSR», Presse Sowjet., a. a. O., 1960, Nr. 15, S. 327–330.

[105] «Dostiženija sovetskoj vlasti za sorok let v cifrach. Statističeskij sbornik» (Die Errungenschaften der Sowjetmacht während der 40 Jahre. Statistische Sammlung), hrsg. v. Central'no statističeskoe upravlenie pri Sovete Ministrov SSSR (Zentrale Statistische Verwaltung beim Ministerrat der UdSSR), Moskau, Gosudarstvennoe Statističeskoe Izdatel'stvo (Statistischer Staatsverlag), 1957, S. 328, 349. – «Narodnoe chozjajstvo SSSR v 1958 godu. Statističeskij ežegodnik» (Die Volkswirtschaft der UdSSR im Jahre 1958. Statistisches Jahrbuch), Moskau, Gosstatizdat (Statistischer Staatsverlag), 1959, S. 108.

[106] CHRUSTSCHOW, «Die Kontrollziffern für die Entwicklung der Volkswirtschaft der UdSSR in den Jahren 1959–1965», a. a. O., S. 63. – Bei der Wohnraumverteilung wurden durchaus auch solche Aspekte berücksichtigt, die die Stellung im beruflichen und gesellschaftlichen Leben bestimmen. – BECKER, «Die kommunistische Verteilung als Ideal und Wirklichkeit», a. a. O., S. 15.

[107] CHRUSTSCHOW, «Die Kontrollziffern für die Entwicklung der Volkswirtschaft der UdSSR in den Jahren 1959–1965», a. a. O., S. 64.

[108] Vgl. das Buch des Verfassers «Studien zum Wirtschaftswachstum Südosteuropas», a. a. O., S. 190 ff.

[109] LIESS, «Planwirtschaft und Sozialismus in Rumänien», a. a. O., S. 167.

[110] Ebd., S. 168.

[111] JÁVORKA und BERÉNYI, «Jövedelmek a munkabéren felül», a. a. O., S. 32 f. – FÖLDES, K., «Érték – nemzeti jövedelem – szolgáltatás» (Werte – Nationaleinkommen – Dienstleistungen), Közgazd. Szle, Jg. 11, a. a. O., Nr. 1, S. 36–41.

[112] JÁVORKA und BERÉNYI, «Jövedelmek a munkabéren felül», a. a. O., S. 69 ff.

[113] SCHWANKE, «Die Verwirklichung der Sowjetwirtschaft in Albanien», a. a. O., S. 286.

[114] HAAS und LEUTWEIN, «Die rechtliche und soziale Lage der Arbeitnehmer in der sowjetischen Besatzungszone», a. a. O., S. 257 f.

[115] MAMPEL und HAUCK, «Sozialpolitik in Mitteldeutschland», a. a. O., S. 60 ff.

[116] HAAS und LEUTWEIN, «Die rechtliche und soziale Lage der Arbeitnehmer in der sowjetischen Besatzungszone», a. a. O., S. 257.

[117] THALHEIM, K. C., «Die Rezeption des Sowjetmodells in Mitteldeutschland», JAHN (Hrsg.), Die Wirtschaftssysteme der Staaten Osteuropas und der Volksrepublik China usw., a. a. O., Bd. 23/II, S. 335.

[118] KORKISCH, F., «Staatsaufbau und Gesetzgebung der Volksrepublik Polen», MARKERT (Hrsg.), Osteuropa Handbuch. Polen, a. a. O., S. 355.

[119] DOUGLAS, D. W., «Transitional Economic Systems. The Polish-Czech Example», London, Routledge and Kegan Paul, 1953, S. 243.

[120] ZAGORIA, D. S., «Der chinesisch-sowjetische Konflikt» (aus dem Engl.), München, Rütten und Loening, 1964, S. 95 ff.

[121] «Das Musterstatut», Ost-Prob., Jg. 10, a. a. O., Nr. 21, S. 702, Art. 17–20.

[122] Verwirklichung der Zielsetzung: hohes wirtschaftliches Wachstum unter der Nebenbedingung einer möglichst gleichmäßigen Einkommensverteilung.

[123] Eine Gleichmacherei bei der Prämienzuweisung wird ausdrücklich abgelehnt.

Notes to Chapter XIV

1 Die vorliegende Analyse bezieht sich auf vielschichtige Strömungen zwischen gegensätzlich erscheinenden Theorien.

2 BRECHT, «Die Wirtschaft, das Geld und das Denken usw.», a. a. O., S. 17 ff. – WILLEKE, H., «Die Wirtschaftspolitik als Gegenstand wissenschaftlicher Betrachtung. Eine grundsätzliche Stellungnahme zur Bestimmbarkeit wirtschaftspolitischer Ziele», Stuttgart, Kohlhammer, 1958 (Veröffentlichungen der Wirtschaftshochschule Mannheim, Reihe 2, Nr. 2), passim. – WEIGAND, G., «Die Berechtigung sittlicher Werturteile in den Sozialwissenschaften», Berlin, Duncker und Humblot, 1960, S. 33–59.

3 Vgl. v. MERKATZ, H.-J., «In der Mitte des Jahrhunderts. Politische Lebensfragen unserer Zeit», München-Wien, Langen und Müller, 1963, S. 7 ff., 92 ff., 110 ff.

4 PANIKKAR, «In Defence of Liberalism», a. a. O., S. 120 ff.

5 BASSO-BERT, V., «Social Liberalism», New York-Washington-Hollywood, Vantage Press, 1960, S. 28 ff., 71 ff.

6 ROBINSON, «Doktrinen der Wirtschaftswissenschaft», a. a. O., S. 45–53.

7 WALTER, E., «Kapitalismus im Übergang. Die freie Wirtschaft auf dem Weg zum Volkskapitalismus», München, Rütten und Loening, 1963, S. 115–125.

8 Vgl. v. HAYEK, F. A., «Der Weg zur Knechtschaft» (aus dem Engl.), Erlenbach-Zürich, Rentsch, 1943, S. 32 ff., 84 f., 98 ff., 102 ff., 135 ff., 162 f., 253 f.

9 DIEHL, «Der Einzelne und die Gemeinschaft usw.», a. a. O., 1. Teil, 4. bis 7. Abschn. – BARTH, H., «Die Idee der Ordnung. Beiträge zu einer politischen Philosophie», Erlenbach-Zürich-Stuttgart, Rentsch, 1958, S. 229 ff. – FREYER, «Weltgeschichte Europas», Bd. 2, a. a. O., S. 886 f.

10 HANDLIN, O. und HANDLIN, M., «The Dimensions of Liberty», Cambridge/Mass., Harvard University Press, 1961, S. 89–112.

11 SELEKMAN, B. M., «A Moral Philosophy for Management», New York-London, McGraw-Hill, 1959, S. 3 ff., 11, 45 f., 166 ff., 188, 215, passim.

12 FREYER, «Weltgeschichte Europas», Bd. 2, a. a. O., S. 947, passim.

13 HEIMANN, «Soziale Theorie der Wirtschaftssysteme», a. a. O., S. 21–24.

14 Vgl. v. NELL-BREUNING, O., «Wirtschaftsethik. Zum gleichnamigen Buch von Walter Weddigen», in: Scholastik. Vierteljahresschrift für Theologie und Philosophie, Jg. 28, Freiburg, 1953, S. 65.

15 DATTA, A., «Socialism, Democracy, and Industrialization. A Collection of Essays», London, Allen and Unwin, 1962, S. 24–31. – BOETTCHER, «Die sowjetische Wirtschaftspolitik am Scheidewege», a. a. O., S. 280 ff.

16 MÜLLER, W., «Die marxistisch-leninistische Freiheitsauffassung und die soziale Funktion der reaktionären bürgerlichen Freiheitskonzeption (dargestellt am Beispiel Theodor Litts)», Wiss. Z. Univ. Leipzig, Gesellschafts- und Sprachwissenschaftliche Reihe, Jg. 8, Leipzig, 1958/59, Nr. 3, S. 427 ff. – Ost-Prob., Jg. 13, Bonn, 1961, Nr. 21 und ebd., Jg. 15, a. a. O., Nr. 24 (in beiden Heften die Rubrik «Ideologie»).

17 SARTRE, J.-P., «Critique de la raison dialectique», Bd. 1, Paris, Gallimard, 1960, S. 63 ff., passim.

18 HEILBRONER, «Wirtschaft und Wissen usw.», a. a. O., S. 316–361. – RITTIG, G., «Sozialismus und Liberalismus. Eine Studie über das grundsätzliche Verhältnis ihrer wirtschaftspolitischen Konzeption», SCHMID, C., SCHILLER, K., POTTHOFF, E. (Hrsg.), Grundfragen moderner Wirtschaftspolitik, Frankfurt, Europäische Verlagsanstalt, o. J. (Schriftenreihe der Gesellschaft zur Förderung der Politischen Wissenschaft, Bd. 1), S. 107–125. – RÖPKE, W., «Marktwirtschaft ist nicht genug», RÖPKE, W., ILAU, H., BÖHM, F., u. a. (Hrsg.), «Hat der Westen eine Idee?», Ludwigsburg, Hoch, 1957, S. 9–20. – SCHELSKY, H., «Zukunftsaspekte

der industriellen Gesellschaft», Hamburger Jb. Wirt. Gesellpol., Jg. 1, Tübingen, Mohr (Siebeck), 1956, S. 34–41.

[19] WALTER, «Kapitalismus im Übergang usw.», a. a. O., S. 19 f., 33, 59, 96 f., 115, 147 f., 169 ff. – HEIMANN, «Soziale Theorie der Wirtschaftssysteme», a. a. O., S. 125–138, S. 201 bis 211. – SCHUMPETER, J. A., «Kapitalismus, Sozialismus und Demokratie» (aus dem Engl.), Bern, Francke, 1946, S. 174 f., 213–230, 261 ff. – SPIEGEL, H. W., «Current Economic Problems», 3. Aufl., Homewood/Ill., Irwin, 1961, S. 390–417.

[20] RIESMAN, «Die einsame Masse», a. a. O., S. 201 f., 210 f., passim. – SCHUMPETER, «Kapitalismus, Sozialismus und Demokratie», a. a. O., S. 297–433.

[21] ORTLIEB, H.-D., «Klassenkampf oder Sozialpartnerschaft», Hamburger Jb. Wirt. Gesellpol., Jg. 1, a. a. O., S. 56–71.

[22] SPINDLER, G. P., «Neue Antworten im sozialen Raum. Leitbilder für Unternehmer», Düsseldorf-Wien, Econ-Verlag, 1964, S. 135–156. – NIEHAUS, H., «Zeitbilder der Wirtschafts- und Agrarpolitik in einer modernen Gesellschaft», Stuttgart, Seewald, 1957, Abschn. 1, 2. – KLOTH, H., «Das Sozialbewußtsein in der westdeutschen Gesellschaft», SCHMID, SCHILLER, POTTHOFF (Hrsg.), Grundfragen moderner Wirtschaftspolitik, a. a. O., S. 9, 14 ff.

[23] TAUT, «Arbeit und Bedürfnisse im Kapitalismus», a. a. O., S. 944–969. – (o. Verf.), «Gedanken zur Auseinandersetzung mit der bürgerlichen Philosophie», Dtsche Z. Philos., Jg. 9, a. a. O., Nr. 9, S. 1119 ff. – HEISE, W., «Besprechung von: Freyer, ‹Theorie des gegenwärtigen Zeitalters›», ebd., Jg. 6, a. a. O., Nr. 1, S. 159–164. – HEYDEN, G., «Zur Situation der bürgerlichen Philosophie Westdeutschlands», ebd., Jg. 10, a. a. O., Nr. 7, S. 830–845.

[24] KRAUSE, W., «Economic Development. The Underdeveloped World and the American Interest», San Francisco, Wadsworth Publishing Company, 1961, S. 278 ff. – BEHRENDT, R. F. (Hrsg.), «Die wirtschaftlich und gesellschaftlich unterentwickelten Länder und wir», Bern, Haupt, 1961, S. 19–56. – HUNOLD, A. (Hrsg.), «Entwicklungsländer, Wahn und Wirklichkeit», Erlenbach-Zürich-Stuttgart, Rentsch, 1961, S. 83–110.

[25] ACHINGER, H., «Sozialpolitik als Gesellschaftspolitik. Von der Arbeiterfrage zum Wohlstandsstaat», Hamburg, Rowohlt, 1958, S. 147–159.

[26] Hier sind in philosophisch-anthropologischer Hinsicht auch die vielen bedeutenden Stimmen aufzuführen, welche die Frage nach Recht und Sinn der westlichen Freiheit stellen. – VEIT, O., «Soziologie der Freiheit», Frankfurt, Klostermann, 1957, S. 233–237, 259 ff. – Ferner v. MARTIN, A., «Zur Soziologie der Freiheit», Kölner Z. Soz. Sozpsychol., Jg. 10, Köln, 1958, S. 674–682. – FREYER, H., «Theorie des gegenwärtigen Zeitalters», 2. Aufl., Stuttgart, Deutsche Verlagsanstalt, 1958, S. 234–247. – HOMMES, J., «Krise der Freiheit. Hegel-Marx-Heidegger», Regensburg, Pustet, 1958, S. 313 ff., passim. – MICHEL, «Der Prozeß ‹Gesellschaft contra Person› usw.», a. a. O., S. 135–175. – SCHUMPETER, «Kapitalismus, Sozialismus und Demokratie», a. a. O., S. 198–212, 479 f. – GRANT, G. P., «Philosophy in the Mass Age. An Essay on the Fabric of Western Culture and the Need for a New Moral Philosophy», New York, Hill and Wang, 1960, S. 111 ff.

[27] WEBER, A., «Sowjetwirtschaft heute. Schwächen und Stärken», Berlin, Duncker und Humblot, 1962, S. 59–62, 116 f.

[28] Von liberaler Seite werden die günstigen Entwicklungen der Wohlstandsgesellschaft weitgehend mit Recht als Erfolg liberalen Wirtschaftens ausgegeben. – KARRENBERG, F., «Gestalt und Kritik des Westens. Beiträge zur christlichen Sozialethik heute», Stuttgart, Kreuz Verlag, 1959, S. 201–224. – WEDDIGEN, W., «Primat der Wirtschaft?», Schmollers Jb., Jg. 49, Berlin, 1961, Nr. 3, S. 269–283.

[29] GRANT, «Philosophy in the Mass Age usw.», a. a. O., S. 26–39. – LITT, T., «Berufsbildung, Fachbildung, Menschenbildung», 2. Aufl., Bonn, Bundeszentrale für Heimatdienst, 1960, S. 76–88.

[30] Pluralismus wird hier als Vielfalt sozialphilosophischer Denkrichtungen verstanden.

[31] MULLER, «Issues of Freedom», a. a. O., S. 134–143.

[32] Vgl. DE TOCQUEVILLE, A., «Die Demokratie in Amerika» (aus dem Franz.), Frankfurt/M.-Hamburg, Fischer, 1956, S. 149 f., 180 ff., 206 ff. – GARDNER, J. W., «Excellence.

Can We Be Equal and Excellent too?», New York, Harper and Brothers, 1961, S. 11–20, 135, 156.

³³ MYRDAL, «Das politische Element in der nationalökonomischen Doktrinbildung», a. a. O., S. 112 ff., passim. – BOETTCHER, «Die sowjetische Wirtschaftspolitik am Scheidewege», a. a. O., S. 281.

³⁴ Es wird nicht geleugnet, daß manche Gedankenzüge der Wirtschaftslehre anderen Ursprungs sind; im Hinblick auf den heute alles beherrschenden Ost-West-Konflikt liefern sie aber nur vergleichsweise am Rande liegende Abwandlungen der grundlegenden Thematik.

³⁵ MYRDAL spricht aus diesem Grunde davon, daß der Liberalismus selbst sich in einen «konservativen» und einen «sozialrevolutionären Liberalismus» gespalten habe.

³⁶ KEYNES, J. M., «Politik und Wirtschaft. Männer und Probleme. Ausgewählte Abhandlungen» (aus dem Engl.), Tübingen-Zürich, Mohr (Siebeck)-Polygraphischer Verlag, 1956, S. 238 ff., 252–254, 258. – DAHRENDORF, «Gesellschaft und Freiheit», a. a. O., S. 237 ff., 356 ff., 414 f. – MICHEL, «Der Prozeß ‹Gesellschaft contra Person› usw.», a. a. O., S. 129. – Vgl. auch v. NELL-BREUNING, O., «Gemeinsames und Trennendes in den Hauptrichtungen der Wirtschaftswissenschaft» sowie «Sinnbestimmung der Wirtschaft aus letzten Gründen», Grundsatzfragen der Wirtschaftsordnung. Ein Vortragszyklus veranstaltet von der Wirtschafts- und Sozialwissenschaftlichen Fakultät der Freien Universität Berlin, a. a. O., S. 220, 228 f., 250 f. – ÅKERMAN, J., «Das Problem der sozialökonomischen Synthese», Lund, Gleerup, 1938, S. 74–90, 92–111.

³⁷ Im Osten wird jeder Versuch, dortige Probleme als industriegesellschaftliche Erscheinungen zu interpretieren, zurückgewiesen. – Vgl. (o. Verf.), «Gedanken zur Auseinandersetzung mit der bürgerlichen Philosophie», a. a. O., S. 1119 ff. – SÖDER, G., «Verrat an der Freiheit. Zur Kritik der Freiheitskonzeption des ‹demokratischen Sozialismus›», Berlin, Dietz, 1961, S. 69 ff.

³⁸ KEYNES, «Politik und Wirtschaft usw.», a. a. O., S. 267 f., 272.

³⁹ SCHMÖLDERS, G., «Konjunkturen und Krisen», Hamburg, Rowohlt, 1955 (Rowohlts deutsche Enzyklopädie, Bd. 3), S. 54 f.

⁴⁰ STERNBERG, F., «Marx und die Gegenwart», Köln, Verlag für Politik und Wirtschaft, 1955, S. 105 ff. – Vgl. auch v. NELL-BREUNING, O., MÜLLER, J. H., «Vom Geld und vom Kapital», Freiburg, Herder, 1962, S. 147–153.

⁴¹ KEYNES, «Politik und Wirtschaft usw.», a. a. O., S. 243 ff., 270.

⁴² VEIT, «Soziologie der Freiheit», a. a. O., S. 76 ff., 207 ff.

⁴³ KEYNES, «Politik und Wirtschaft usw.», a. a. O., S. 267, 272.

⁴⁴ STRACHEY, J., «Kapitalismus heute und morgen» (aus dem Engl.), Düsseldorf, Econ, 1957, Abschn. 12, 13. – SCHILLER, K., «Der Ökonom und die Gesellschaft», Hamburger Jb. Wirt. Gesellpol., Jg. 1, a. a. O., S. 11–18.

⁴⁵ KEYNES, «Politik und Wirtschaft usw.», a. a. O., S. 244 f.

⁴⁶ Zur Kritik des Marginalismus: MYRDAL, «Das politische Element in der nationalökonomischen Doktrinbildung», a. a. O., S. 20.

⁴⁷ MYINT, H., «Theories of Welfare Economics», New York, Kelley, 1962, passim. – JONAS, «Das Selbstverständnis der ökonomischen Theorie», a. a. O., S. 185–191.

⁴⁸ JANTKE, C., «Hochschule und Sozialwissenschaft», Hamburger Jb. Wirt. Gesellpol., Jg. 1, a. a. O., S. 22 ff.

⁴⁹ MYRDAL, «Das politische Element in der nationalökonomischen Doktrinbildung», a. a. O., S. 161.

⁵⁰ SOMBART, «Sozialismus und soziale Bewegung», a. a. O., S. 302–308.

⁵¹ GAMBS, J. S., WERTIMER jr., S., «Economics and Man», Homewood/Ill., Irwin, 1959, S. 170–193. – BAGLEY jr., W. C., «The Task of Institutionalism», SOLO, R. A. (Hrsg.), Economics and the Public Interest, New Brunswick/N. J., Rutgers University Press, 1955, S. 15 ff. – HEILBRONER, «Wirtschaft und Wissen usw.», a. a. O., S. 228–269.

⁵² KEYNES, «Politik und Wirtschaft usw.», a. a. O., S. 253. – DAHRENDORF, «Gesellschaft

und Freiheit», a. a. O., S. 414 f. – STRACHEY, «Kapitalismus heute und morgen», a. a. O., S. 211–250.

⁵³ DAHRENDORF, «Gesellschaft und Freiheit», a. a. O., S. 13–26, 336 ff., 356 ff. – Ferner v. KNOERINGEN, W., «Utopie und Wirklichkeit. Die Krise des Kommunismus», in: Die neue Gesellschaft, Bd. 8, Bielefeld, 1961, Nr. 3, S. 170. – Weiterhin v. NELL-BREUNING, «Sinnbestimmung der Wirtschaft aus letzten Gründen», a. a. O., S. 246. – HEIMANN, «Soziale Theorie der Wirtschaftssysteme», a. a. O., S. 323 ff.

⁵⁴ KAHL, J., «Macht und Markt. Vom Ausbau unserer Wirtschaftsordnung», Berlin, Duncker und Humblot, 1956, S. 11–20, passim.

⁵⁵ HUGHES, H. S., «Consciousness and Society. The Reorientation of European Social Thought, 1890–1920», New York, Knopf, 1961, S. 401 ff.

⁵⁶ Allerdings dürfen die Zusammenhänge mit den entsprechenden politisch-philosophischen Auffassungen nicht unbeachtet bleiben.

⁵⁷ Vgl. v. MISES, «Die Wurzeln des Antikapitalismus», a. a. O., S. 43–52, 95, 125. – Ferner v. HAYEK, «Der Weg zur Knechtschaft», a. a. O., S. 62–66. – NAWROTH, E., «Die wirtschaftspolitischen Ordnungsvorstellungen des Neoliberalismus», Köln-Berlin-Bonn-München, Heymann, 1962, S. 12–14.

⁵⁸ So wird z. B. gegenüber der Behauptung größerer «Gerechtigkeit» der Verteilung durch Krisenfestigkeit geltend gemacht, daß der dafür zu zahlende Preis – Einbußen an Freiheit – zu hoch sei.

⁵⁹ Vgl. v. MARTIN, «Ordnung und Freiheit usw.», a. a. O., S. 15 f., 19 f. – WELTY, E., «Die Sozialencyklika Papst Johannes XXIII., Mater et Magistra. Über die Ordnung des gesellschaftlichen Lebens der Gegenwart im Sinn der christlichen Lehre», Freiburg, Herder, 1961, S. 34.

⁶⁰ HEIMANN, «Soziale Theorie der Wirtschaftssysteme», a. a. O., S. 201–211.

⁶¹ EUCKEN, W., «Grundsätze der Wirtschaftspolitik», Hamburg, Rowohlt, 1959 (Rowohlts deutsche Enzyklopädie, Bd. 81), S. 160, passim.

⁶² BÖHM, F., «Freiheitsordnung und soziale Frage» sowie «Der Rechtsstaat und der soziale Wohlfahrtsstaat», Grundsatzfragen der Wirtschaftsordnung. Ein Vortragszyklus, veranstaltet von der Wirtschafts- und Sozialwissenschaftlichen Fakultät der Freien Universität Berlin, a. a. O., S. 71–174, insbesondere S. 130 ff. – RÜSTOW, A., «Zwischen Kapitalismus und Kommunismus», Bad Godesberg, Küpper vorm. Bondi, 1949, S. 31–41. – EUCKEN, «Grundsätze der Wirtschaftspolitik», a. a. O., S. 188 ff. – Ferner v. HAYEK, «Der Weg zur Knechtschaft», a. a. O., S. 102 ff. – NAWROTH, «Die wirtschaftspolitischen Ordnungsvorstellungen des Neoliberalismus», a. a. O., S. 18, 21.

⁶³ FRICKHÖFFER, W., «Konsequente Wirtschaftspolitik», in: Was muß die freie Welt tun?, Vorträge auf der dreizehnten Tagung der Aktionsgemeinschaft Soziale Marktwirtschaft am 10. Juni 1959 in Bad Godesberg, Ludwigsburg, Hoch, 1959, S. 62.

⁶⁴ Dagegen wendet sich HEIMANN, «Soziale Theorie der Wirtschaftssysteme», a. a. O., S. 140 ff., 149 ff., 171 ff., 327–331.

⁶⁵ MEINHOLD, H., «Widersprüche in unserer Wirtschaftsverfassung», Grundsatzfragen der Wirtschaftsordnung. Ein Vortragszyklus veranstaltet von der Wirtschafts- und Sozialwissenschaftlichen Fakultät der Freien Universität Berlin, a. a. O., S. 191, passim.

⁶⁶ WEISSER, «Die Überwindung des Ökonomismus in der Wirtschaftswissenschaft», ebd., S. 9–40.

⁶⁷ RÜSTOW, «Zwischen Kapitalismus und Kommunismus», a. a. O., S. 5 f., 56 f. – MICHEL, «Der Prozeß ‹Gesellschaft contra Person› usw.», a. a. O., S. 103–134.

⁶⁸ HEILBRONER, «Wirtschaft und Wissen usw.», a. a. O., S. 319 ff.

⁶⁹ MUELLER, F. H., «Was wollte Adam Smith?», HÖFNER, I., VERDROSS, A., VITO, F. (Hrsg.), Naturordnung in Gesellschaft, Staat und Wirtschaft, Innsbruck-Wien-München, Tyrolia-Verlag, 1961, S. 571–588.

⁷⁰ SCHUMPETER, «Kapitalismus, Sozialismus und Demokratie», a. a. O., S. 451 ff. – NAW-

ROTH, «Die wirtschaftspolitischen Ordnungsvorstellungen des Neoliberalismus», a. a. O., S. 19 f. – Ferner v. MARTIN, «Ordnung und Freiheit usw.», a. a. O., S. 26 f.

71 DÖRGE, F.-W., «Bericht über einführende Literatur zur neuliberalen Wirtschaftspolitik», Hamburger Jb. Wirt. Gesellpol., Jg. 1, a. a. O., S. 199–209.

72 NAWROTH, «Die wirtschaftspolitischen Ordnungsvorstellungen des Neoliberalismus», a. a. O., S. 29–32.

73 PREISER, E., «Die Zukunft unserer Wirtschaftsordnung», 3. Aufl., Göttingen, Vandenhoeck und Ruprecht, 1960 (Kleine Vandenhoeck-Reihe Nr. 19/19a), S. 26 ff., 62 ff.

74 «Sozialismus 1964. Die wirtschaftspolitischen Ideen der europäischen Sozialdemokraten», in: Frankfurter Allgemeine Zeitung, Wirtschaftsblatt, Nr. 39 vom 15. 2. 1964.

75 NEMITZ, K., «Sozialistische Marktwirtschaft. Die wirtschaftspolitischen Konzeptionen der deutschen Sozialdemokratie», Frankfurt, Europäische Verlagsanstalt, 1960, S. 64 ff.

76 Als unausweichliche Zukunft charakterisieren den Sozialismus SCHUMPETER, «Kapitalismus, Sozialismus und Demokratie», a. a. O., passim. – HEIMANN, «Soziale Theorie der Wirtschaftssysteme», a. a. O., S. 199–201. – DEIST, H., «Wirtschaftsdemokratie», SCHMID, SCHILLER, POTTHOFF (Hrsg.), Grundfragen moderner Wirtschaftspolitik, a. a. O., S. 216–226. – SPINDLER, «Neue Antworten im sozialen Raum usw.», a. a. O., S. 255–280.

77 PRELLER, «Sozialpolitik usw.», a. a. O., S. 229 ff.

78 PONSIOEN, J. A. (Hrsg.), «Social Welfare Policy. First Collection: Contribution to Theory», 's Gravenhage, Mouton, 1962 (Publications of the Institute of Social Studies, Series Mayor, Bd. 3), S. 72–82.

79 FISCHER, L., «Russia, America, and the World», New York, Harper and Brothers, 1960/61, S. 201–215.

80 Daß hier zwischen «rechter» SPD und den Gewerkschaften in der Bundesrepublik Deutschland Auffassungsdifferenzen bestehen, zeigen folgende zwei Artikel: BRIEFS, G., «Irrtümer der Gewerkschaft. Bemerkungen zum neuen Grundsatzprogramm des DGB», in: Frankfurter Allgemeine Zeitung, Nr. 198 vom 28. 8. 1963. – «Sozialismus 1964. Die wirtschaftspolitischen Ideen der europäischen Sozialdemokraten», a. a. O.

81 TAUTSCHER, A., «Die öffentliche Wirtschaft im Spannungsfeld von Sicherheit und Freiheit», Inaugurationsrede, Graz, Kienreich, 1957, passim.

82 ROSSADE, W., «‹Kultur›-Ideologie der rechten SPD-Führung und ‹human relations›», Dtsche Z. Philos., Jg. 9, a. a. O., Nr. 12, S. 1461–1477. – MILLER, R., «Kritische Bemerkungen zum ‹demokratischen Sozialismus›», ebd., Jg. 6, a. a. O., Nr. 5, S. 733–745.

83 Vgl. v. NELL-BREUNING, O., «Einführung in die Literatur der katholischen Sozialiehre», Hamburger Jb. Wirt. Gesellpol., Jg. 1, a. a. O., S. 127–135.

84 PFISTER, B., «Ist die Gesellschaftspolitik auf die Wirtschaftstheorie angewiesen?», HÖFFNER, VERDROSS, VITO (Hrsg.), Naturordnung in Gesellschaft, Staat und Wirtschaft, a. a. O., S. 589 ff. – WELTY, «Die Socialencyklika usw.», a. a. O., S. 26 f., 32 f.

85 TAUTSCHER, A., «Wirtschaftsethik», München, Hueber, 1957 (Handbücher der Moraltheologie, Bd. 11), S. 23 ff., 81, passim.

86 WELTY, «Die Sozialencyklika usw.», a. a. O., S. 26 f., 30.

87 JÖHR, W. A., «Solidaritätsprinzip und Marktwirtschaft», HÖFFNER, VERDROSS, VITO (Hrsg.), Naturordnung in Gesellschaft, Staat und Wirtschaft, a. a. O., S. 616 ff. – UTZ, A. F., «Die philosophischen Grundlagen der Wirtschafts- und Sozialpolitik», Freiburg/Schweiz, Internationales Institut für Sozialwissenschaft und Politik, 1961, S. 31 f.

88 WELTY, «Die Sozialencyklika usw.», a. a. O., S. 33 f., 44 f., 61.

89 JOSTOCK, P., «Eigentum als Ordnungs- und Unordnungsmacht», HÖFFNER, VERDROSS, VITO (Hrsg.), Naturordnung in Gesellschaft, Staat und Wirtschaft, a. a. O., S. 326–336.

90 Vgl. v. NELL-BREUNING, «Gemeinsames und Trennendes in den Hauptrichtungen der Wirtschaftswissenschaft», a. a. O., S. 215–231. – KLÜBER, F., «Individuum und Gemeinschaft in katholischer Sicht», Hannover, 1963 (Schriften der Niedersächsischen Landeszentrale für politische Bildung. Individuum und Gemeinschaft, Nr. 2), passim.

[91] Vgl. v. NELL-BREUNING, O., «Wirtschaft und Gesellschaft heute», Bd. 3: Zeitfragen. 1955–1959, Freiburg, Herder, 1960, S. 75 f., 192 ff., 235, 247.

[92] WESTPHALEN, F. A., «Die Renaissance der konservativen Idee», HÖFFNER, VERDROSS, VITO (Hrsg.), Naturordnung in Gesellschaft, Staat und Wirtschaft, a. a. O., S. 82 ff. – CRONIN, J. F., «Social Principles and Economic Life», Milwaukee, The Bruce Publishing Company, 1959, S. 120 ff. – WIRZ, L., «Wirtschaftsphilosophie. Rekonstruktion der Wirtschaftstheorie», Heidelberg-Löwen, Kerle-Nauwelaerts, 1965, S. 190 ff.

[93] HEIMANN, «Soziale Theorie der Wirtschaftssysteme», a. a. O., S. 83.

[94] Vgl. den Aufsatz des Verfassers «Individual and Collective Wants», J. Pol. Econ., Jg. 56, Chicago, 1948, Nr. 1, S. 8.

[95] HALLER, H., «Finanzpolitik», 3. Aufl., Tübingen-Zürich, Mohr (Siebeck)-Polygraphischer Verlag, 1965, S. 135 f.

[96] HENSEL, K. P., «Wirtschaftliche Ordnungsformen und das Problem des Eigentums, der Leitung und Kontrolle», in: Moderne Welt, Jg. 1, Köln-Marienburg, 1959/60, Nr. 3/4, S. 339 f.

[97] ARROW, K. J., «Social Choice and Individual Values», 2. Aufl., New York-London-Sidney, Wiley and Sons, 1963, S. 61 ff., 71 ff.

[98] Vgl. supra, Abschnitt VIII.

[99] Hier kommen vorwiegend die Begründungen für eine moderne Sozialpolitik in Betracht, die eine gemeinsame Verantwortung betonen. – ACHINGER, «Sozialpolitik als Gesellschaftspolitik usw.», a. a. O., S. 106 ff.

[100] WHYTE, «Herr und Opfer der Organisation», a. a. O., S. 13 f., passim.

[101] KATONA, G., «Die Macht des Verbrauchers» (aus dem Engl.), Düsseldorf-Wien, Econ, 1962, S. 43 ff., 219.

[102] DUESENBERRY, J. S., «Income, Saving, and the Theory of Consumer Behavior», Cambridge/Mass., Harvard University Press, 1949, S. 27.

[103] Vgl. das Buch des Verfassers «Comparative Economic Systems», New York-Toronto-London, McGraw-Hill, 1952, S. 293.

[104] RÖPKE, W., «Maß und Mitte», Erlenbach-Zürich, Rentsch, 1950, S. 203.

[105] Eine konjunkturpolitische Flexibilität der Steuersätze wird z. B. in den USA betont. – KÖHLER-RIECKENBERG, I., «Wachstumsprobleme der USA», SCHILCHER, R. (Hrsg.), Wirtschaftswachstum. Beiträge zur ökonomischen Theorie und Politik, Berlin, de Gruyter, 1964, S. 180 ff.

[106] Vgl. das Buch des Verfassers «Philosophie in der Volkswirtschaftslehre usw.», Bd. 1, a. a. O., S. 361 f.

[107] Vgl. v. HAYEK, F. A., «Wahrer und falscher Individualismus», Ordo, Bd. 1, Opladen, 1948, S. 22 f.

[108] Ebd., S. 28.

[109] SCHILLER, K., «Sozialismus und Wettbewerb», SCHMID, SCHILLER, POTTHOFF (Hrsg.), Grundfragen moderner Wirtschaftspolitik, a. a. O., S. 245 ff.

[110] Vgl. supra, Abschnitt XII und infra, Abschnitt XVI.

[111] WALTER, «Kapitalismus im Übergang usw.», a. a. O., S. 19.

[112] ALBERT, «Ökonomische Ideologie und politische Theorie usw.», a. a. O., S. 101 ff.

[113] REDLICH, F., «Der Unternehmer. Wirtschafts- und Sozialgeschichtliche Studien», Göttingen, Vandenhoeck und Ruprecht, 1964, Teil II, S. 95 ff.

[114] PREISER, E., «Die ökonomische Problematik der Eigentumsverteilung», KARRENBERG und ALBERT (Hrsg.), Sozialwissenschaft und Gesellschaftsgestaltung. Festschrift für Gerhard Weisser, a. a. O., S. 308 f.

[115] Vgl. v. BECKERATH, H., «Großindustrie und Gesellschaftsordnung. Industrielle und politische Dynamik», Tübingen-Zürich, Mohr (Siebeck)-Polygraphischer Verlag, 1954, S. 209 ff.

[116] Dazu trägt insbesondere die mit wachsenden technisch bedingten optimalen Ausstoßgrößen zunehmende Abhängigkeit der Produzenten von Absatzmöglichkeiten bei. –

FOOTNOTES PP. 223–28

TRITSCH, W., «Die Wirtschaftsdynamik unserer Zeit», 1. Aufl., Stuttgart, Schwab, 1959, S. 105.
117 WALTER, «Kapitalismus im Übergang usw.», a. a. O., S. 152.
118 HEIMANN, «Soziale Theorie der Wirtschaftssysteme», a. a. O., S. 127.
119 Vgl. das Buch des Verfassers «Comparative Economic Systems», a. a. O., S. 145.
120 RITSCHL, H., «Die Grundlagen der Wirtschaftsordnung», ders., Gesammelte Aufsätze zur Wirtschaftsordnung, Tübingen, Mohr (Siebeck), 1954 (Veröff. Akad. Gemeinw., Hamburg), S. 41.
121 MOLITOR, B., «Vermögensbildung als wirtschaftspolitisches Problem», Tübingen, Mohr (Siebeck), 1965 (Veröff. Akad. Wirt. Pol., Hamburg), S. 67 f.
122 Ebd., S. 29.
123 Vgl. supra, Abschnitt X.
124 RÖPKE, W., «Jenseits von Angebot und Nachfrage», Erlenbach-Zürich-Stuttgart, Rentsch, 1958, S. 135.

Notes to Chapter XV

1 Eine Definition des Begriffes Bolschewismus gibt J. PLAMENATZ, «German Marxism and Russian Communism», London-New York, Longmans-Green, 1954, S. 317–322.
2 Über PLECHANOV siehe ANDERSON, T., «Masters of Russian Marxism», New York, Appleton-Century-Crofts, 1963, S. 21–41. – Über KAUTSKY siehe MATTHIAS, «Kautsky und der Kautskyanismus usw.», a. a. O., S. 151 ff. – Die Geschichte des LENINschen Denkens beschreibt LANGE, «Marxismus, Leninismus, Stalinismus usw.», a. a. O., S. 87–99.
3 KOCH, W., «Geschichtsgesetz und Strategie bei Lenin», MARKERT, W. (Hrsg.), Der Mensch im kommunistischen System. Tübinger Vorträge über Marxismus und Sowjetstaat, Tübingen, Mohr (Siebeck), 1957, S. 39–52.
4 Ost-Prob., Jg. 14, a. a. O., Nr. 22, S. 677.
5 HERMENS, «Der Ost-West-Konflikt. Gründe und Scheingründe», a. a. O., S. 7.
6 NÜRNBERGER, R., «Lenins Revolutionstheorie. Eine Studie über ‹Staat und Revolution›», Marxismusstudien, 1. Folge, a. a. O., S. 161–172. – Vgl. auch v. PÁSZTORY, T., «Von marxistischer Ideologie zur Planwirtschaft (Darstellung, Analyse und Kritik)», Berlin, Duncker und Humblot, 1964, S. 23–30.
7 LANGE, «Marxismus, Leninismus, Stalinismus usw.», a. a. O., S. 89, 100.
8 Hauptvertreter dieser dann in den westlichen Sozialdemokratien siegenden Einstellung war E. BERNSTEIN. – GNEUSS, C., «Vorbote. Eduard Bernstein», LABEDZ, L. (Hrsg.), Der Revisionismus (aus dem Engl.), Köln-Berlin, Kiepenheuer und Witsch, 1965, S. 37–50.
9 Gegen ein vorläufiges Bündnis wandte sich später TROTZKIJ. – LEHMBRUCH, G., «Kleiner Wegweiser zum Studium der Sowjetideologie», Bonn, Deutscher Bundesverlag, 1958, S. 54.
10 LIEBER, H. J., «Individuum und Gesellschaft in der Sowjetideologie», Hannover, Niedersächsische Landeszentrale für politische Bildung, 1964, S. 44 ff., 74 ff.
11 Daß die sozialdemokratische Arbeiterschaft eine zunehmende Legalität zum «kapitalistischen» Staat entwickelte, erklärte LENIN aus deren Korruption. – PLAMENATZ, «German Marxism and Russian Communism», a. a. O., S. 303. – PERROUX, F., «Feindliche Koexistenz?» (aus dem Franz.), Stuttgart, Schwab, 1961, S. 48 ff.
12 Über die Ausgestaltung der Theorie von der historischen Möglichkeit und Legitimität einer russischen Revolution durch TROTZKIJ und LENIN (1905) siehe PLAMENATZ, «German Marxism and Russian Communism», a. a. O., S. 283 ff. – STERNBERG, F., «Zwei Großmächte im totalitären Block», GAITANIDES (Hrsg.), Die Zukunft des Kommunismus, a. a. O., S. 98 f.
13 MARKERT, W., «Marxismus und russisches Erbe im Sowjetsystem», ders. (Hrsg.), Der Mensch im kommunistischen System, a. a. O., S. 53–71. – FETSCHER, «Von Marx zur Sowjet-

ideologie», a. a. O., S. 56. – TSCHIŽEWSKIJ, D. und GROH, D. (Hrsg.), «Europa und Rußland. Texte zum Problem des westeuropäischen und russischen Selbstverständnisses», Darm-
stadt, Wissenschaftliche Buchgesellschaft, 1960, passim.

14 FREUND, M., «Welche Zukunft hat der Kommunismus?», GAITANIDES (Hrsg.), Die
Zukunft des Kommunismus, a. a. O., S. 119–131. – DIRKS, W., «Spekulationen», ebd., S. 12 f. –
GERSTENMAIER, E., «Feinde für immer?», ebd., S. 114. – HEER, F., «Visionen», ebd., S. 176. –
WILES, «The Political Economy of Communism», a. a. O., S. 253–271. – Die Krise des Kom-
munismus dürfte folglich immer dann eintreten, wenn der Nachholbedarf an Industrialisie-
rung einigermaßen befriedigt ist.

15 LENIN, W. I., «Antwort auf die Fragen des Korrespondenten der englischen Zeitung
‹Daily Express›», ders., Werke, Bd. 30, Berlin, Dietz, 1960, S. 360.

16 LENIN verstand unter «Sowjetmacht» natürlich nicht oder wenigstens nicht endgültig
das, was wir damit verbinden, und was ja auch allzubald daraus wurde, nämlich eine streng
zentralistische Reglementierung. Er dachte an eine föderative Selbstverwaltung der Betriebs-
räte. – GAITANIDES, «Die Vergangenheit des (Welt-)Kommunismus hat schon begonnen»,
ders. (Hrsg.), Die Zukunft des Kommunismus, a. a. O., S. 133.

17 Wenn auch dessen Gemeinschaftsbegriff vom Kopf (der Idee, des Volks- und Weltgei-
stes) auf die Füße (der Arbeitsgruppe) gestellt wurde.

18 Zum Verhältnis von Ideologie und Strategie vgl. HEIMANN, «Soziale Theorie der Wirtschaftssysteme», a. a. O., S. 233–247.

19 MARX' Synthese von Theorie und Praxis wird allzu oft bagatellisiert. Aber könnte es
nicht sein, daß die evolutionäre Sozialisierung im Westen ihm Recht gibt?

20 Unzutreffend wäre es allerdings, LENIN als einen reinen Voluntaristen anzugeben. Er
verstand sich – wie so viele große Handelnde – auch als Vollstrecker eines geschichtlichen
Auftrages. – BAUERMEISTER, «Die russische kommunistische Theorie usw.», a. a. O., S. 20 f., 31 ff.

21 Anderseits ist diese «Revolution von oben» kein absoluter Bruch mit MARX' Lehre.
Schon MARX hatte nämlich betont, daß das Proletariat der Führung der Philosophie bedürfe,
um das zur Revolution provozierende Selbst- und Sozialbewußtsein zu gewinnen.

22 PLAMENATZ, «German Marxism and Russian Communism», a. a. O., S. 285 f.

23 Bemerkenswert ist in diesem Zusammenhang, wie sehr LENIN über MARX hinaus auf
HEGEL zurückgreift. – FETSCHER, «Das Verhältnis des Marxismus zu Hegel», ders. (Hrsg.),
Marxismusstudien, 3. Folge, a. a. O., S. 95 f.

24 Die Frage, die sich heute stellt, lautet, ob diese Gefahr von systemimmanenten Kräf-
ten überwunden werden kann. Der Marxismus steht selber in der Geschichte. Wird sich darum nicht auch sein Überbau mit den besonderen Verhältnissen wandeln müssen? Was wird
die Ideologie eines sowjetischen Industrie-Menschentums sein? Ja, wird nicht gerade jetzt,
da der Aufbau im wesentlichen beendet sein soll, die virulent gebliebene MARXsche Humani-
tätsidee sich gegen ihre falschen Verwirklicher richten und das System korrigieren?

25 Die Errichtung des Zentralverwaltungsstaates und der Zentralverwaltungswirtschaft
war, pragmatisch gesehen, die Antwort auf die Schwierigkeiten der russischen Ausgangslage.
Sie wurde bald nach dem Zusammenbruch des Sowjetsystems der Betriebsverwaltung die
allein herrschende Organisationsform.

Von der Idee eines Kollektivs von lauter gleichen, allseitigen Menschen ist die heutige
Wirklichkeit aber immer noch fern. Neuere «liberalisierende» Züge in der Ostgesellschaft
bleiben doppeldeutig: Sind sie die Folge ökonomischer Zwänge, bedeuten sie ein Nachlassen
des kommunistischen Elans, Annäherung an den Westen oder sind sie – wie das neue Parteiprogramm von 1962 behauptet – ein effektiver Durchbruch in Richtung auf die Verwirklichung des marxistischen Zukunftsbildes?

26 FETSCHER, «Von Marx zur Sowjetideologie», a. a. O., S. 18 f., 71 f.

27 Ebd., S. 72 f., 86, 105 f. – LANGE, «Marxismus, Leninismus, Stalinismus usw.», a. a. O.,
S. 160, 165 ff. – CORNFORTH, «Dialectical Materialism usw.», a. a. O., S. 130–147. – GASTEYGER
(Hrsg.), «Perspektiven der sowjetischen Politik usw.», a. a. O., S. 52 ff. – BRONSKA-PAMPUCH,
«Kommunismus, gibt es das überhaupt?», GAITANIDES (Hrsg.), Die Zukunft des Kommunis-
mus, a. a. O., S. 67 f. – FREUND, «Welche Zukunft hat der Kommunismus?», ebd., S. 120. –

GAITANIDES, «Die Vergangenheit des (Welt-)Kommunismus hat schon begonnen», ebd., S. 133. – HEER, «Visionen», ebd., S. 172.

[28] Die Gründe dürften im mangelnden Kenntnis- und Fähigkeitsstand, gebliebenen Privatinteressen, Nepotismus usw. zu suchen sein.

[29] Er soll die Sowjetunion kurz vor seinem Tode als «bürokratisches Utopia» charakterisiert haben.

[30] MARX, K., «Das Kapital», Bd. 1, Berlin, Dietz, 1951, S. 84.

[31] Es wird damit nicht behauptet, daß es eine westliche Ideologie in dem Sinne gibt, wie der Osten sie besitzt.

[32] ARENDT, «Vita activa usw.», a. a. O., S. 15.

[33] Wie umgekehrt der Individualismus westlicher Provenienz in das «Sozialethos» eines Organisationsmenschentums umschlug. – SCHACK, H., «Die Revision des Marxismus-Leninismus», Berlin, Duncker und Humblot, 1959, S. 32.

[34] Auch im Osten ist ein entsprechender Zug anthropologischen Denkens entstanden. – SCHAFF, A., «Marx oder Sartre? Versuch einer Philosophie des Menschen», Wien, Europa-Verlag, 1964, passim.

[35] Daß ein Humanismus des aus Autonomie sozial verantwortlich handelnden Menschen auch im Osten sich meldet, zeigt die politische Entwicklung. – Ost-Prob., Jg. 14, a. a. O., Nr. 3, S. 74.

[36] SCHACK, «Die Revision des Marxismus-Leninismus», a. a. O., S. 24, 28. – LEHMBRUCH, «Kleiner Wegweiser zum Studium der Sowjetideologie», a. a. O., S. 68 f. – PLAMENATZ, «German Marxism and Russian Communism», a. a. O., S. 285 f. – DEUTSCHER, I., «Russia in Transition and Other Essays», New York, Coward and McCann, 1957, S. 168 ff.

[37] SCHACK, «Die Revision des Marxismus-Leninismus», a. a. O., S. 12 f.
Die ursprüngliche und lang andauernde Verurteilung der bürgerlichen Wissenschaft als Interessenüberbau ist heute suspendiert. Die Wendemarke setzte STALINS Sprachphilosophie-Schrift. – GAITANIDES, «Die Vergangenheit des (Welt-)Kommunismus hat schon begonnen», ders. (Hrsg.), Die Zukunft des Kommunismus, a. a. O., S. 139.

[38] LENIN charakterisiert diesen Ursprung so: «Die Lehre von Marx … ist die rechtmäßige Erbin des Besten, was die Menschheit im 19. Jahrhundert in Gestalt der deutschen Philosophie, der englischen politischen Ökonomie und des französischen Sozialismus geschaffen hat.» – LENIN, «Drei Quellen und drei Bestandteile des Marxismus», a. a. O., S. 3 f.

[39] Dies bedeutet ferner, daß der Mensch niemals primär einzelner, sondern zuvörderst Mitglied einer Klasse ist.

[40] FROMM, «Das Menschenbild bei Marx», a. a. O., S. 34–48. – BOCKMÜHL, K. E., «Leiblichkeit und Gesellschaft. Studien zur Religionskritik und Anthropologie im Frühwerk von Ludwig Feuerbach und Karl Marx», Göttingen, Vandenhoeck und Ruprecht, 1961, S. 234 ff.

[41] In dieser – atheistischen – Philosophie des grenzenlos selbstsüchtigen Menschen sieht neben L. LANDGREBE («Hegel und Marx», Marxismusstudien, 1. Folge, a. a. O., S. 42 ff.) auch J. HOMMES («Der technische Eros. Das Wesen der materialistischen Geschichtsauffassung», Freiburg, Herder, 1955, S. 23–37, 114–133, 314–337) das Zentrum von MARX.

[42] Dieses Theorem übernahm der junge MARX von HEGEL. – WETTER, G. A., «Die Umkehrung Hegels. Grundzüge und Ursprünge der Sowjetphilosophie», Köln, Verlag Wissenschaft und Politik, 1963, S. 13 f., 16 f.

[43] Es ist dies das romantische Erbe von MARX, welches sich zum anderen auch in seinem sozialen Ganzheits-Pathos bemerkbar macht.

[44] Der Mensch ist gesellschaftlich arbeitendes Wesen. Pluralität und Aktivität sind die beiden Ur-Tatsachen, aus denen dann geschichtlich alles konkret Menschhafte wird und sich mit den Verhältnissen wandelt.

[45] MARXens Ausführungen sind weniger eine realistische Schilderung der Verhältnisse im Frühkapitalismus (wenngleich sie dies auch sind, vgl. PERROUX, «Feindliche Koexistenz?», a. a. O., S. 58), sondern vornehmlich das idealtypische Modell eines unbeschränkten Kapitalismus und seiner Eigendynamik (vgl. ebd., S. 75). Es ist nicht abwegig zu sagen, daß MARX ebenso sehr ein «umgestülpter RICARDO» wie er – nach seinen eigenen Worten – ein umgestülpter HEGEL ist.

[46] WETTER, «Die Umkehrung Hegels usw.», a. a. O., S. 19–26.

[47] LANGE, «Marxismus, Leninismus, Stalinismus usw.», a. a. O., S. 17, 40 ff. – MARX, K., «Die Frühschriften», LANDSHUT, S. (Hrsg.), Stuttgart, Kröner, 1955, S. 222 ff., 317 ff.

[48] Hier zeigt sich eine Doppelsinnigkeit der MARXschen Gedanken, in welcher die spätere Überwucherung des humanen Prinzips durch wirtschaftliches Progreßdenken vorgebahnt ist. – FETSCHER, «Von Marx zur Sowjetideologie», a. a. O., S. 17 f.

[49] Dieser Punkt sollte später dazu führen, daß in Sowjetrußland ein staatskapitalistisches Zwischenstadium anberaumt wurde, um diese ökonomische Basis nachzuholen. – BOETTCHER, «Die sowjetische Wirtschaftspolitik am Scheidewege», a. a. O., S. 207 ff., 256 ff.

[50] Bemerkenswert ist, wie sehr die gesamte Wirtschaftslehre und Sozialphilosophie des Marxismus seinem Gegner, dem Liberalismus, verhaftet blieben – gerade weil der Marxismus als dessen dialektische Kehrseite entstand. – Vgl. zu diesen Homologien MICHEL, «Der Prozeß ‹Gesellschaft contra Person› usw.», a. a. O., S. 106. – LEHMBRUCH, «Kleiner Wegweiser zum Studium der Sowjetideologie», a. a. O., S. 47. – SCHACK, «Die Revision des Marxismus-Leninismus», a. a. O., S. 43. – BECHTEL, H., «Wirtschaftsgeschichte Deutschlands im 19. und 20. Jahrhundert», München, Callwey, 1956, S. 132.

[51] WETTER, «Die Umkehrung Hegels usw.», a. a. O., S. 25 ff.

[52] ARENDT, «Vita activa usw.», a. a. O., S. 336, Anm. 18.

[53] Es ist ein Reich, in dem Humanismus gleich Kommunismus gleich Naturalismus geworden ist. Ob aber dieser Traum von der allumfassenden Harmonie der Interessen und Identität der einzelnen wirklich der einer sogar optimal menschenwürdigen Existenz ist, darf füglich bezweifelt werden. – ARENDT, «Vita activa usw.», a. a. O., S. 152 f., 313 f.

[54] MARX, K., «Das Kapital. Kritik der politischen Ökonomie», Bd. 3, Berlin, Dietz, 1949, S. 873 f.

[55] LITT, «Das Bildungsideal der deutschen Klassik usw.», a. a. O., S. 117, 124. – Ost-Prob., Jg. 14, a. a. O., Nr. 3, S. 74.

[56] Es sind Anzeichen dafür vorhanden, daß eine neue, gereiftere Humanität in Ost und West heraufdrängt: Ein Kommunismus ohne Zwang und eine individuelle Freiheit ohne Privatwillkür. – Ost-Prob., Jg. 14, a. a. O., Nr. 3, S. 66–74. – HEER, «Visionen», GAITANIDES (Hrsg.), Die Zukunft des Kommunismus, a. a. O., S. 179. – SCHACK, «Die Revision des Marxismus-Leninismus», a. a. O., S. 45 ff. – Ferner v. RIMSCHA, H., «Geschichte Rußlands», Wiesbaden, Rheinische Verlagsanstalt, o. J. (Sammlung Wissen und Leben, Nr. 8), S. 582–587.

[57] LANGE, «Marxismus, Leninismus, Stalinismus usw.», a. a. O., S. 11. – PERROUX, «Feindliche Koexistenz?», a. a. O., S. 28, 68.

[58] Die gemeinsame Grundlage ist der Aufklärungs-Humanismus.

[59] Vgl. supra, Abschnitt XIV.

[60] HARTMANN, N., «Das Ethos der Persönlichkeit», in: Actas del primer congreso nacional de Filosofia, Mendoza/Argentina, Bd. 1, Buenos Aires, Instituto de Estética, 1949, passim.

[61] Wobei schon dieser Begriff zwischen Gesellschaft als Zweckverband von Privatinteressenten und Gesellschaft im Sinne der TÖNNIESschen ‹Gemeinschaft› schillert.

[62] STALIN, «Ekonomičeskie problemy socializma v SSSR», a. a. O., S. 87 f.

[63] DAHRENDORF, «Homo Sociologicus usw.», a. a. O., S. 28 ff.

[64] PERROUX, «Feindliche Koexistenz?», a. a. O., S. 61 f.

[65] Es ist genau diese Problematik, die das heutige sozialphilosophische Denken der verschiedenen Provenienzen und Schattierungen bestimmt.

[66] Die hier angestellten Überlegungen sind an den Gedanken solcher Autoren orientiert, welche das Ineinandergreifen, die «Einheit von Einheit und Nichteinheit» (HEGEL) dieser beiden Momente der menschlichen Existenz ernstnehmen.

[67] Eine eigenständige Einleitung in die Komplexität und Problematik des Ost-West-Gegensatzes liefert PERROUX. Darin werden vor allem die Verflechtungen von Wirtschaft und Gesamtkultur sowie die Gleich-Ursprünglichkeit beider Systeme betont. – PERROUX, «Feindliche Koexistenz?», a. a. O., S. 13 ff., 22, 25 f.

[68] Diese Gegenüberstellung ist zugespitzt, dürfte aber eben darum die bedenkenswerten, zeitgenössischen Trends gut zum Vorschein bringen.

343

69 «Der selbstsüchtige Zweck in seiner Verwirklichung, so durch die Allgemeinheit bedingt, begründet ein System allseitiger Abhängigkeit ...», HEGEL, «Grundlinien der Philosophie des Rechts», a. a. O., § 183.

70 Hier nach Lösungsmöglichkeiten zu suchen, erscheint als vornehmste Aufgabe einer Sozialphilosophie, die auf der Höhe der heutigen Weltlage stehen soll.

71 HEIMANN, «Soziale Theorie der Wirtschaftssysteme», a. a. O., S. 44, passim.

72 Mit dieser Bemerkung wird nicht die Selbstgefährdung des Westens mit den Inhumanitäten des Ostens auf eine Stufe gestellt. Wohl aber stellt sie die These zur Diskussion, ob nicht der nur mehr funktionierende Konsumbürger eine akute Gefahr für die Menschlichkeit des Menschen darstellt, der es zu begegnen gilt.

73 Die MARXsche Nationalökonomie kann als Umkehrung der klassischen Sozialphilosophie aufgefaßt werden. Bei SMITH betreibt der Privategoismus, weil er immer schon von sittlicher Sympathie formiert ist, das Wohl aller. Bei MARX hingegen verhilft die kommunistische Assoziation, weil ihr das Streben nach individueller Wohlfahrt zugehört, dem einzelnen zur vollen Entfaltung.

74 Konsumaufblähung der fortgeschritteneren Wirtschaft des Westens, Vorrang der Produktionsgüterindustrie in der nachziehenden Ost-Wirtschaft: hier wird der Mensch verdinglicht an eine Warenwelt, dort entmenscht zur Arbeitskraft des Nachholens. Wohin wird die Ost-Welt fortschreiten?

75 Es geht um die optimale Angleichung von Produktivkräften und Produktionsverhältnissen, um die bestmögliche Befriedigung der materiellen und kulturellen Bedürfnisse der größtmöglichen Zahl. – THALHEIM, «Grundzüge des sowjetischen Wirtschaftssystems», a. a. O., S. 17 f.

76 HEIMANN, «Soziale Theorie der Wirtschaftssysteme», a. a. O., S. 323–331.

77 ACHINGER, «Sozialpolitik als Gesellschaftspolitik usw.», a. a. O., S. 79 ff., 140 ff. – DERS., «Sozialpolitik und Wissenschaft», a. a. O., passim. – PREISER, «Die Zukunft unserer Wirtschaftsordnung», a. a. O., S. 32 f., 58 ff., passim.

78 KARRENBERG, «Gestalt und Kritik des Westens», a. a. O., passim.

79 Eine interessante östliche Entwicklung in dieser Richtung zu Beginn der 1960er Jahre dürfte in Polen vorliegen. – Ost-Prob., Jg. 14, a. a. O., Nr 3, S. 86 ff.

80 Zur Einteilung dieses Unterabschnittes vgl. den Aufsatz des Verfassers «Scope and Problems of Economic Philosophy», a. a. O., S. 399 f.

81 «Gewaltenvereinigung, Zentralismus, einheitliche Befehlsgewalt und Planprinzip sind die bestimmenden Grundsätze, auf denen die Organisation des Sowjetstaates beruht.» – MEISSNER, «Rußland im Umbruch usw.», a. a. O., S. 19.

82 Zur allgemeinen Problematik des russisch-marxistischen Chiliasmus vgl. LANGE, «Marxismus, Leninismus, Stalinismus usw.», a. a. O., S. 181 ff.

83 BECKER, H. und BARNES, H. E., «Social Thought from Lore to Science», Bd. 3, New York, Dover Publications, 1961, S. 1029–1059.

84 MEISSNER, «Rußland im Umbruch usw.», a. a. O., S. 19.

85 Das Problem von Reform und Orthodoxie liegt in diesem Falle darin, daß die Partei das wahre Wissen um Natur und Mensch zu besitzen beansprucht.

86 Daß sich eine Lockerung des autokratischen Systems bereits zu Lebzeiten STALINS anbahnte, zeigt MEISSNER, «Rußland im Umbruch usw.», a. a. O., S. 4 f., 18 f.

87 PERROUX, «Feindliche Koexistenz?», a. a. O., S. 12 f., 191 f.

88 HAENSEL, P., «Die Wirtschaftspolitik Sowjetrußlands», Tübingen, Mohr (Siebeck), 1930, S. 27–44. – WILES, «The Political Economy of Communism», a. a. O., S. 28–33. – THALHEIM, «Grundzüge des sowjetischen Wirtschaftssystems», a. a. O., S. 25–32. – STUCKI, L., «Die Quadratur des roten Kreises», GAITANIDES (Hrsg.), Die Zukunft des Kommunismus, a. a. O., S. 76.

89 LENIN entschloß sich sehr bald, nach 1905, ausgehend von dem Theorem, daß die russische Revolution westliche Revolutionen nach sich ziehen werde, zur Revolution in einem Lande. Seiner Fraktion der Bolschewiki, die ihm darin folgte, unterlagen die den ursprüng-

lichen Internationalismus bewahrenden Menschewiki. Immerhin erwartete LENIN noch das sofortige Überspringen des revolutionären Funkens. Das sollte erst unter STALIN anders werden.

⁹⁰ DEUTSCHER, I., «Stalin. Die Geschichte des modernen Rußland» (aus dem Engl.), Stuttgart, Kohlhammer, 1951. – CONQUEST, R., «Sowjetrußland, das System und die Menschen», Köln, Verlag Wissenschaft und Politik, 1961.

⁹¹ Diese Kontroverse ist primär eine ontologische und wird darum ausführlich im Abschnitt VI behandelt. Hier ist sie nur mit einem ihrer Aspekte einschlägig, nämlich mit der Frage nach den Gesetzmäßigkeiten der Entwicklung des Sozialismus-Kommunismus.

⁹² Ihre anti-planwirtschaftliche Konzeption ging von dem Gedanken eines Gleichgewichts der Kräfte aus. – AHLBERG, «Der vergessene Philosoph. Abram Moissevitsch Deborin», LABEDZ (Hrsg.), Der Revisionismus, a. a. O., S. 162–188.

⁹³ Beide Gruppen konnten sich auf MARX berufen, bei dem sowohl die These von der Naturgesetzlichkeit der Entwicklung als auch die Lehre von den dialektischen Sprüngen vorkommt.

⁹⁴ Vgl. supra, Abschn. VI.

⁹⁵ AHLBERG, «‹Dialektische Philosophie› und Gesellschaft in der Sowjetunion», a. a. O., S. 102. – Zur STALINschen Produktionspolitik: STALIN, J. W., «Über die Aufgaben der Wirtschaftler. Rede auf der ersten Unionskonferenz der Funktionäre der sozialistischen Industrie, 4. Februar 1931», ders., Werke, Bd. 13, a. a. O., S. 35, 38. – «Geschichte der Kommunistischen Partei der Sowjetunion (Bolschewiki)», Kurzer Lehrgang, 10. Aufl., a. a. O., S. 420.

⁹⁶ MEISSNER, «Rußland im Umbruch usw.», a. a. O., S. 17 f. – FETSCHER, «Von Marx zur Sowjetideologie», a. a. O., S. 131 f.

⁹⁷ PLAMENATZ, «German Marxism and Russian Communism», a. a. O., S. 289 ff.

⁹⁸ Ebd., S. 296 ff. – LÖWENTHAL, «Das kommunistische Experiment usw.», a. a. O., S. 173–177.

⁹⁹ Ebd., S. 164–167. – Heute werden diese Theoreme STALINS abgelehnt; vgl. Ost-Prob., Jg. 14, a. a. O., Nr. 22, S. 675.

¹⁰⁰ Auf dieser nationalistischen Linie lag denn auch STALINS 1939 verkündete Lehre vom «Aufbau des Kommunismus in einem Lande». – MEISSNER, «Rußland im Umbruch usw.», a. a. O., S. 18.

¹⁰¹ Im Kapitalismus wirken die Sachgesetzlichkeiten der Produktionssphäre wie Naturgesetze, obwohl sie doch das Werk von Menschen sind.

¹⁰² MEISSNER, «Rußland im Umbruch usw.», a. a. O., S. 13 f. – GASTEYGER (Hrsg.), «Perspektiven der sowjetischen Politik usw.», a. a. O., S. 54 f.

¹⁰³ BRONSKA-PAMPUCH, «Kommunismus, gibt es das überhaupt?», GAITANIDES (Hrsg.), Die Zukunft des Kommunismus, a. a. O., S. 70.

¹⁰⁴ MEISSNER, «Rußland im Umbruch usw.», a. a. O., S. 2 f.

¹⁰⁵ STALIN, «Ekonomičeskie problemy socializma v SSSR», a. a. O., passim.

¹⁰⁶ Hier wirkte sich die Theorie der «Revolution von oben» aus. – MEISSNER, «Rußland im Umbruch usw.», a. a. O., S. 18.

¹⁰⁷ Es hatte sich eine neue Klassenschichtung zwischen bürokratischer Herrenkaste einerseits und Arbeitern und Bauern anderseits verfestigt. Daß die politische und wirtschaftliche Oberschicht Staatseigentum für sozialer ansah als genossenschaftliches, zeigt nur zum andern Male die notdürftig verbrämte Abkehr von den Idealen des Ursprungs.

¹⁰⁸ FETSCHER, «Von Marx zur Sowjetideologie», a. a. O., S. 142 ff.

¹⁰⁹ GASTEYGER (Hrsg.), «Perspektiven der sowjetischen Politik usw.», a. a. O., S. 22 f. – DANILOWICZ, R. J., «Die Arbeiterräte in Jugoslawien», Hinter dem Eisernen Vorhang, Jg. 9, München, 1963, Nr. 7/8, S. 7–14.

¹¹⁰ SHERMAN, A., «Revisionist wider Willen. Tito», LABEDZ (Hrsg.), Der Revisionismus, a. a. O., S. 439–454. – WILES, «The Political Economy of Communism», a. a. O., S. 4 f., 10 f., 36–41, 336 f. – SCHACK, «Die Revision des Marxismus-Leninismus», a. a. O., S. 36 f., 44. – LÖWENTHAL, R., «Das kommunistische Schisma», GAITANIDES (Hrsg.), Die Zukunft des Kom-

munismus, a. a. O., S. 30, 45 f. und GAITANIDES, «Die Vergangenheit des (Welt-)Kommunismus hat schon begonnen», ebd., S. 133. – GASTEYGER (Hrsg.), «Perspektiven der sowjetischen Politik usw.», a. a. O., S. 91. – BAUDIN, L., «La Yougoslavie et le Communisme», Kyklos, Bd. 13, Basel, 1960, Nr. 3, S. 327–345. – PASIC, N., «Jugoslawischer Sozialismus und Moskauer Programm», Ost-Prob., Jg. 14, a. a. O., Nr. 13, S. 407–413.

111 LÖWENTHAL, «Das kommunistische Schisma», GAITANIDES (Hrsg.), Die Zukunft des Kommunismus, a. a. O., S. 47 f.

112 RÜHLE, J., «Das gefesselte Theater. Vom Revolutionstheater zum Sozialistischen Realismus», Köln-Berlin, Kiepenheuer und Witsch, 1957, S. 425. – ROSTOW und LEVIN, «The Dynamics of Soviet Society», a. a. O., S. 218 f., 238 ff. – GAITANIDES, «Die Vergangenheit des (Welt-)Kommunismus hat schon begonnen», ders. (Hrsg.), Die Zukunft des Kommunismus, a. a. O., S. 139 f.

113 STUCKI, «Die Quadratur des roten Kreises», GAITANIDES (Hrsg.), Die Zukunft des Kommunismus, a. a. O., S. 79 ff.

114 THALHEIM, «Grundzüge des sowjetischen Wirtschaftssystems», a. a. O., S. 41 f. – RÜHLE, «Das gefesselte Theater usw.», a. a. O., S. 425–440. – Vgl. v. RIMSCHA, «Geschichte Rußlands», a. a. O., S. 584 f. – DEUTSCHER, «Russia in Transition and Other Essays», a. a. O., S. 52–70. – GASTEYGER (Hrsg.), «Perspektiven der sowjetischen Politik usw.», a. a. O., S. 12 f. – Ost-Prob., Jg. 14, a. a. O., Nr. 17, S. 534 f., 542. – Ost-Prob., Jg. 14, a. a. O., Nr. 4, S. 109 ff. – LABEDZ, L., «Sociology as a Vocation», Survey, New York, 1963, Nr. 48, S. 59 bis 64. – Zu den östlichen philosophischen Bewegungen vgl. BUCHHOLZ, A., «Problems of the Ideological East-West-Conflict», BOCHENSKI und BLAKELY (Hrsg.), Studies in Soviet Thought, Bd. 1, a. a. O., S. 120–131.

115 Vgl. v. RIMSCHA, «Geschichte Rußlands», a. a. O., S. 582 ff.

116 CHRUSCHTSCHOW, «Rechenschaftsbericht des Zentralkomitees der KPdSU an den XX. Parteitag usw.», a. a. O., S. 18 ff., 43 ff., 81, 121, 126. – GASTEYGER (Hrsg.), «Perspektiven der sowjetischen Politik usw.», a. a. O., S. 13–18. – SCHACK, «Die Revision des Marxismus-Leninismus», a. a. O., S. 33 f., 38 f. – NOVE, A., «The Soviet Industrial Reorganization», Prob. Comm., Bd. 6, a. a. O., Nr. 6, S. 19–25. – SWEARER, «Decentralization in Recent Soviet Administrative Practice», a. a. O., S. 456–470.

117 GOLLWITZER, «Die totalitäre Utopie relativiert sich», GAITANIDES (Hrsg.), Die Zukunft des Kommunismus, a. a. O., S. 48.

118 FETSCHER, «Von Marx zur Sowjetideologie», a. a. O., S. 146. – RÜHLE, «Das gefesselte Theater usw.», a. a. O., S. 436 f.

119 CHRUSCHTSCHOW, «Rechenschaftsbericht des Zentralkomitees der KPdSU an den XX. Parteitag usw.», a. a. O., S. 66–92. – WILES, «The Political Economy of Communism», a. a. O., S. 9 ff., 41, 50, 340 f.

120 GASTEYGER (Hrsg.), «Perspektiven der sowjetischen Politik usw.», a. a. O., S. 16 f. – CHRUSCHTSCHOW, «Rechenschaftsbericht des Zentralkomitees der KPdSU an den XX. Parteitag usw.», a. a. O., S. 62 ff., 118 ff., 121.

121 THALHEIM, «Grundzüge des sowjetischen Wirtschaftssystems», a. a. O., S. 42–49, 167.

122 «Chruschtschёw vor dem XXI. Parteitag», Ost-Prob., Jg. 11, a. a. O., Nr. 4, S. 98 ff. – GASTEYGER (Hrsg.), «Perspektiven der sowjetischen Politik usw.», a. a. O., S. 52 f.

123 NOLLAU, «Zerfall des Weltkommunismus usw.», a. a. O., passim. – WHITING, A.S., «Differenzen zwischen Moskau und Peking?», Ost-Prob., Jg. 11, a. a. O., Nr. 23, S. 722 ff. – NORTH, R. C., «Moscow and Chinese Communists», 2. Aufl., Stanford, Stanford University Press, 1963, S. 266–291.

124 Vgl. v. RIMSCHA, «Geschichte Rußlands», a. a. O., S. 586. – FEDOSSEJEW, «Sozialismus und Humanismus», a. a. O., S. 43–50.

125 THALHEIM, «Grundzüge des sowjetischen Wirtschaftssystems», a. a. O., S. 56 f., 60 ff. – SCHACK, «Die Revision des Marxismus-Leninismus», a. a. O., S. 37 f.

126 Ebd., S. 38. – Über den entsprechenden sozialphilosophischen Revisionismus in Polen unterrichten: Ost-Prob., Jg. 14, a. a. O., Nr. 3, S. 66–74. – MONTIAS, J. H., «The Polish ‹Economic Model›», Prob. Comm., Bd. 9, a. a. O., Nr. 2, S. 16–24.

[127] Neben dem sozialphilosophischen Gegensatz steht der außenpolitische zwischen dem Koexistenz-Theorem und der chinesischen Doktrin der gewaltsamen Revolution. – NOLLAU, «Zerfall des Weltkommunismus usw.», a. a. O., S. 50 ff.

[128] GASTEYGER (Hrsg.), «Perspektiven der sowjetischen Politik usw.», a. a. O., S. 20 ff. – Es gab auch in China kurzfristig (1957) den Versuch einer Liberalisierung, der aber bald beendet wurde. – SCHACK, «Die Revision des Marxismus-Leninismus», a. a. O., S. 26. – ULAM, «The New Face of Soviet Totalitarianism», a. a. O., S. 197–206. – WILES, «The Political Economy of Communism», a. a. O., S. 9, 12, 44, 342 ff.

[129] SOLICH, E. J., «Der Osten bleibt ein Block», GAITANIDES (Hrsg.), Die Zukunft des Kommunismus, a. a. O., S. 85 ff.

[130] SINICYN, V., «Formirovanie kommunističeskogo byta» (Formierung der kommunistischen Lebensweise), Kommunist, Jg. 40, Moskau, 1963, Nr. 11. – Ost-Prob., Jg. 14, a. a. O., Nr. 17, S. 515–542. – GASTEYGER (Hrsg.), «Perspektiven der sowjetischen Politik usw.», a. a. O., S. 55 f.

[131] Ebd., S. 51 f.

[132] STUCKI, «Die Quadratur des roten Kreises», GAITANIDES (Hrsg.), Die Zukunft des Kommunismus, a. a. O., S. 82 f. – STERNBERG, «Zwei Großmächte im totalitären Block», ebd., S. 103.

[133] GASTEYGER (Hrsg.), «Perspektiven der sowjetischen Politik usw.», a. a. O., S. 71 ff.

[134] Ebd., S. 54 f. – Bei dem System der Einheits-Weltanschauung soll es, trotz aller Abkehr vom Terror, bleiben. Ist aber «innerparteiliche Freiheit» dieser Art schon Freiheit? – Ost-Prob., Jg. 14, a. a. O., Nr. 22, S. 678 und ebd., Nr. 23, S. 722 f.

[135] GASTEYGER (Hrsg.), «Perspektiven der sowjetischen Politik usw.», a. a. O., S. 67 f. – WILES, «The Political Economy of Communism», a. a. O., S. 331–349, 381–397.

[136] THALHEIM, «Grundzüge des sowjetischen Wirtschaftssystems», a. a. O., S. 143–155. – Schließlich stellt sich die Frage, ob es sich bei alledem «nur» um ein amerikanisches Lebensideal handelt. BRONSKA-PAMPUCH, «Kommunismus, gibt es das überhaupt?», GAITANIDES (Hrsg.), Die Zukunft des Kommunismus, a. a. O., S. 67 f. – ULAM, A. B., «The Unfinished Revolution. An Essay on the Sources of Influence of Marxism and Communism», New York, Random House, 1960, S. 264–277. – DERS., «The New Face of Soviet Totalitarianism», a. a. O., S. 206–217. – SCHAPIRO, L., «Towards a ‹Communist Welfare State›? (Discussion)», Prob. Comm., Bd. 9, a. a. O., Nr. 3, S. 44–51.

[137] HERMENS, «Der Ost-West-Konflikt. Gründe und Scheingründe», a. a. O., S. 73.

[138] SCHELER, H., «Philosophische Probleme des Übergangs vom Kapitalismus zum Kommunismus», Berlin, Deutscher Verlag der Wissenschaften, 1959, S. 19, 34, passim.

[139] TREUE, «Wirtschaftsgeschichte der Neuzeit usw.», a. a. O., S. 710.

[140] Zum Fragenkreis Änderung des Systems oder Änderung im System vgl. HERMENS, «Der Ost-West-Konflikt. Gründe und Scheingründe», a. a. O., S. 48 ff.

Notes to Chapter XVI

[1] «Ob ulučšenii upravlenija promyšlennost'ju, soveršenstvovanii planirovanija i usilenii ekonomičeskogo stimulirovanija promyšlennogo proizvodstva» (Über die Verbesserung der Industrielenkung, über die Vervollkommnung der Planung und die Hebung des ökonomischen Anreizes der Industrieproduktion), Rede im Plenum des Zentralkomitees der Kommunistischen Partei der Sowjetunion, Pravda, Moskau, Nr. 271 vom 29. 9. 1965, S. 1–3.

[2] Ekonomičeskaja Gazeta (Wirtschaftszeitung), Jg. 33, Moskau, 1965, Nr. 42, S. 1 ff.

[3] Vgl. insbesondere die Zusammenfassungen über die Liberman-Diskussion in «Problems of Economics», Jg. 5, New York, 1962/63, Nr. 12, S. 3–27. – Ebd., Jg. 7, a. a. O., Nr. 9, S. 3–17 (mit Beiträgen von LIBERMAN, LEONT'EV, TRAPEZNIKOV, ZVEREV, AL'TER u. a.).

4 THALHEIM, K. C., «Die Wirtschaft der Sowjetzone in Krise und Umbau», Berlin, Duncker und Humblot, 1964 (Wirtschaft und Gesellschaft in Mitteldeutschland, 1), S. 62 ff.

5 «Neues Wirtschaftsmodell in der ČSSR», Hinter dem Eisernen Vorhang, Jg. 10, München, 1964, Nr. 11, S. 3–11.

6 MEISSNER, B., «Das Parteiprogramm der KPdSU 1903–1961», Köln, Verlag Wissenschaft und Politik, 1962 (Dokumente zum Studium des Kommunismus, Bundesinstitut zur Erforschung des Marxismus-Leninismus (Hrsg.), 1), S. 207 ff.

7 Népszabadság (Volksfreiheit), Budapest, Nr. 14 vom 17. 1. 1965.

8 PIRITYI, O., «Az ármechanizmusról» (Über den Preismechanismus), Közgazd. Szle (Volkswirtschaftliche Rundschau), Jg. 12, Budapest, 1965, Nr. 10, S. 1182 ff. – FOCK, J., «Gazdasági fejlödésünk idöszerü kérdései» (Aktuelle Fragen unserer wirtschaftlichen Entwicklung), Társad. Szle (Gesellschaftliche Rundschau), Jg. 20, Budapest, 1965, Nr. 10, S. 1–16.

9 Dabei geht man allgemein von den Ware-Geld-Beziehungen und den materiellen Anreizen aus, deren Ausnutzung z. B. im Parteiprogramm der KPdSU von 1961 nachdrücklich betont wurden. – MEISSNER, «Das Parteiprogramm der KPdSU 1903–1961», a. a. O., S. 206.

10 Man stützt sich dabei auf das «sozialistische Gesetz der Verteilung nach der Arbeitsleistung». – «Politische Ökonomie. Lehrbuch», 7. Aufl., nach der vierten, überarbeiteten und ergänzten russ. Ausgabe, Berlin, Dietz, 1965, S. 529 ff. – Zur jüngsten Entwicklung der Lohnpolitik in Ungarn vgl. RÓZSA, I., «Differenciáltság vagy nivelláció a jövedelmekben» (Differenziertheit oder Nivellierung in den Einkommen), Közgazd. Szle, Jg. 12, a. a. O., Nr. 6, S. 680 ff.

11 SEBESTYÉN, T., «A minöség védelmében» (Zum Schutze der Qualität), Figyelö (Beobachter), Jg. 7, Budapest, 1963, Nr. 30, S. 5.

12 NICK, H., «Mehr Aufmerksamkeit der Ökonomie der vergegenständlichten Arbeit», Einheit, Jg. 19, Berlin, 1964, Nr. 7, S. 37 ff.

13 So machte im Jahre 1963 der seit dem Beginn der 1950er Jahre ständig angestiegene Anteil der unvollendeten an den gesamten Investitionen bereits nahezu 45 % aus (in den Jahren 1950–1954 waren es nur ca. 16 %, 1955–1957 ca. 28 %). – «Statisztikai Évkönyv 1963» (Statistisches Jahrbuch 1963), Budapest, Központi Statisztikai Hivatal (Statistisches Zentralamt), 1964, S. 45.

14 BALÁZSY, S., «Die Grund- und Umlaufmittelfonds in der Ungarischen Volksrepublik», Wirtsch. wiss., Jg. 12, Berlin, 1964, Nr. 7, S. 1175–1181.

15 «Economic Survey for Europe in 1962, Part 2: Economic Planning in Europe», Prepared by the Secretariat of the Economic Commission for Europe, Geneva, 1965, insbes. Abschn. 1.

16 Die verschiedenen Interpretationsmöglichkeiten kamen z. B. in Diskussionsbeiträgen auf der Jahrestagung der Deutschen Gesellschaft für Osteuropakunde im Oktober 1965 deutlich zum Ausdruck. – Vgl. die Berichterstattung in der deutschen Tagespresse, z. B. «Die Welt», Hamburg, Nr. 247 vom 23. 10. 1965, S. 28. – «Handelsblatt», Düsseldorf, Nr. 206 vom 25. 10. 1965, S. 5.

17 Ebendies hatte A. SMITH im Auge, wenn er von der «invisible hand» sprach.

18 Dabei wirkt ein solcher «Gewinn» allerdings nur teilweise wie sein marktwirtschaftliches Gegenstück. So fehlt ihm insbesondere die Koordinations- und Investitionslenkungsfunktion; solche makroökonomischen Aufgaben, die der Gewinn in der Marktwirtschaft wahrzunehmen hat, sind im Osten nach wie vor einer Planung der öffentlichen Hand vorbehalten.

19 Vgl. den Aufsatz des Verfassers «The Eastern European Economic Cycle», World Aff. Quart., Los Angeles, 1955, S. 275–301. – (ohne Verf.), «Vita a növekedési ütem idöszakos hullámzásának okairól» (Diskussion über die Gründe der periodischen Schwankungen des Wachstumstempos), Közgazd. Szle, Jg. 12, a. a. O., Nr. 9, S. 1132–1139.

20 Die Anlage der Neuen Ökonomischen Politik und die Grundlinien der gegenwärtigen Reformen weisen aufschlußreiche Ähnlichkeiten auf. – LENIN, W. I., «Entwurf einer Resolution zu den Fragen der Neuen Ökonomischen Politik», ders., Werke, Bd. 32, Berlin, Dietz, S. 454 ff.

21 RAUPACH, «Geschichte der Sowjetwirtschaft», a. a. O., S. 47–61.

22 Vgl. das Buch des Verfassers «Comparative Economic Systems», a. a. O., S. 376 f. – JASNY, N., «The Soviet Price System», Stanford/Calif., Stanford University Press, 1951, S. 8 ff., 15 ff.

23 Zur Entwicklung in Südosteuropa vgl. das Buch des Verfassers «Studien zum Wirtschaftswachstum Südosteuropas», Stuttgart, Fischer, 1964, passim.

24 Versuche in dieser Richtung wurden bekanntlich seit dem Tode STALINs wiederholt unternommen; sie machten bereits ein wesentliches Kennzeichen des Neuen Kurses im Jahre 1953 aus. Bislang wurden sie jedoch in allen Ostblockländern nach kurzer Zeit wieder mehr oder weniger aufgegeben.

25 SCHILLER, K., «Sozialismus und Wettbewerb», Hamburg, Verlagsgesellschaft deutscher Konsumgenossenschaften, 1955, S. 14. – Zum Problem einer ökonomischen Theorie des Sozialismus vgl. v. WIESER, F., «Der natürliche Werth», Wien, Hölder, 1889, S. 64 ff., 77 ff. – MENGER, A., «Volkspolitik», Jena, Fischer, 1906, S. 58–62, 84–87. – BARONE, E., «The Ministry of Production in the Collectivist State» (Nachdruck), v. HAYEK, F. A. (Hrsg.), Collectivist Economic Planning, 3. Aufl., London, Routledge and Sons, 1947, S. 245–290, insbes. S. 265–290. – SOMBART, «Sozialismus und Soziale Bewegung», a. a. O., S. 62–108. – HALM, G., «Ist der Sozialismus wirtschaftlich möglich?», Berlin, Junker und Dünnhaupt, 1929, S. 13–37. – LIEPMANN, R., «Geschichte und Kritik des Sozialismus», Leipzig, Quelle und Meyer, 1922, S. 162–188.

26 WETTER, «Die Umkehrung Hegels usw.», a. a. O., S. 16 ff. – Zur neueren Entwicklung in der Sowjetphilosophie vgl. DEMAITRE, E., «In Search of Humanism», Prob. Comm., Bd. 14, a. a. O., Nr. 5, S. 18–30.

27 GERÖ, E., «Országépitö munkásifjuság» (Arbeiterjugend beim Aufbau des Landes), Válogatott beszédek és cikkek 1944–1950 (Ausgewählte Reden und Aufsätze 1944–1950), Budapest, Szikra Kiadó, 1950, S. 274. – SZARKA, J., «A szocialista ember neveléséröl» (Über die Erziehung des sozialistischen Menschen), Társad. Szle, Jg. 19, a. a. O., Nr. 8–9, S. 48. – MEISSNER, «Das Parteiprogramm der KPdSU 1903–1961», a. a. O., S. 186 ff.

28 Vgl. supra Abschnitt II, sowie DAHM, «Die Dialektik im Wandel der Sowjetphilosophie», a. a. O., S. 29 ff. – KWANT, «Philosophy of Labor», a. a. O., S. 66 ff. – LANGE, «Marxismus, Leninismus, Stalinismus usw.», a. a. O., S. 85 ff. – HOMMES, «Der technische Eros usw.», a. a. O., S. 314–337.

29 FROMM, «Das Menschenbild bei Marx», a. a. O., S. 44–48, 57, 69 f. – PLAMENATZ, «German Marxism and Russian Communism», a. a. O., S. 74 ff. – NÜRNBERGER, R., «Die französische Revolution im revolutionären Selbstverständnis des Marxismus», FETSCHER (Hrsg.), Marxismusstudien, 2. Folge. a. a. O., S. 65 ff.

30 MARX, «Die Frühschriften», LANDSHUT (Hrsg.), a. a. O., S. 547 f.

31 Vgl. das Buch des Verfassers «Comparative Economic Systems», a. a. O., S. 292–308. – HALM, G., «Wirtschaftssysteme», Berlin, Duncker und Humblot, 1960, S. 12 ff. – «Der Witz der bürgerlichen Gesellschaft besteht ja eben darin, daß a priori keine bewußte gesellschaftliche Regelung der Produktion stattfindet.» MARX, K. und ENGELS, F., «Ausgewählte Schriften in zwei Bänden», Berlin, Dietz, 1953, S. 434.

32 BAUERMEISTER, «Die russische kommunistische Theorie usw.», a. a. O., S. 23 ff.

33 JÖHR und SINGER, «Die Nationalökonomie im Dienste der Wirtschaftspolitik», a. a. O., S. 150.

34 WEBER, A., «Sowjetwirtschaft und Weltwirtschaft», Berlin, Duncker und Humblot, 1959, S. 12.

35 «Politische Ökonomie. Lehrbuch», a. a. O., S. 471 f., 490 f.

36 Ebd., S. 484.

37 Vgl. das Buch des Verfassers «Comparative Economic Systems», a. a. O., S. 153 ff.

38 Nach kommunistischen Anschauungen führt eine an individualistischen Maximen orientierte Wirtschaft zur Konzentration der Macht in wenigen Händen, d. h. zur Monopolbildung und zur Ausbeutung der Massen. – «Politische Ökonomie. Lehrbuch», a. a. O., S. 254–273.

39 BECKER, R., «Die kommunistische Verteilung als Ideal und Wirklichkeit», Osteuropa Wirtsch., Jg. 9, Stuttgart, 1964, Nr. 1, S. 1 ff. – MSTISLAVSKIJ, P., «Pod-em narodnogo blagosostojanija – zakon socializma» (Die Erhöhung des Volkswohlstandes – Gesetz des Sozialismus), Kommunist, Jg. 40, a. a. O., Nr. 4, S. 44. – In Ungarn betrug der Anteil des ausgezahlten Lohnes 1955 = 55,5 v.H., 1958 = 56,2 v.H. Der übrige Anteil kam den Arbeitern in Form von indirekten Zuwendungen kollektiv zugute. – Errechnet aus: JÁVORKA, E. und BERÉNYI, J., «Jövedelmek a munkabéren felül» (Einkommen über dem Arbeitslohn), Budapest, Kossuth Könyvkiadó (Kossuth Buchverlag), 1960, S. 81 ff.

40 MEISSNER, «Das Parteiprogramm der KPdSU 1903–1961», a. a. O., S. 89.

41 Ebd., S. 207 ff.

42 «Dekrety sovetskoj vlasti» (Dekrete der Sowjetmacht), Bd. 1: 25. Oktober 1917 bis 16. März 1918, Moskau, Gospolitizdat (Staatsverlag für politische Literatur), 1957, S. 17–19, 77 f., 82 f., 225–231, 407. – Ebd., Bd. 2: 17. März bis 10. Juli 1918, a. a. O., 1958, S. 498 bis 503. – GLADKOV, I. A., «Očerki sovetskoj ekonomiki 1917–1920» (Studien zur sowjetischen Ökonomie 1917–1920), Moskau, Gospolitizdat (Staatsverlag für politische Literatur), 1956, S. 211 f. – WILES, «The Political Economy of Communism», a. a. O., S. 28 ff. – TUMANJAN, O. E., «Razvitie planirovanija v SSSR. Kratkij očerk» (Die Entwicklung der Planung in der UdSSR. Kurzes Studium), Jerewan, Izdatel'stvo Erevanskogo Universiteta (Verlag der Universität Jerewan), 1958, S. 16 f.

43 LENIN, W. I., «Die proletarische Revolution und der Renegat Kautsky», ders., Werke, Bd. 28, a. a. O., 1959, S. 252 f.

44 HEITMANN, S., «Zwischen Lenin und Stalin. Nikolai I. Bucharin», LABEDZ (Hrsg.), Der Revisionismus, a. a. O., S. 96 ff.

45 «Die Forderungen und Wünsche der Menschen werden bei all ihrer Vielfalt ein Ausdruck der gesunden, vernünftigen Bedürfnisse des allseitig entwickelten Menschen sein.» – MEISSNER, «Das Parteiprogramm der KPdSU 1903–1961», a. a. O., S. 207.

46 Z. B. führte Ungarn zunächst eine Verstaatlichung des Bergbaus, der Stahl- und Eisenindustrie, der Energiewirtschaft und der Banken ein, die bis 1947 in öffentliches Eigentum übergingen. In ähnlicher Weise wie in Ungarn, wo sich der Kollektivierungsprozeß auch nachher fortsetzte, verfuhr man in Rumänien und Bulgarien. – Vgl. das Buch des Verfassers «Studien zum Wirtschaftswachstum Südosteuropas», a. a. O., S. 138 ff.

47 «Politische Ökonomie. Lehrbuch», a. a. O., S. 364 ff.

48 WETTER, «Sowjetideologie heute usw.», a. a. O., S. 102 f.

49 KOCH, G., «Charakter und Wirkungsweise ökonomischer Gesetze im Sozialismus», Institut für Marxismus-Leninismus der Humboldt-Universität Berlin (Hrsg.), Philosophie im Meinungsstreit, Berlin, Dietz, 1965, S. 75–100. – BUCHARIN, «Ökonomik der Transformationsperiode usw.», a. a. O., S. 73 f.

50 «Politische Ökonomie. Lehrbuch», a. a. O., S. 488 ff.

51 Ebd., S. 565.

52 SCHULZ, H.-J., «Über die Grundlagen der Produktionsfondsabgabe», Wirtsch. wiss., Jg. 13, a. a. O., Nr. 10, S. 1610. – STALIN, J. W., «Politischer Rechenschaftsbericht des Zentralkomitees an den XVI. Parteitag der KPdSU (B), 27. 6. 1930», ders., Werke, Bd. 12, a. a. O., 1954, S. 323. – Eine solche Erklärung verliert aber dadurch an Wahrscheinlichkeit, daß in neuerer Zeit eher das Hinüberentwickeln zum Kommunismus betont wird.

53 STALIN, «Über die rechte Abweichung in der KPdSU (B)», a. a. O., S. 38 f.

54 LENIN, W. I., «Brief über den Plan für den politischen Bericht auf dem XI. Parteitag an Molotow», ders., Werke, Bd. 33, a. a. O., 1963, S. 237 f. – DERS., «Friedrich Engels (1895)», ders., Werke, Bd. 2, a. a. O., 1963, S. 6. – DERS., «4000 Rubel im Jahr und sechsstündiger Arbeitstag (1914)», ders., Werke, Bd. 20, a. a. O., 1961, S. 57. – DERS., «Rede über Krieg und Frieden», ders., Ausgewählte Werke, Bd. 2, Berlin, Dietz, 1952, S. 333.

55 LENIN, W. I., «VIII. Gesamtrussischer Sowjetkongreß. Bericht über die Tätigkeit der Volkskommissare, 22. Dezember 1920», ders., Werke, Bd. 31, a. a. O., 1959, S. 508. – «Dekret Soveta Narodnych Komissarov» (Dekret des Rates der Volkskommissare), 22 fevralja 1921 g. (vom 22. Februar 1921), Položenie o gosudarstvennoj obščeplanovoj komissii (Verfügung über die Staatliche Plankommission), in: Direktivy KPSS i Sovetskogo pravitel'stva po chozjajstvennym voprosam (Direktiven der Kommunistischen Partei der SU und der Sowjetischen Regierung zu Wirtschaftsfragen), Bd. 1, Moskau, Gospolitizdat (Staatsverlag für politische Literatur), 1957, S. 203 f.

[56] GERGELY, I., «Eszközgazdálkodás és használati díj» (Das Wirtschaften mit den Mitteln und Nutzungsgebühr), Közgazd. Szle, Jg. 10, a. a. O., Nr. 8, S. 889–904.

[57] Aus diesem Postulat hat man den Schluß gezogen, mathematischen Planungs- und Lenkungsmethoden verstärkte Aufmerksamkeit zuzuwenden. Insbesondere wird seit einiger Zeit die Kybernetik stark betont. Vgl. u. a. «Filosofskie voprosy kibernetiki» (Philosophische Fragen der Kybernetik), Moskau, Izdatel'stvo social'no-ekonomičeskoj literatury (Verlag für Sozialwesen und Ökonomik), 1961, passim. – SIMON, G., «Matematikai módszerek közgazdasági alkalmazása» (Die Verwendung mathematischer Methoden in der Volkswirtschaft), Szle, Jg. 18, a. a. O., Nr. 11, S. 72 ff. – CSATÓ, I., «Az elektronikus közgazdász» (Der elektronische Volkswirt), Figyelö, Jg. 8, a. a. O., Nr. 11, S. 1.

[58] SCHELER, «Philosophische Probleme des Übergangs vom Kapitalismus zum Kommunismus», a. a. O., S. 43. – CHRUSTSCHOW (CHRUŠČEV), N. S., «Die Kontrollziffern für die Entwicklung der Volkswirtschaft der UdSSR in den Jahren 1959–1965», Moskau, Verlag für fremdsprachige Literatur, 1959, S. 127 ff.

[59] KADE, G. und KRENGEL, R., «Chruschtschow und die Folgen. Über die voraussichtliche Entwicklung der sowjetischen Wirtschaftspolitik nach dem Sturze Chruschtschows», Konjunk. pol., Jg. 10, Berlin, 1964, Nr. 5, S. 282. – CHRUSCHTSCHOW (CHRUŠČEV), N. S., «Die Entwicklung der Wirtschaft der UdSSR und die Leitung der Volkswirtschaft durch die Partei», Bericht auf dem Plenum des ZK der KPdSU am 19. November 1962, Presse Sowjet., Berlin, 1962, Nr. 134, S. 2919 f. – LIBERMAN, J., «Plan, Gewinn, Prämie», Presse Sowjet., a. a. O., 1962, Nr. 108, S. 2331–2335. – DERS., «Noch einmal über Plan, Gewinn, Prämie», Presse Sowjet., a. a. O., 1964, Nr. 114, S. 2525 ff. – TINBERGEN, J., «Do Communist and Free Economies Show a Converging Pattern?», Sov. Stud., Bd. 12, Oxford, 1960/61, Nr. 4, S. 334.

[60] BOETTCHER, «Die sowjetische Wirtschaftspolitik am Scheidewege», a. a. O., S. 196. – MEIMBERG, R., «Über die Möglichkeiten eines Übergangs von der zentralen Kommandowirtschaft zur Marktwirtschaft», JÜRGENSEN, H. (Hrsg.), Gestaltungsprobleme der Weltwirtschaft. Andreas Predöhl aus Anlaß seines 70. Geburtstages gewidmet, Göttingen, Vandenhoeck und Ruprecht, 1964, S. 117–125.

[61] GOLDMAN, M. I., «Markt und Marketing der Sowjets. Verbraucherversorgung in der Sowjetunion», Frankfurt/M., Lorch, 1964, S. 72 ff.

[62] «Vorrang der Konsumtion ist ungefährlich», Ost-Prob., Jg. 16, a. a. O., S. 195: «Die Partei bekämpft entschlossen den Dogmatismus in der Planung, in den Planungsmethoden, die Anhänglichkeit an irgendwann einmal richtig gewesene, heute aber sichtlich überholte Formeln.» – CHRUSCHTSCHOW, «Die Entwicklung der Wirtschaft der UdSSR usw.», a. a. O., S. 2903.

[63] Nachdem einige Volksrepubliken – z. T. versuchsweise – bereits unter verschiedenen Bezeichnungen westliche Merkmale des Kapitalzinses eingeführt hatten, wurde ein gleicher Schritt nun auch in der Sowjetunion beschlossen.

[64] Agerpres (Dokumente, Artikel und Informationen über Rumänien), Jg. 16, Bukarest, 1965, Nr. 12, S. 6 ff.

[65] «Rechenschaftsbericht des Zentralkomitees der Rumänischen Kommunistischen Partei über die Tätigkeit der Partei in der Zeitspanne zwischen dem VIII. Parteitag (III. Parteitag der Rumänischen Arbeiter-Partei) und dem IX. Parteitag», Agerpres (Nachrichten aus Rumänien), Jg. 2, Bukarest, 1965, Nr. 30, 1–49.

[66] Rumänien lehnt sich in seiner Industrialisierungspolitik noch deutlich an das frühere Modell einer möglichst autarken Wirtschaft jedes einzelnen sozialistischen Landes an.

[67] Vgl. das Buch des Verfassers «Studien zum Wirtschaftswachstum Südosteuropas», a. a. O., S. 115 ff. – NYERS, R., «Az új Magyarország két évtizede» (Zwei Jahrzehnte des neuen Ungarn), Közgazd. Szle, Jg. 12, a. a. O., Nr. 4, S. 389 ff.

[68] Ajtai, M., «Az 1965. évi népgazdasági terv fö kérdései» (Die Hauptprobleme des

Volkswirtschaftsplanes für das Jahr 1965), Népszabadság, Budapest, Nr. 11 vom 14. 1. 1965, S. 4 f. – Dabei wurde u. a. eine Neuregelung des Prämiensystems in der Industrie vorgenommen, um die materielle Interessiertheit vermehrt in den Dienst des volkswirtschaftlichen Aufbaus zu stellen. – HORVÁTH, S., «Az új prémiumrendszer – közelröl» (Das neue Prämiensystem aus der Nähe), Figyelö, Jg. 9, a. a. O., Nr. 39, S. 5.

⁶⁹ FOCK, «Gazdasági fejlödésünk idöszerü kérdései», a. a. O., S. 1 ff.

⁷⁰ «A VIII. kongresszus útján» (Auf dem Pfad des 8. Parteitages), Társad. Szle, Jg. 19, a. a. O., Nr. 1, S. 1 ff. – «A Központi Statisztikai Hivatal jelentése az 1963. évi népgazdasági terv teljesitéséröl» (Bericht des Statistischen Zentralamtes über die Erfüllung des Volkswirtschaftsplanes im Jahre 1963), Népszabadság, a. a. O., Nr. 15 vom 19. 1. 1964, S. 1 f.

⁷¹ «Megmentett százmilliók» (Gerettete Hundertmillionen), Figyelö, Jg. 9, a. a. O., Nr. 24, S. 5.

⁷² Vgl. zur Problematik des ungarischen Preissystems u. a. CSIKÓS-NAGY, B., «Diskussion über eine neue ungarische Preisregelung», Wirtsch. wiss., Jg. 11, a. a. O., Nr. 10, S. 1639 ff.

⁷³ So wurde z. B. in der DDR versuchsweise für einige Vereinigungen Volkseigener Betriebe und auch für Einzelbetriebe eine «Produktionsfondsabgabe» eingeführt.

⁷⁴ KARDOS, G., «Az eszközlekötési járulék» (Die Nutzungsgebühr), Népszabadság, a. a. O., Nr. 283 vom 4. 12. 1963, S. 9.

⁷⁵ HORVÁTH, L., «Vállalati önállóság – központi irányitás» (Selbständigkeit des Unternehmens – zentrale Lenkung), Népszabadság, a. a. O., Nr. 251 vom 24. 10. 1965, S. 5.

⁷⁶ Zu den Beschlüssen der Plenarsitzung des ZK der Bulgarischen Kommunistischen Partei im Mai 1963, insbesondere den dort vorgetragenen Thesen von T. ŽIVKOV, vgl. «Organizacijata i metodikata na planiraneto – na ošče po-visoko ravnišče» (Die Organisation und Methodik der Planung – auf einem noch höheren Niveau), Planovo stopanstvo i statistika (Planwirtschaft und Statistik), Jg. 18, Sofia, 1965, Nr. 6, S. 3–9.

⁷⁷ Das Plan-Gewinn-Prämie-Problem kommt in Bulgarien sowohl auf volkswirtschaftlicher als auch auf betrieblicher Ebene zur Geltung. Für eine Hebung der Rentabilität und der Wirtschaftlichkeit durch stärkere Betonung der materiellen Interessiertheit sieht man in Bulgarien in steuerpolitischen Maßnahmen die wichtigste Lösung. Darauf weisen die Formen der Besteuerung hin: «Steuer zur Regulierung der Rentabilität», «Produktionsfondssteuer» und (z. T.) «Progressive Einkommenssteuer». – JANEV, J., «Danǔčno oblagane pri novata sistema na planirane i rūkovodstvo na narodnoto stopanstvo» (Die Besteuerung in dem neuen Planungs- und Lenkungssystem der Volkswirtschaft), Finansi i Kredit (Finanzen und Kredit), Jg. 16, Sofia, 1965, Nr. 5, S. 14–20.

⁷⁸ «Reformversuche», Wiss. D. Südosteuropa, Jg. 14, München, 1965, Nr. 8/9, S. 126. Hinter dem Eisernen Vorhang, Jg. 10, a. a. O., Nr. 2, S. 37 f.

⁷⁹ «Konsumgüterindustrie marktorientiert», ebd., Nr. 7/8, S. 46 f.

Notes to Chapter XVII

¹ Vgl. das Buch des Verfassers «Comparative Economic Systems», a. a. O., S. 49 ff. – HEIMANN, «Soziale Theorie der Wirtschaftssysteme», a. a. O., S. 323.

² Ebd., S. 325.

³ Zu geistesgeschichtlicher Entgegensetzung und Zusammengehörigkeit von Liberalismus und Marxismus vgl. FREYER, «Weltgeschichte Europas», Bd. 2, a. a. O., S. 941 f., 949 ff.

⁴ RITSCHL, «Die Grundlagen der Wirtschaftsordnung», a. a. O., S. 95.

⁵ Soziologie als Kulturkritik betont dieses Gefahrenmoment gegenüber einer Rollen-Soziologie, deren exakte Methodik eher als Rechtfertigung der bestehenden Verhältnisse wirkt.

6 Vgl. (o. Verf.) «Gedanken zur Auseinandersetzung mit der bürgerlichen Philosophie», Dtsche Z. Philos., Jg. 9, a. a. O., Nr. 9, S. 1119 ff.

7 Ost-Prob., Jg. 13, a. a. O., Nr. 21, S. 666–692. – Ebd., Jg. 15, a. a. O., Nr. 24, S. 738–750.

8 Aber die Totalität der fremdbestimmten (von «der Partei» betriebenen) Beanspruchung des Menschen (PRELLER, «Sozialpolitik usw.», a. a. O., S. 53), die eine revolutionäre Antwort auf die westlichen «Entfremdungs»-Erscheinungen sein sollte (ebd., S. 40 ff.), erweist sich nur noch massiver als Ausschließung der selbständigen Persönlichkeit.

9 Ebd., S. 39 f. – Vgl. ferner die Abhandlung des Verfassers «Volkswirtschaftliche Leistungen der Automation», Göttingen, Vandenhoeck und Ruprecht, 1959 (Göttinger Universitätsreden), passim.

10 Negative Folgen für den Westen betont MONTAG, R. und Autorenkollektiv, «Ökonomische Probleme der Automatisierung im Kapitalismus», Wiss. Z. Univ. Leipzig, Jg. 8, Leipzig, 1958/59 (Gesellschafts- und Sprachwissenschaftliche Reihe, Nr. 5), S. 831 ff.

11 DAHRENDORF, «Homo Sociologicus usw.», a. a. O., passim.

12 PRELLER, «Sozialpolitik usw.», a. a. O., S. 27, 33. – Über die Frage, vor der der Osten unausweichlich steht, siehe BARTSCH, G., «Die Kommunisten und das Generationsproblem», Osteuropa, Jg. 14, Stuttgart, 1964, Nr. 5, S. 329–340. – SCHMOLLACK, J. und SWOBODA, H., «Über die Verbindung von materieller Interessiertheit und ideellen Anreizen zur Arbeit», Wirtsch. wiss., Jg. 12, a. a. O., Nr. 2, S. 177–189.

13 Hiermit ist die dialektische Einheit von Individualfreiheit und Sozialbestimmtheit, von materiellen und geistigen Interessen usw. gemeint.

14 Eine Abwägung der nächsten Chancen bietet HEIMANN, «Soziale Theorie der Wirtschaftssysteme», a. a. O., S. 324–328.

15 Diese Lagebeurteilung vermittelt zwischen einer Angleichungstheorie und der Betonung eines unversöhnlichen Dualismus. – Zu letzterem vgl. STEINISCH, J., «Angleichung der Wirtschaftssysteme von Ost und West?», Marburg, Mauersberger, 1962, S. 146 ff., passim.

16 FREYER, «Theorie des gegenwärtigen Zeitalters», a. a. O., S. 79 ff.

17 Die These, daß der angeblich nihilistische «Idealmangel» des Westens den Kommunismus als Heilsidee marktgängig machen könnte, hat allerdings wohl nur für einige Moralisten recht und darf hier unbeachtet bleiben.

18 PRELLER, «Sozialpolitik usw.», a. a. O., S. 28, 31.

19 Unter ethischem Blickwinkel wird diese Antithetik abgehandelt bei CALLIE, W. B., «Liberal Morality and Socialist Morality», LASLETT, P. (Hrsg.), Philosophy, Politics, and Society, 3. Aufl., Oxford, Basil Blackwell, 1963, S. 123–128.

20 Der Westen bedarf allerdings einer philosophischen Anthropologie, welche die Vorzüge seines Menschenbildes gegenüber dem des Ostens sichtbar macht. – Untereinander höchst heterogene Ansätze zu einer MARX gewachsenen Anthropologie finden sich bei A. GEHLEN, H. PLESSNER, H. FREYER, J.-P. SARTRE, H. MARCUSE, T. ADORNO, J. HABERMAS und anderen.

21 Spätestens seit der Weltwirtschaftskrise, aber auch schon vorher, war in den Liberalismus immer stärker das Moment staatlicher Sozialpolitik eingezogen. – FREYER, «Weltgeschichte Europas», Bd. 2, a. a. O., S. 944 ff. – TREUE, «Wirtschaftsgeschichte der Neuzeit», a. a. O., S. 646, 660 ff. – MÄRZ, «Die Marxsche Wirtschaftslehre im Widerstreit der Meinungen usw.», a. a. O., S. 207 f., 222 ff. – RITSCHL, «Die Grundlagen der Wirtschaftsordnung», a. a. O., S. 80–89.

22 In beiden Fällen zeigte sich das Scheitern der extremen «Patentlösungen» aller Probleme der menschlich-gesellschaftlichen Angelegenheiten. Stattdessen drängt sich der Gedanke einer dialektischen Form menschlicher Aktionstendenzen auf.

23 PRELLER, «Sozialpolitik usw.», a. a. O., S. 2 ff., 8, 21, 28, passim.

24 THALHEIM, K. C., «Die Unterschiede zwischen der Zentralverwaltungswirtschaft sowjetischen Typs und marktwirtschaftlich organisierten Volkswirtschaften», in: Vergleich zwischen den Wirtschaftssystemen in der Welt, a. a. O., S. 11–33 und KRENGEL, R., «Ähnlichkeiten zwischen der sowjetischen und der westdeutschen Wirtschaftsentwicklung nach dem Kriege», ebd., S. 34–52. – BARTSCH, «Die Kommunisten und das Generationsproblem», a. a. O.,

S. 329 ff. – MÄRZ, «Die Marxsche Wirtschaftslehre im Widerstreit der Meinungen usw.», a. a. O., S. 224 ff. – HEIMANN, «Soziale Theorie der Wirtschaftssysteme», a. a. O., S. 247–257, 289–293.

25 PRELLER, «Sozialpolitik usw.», a. a. O., S. 40 ff.

26 RITSCHL, «Die Grundlagen der Wirtschaftsordnung», a. a. O., S. 90 f. – FREYER, «Weltgeschichte Europas», Bd. 2, a. a. O., S. 941 f.

27 GEHLEN, A., «Die Seele im technischen Zeitalter. Sozialpsychologische Problematik der Industriegesellschaft», Reinbek, Rowohlt, 1964, das Schlußkapitel.

INDEX OF PROPER NAMES

355